A Book
of
Drama - 2

PERSPECTIVES IN LITERATURE

A Book of Short Stories—1
A Book of Poetry—1
A Book of Nonfiction—1
A Book of Drama—1

A Book of Short Stories—2
A Book of Poetry—2
A Book of Nonfiction—2
A Book of Drama—2

American Literature to 1900
Modern American Prose
A Book of Modern American Poetry
A Book of Drama—3

English Literature—500 to 1500
English Literature—1500 to 1700
English Literature—1700 to 1900
Modern British Prose
A Book of Modern British Poetry
A Book of Drama—4

A Book of Mythology (in preparation)

Bridges to Understanding: Essays on the Novel
  (in preparation)

PERSPECTIVES IN LITERATURE

A Book of Drama - 2

MARION A. HOCTOR
BLANCHE V. SCHWARTZ

HARCOURT, BRACE & WORLD, INC.
New York   Chicago   San Francisco   Atlanta   Dallas

Cover Photos: The cover photographs are from a production of Shakespeare's Julius Caesar at the Stratford Shakespearean Festival, Stratford, Ontario, Canada. The front cover shows Caesar about to be stabbed (Act III, Scene 1); the back cover shows Mark Antony about to remove the mantle from Caesar's body (Act III, Scene 2).

ACKNOWLEDGMENTS: For permission to reprint copyrighted material, grateful acknowledgment is made to the following publishers, authors, and agents:

Arms and the Man by George Bernard Shaw, 1898 version. Reprinted by permission of The Society of Authors, Agents for the Bernard Shaw Estate.

Julius Caesar from Shakespeare: The Complete Works, edited by G. B. Harrison, copyright 1948, 1952 by Harcourt, Brace & World, Inc., and reprinted with their permission.

As You Like It from Shakespeare: The Complete Works, edited by G. B. Harrison, copyright 1948, 1952 by Harcourt, Brace & World, Inc., and reprinted with their permission.

Contents

INTRODUCTION

T HE PLAYS IN A *Book of Drama—2* (Henrik Ibsen's *An Enemy of the People*, George Bernard Shaw's *Arms and the Man*, and Shakespeare's *Julius Caesar* and *As You Like It*) were, like all dramas, written to be presented in a theater and seen by an audience, but they may also be read and discussed with pleasure. Although it is true that a theater audience often has the more rewarding experience, the reader of a play has one or two advantages. For example, the reader can follow a play at his own pace, never rushed or slowed down. He can pause and think about what is being said or done. He can look back at something that *has* happened already in order to connect it with something that *is* happening right there on the page in front of him. He can so enrich his understanding of the play by careful reading that when the time comes for him to see it presented in a theater, his experience will be greatly enlarged.

What's In a Play?

Plays present the world of the writer's imagination (even when plots are based on history or biography); we turn to this world rather than to the factual one for a variety of reasons. We may use it as an escape from our everyday world or as a distraction from its worries. We may watch drama with fascination because we are curious to see how things will turn out for the characters we met when the play began. We may even be seeking knowledge—not the sort of information and understanding that comes from formal schooling, but rather the particular kind of insight that direct experience can give us. Such experience, of course, is not our own personal experience. It is the experience of others, the characters in the play. But because their experience is related in some way to the kind we have had, are having, or may someday have, it can help us to better understand ourselves and our lives.

In addition to presenting experiences and events, drama—like other forms of literature—tries to find some meaning in these events and experiences. We have, for example, a certain amount of historical information about the murder of the real Julius Caesar in the Roman Senate. Why then, we might ask, should Shakespeare write a play about Caesar's assassination? Was he, perhaps, interested in telling us *why* Caesar was killed, and then giving us his view of the consequences? Or is there something more than this?

After reading *Julius Caesar* or seeing it acted on the stage, we have experienced directly some of the meaning of the title character's life and death. We may have known beforehand the fact that Caesar was killed, and we may have had some ideas why. But now our understanding of these events is enhanced because we have watched, through the actors, the human beings who were involved in these events as they have been interpreted by the playwright. We have seen that men have always been concerned with power and the control of power, and with government and the eternal quest to achieve a just government. We have seen the Romans' doubts and decisions, their strengths and their weaknesses, their good intentions and their evil motives. Caesar's murder is no longer only a historical fact to us. It is a reality. But perhaps even more important, through the play we have been led to consider moral and political questions we are all faced with at one time or another in contemporary life.

Shaw's *Arms and the Man* also teaches as well as entertains. In addition to telling a delightful story, it offers comments about honesty and dishonesty, about sentimentality and real love, and about people making themselves ridiculous and being saved in spite of themselves. *An Enemy of the People*, a realistic drama, examines the relationship between ethics and money when the people of a town learn of the pollution of their spa, or mineral spring, which contributes so much to their prosperity. *As You Like It* offers perceptions about love in its many guises. In this sense, all four plays in *A Book of Drama—2* are alike: each presents an aspect of life and tries to reveal some new facet of its inner meaning.

The Kinds of Drama

Ever since early drama in ancient Greece, playwrights have used the terms *comedy* and *tragedy* to describe the kinds of plays they were writing. Although today the term *comedy* is generally applied to drama that amuses and diverts an audience, historically the term *comedy* is not applied solely to plays that are funny. A comedy by tradition is a play that ends happily. It presents sympathetically that which is ludicrous in man. The adventures of the characters may amuse and entertain us. But the characters themselves, in comedy, will have something to learn from their experience. They will have to pay a price for what they learn about themselves and about life in the course of the play, but this price will usually be easy enough to pay. They will have to learn to laugh at themselves or at the selves they used to be. The world of comedy usually seems to be a pretty good world, a world in which matters tend to work out for the best, and the happy ending is often expressed in a wedding, dance, or feast.

For the playwright who is interested in another aspect of human experience (or in treating similar aspects in different ways), there is the world of *tragedy*. This is a world in which people suffer, and one in which the individual usually suffers alone. A tragedy is a play that ends unhappily. But if tragedies were merely plays about suffering and death, we would neither go to see them nor bother to read them. The experience would be too painful. A tragedy, then, must be something more than a play that ends in death or failure. It is a drama about the individual at war with his society or with himself or about man alone on some great quest. Tragedy is a kind of drama that makes it possible for us to find some meaning in unhappiness and in the factors that cause it. It shows us a world in which we must pay a high price for what we learn about ourselves and about life.

There are many different sorts of comedies and tragedies. Although those plays that fall heavily at one end or another of the scale are easy enough to classify as comedy or tragedy, many near the middle are not so simple to categorize. Shakespeare's *As You Like It* can be called "romantic" comedy because it takes place in an idyllic world where good men are handsome and brave, and where good women are beautiful and clever. Shaw's *Arms and the Man* is usually seen as "anti-romantic" comedy because it deliberately and consistently undercuts those same qualities.

And Shakespeare's *Julius Caesar* is clearly a tragedy. But Ibsen's *An Enemy of the People* leaves us puzzled in ways that classic tragedy, which centers on an almost wholly admirable hero, does not. In *An Enemy of the People* we are not really certain whether the main character in the play is a hero or not, and without a hero it is hard to have tragedy. For this and other reasons, Ibsen's play can, perhaps, be better described as serious social drama, or as a problem play.

AN ENEMY
OF THE PEOPLE

Henrik Ibsen
[1828–1906]

The little seaport town of Skien in Norway was the birthplace of Henrik Ibsen, and there he was educated and lived until he was fifteen, when he became a druggist's apprentice. Later, living in the capital city of Oslo * and studying to enter the university, he met the violinist Ole Bull, through whom he was given the opportunity of working as instructor and dramatic author at the national theater at Bergen. Ibsen then gave up all thought of continuing to study for university entrance and remained at Bergen for six years. During this period he visited Copenhagen and Dresden, where he learned stage production.

Ibsen spent the next seven years in Oslo, associated with various theaters and receiving small government grants from time to time. One might have thought him settled there for life, but Norway's refusal to honor its agreement to support Denmark in her war with Germany led him to exile himself from his native country for more than twenty-five years—1864 to 1891. During this time he lived in various European countries, but it was to Italy he most often returned. All but a few of his plays were written in exile and were produced in countries other than his own before being presented in their original language. By the time he returned to Norway, he was reported to be a very rich man and his reputation was international.

* **Oslo:** then called Kristiania; changed to Oslo in 1925.

4

(In England, the critic and playwright George Bernard Shaw, was one of Ibsen's greatest admirers as a critic, and one of his greatest disciples as a playwright.) Ibsen remained in Oslo until his death.

Although Ibsen is acknowledged as the originating master of social, realistic drama, his first two well-known plays were poetic dramas—*Brand* (1866) and *Peer Gynt* (1867). (It was for the latter that Grieg wrote his famous musical suite.) His social dramas dealt with topics that were then taboo and that still evoke controversy. Typical of them was *The Doll's House* (1879), which considered the role of women in marriage. *Ghosts* (1881) showed a son paying for the sins of his father. *An Enemy of the People* (1882) came next, attacking corruption. Ibsen's later plays, such as *Hedda Gabler* (1890), *The Master Builder* (1892), and *John Gabriel Borkman* (1896), were concerned more with the problems of the individual than with the social forces surrounding him. The theme of *The Wild Duck* (1884) seemingly is that man needs to live by his illusions.

Although the issues over which the characters become embroiled in *An Enemy of the People* may for a moment or two seem remote, they are as current and topical as today's newspaper. Until we no longer read about crooked politicians, dishonest journalism, polluted water, and selfish businessmen, we shall find that the play talks directly to us despite its distance in time and place.

CHARACTERS

Doctor Thomas Stockmann,
Medical Officer of the Municipal Baths *

Mrs. Stockmann,
his wife

Petra,
their daughter, a teacher

Eilif } their sons, aged thirteen
Morten } and ten, respectively

Peter Stockmann,
the Doctor's older brother; Mayor of the Town and Chief Constable, Chairman of the Baths' Committee, etc., etc.

Morten Kiil,
owner of a tannery,† Mrs. Stockmann's adoptive father

Hovstad,
editor in chief of the *People's Messenger*, the local newspaper

Billing,
assistant editor of the *People's Messenger*

Captain Horster,
a sea captain

Aslaksen,
a printer of the *People's Messenger*

Men of various occupations, a few women, and some schoolboys—the audience at a public meeting

Place.   A coast town in southern Norway.

---

* **Baths:** a place with natural mineral springs, usually called spas, frequented by people for medical treatment, especially by bathing.

Ever since Roman times—and perhaps before—the waters of natural mineral springs have been considered restorative and health-giving, especially for the ill and the weak. During the eighteenth and nineteenth centuries, spas—or health resorts—sprang up all over Europe. Wherever these springs were found, the resource was exploited, and "baths" were built. Many individuals and towns became wealthy in the process, just as resort developers might today.

† **tannery:** a place where animal hides are tanned and made into leather.

Act I

DR. STOCKMANN'S *sitting room. It is evening. The room is plainly but neatly arranged and furnished. In the right-hand wall are two doors; the farther leads out to the hall, the nearer to the doctor's study. In the left-hand wall, opposite the door leading to the hall, is a door leading to the other rooms occupied by the family. In the middle of the same wall stands the stove used for heating the room, and, farther forward, a couch with a mirror hanging over it and an oval table in front of it. On the table, a lighted lamp, with a lamp shade. At the back of the room, an open door leads to the dining room.* BILLING *is seen sitting at the dining table, on which a lamp is burning. He has a napkin tucked under his chin, and* MRS. STOCK- MANN *is standing by the table handing him a large plateful of roast beef. The other places at the table are empty, and the table some- what in disorder, a meal having evidently recently been finished.*

MRS. STOCKMANN.   You see, if you come an hour late, Mr. Billing, you have to put up with cold meat.

BILLING.   (*As he eats.*)   It is uncommonly good, thank you—remark- ably good.

MRS. STOCKMANN.   My husband makes such a point of having his meals punctually, you know—

BILLING.   That doesn't affect me a bit. Indeed, I almost think I enjoy a meal all the better when I can sit down and eat all by my- self and undisturbed.

MRS. STOCKMANN.   Oh well, as long as you are enjoying it—(*Turns to the hall door, listening.*) I expect that is Mr. Hovstad coming, too.

BILLING.   Very likely.

(PETER STOCKMANN *comes in. He wears an overcoat and his official hat, and carries a walking stick.*)

PETER STOCKMANN.   Good evening, Katherine.

MRS. STOCKMANN.   (*Coming forward into the sitting room.*)   Ah, good evening—is it you? How good of you to come up and see us!

PETER STOCKMANN.   I happened to be passing, and so—(*Looks into the dining room.*) But you have company with you, I see.

MRS. STOCKMANN.   (*A little embarrassed.*)   Oh, no—it was quite by chance he came in. (*Hurriedly.*) Won't you come in and have something, too?

PETER STOCKMANN.   I! No, thank you. Good gracious—hot meat at night! [1] Not with my digestion.

MRS. STOCKMANN.   Oh, but just once in a while—

PETER STOCKMANN.   No, no, my dear lady; I stick to my tea and bread and butter. It is much more wholesome in the long run—and a little more economical, too.

1. hot . . . night: The main meal was eaten in the middle of the day.

MRS. STOCKMANN. (*Smiling.*)   Now you mustn't think that Thomas and I are spendthrifts.

PETER STOCKMANN.   Not you, my dear; I would never think that of you. (*Points to the* DOCTOR's *study.*) Is he not at home?

MRS. STOCKMANN.   No, he went out for a little turn after supper—he and the boys.

PETER STOCKMANN.   I doubt if that is a wise thing to do. (*Listens.*) I fancy I hear him coming now.

MRS. STOCKMANN.   No, I don't think it is he. (*A knock is heard at the door.*) Come in! (HOVSTAD *comes in from the hall.*) Oh, it is you, Mr. Hovstad!

HOVSTAD.   Yes, I hope you will forgive me, but I was delayed at the printer's. Good evening, Mr. Mayor.

PETER STOCKMANN. (*Bowing a little distantly.*)   Good evening. You have come on business, no doubt.

HOVSTAD.   Partly. It's about an article for the paper.

PETER STOCKMANN.   So I imagined. I hear my brother has become a prolific [2] contributor to the *People's Messenger*.

HOVSTAD.   Yes, he is good enough to write in the *People's Messenger* when he has any home truths to tell.

MRS. STOCKMANN. (*To* HOVSTAD.)   But won't you—? (*Points to the dining room.*)

PETER STOCKMANN.   Quite so, quite so. I don't blame him in the least, as a writer, for addressing himself to the quarters where he will find the readiest sympathy. And, besides that, I personally have no reason to bear any ill will to your paper, Mr. Hovstad.

HOVSTAD.   I quite agree with you.

PETER STOCKMANN.   Taking one thing with another, there is an excellent spirit of toleration in the town—an admirable municipal spirit. And it all springs from the fact of our having a great common interest to unite us—an interest that is in an equally high degree the concern of every right-minded citizen—

HOVSTAD.   The Baths, yes.

PETER STOCKMANN.   Exactly—our fine, new, handsome Baths. Mark my words, Mr. Hovstad—the Baths will become the focus of our municipal life! Not a doubt of it!

MRS. STOCKMANN.   That is just what Thomas says.

PETER STOCKMANN.   Think how extraordinarily the place has de-

---

2. **prolific:** frequent; marked by abundant productivity.

veloped within the last year or two! Money has been flowing in, and there is some life and some business doing in the town. Houses and landed property are rising in value every day.

HOVSTAD.   And unemployment is diminishing.

PETER STOCKMANN.   Yes, that is another thing. The burden of the poor-rates has been lightened, to the great relief of the propertied classes; and that relief will be even greater if only we get a really good summer this year, and lots of visitors—plenty of invalids, who will make the Baths talked about.

HOVSTAD.   And there is a good prospect of that, I hear.

PETER STOCKMANN.   It looks very promising. Enquiries about apartments and that sort of thing are reaching us every day.

HOVSTAD.   Well, the Doctor's article will come in very suitably.

PETER STOCKMANN.   Has he been writing something just lately?

HOVSTAD.   This is something he wrote in the winter, a recommendation of the Baths—an account of the excellent sanitary conditions here. But I held the article over, temporarily.

PETER STOCKMANN.   Ah, some little difficulty about it, I suppose?

HOVSTAD.   No, not at all; I thought it would be better to wait till the spring, because it is just at this time that people begin to think seriously about their summer quarters.

PETER STOCKMANN.   Quite right; you were perfectly right, Mr. Hovstad.

MRS. STOCKMANN.   Yes, Thomas is really indefatigable [3] when it is a question of the Baths.

PETER STOCKMANN.   Well—remember, he is the Medical Officer to the Baths.

HOVSTAD.   Yes, and what is more, they owe their existence to him.

PETER STOCKMANN.   To him? Indeed! It is true I have heard from time to time that some people are of that opinion. And at the same time I must say I imagined that I took a modest part in the enterprise.

MRS. STOCKMANN.   Yes, that is what Thomas is always saying.

HOVSTAD.   But who denies it, Mr. Stockmann? You set the thing going and made a practical concern of it; we all know that. I only meant that the idea of it came first from the Doctor.

PETER STOCKMANN.   Oh, ideas—yes! My brother has had plenty of them in his time—unfortunately. But when it is a question of put-

---

3. **indefatigable** (in'də·fat'ə·gə·bəl): tireless; unflagging.

ting an idea into practical shape, you have to apply to a man of different mettle,[4] Mr. Hovstad. And I certainly should have thought that in this house at least—

MRS. STOCKMANN. My dear Peter—

HOVSTAD. How can you think that—?

MRS. STOCKMANN. Won't you go in and have something, Mr. Hovstad? My husband is sure to be back directly.

HOVSTAD. Thank you, perhaps just a morsel. (*Goes into the dining room.*)

PETER STOCKMANN. (*Lowering his voice a little.*) It is a curious thing that these farmers' sons never seem to lose their want of tact.[5]

MRS. STOCKMANN. Surely it is not worth bothering about! Cannot you and Thomas share the credit as brothers?

PETER STOCKMANN. I should have thought so; but apparently some people are not satisfied with a share.

MRS. STOCKMANN. What nonsense! You and Thomas get on so capitally [6] together. (*Listens.*) There he is at last, I think. (*Goes out and opens the door leading to the hall.*)

DR. STOCKMANN. (*Laughing and talking outside.*) Look here—here is another guest for you, Katherine. Isn't that jolly? Come in, Captain Horster; hang your coat up on this peg. Ah, you don't wear an overcoat. Just think, Katherine; I met him in the street and could hardly persuade him to come up! (CAPTAIN HORSTER *comes into the room and greets* MRS. STOCKMANN. *He is followed by* DR. STOCKMANN.) Come along in, boys. They are ravenously hungry again, you know. Come along, Captain Horster; you must have a slice of beef.

(*Pushes* HORSTER *into the dining room,* EJLIF *and* MORTEN *go in after them.*)

MRS. STOCKMANN. But, Thomas, don't you see—?

DR. STOCKMANN. (*Turning in the doorway.*) Oh, is it you, Peter? (*Shakes hands with him.*) Now that is very delightful.

PETER STOCKMANN. Unfortunately, I must go in a moment—

DR. STOCKMANN. Rubbish! There is some toddy [7] just coming in. You haven't forgotten the toddy, Katherine?

4. **mettle:** quality of character, or temperament.
5. **want of tact:** lack of delicacy; lack of sensitivity to a situation.
6. **capitally:** very well; excellently.
7. **toddy:** hot drink made with brandy or whiskey and hot water, sugar, and a slice of lemon.

MRS. STOCKMANN. Of course not; the water is boiling now. (*Goes into the dining room.*)

PETER STOCKMANN. Toddy, too!

DR. STOCKMANN. Yes, sit down and we will have it comfortably.

PETER STOCKMANN. Thanks, I never care about an evening's drinking.

DR. STOCKMANN. But this isn't an evening's drinking.

PETER STOCKMANN. It seems to me—(*Looks toward the dining room.*) It is extraordinary how they can put away all that food.

DR. STOCKMANN. (*Rubbing his hands.*) Yes, isn't it splendid to see young people eat? They have always got an appetite, you know! That's as it should be. Lots of food—to build up their strength! They are the people who are going to stir up the fermenting [8] forces of the future, Peter.

PETER STOCKMANN. May I ask what they will find here to "stir up," as you put it?

DR. STOCKMANN. Ah, you must ask the young people that—when the time comes. We shan't be able to see it, of course. That stands to reason—two old fogies, like us—

PETER STOCKMANN. Really, really! I must say that is an extremely odd expression to—

DR. STOCKMANN. Oh, you mustn't take me too literally, Peter. I am so heartily happy and contented, you know. I think it is such an extraordinary piece of good fortune to be in the middle of all this growing, germinating [9] life. It is a splendid time to live in! It is as if a whole new world were being created around one.

PETER STOCKMANN. Do you really think so?

DR. STOCKMANN. Ah, naturally you can't appreciate it as keenly as I. You have lived all your life in these surroundings, and your impressions have got blunted. But I, who have been buried all these years in my little corner up north, almost without ever seeing a stranger who might bring new ideas with him—well, in my case it has just the same effect as if I had been transported into the middle of a crowded city.

PETER STOCKMANN. Oh, a city—!

DR. STOCKMANN. I know, I know; it is all cramped enough here, compared with many other places. But there is life here—there is promise—there are innumerable things to work for and fight for;

---

8. **fermenting**: exciting or agitating; causing unrest and change.
9. **germinating**: sprouting; beginning to develop.

and that is the main thing. (*Calls.*) Katherine, hasn't the postman
been here?

MRS. STOCKMANN. (*From the dining room.*)   No.

DR. STOCKMANN.   And then to be comfortably off, Peter! That is
something one learns to value, when one has been on the brink of
starvation, as we have.

PETER STOCKMANN.   Oh, surely—

DR. STOCKMANN.   Indeed I can assure you we have often been very
hard put to it, up there. And now to be able to live like a lord!
Today, for instance, we had roast beef for dinner—and, what is
more, for supper, too. Won't you come and have a little bit? Or let
me show it to you, at any rate? Come here—

PETER STOCKMANN.   No, no—not for worlds!

DR. STOCKMANN.   Well, but just come here then. Do you see, we
have got a tablecover?

PETER STOCKMANN.   Yes, I noticed it.

DR. STOCKMANN.   And we have got a lamp shade too. Do you see?
All out of Katherine's savings! It makes the room so cosy. Don't
you think so? Just stand here for a moment—no, no, not there—
just here, that's it! Look now, when you get the light on it altogether—I really think it looks very nice, doesn't it?

PETER STOCKMANN.   Oh, if you can afford luxuries of this kind—

DR. STOCKMANN.   Yes, I can afford it now. Katherine tells me I earn
almost as much as we spend.

PETER STOCKMANN.   Almost—yes!

DR. STOCKMANN.   But a scientific man must live in a little bit of style.
I am quite sure an ordinary civil servant spends more in a year than
I do.

PETER STOCKMANN.   I daresay. A civil servant—a man in a well-paid
position—

DR. STOCKMANN.   Well, any ordinary merchant, then! A man in that
position spends two or three times as much as—

PETER STOCKMANN.   It just depends on circumstances.

DR. STOCKMANN.   At all events I assure you I don't waste money
unprofitably. But I can't find it in my heart to deny myself the
pleasure of entertaining my friends. I need that sort of thing, you
know. I have lived for so long shut out of it all that it is a necessity
of life to me to mix with young, eager, ambitious men, men of liberal and active minds; and that describes every one of those fellows
who are enjoying their supper in there. I wish you knew more of
Hovstad—

PETER STOCKMANN. By the way, Hovstad was telling me he was going to print another article of yours.

DR. STOCKMANN. An article of mine?

PETER STOCKMANN. Yes, about the Baths. An article you wrote in the winter.

DR. STOCKMANN. Oh, that one! No, I don't intend that to appear just for the present.

PETER STOCKMANN. Why not? It seems to me that this would be the most opportune [10] moment.

DR. STOCKMANN. Yes, very likely—under normal conditions. (*Crosses the room.*)

PETER STOCKMANN. (*Following him with his eyes.*) Is there anything abnormal about the present conditions?

DR. STOCKMANN. (*Standing still.*) To tell you the truth, Peter, I can't say just at this moment—at all events not tonight. There may be much that is very abnormal about the present conditions—and it is possible there may be nothing abnormal about them at all. It is quite possible it may be merely my imagination.

PETER STOCKMANN. I must say it all sounds most mysterious. Is there something going on that I am to be kept in ignorance of? I should have imagined that I, as Chairman of the governing body of the Baths—

DR. STOCKMANN. And I should have imagined that I— Oh, come, don't let us fly out at one another, Peter.

PETER STOCKMANN. Heaven forbid! I am not in the habit of flying out at people, as you call it. But I am entitled to request most emphatically that all arrangements shall be made in a businesslike manner, through the proper channels, and shall be dealt with by the legally constituted [11] authorities. I can allow no going behind our backs by any roundabout means.

DR. STOCKMANN. Have I ever at any time tried to go behind your backs?

PETER STOCKMANN. You have an ingrained tendency to take your own way, at all events; and that is almost equally inadmissible in a well-ordered community. The individual ought undoubtedly to acquiesce [12] in subordinating himself to the community—or, to speak more accurately, to the authorities who have the care of the community's welfare.

10. **opportune:** fitting; well-timed.
11. **constituted:** established.
12. **acquiesce:** submit; agree.

DR. STOCKMANN.   Very likely. But what the deuce has all this got to do with me?

PETER STOCKMANN.   That is exactly what you never appear to be willing to learn, my dear Thomas. But, mark my words, some day you will have to suffer for it—sooner or later. Now I have told you. Good-bye.

DR. STOCKMANN.   Have you taken leave of your senses? You are on the wrong scent [13] altogether.

PETER STOCKMANN.   I am not usually that. You must excuse me now if I— (*Calls into the dining room.*) Good night, Katherine. Good night, gentlemen. (*Goes out.*)

MRS. STOCKMANN. (*Coming from the dining room.*)   Has he gone?

DR. STOCKMANN.   Yes, and in such a bad temper.

MRS. STOCKMANN.   But, dear Thomas, what have you been doing to him again?

DR. STOCKMANN.   Nothing at all. And, anyhow, he can't oblige me to make my report before the proper time.

MRS. STOCKMANN.   What have you got to make a report to him about?

DR. STOCKMANN.   Hm! Leave that to me, Katherine. It is an extraordinary thing that the postman doesn't come.

(HOVSTAD, BILLING, *and* HORSTER *have got up from the table and come into the sitting room.* EJLIF *and* MORTEN *come in after them.*)

BILLING. (*Stretching himself.*)   Ah! One feels a new man after a meal like that.

HOVSTAD.   The mayor wasn't in a very sweet temper tonight, then.

DR. STOCKMANN.   It is his stomach; he has a wretched digestion.

HOVSTAD.   I rather think it was us two of the *People's Messenger* that he couldn't digest.

MRS. STOCKMANN. I thought you came out of it pretty well with him.

HOVSTAD.   Oh yes; but it isn't anything more than a sort of truce.

BILLING.   That is just what it is! That word sums up the situation.

DR. STOCKMANN.   We must remember that Peter is a lonely man, poor chap. He has no home comforts of any kind; nothing but everlasting business. And all that infernal weak tea wash that he pours into himself! Now then, my boys, bring chairs up to the table. Aren't we going to have that toddy, Katherine?

13. scent: odor; here used figuratively to mean thinking along the wrong lines.

MRS. STOCKMANN. (*Going into the dining room.*)   I am just getting it.

DR. STOCKMANN.   Sit down here on the couch beside me, Captain Horster. We so seldom see you. Please sit down, my friends.

(*They sit down at the table.* MRS. STOCKMANN *brings a tray, with a spirit-lamp,[14] glasses, bottles, etc., upon it.*)

MRS. STOCKMANN.   There you are! This is arrack,[15] and this is rum, and this one is the brandy. Now every one must help himself.

DR. STOCKMANN. (*Taking a glass.*)   We will. (*They all mix themselves some toddy.*) And let us have the cigars. Ejlif, you know where the box is. And you, Morten, can fetch my pipe. (*The two boys go into the room on the right.*) I have a suspicion that Ejlif pockets a cigar now and then, but I take no notice of it. (*Calls out.*) And my smoking cap too, Morten. Katherine, you can tell him where I left it. Ah, he has got it. (*The boys bring the various things.*) Now, my friends. I stick to my pipe, you know. This one has seen plenty of bad weather with me up north. (*Touches glasses with them.*) Your good health! Ah! It is good to be sitting snug and warm here.

MRS. STOCKMANN. (*Who sits knitting.*)   Do you sail soon, Captain Horster?

HORSTER.   I expect to be ready to sail next week.

MRS. STOCKMANN.   I suppose you are going to America?

HORSTER.   Yes, that is the plan.

MRS. STOCKMANN.   Then you won't be able to take part in the coming election.

HORSTER.   Is there going to be an election?

BILLING.   Didn't you know?

HORSTER.   No, I don't mix myself up with those things.

BILLING.   But do you not take an interest in public affairs?

HORSTER.   No, I don't know anything about politics.

BILLING.   All the same, one ought to vote, at any rate.

HORSTER.   Even if one doesn't know anything about what is going on?

BILLING.   Doesn't know! What do you mean by that? A community is like a ship; everyone ought to be prepared to take the helm.

---

14. **spirit-lamp:** an old-fashioned lamp using alcohol for fuel.
15. **arrack** (ar'ək): from the Arabic *'araq*, juice; a strong Oriental liquor made from a mash of rice and molasses.

HORSTER. Maybe that is all very well on shore, but on board ship it wouldn't work.

HOVSTAD. It is astonishing how little most sailors care about what goes on on shore.

BILLING. Very extraordinary.

DR. STOCKMANN. Sailors are like birds of passage; they feel equally at home in any latitude. And that is only an additional reason for our being all the more keen, Hovstad. Is there to be anything of public interest in tomorrow's *Messenger?*

HOVSTAD. Nothing about municipal affairs. But the day after tomorrow I was thinking of printing your article—

DR. STOCKMANN. Ah, devil take it—my article! Look here, that must wait a bit.

HOVSTAD. Really? We had just got convenient space for it, and I thought it was just the opportune moment—

DR. STOCKMANN. Yes, yes, very likely you are right; but it must wait all the same. I will explain to you later.

(PETRA *comes in from the hall, in hat and cloak and with a bundle of exercise books* [16] *under her arm.*)

PETRA. Good evening.

DR. STOCKMANN. Good evening, Petra; come along.

(*Mutual greetings;* PETRA *takes off her things and puts them down on a chair by the door.*)

PETRA. And you have all been sitting here enjoying yourselves, while I have been out slaving!

DR. STOCKMANN. Well, come and enjoy yourself, too!

BILLING. May I mix a glass for you?

PETRA. (*Coming to the table.*) Thanks, I would rather do it; you always mix it too strong. But I forgot, Father—I have a letter for you.

(*Goes to the chair where she has laid her things.*)

DR. STOCKMANN. A letter? From whom?

PETRA. (*Looking in her coat pocket.*) The postman gave it to me just as I was going out—

DR. STOCKMANN. (*Getting up and going to her.*) And you only give it to me now!

PETRA. I really had not time to run up again. There it is!

16. **exercise books:** students' workbooks.

DR. STOCKMANN. (*Seizing the letter.*)   Let's see, let's see, child!
(*Looks at the address.*) Yes, that's all right!

MRS. STOCKMANN.   Is it the one you have been expecting so anxiously, Thomas?

DR. STOCKMANN.   Yes, it is. I must go to my room now and—Where
shall I get a light, Katherine? Is there no lamp in my room again?

MRS. STOCKMANN.   Yes, your lamp is all ready lit on your desk.

DR. STOCKMANN.   Good, good. Excuse me for a moment—(*Goes into
his study.*)

PETRA.   What do you suppose it is, Mother?

MRS. STOCKMANN.   I don't know; for the last day or two he has always
been asking if the postman has not been.

BILLING.   Probably some country patient.

PETRA.   Poor old dad! He will overwork himself soon. (*Mixes a glass
for herself.*) There, that will taste good!

HOVSTAD.   Have you been teaching in the evening school again
today?

PETRA. (*Sipping from her glass.*)   Two hours.

BILLING.   And four hours of school in the morning—

PETRA.   Five hours.

MRS. STOCKMANN.   And you have still got exercises to correct, I see.

PETRA.   A whole heap, yes.

HORSTER.   You are pretty full up with work too, it seems to me.

PETRA.   Yes—but that is good. One is so delightfully tired after it.

BILLING.   Do you like that?

PETRA.   Yes, because one sleeps so well then.

MORTEN.   You must be dreadfully wicked, Petra.

PETRA.   Wicked?

MORTEN.   Yes, because you work so much. Mr. Rörlund says work
is a punishment for our sins.

EJLIF.   Pooh, what a duffer [17] you are, to believe a thing like that!

MRS. STOCKMANN.   Come, come, Ejlif!

BILLING. (*Laughing.*)   That's capital!

HOVSTAD.   Don't you want to work as hard as that, Morten?

MORTEN.   No, indeed I don't.

HOVSTAD.   What do you want to be, then?

MORTEN.   I should like best to be a viking.[18]

EJLIF.   You would have to be a pagan, then.

17. **duffer:** an informal term for a dull-witted person.
18. **viking:** a Scandinavian warrior pirate. Vikings plundered the coasts of Europe in the eighth, ninth, and tenth centuries.

MORTEN. Well, I could become a pagan, couldn't I?

BILLING. I agree with you, Morten! My sentiments, exactly.

MRS. STOCKMANN. (*Signaling to him.*)   I am sure that is not true, Mr. Billing.

BILLING. Yes, I swear it is! I am a pagan, and I am proud of it. Believe me, before long we shall all be pagans.

MORTEN. And then shall be allowed to do anything we like?

BILLING. Well, you see, Morten—

MRS. STOCKMANN. You must go to your room now, boys; I am sure you have some lessons to learn for tomorrow.

EJLIF. I should like so much to stay a little longer—

MRS. STOCKMANN. No, no; away you go, both of you.

(*The boys say good night and go into the room on the left.*)

HOVSTAD. Do you really think it can do the boys any harm to hear such things?

MRS. STOCKMANN. I don't know, but I don't like it.

PETRA. But you know, Mother, I think you really are wrong about it.

MRS. STOCKMANN. Maybe, but I don't like it—not in our own home.

PETRA. There is so much falsehood both at home and at school. At home one must not speak, and at school we have to stand and tell lies to the children.

HORSTER. Tell lies?

PETRA. Yes, don't you suppose we have to teach them all sorts of things that we don't believe?

BILLING. That is perfectly true.

PETRA. If only I had the means I would start a school of my own, and it would be conducted on very different lines.

BILLING. Oh, bother the means—!

HORSTER. Well if you are thinking of that, Miss Stockmann, I shall be delighted to provide you with a schoolroom. The great big old house my father left me is standing almost empty; there is an immense dining room downstairs—

PETRA. (*Laughing.*)   Thank you very much; but I am afraid nothing will come of it.

HOVSTAD. No, Miss Petra is much more likely to take to journalism, I expect. By the way, have you had time to do anything with that English story you promised to translate for us?

PETRA.   No, not yet; but you shall have it in good time.

(DR. STOCKMANN *comes in from his room with an open letter in his hand.*)

DR. STOCKMANN.   (*Waving the letter.*)   Well, now the town will have something new to talk about, I can tell you!

BILLING.   Something new?

MRS. STOCKMANN.   What is this?

DR. STOCKMANN.   A great discovery, Katherine.

HOVSTAD.   Really?

MRS. STOCKMANN.   A discovery of yours?

DR. STOCKMANN.   A discovery of mine. (*Walks up and down.*) Just let them come saying, as usual, that it is all fancy and a crazy man's imagination! But they will be careful what they say this time, I can tell you!

PETRA.   But, Father, tell us what it is.

DR. STOCKMANN.   Yes, yes—only give me time, and you shall know all about it. If only I had Peter here now! It just shows how we men can go about forming our judgments, when in reality we are as blind as any moles—

HOVSTAD.   What are you driving at, Doctor?

DR. STOCKMANN.   (*Standing still by the table.*)   Isn't it the universal opinion that our town is a healthy spot?

HOVSTAD.   Certainly.

DR. STOCKMANN.   Quite an unusually healthy spot, in fact—a place that deserves to be recommended in the warmest possible manner either for invalids or for people who are well—

MRS. STOCKMANN.   Yes, but my dear Thomas—

DR. STOCKMANN.   And we have been recommending it and praising it—I have written and written, both in the *Messenger* and in pamphlets—

HOVSTAD.   Well, what then?

DR. STOCKMANN.   And the Baths—we have called them the "main artery of the town's lifeblood," the "nerve center of our town," and the devil knows what else—

BILLING.   "The town's pulsating heart" was the expression I once used on an important occasion—

DR. STOCKMANN.   Quite so. Well, do you know what they really are, these great, splendid, much-praised Baths, that have cost so much money—do you know what they are?

HOVSTAD.   No, what are they?

MRS. STOCKMANN.   Yes, what are they?

DR. STOCKMANN.   The whole place is a pesthouse! [19]

PETRA.   The Baths, Father?

MRS. STOCKMANN.   (*At the same time.*)   Our Baths!

HOVSTAD.   But, Doctor—

BILLING.   Absolutely incredible!

DR. STOCKMANN.   The whole Bath establishment is a whited, poisoned sepulcher,[20] I tell you—the gravest possible danger to the public health! All the nastiness up at Mölledal, all that stinking filth, is infecting the water in the conduit pipes [21] leading to the reservoir; and the same cursed, filthy poison oozes out on the shore too—

HORSTER.   Where the bathing place is?

DR. STOCKMANN.   Just there.

HOVSTAD.   How do you come to be so certain of all this, Doctor?

DR. STOCKMANN.   I have investigated the matter most conscientiously. For a long time past I have suspected something of the kind. Last year we had some very strange cases of illness among the visitors—typhoid [22] cases, and cases of gastric [23] fever—

MRS. STOCKMANN.   Yes, that is quite true.

DR. STOCKMANN.   At the time, we supposed the visitors had been infected before they came; but later on, in the winter, I began to have a different opinion; and so I set myself to examine the water, as well as I could.

MRS. STOCKMANN.   Then that is what you have been so busy with?

DR. STOCKMANN.   Indeed I have been busy, Katherine. But here I had none of the necessary scientific apparatus, so I sent samples, both of the drinking water and of the sea water, up to the University, to have an accurate analysis made by a chemist.

HOVSTAD.   And have you got that?

19. **pesthouse:** *formerly,* a public hospital for persons suffering from plague or other infectious disease.
20. **sepulcher** (sep'əl·kər): burial place. Stockmann is suggesting that its appearances are deceiving. His thought is similar to the following passage in the New Testament: ". . . for ye are like unto whited sepulchers, which indeed appear beautiful outward, but are within full of dead men's bones, and of all uncleanness" (Matthew 23:27).
21. **conduit** (kon'dit, kon'dōō·it) **pipes:** channels or pipes for carrying water.
22. **typhoid:** a severe infectious disease characterized by fever and intestinal illness, caused by drinking infected milk or water.
23. **gastric:** in or near the stomach.

DR. STOCKMANN. (*Showing him the letter.*)   Here it is! It proves the presence of decomposing organic matter in the water—it is full of infusoria.[24] The water is absolutely dangerous to use, either internally or externally.

MRS. STOCKMANN.   What a mercy you discovered it in time.

DR. STOCKMANN.   You may well say so.

HOVSTAD.   And what do you propose to do now, Doctor?

DR. STOCKMANN.   To see the matter put right—naturally.

HOVSTAD.   Can that be done?

DR. STOCKMANN.   It must be done. Otherwise the Baths will be absolutely useless and wasted. But we need not anticipate that; I have a very clear idea what we shall have to do.

MRS. STOCKMANN.   But why have you kept this all so secret, dear?

DR. STOCKMANN.   Do you suppose I was going to run about the town gossiping about it, before I had absolute proof? No, thank you. I am not such a fool.

PETRA.   Still, you might have told us—

DR. STOCKMANN.   Not a living soul. But tomorrow you may run round to the old Badger [25]—

MRS. STOCKMANN.   Oh, Thomas! Thomas!

DR. STOCKMANN.   Well, to your grandfather, then. The old boy will have something to be astonished at! I know he thinks I am cracked —and there are lots of other people think so, too, I have noticed. But now these good folks shall see—they shall just see—! (*Walks about, rubbing his hands.*) There will be a nice upset in the town, Katherine; you can't imagine what it will be. All the conduit pipes will have to be relaid.

HOVSTAD. (*Getting up.*)   All the conduit pipes—?

DR. STOCKMANN.   Yes, of course. The intake is too low down; it will have to be lifted to a position much higher up.

PETRA.   Then you were right after all.

DR. STOCKMANN.   Ah, you remember, Petra—I wrote opposing the plans before the work was begun. But at that time no one would listen to me. Well, I am going to let them have it, now! Of course I have prepared a report for the Baths' Committee; I have had it ready for a week, and was only waiting for this to come. (*Shows the letter.*) Now it shall go off at once. (*Goes into his room and*

24. **infusoria:** microscopic bodies living in decayed matter or in stagnant water.
25. **Badger:** a burrowing animal; used here to indicate the type of person who nags or annoys another.

comes back with some papers.) Look at that! Four closely written sheets! And the letter shall go with them. Give me a bit of paper, Katherine—something to wrap them up in. That will do! Now give it to—to— (*Stamps his foot.*)—what the deuce is her name? Give it to the maid, and tell her to take it at once to the Mayor.

(MRS. STOCKMANN *takes the packet and goes out through the dining room.*)

PETRA.   What do you think Uncle Peter will say, Father?

DR. STOCKMANN.   What is there for him to say? I should think he would be very glad that such an important truth has been brought to light.

HOVSTAD.   Will you let me print a short note about your discovery in the *Messenger?*

DR. STOCKMANN.   I shall be very much obliged if you will.

HOVSTAD.   It is very desirable that the public should be informed of it without delay.

DR. STOCKMANN.   Certainly.

MRS. STOCKMANN. (*Coming back.*)   She has just gone with it.

BILLING.   Upon my soul, Doctor, you are going to be the foremost man in the town!

DR. STOCKMANN. (*Walking about happily.*)   Nonsense! As a matter of fact I have done nothing more than my duty. I have only made a lucky find—that's all. Still, all the same—

BILLING.   Hovstad, don't you think the town ought to give Dr. Stockmann some sort of testimonial?

HOVSTAD.   I will suggest it, anyway.

BILLING.   And I will speak to Aslaksen about it.

DR. STOCKMANN.   No, my good friends, don't let us have any of that nonsense. I won't hear of anything of the kind. And if the Baths' Committee should think of voting me an increase of salary, I will not accept it. Do you hear, Katherine?—I won't accept it.

MRS. STOCKMANN.   You are quite right, Thomas.

PETRA. (*Lifting her glass.*)   Your health, Father!

HOVSTAD *and* BILLING.   Your health, Doctor! Good health!

HORSTER. (*Touches glasses with* DR. STOCKMANN.)   I hope it will bring you nothing but good luck.

DR. STOCKMANN.   Thank you, thank you, my dear fellows! I feel tremendously happy! It is a splendid thing for a man to be able to feel that he has done a service to his native town and to his fellow citizens. Hurrah, Katherine!

(*He puts his arms round her and whirls her round and round, while she protests with laughing cries. They all laugh, clap their hands and cheer the* DOCTOR. *The boys put their heads in at the door to see what is going on.*)

Curtain.

Meaning and Method: Act I

1. Before Dr. Stockmann appears on stage Ibsen prepares the way for him by revealing the opinions of others about his character. What do his wife's lines tell us? Why does Hovstad admire him? For what traits does his elder brother, Peter, criticize the Doctor? Is he jealous? Cite evidence to prove your answers.

2. By means of the dialogue between Dr. Stockmann and his brother, Ibsen is able to present their basic areas of conflict. On what issues do the two disagree? Which man is opposed to independent action? Which supports the status quo and which looks forward to change? In what other characteristics do they differ? How is sympathy built for one brother, unfriendliness for the other?

3. In the kind of life she leads and in her manner of expressing herself, Petra seems similar to her father. Cite the lines that allow this conclusion to be drawn. In what way does Mrs. Stockmann seem different from her husband and her daughter?

4. After describing the discovery he has made about the dangers of the Baths to public health, Dr. Stockmann walks about cheerfully, "rubbing his hands." Why is he delighted with his unpleasant discovery? What reaction does he expect from the local government, the Baths' Committee, and the public? Why does Hovstad want to publish the Doctor's discovery? What do you expect the reaction of Peter Stockmann and the other powers in the town to be? Why? What do you think the Doctor's motives are for wanting to tell the public the truth about the Baths?

5. *Exposition*—the presentation of background material—gives the audience the information it needs to know. Since the Baths are completed before the play opens, Ibsen had to devise a way to give the audience the history of the Baths: whose idea they were; who set the project in motion; what conflicts arose in the construction; and the effect of the project on the town as a whole.

   Peter Stockmann speaks of the Baths first. What aspect does he tell about? How are the other facts presented? At what point does the exposition end and the real action of the play begin?

Act II

The same. The door into the dining room is shut. It is morning.
MRS. STOCKMANN, *with a sealed letter in her hand, comes in from the dining room, goes to the door of the* DOCTOR's *study and peeps in.*

MRS. STOCKMANN.   Are you in, Thomas?
DR. STOCKMANN. (*From within his room.*)   Yes, I have just come in. (*Comes into the room.*) What is it?
MRS. STOCKMANN.   A letter from your brother.
DR. STOCKMANN.   Aha, let us see! (*Opens the letter and reads.*) "I return herewith the manuscript you sent me"— (*Reads on in a low murmur.*) Hm!—
MRS. STOCKMANN.   What does he say?
DR. STOCKMANN. (*Putting the papers in his pocket.*)   Oh, he only writes that he will come up here himself about midday.
MRS. STOCKMANN.   Well, try and remember to be at home this time.
DR. STOCKMANN.   That will be all right; I have got through all my morning visits.
MRS. STOCKMANN.   I am extremely curious to know how he takes it.
DR. STOCKMANN.   You will see he won't like its having been I and not he, that made the discovery.
MRS. STOCKMANN.   Aren't you a little nervous about that?
DR. STOCKMANN.   Oh, he really will be pleased enough, you know. But, at the same time, Peter is so confoundedly afraid of anyone's doing any service to the town except himself.
MRS. STOCKMANN.   I will tell you what, Thomas—you should be good natured, and share the credit of this with him. Couldn't you make out that it was he who set you on the scent of this discovery?
DR. STOCKMANN.   I am quite willing. If only I can get the thing set right. I—

(MORTEN KIIL *puts his head in through the door leading from the hall, looks round in an enquiring manner and chuckles.*)

MORTEN KIIL. (*Slyly.*)   Is it—is it true?
MRS. STOCKMANN. (*Going to the door.*)   Father! Is it you?
DR. STOCKMANN.   Ah, Mr. Kiil—good morning, good morning!
MRS. STOCKMANN.   But come along in.
MORTEN KIIL.   If it is true, I will; if not, I am off.
DR. STOCKMANN.   If what is true?

MORTEN KIIL. This tale about the water supply. Is it true?

DR. STOCKMANN. Certainly it is true. But how did you come to hear it?

MORTEN KIIL. (*Coming in.*) Petra ran in on her way to the school—

DR. STOCKMANN. Did she?

MORTEN KIIL. Yes; and she declares that—I thought she was only making a fool of me, but it isn't like Petra to do that.

DR. STOCKMANN. Of course not. How could you imagine such a thing?

MORTEN KIIL. Oh well, it is better never to trust anybody; you may find you have been made a fool of before you know where you are. But it is really true, all the same?

DR. STOCKMANN. You can depend upon it that it is true. Won't you sit down? (*Settles him on the couch.*) Isn't it a real bit of luck for the town—

MORTEN KIIL. (*Suppressing his laughter.*) A bit of luck for the town?

DR. STOCKMANN. Yes, that I made the discovery in good time.

MORTEN KIIL. (*As before.*) Yes, yes, yes!—But I should never have thought you the sort of man to pull your own brother's leg [1] like this!

DR. STOCKMANN. Pull his leg!

MRS. STOCKMANN. Really, Father dear—

MORTEN KIIL. (*Resting his hands and his chin on the handle of his stick and winking slyly at the* DOCTOR.) Let me see, what was the story? Some kind of beast that had got into the water pipes, wasn't it?

DR. STOCKMANN. Infusoria—yes.

MORTEN KIIL. And a lot of these beasts had got in, according to Petra—a tremendous lot.

DR. STOCKMANN. Certainly; hundreds of thousands of them, probably.

MORTEN KIIL. But no one can see them—isn't that so?

DR. STOCKMANN. Yes; you can't see them.

MORTEN KIIL. (*With a quiet chuckle.*) Damme—it's the finest story I have ever heard!

DR. STOCKMANN. What do you mean?

MORTEN KIIL. But you will never get the Mayor to believe a thing like that.

DR. STOCKMANN. We shall see.

1. pull . . . leg: make fun of your own brother; to kid or deceive him.

MORTEN KIIL.   Do you think he will be fool enough to—?

DR. STOCKMANN.   I hope the whole town will be fools enough.

MORTEN KIIL.   The whole town! Well, it wouldn't be a bad thing. It would just serve them right, and teach them a lesson. They think themselves so much cleverer than we old fellows. They hounded me out of the council; they did, I tell you—they hounded me out. Now they shall pay for it. You pull their legs, too, Thomas!

DR. STOCKMANN.   Really, I—

MORTEN KIIL.   You pull their legs! (*Gets up.*) If you can work it so that the Mayor and his friends all swallow the same bait, I will give ten pounds [2] to a charity—like a shot!

DR. STOCKMANN.   That is very kind of you.

MORTEN KIIL.   Yes, I haven't got much money to throw away, I can tell you; but if you can work this, I will give five pounds to a charity at Christmas.

(HOVSTAD *comes in by the hall door.*)

HOVSTAD.   Good morning! (*Stops.*) Oh, I beg your pardon—

DR. STOCKMANN.   Not at all; come in.

MORTEN KIIL.   (*With another chuckle.*)   Oho! Is he in this, too?

HOVSTAD.   What do you mean?

DR. STOCKMANN.   Certainly he is.

MORTEN KIIL.   I might have known it! It must get into the papers. You know how to do it, Thomas! Set your wits to work. Now I must go.

DR. STOCKMANN.   Won't you stay a little while?

MORTEN KIIL.   No, I must be off now. You keep up this game for all it is worth; you won't repent it, I'm damned if you will!

(*He goes out;* MRS. STOCKMANN *follows him into the hall.*)

DR. STOCKMANN.   (*Laughing.*)   Just imagine—the old chap doesn't believe a word of all this about the water supply.

HOVSTAD.   Oh, that was it, then?

DR. STOCKMANN.   Yes, that was what we were talking about. Perhaps it is the same thing that brings you here?

HOVSTAD.   Yes, it is. Can you spare me a few minutes, Doctor?

DR. STOCKMANN.   As long as you like, my dear fellow.

HOVSTAD.   Have you heard from the Mayor yet?

DR. STOCKMANN.   Not yet. He is coming here later.

2. **ten pounds:** British currency.

HOVSTAD.   I have given the matter a great deal of thought since last night.

DR. STOCKMANN.   Well?

HOVSTAD.   From your point of view, as a doctor and a man of science, this affair of the water supply is an isolated matter. I mean, you do not realize that it involves a great many other things.

DR. STOCKMANN.   How do you mean? Let us sit down, my dear fellow. No, sit here on the couch. (HOVSTAD *sits down on the couch,* DR. STOCKMANN *on a chair on the other side of the table.*) Now then. You mean that—?

HOVSTAD.   You said yesterday that the pollution of the water was due to impurities in the soil.

DR. STOCKMANN.   Yes, unquestionably it is due to that poisonous morass [3] up at Mölledal.

HOVSTAD.   Begging your pardon, Doctor, I fancy it is due to quite another morass altogether.

DR. STOCKMANN.   What morass?

HOVSTAD.   The morass that the whole life of our town is built on and is rotting in.

DR. STOCKMANN.   What the deuce are you driving at, Hovstad?

HOVSTAD.   The whole of the town's interests have, little by little, got into the hands of a pack of officials.

DR. STOCKMANN.   Oh, come! They are not all officials.

HOVSTAD.   No, but those that are not officials are at any rate the officials' friends and adherents; it is the wealthy folk, the old families in the town, that have got us entirely in their hands.

DR. STOCKMANN.   Yes, but after all they are men of ability and knowledge.

HOVSTAD.   Did they show any ability or knowledge when they laid the conduit pipes where they are now?

DR. STOCKMANN.   No, of course that was a great piece of stupidity on their part. But that is going to be set right now.

HOVSTAD.   Do you think that will be all such plain sailing?

DR. STOCKMANN.   Plain sailing or no, it has got to be done, anyway.

HOVSTAD.   Yes, provided the press takes up the question.

DR. STOCKMANN.   I don't think that will be necessary, my dear fellow; I am certain my brother—

3. **morass:** swamp; marsh; bog. It may also mean anything that impedes, perplexes, or entraps, as a difficult situation.

HOVSTAD.   Excuse me, Doctor; I feel bound to tell you I am inclined to take the matter up.

DR. STOCKMANN.   In the paper?

HOVSTAD.   Yes. When I took over the *People's Messenger,* my idea was to break up this ring of self-opinionated [4] old fossils [5] who had got hold of all the influence.

DR. STOCKMANN.   But you know you told me yourself what the result had been; you nearly ruined your paper.

HOVSTAD.   Yes, at the time we were obliged to climb down, a peg or two, it is quite true, because there was a danger of the whole project of the Baths coming to nothing if they failed us. But now the scheme has been carried through, and we can dispense with these grand gentlemen.

DR. STOCKMANN.   Dispense with them, yes; but we owe them a great debt of gratitude.

HOVSTAD.   That shall be recognized ungrudgingly. But a journalist of my democratic tendencies cannot let such an opportunity as this slip. The bubble of official infallibility [6] must be pricked. The superstition must be destroyed, like any other.

DR. STOCKMANN.   I am wholeheartedly with you in that, Mr. Hovstad; if it is a superstition, away with it!

HOVSTAD.   I should be very reluctant to bring the Mayor into it, because he is your brother. But I am sure you will agree with me that truth should be the first consideration.

DR. STOCKMANN.   That goes without saying. (*With sudden emphasis.*) Yes, but—but—

HOVSTAD.   You must not misjudge me. I am neither more self-interested nor more ambitious than most men.

DR. STOCKMANN.   My dear fellow—who suggests anything of the kind?

HOVSTAD.   I am of humble origin, as you know; and that has given me opportunities of knowing what is the most crying need in the humbler ranks of life. It is that they should be allowed some part in the direction of public affairs, Doctor. That is what will develop their faculties and intelligence and self-respect—

DR. STOCKMANN.   I quite appreciate that.

HOVSTAD.   Yes—and in my opinion a journalist incurs [7] a heavy re-

4. **self-opinionated:** holding stubbornly to one's own views.
5. **fossils:** traces of ancient plant or animal life preserved in rock formations; used here figuratively to suggest whatever is out of date or antiquated and opposed to change and progress.
6. **infallibility:** inability to make a mistake.
7. **incurs:** brings upon himself.

sponsibility if he neglects a favorable opportunity of emancipating [8] the masses—the humble and oppressed. I know well enough that in exalted circles I shall be called an agitator,[9] and all that sort of thing; but they may call me what they like. If only my conscience doesn't reproach me, then—

DR. STOCKMANN. Quite right! Quite right, Mr. Hovstad. But all the same—devil take it! (*A knock is heard at the door.*) Come in!

(ASLAKSEN *appears at the door. He is poorly but decently dressed, in black, with a slightly crumpled white neckcloth; he wears gloves and has a felt hat in his hand.*)

ASLAKSEN. (*Bowing.*) Excuse my taking the liberty, Doctor—

DR. STOCKMANN. (*Getting up.*) Ah, it is you, Aslaksen!

ASLAKSEN. Yes, Doctor.

HOVSTAD. (*Standing up.*) Is it me you want, Aslaksen?

ASLAKSEN. No; I didn't know I should find you here. No, it was the Doctor I—

DR. STOCKMANN. I am quite at your service. What is it?

ASLAKSEN. Is what I heard from Mr. Billing true, sir—that you mean to improve our water supply?

DR. STOCKMANN. Yes, for the Baths.

ASLAKSEN. Quite so, I understand. Well, I have come to say that I will back that up by every means in my power.

HOVSTAD. (*To the* DOCTOR.) You see!

DR. STOCKMANN. I shall be very grateful to you but—

ASLAKSEN. Because it may be no bad thing to have us small-trades men at your back. We form, as it were, a compact majority in the town—if we choose. And it is always a good thing to have the majority with you, Doctor.

DR. STOCKMANN. That is undeniably true; but I confess I don't see why such unusual precautions should be necessary in this case. It seems to me that such a plain, straightforward thing—

ASLAKSEN. Oh, it may be very desirable, all the same. I know our local authorities so well; officials are not generally very ready to act on proposals that come from other people. That is why I think it would not be at all amiss if we made a little demonstration.

HOVSTAD. That's right.

DR. STOCKMANN. Demonstration, did you say? What on earth are you going to make a demonstration about?

8. **emancipating:** setting free.
9. **agitator:** troublemaker; one who excites or endeavors to incite.

ASLAKSEN. We shall proceed with the greatest moderation, Doctor. Moderation is always my aim; it is the greatest virtue in a citizen —at least, I think so.

DR. STOCKMANN. It is well known to be a characteristic of yours, Mr. Aslaksen.

ASLAKSEN. Yes, I think I may pride myself on that. And this matter of the water supply is of the greatest importance to us small-trades men. The Baths promise to be a regular gold mine for the town. We shall all make our living out of them, especially those of us who are householders.[10] That is why we will back up the project as strongly as possible. And as I am at present Chairman of the Householders' Association—

DR. STOCKMANN. Yes—?

ASLAKSEN. And, what is more, local secretary of the Temperance Society [11]—you know, sir, I suppose, that I am a worker in the temperance cause?

DR. STOCKMANN. Of course, of course.

ASLAKSEN. Well, you can understand that I come into contact with a great many people. And as I have the reputation of a temperate and law-abiding citizen—like yourself, Doctor—I have a certain influence in the town, a little bit of power, if I may be allowed to say so.

DR. STOCKMANN. I know that quite well, Mr. Aslaksen.

ASLAKSEN. So you see it would be an easy matter for me to set on foot some kind of testimonial, if necessary.

DR. STOCKMANN. A testimonial?

ASLAKSEN. Yes, some kind of address of thanks from the townsmen for your share in a matter of such importance to the community. I need scarcely say that it would have to be drawn up with the greatest regard to moderation, so as not to offend the authorities— who, after all, have the reins in their hands. If we pay strict attention to that, no one can take it amiss, I should think!

HOVSTAD. Well, and even supposing they didn't like it—

ASLAKSEN. No, no, no; there must be no discourtesy to the authorities, Mr. Hovstad. It is no use falling foul of those upon whom our welfare so closely depends. I have done that in my time, and no

10. **householders:** homeowners.
11. **Temperance Society:** an organization that urges moderation in the use of alcoholic drinks, and in some cases, forbids their use entirely.

good ever comes of it. But no one can take exception to a reasonable and frank expression of a citizen's views.

DR. STOCKMANN. (*Shaking him by the hand.*)   I can't tell you, dear Mr. Aslaksen, how extremely pleased I am to find such hearty support among my fellow citizens. I am delighted—delighted! Now, you will take a small glass of sherry, eh?

ASLAKSEN.   No, thank you; I never drink alcohol of that kind.

DR. STOCKMANN.   Well, what do you say to a glass of beer, then?

ASLAKSEN.   Nor that either, thank you, Doctor. I never drink anything as early as this. I am going into town now to talk this over with one or two householders, and prepare the ground.

DR. STOCKMANN.   It is tremendously kind of you, Mr. Aslaksen; but I really cannot understand the necessity for all these precautions. It seems to me that the thing should go of itself.

ASLAKSEN.   The authorities are somewhat slow to move, Doctor. Far be it from me to seem to blame them—

HOVSTAD.   We are going to stir them up in the paper tomorrow, Aslaksen.

ASLAKSEN.   But not violently, I trust, Mr. Hovstad. Proceed with moderation, or you will do nothing with them. You may take my advice; I have gathered my experience in the school of life. Well, I must say good-bye, Doctor. You know now that we small-trades men are at your back at all events, like a solid wall. You have the compact majority on your side, Doctor.

DR. STOCKMANN.   I am very much obliged, dear Mr. Aslaksen. (*Shakes hands with him.*) Good-bye, good-bye.

ASLAKSEN.   Are you going my way, toward the printing office, Mr. Hovstad?

HOVSTAD.   I will come later; I have something to settle up first.

ASLAKSEN.   Very well.

(*Bows and goes out;* STOCKMANN *follows him into the hall.*)

HOVSTAD. (*As* STOCKMANN *comes in again.*)   Well, what do you think of that, Doctor? Don't you think it is high time we stirred a little life into all this slackness and vacillation [12] and cowardice?

DR. STOCKMANN.   Are you referring to Aslaksen?

HOVSTAD.   Yes, I am. He is one of those who are floundering in a bog —decent enough fellow though he may be, otherwise. And most of

12. vacillation (vas′ə·lā′shən) : shifting from one viewpoint or loyalty to another.

the people here are in just the same case—seesawing and edging first to one side and then to the other, so overcome with caution and scruple [13] that they never dare to take any decided step.

DR. STOCKMANN.   Yes, but Aslaksen seemed to me so thoroughly well-intentioned.

HOVSTAD.   There is one thing I esteem higher than that; and that is for a man to be self-reliant and sure of himself.

DR. STOCKMANN.   I think you are perfectly right there.

HOVSTAD.   That is why I want to seize this opportunity, and try if I cannot manage to put a little virility [14] into these well-intentioned people for once. The idol of Authority must be shattered in this town. This gross and inexcusable blunder about the water supply must be brought home to the mind of every municipal voter.

DR. STOCKMANN.   Very well; if you are of opinion that it is for the good of the community, so be it. But not until I have had a talk with my brother.

HOVSTAD.   Anyway, I will get a leading article ready; and if the Mayor refuses to take the matter up—

DR. STOCKMANN.   How can you suppose such a thing possible?

HOVSTAD.   It is conceivable.[15] And in that case—

DR. STOCKMANN.   In that case I promise you— Look here, in that case you may print my report—every word of it.

HOVSTAD.   May I? Have I your word for it?

DR. STOCKMANN.   (*Giving him the manuscript.*)   Here it is; take it with you. It can do no harm for you to read it through, and you can give it back to me later on.

HOVSTAD.   Good, good! That is what I will do. And now good-bye, Doctor.

DR. STOCKMANN.   Good-bye, good-bye. You will see everything will run quite smoothly, Mr. Hovstad—quite smoothly.

HOVSTAD.   Hm! We shall see. (*Bows and goes out.*)

DR. STOCKMANN.   (*Opens the dining-room door and looks in.*)   Katherine! Oh, are you back, Petra?

PETRA.   (*Coming in.*)   Yes, I have just come from the school.

MRS. STOCKMANN.   (*Coming in.*)   Has he not been here yet?

DR. STOCKMANN.   Peter? No. But I have had a long talk with Hovstad. He is quite excited about my discovery. I find it has a much wider

---

13. **scruple:** doubt or uncertainty regarding a moral right or duty; reluctance arising from conscientious disapproval.
14. **virility:** manliness or vigor.
15. **conceivable:** imaginable; believable.

bearing than I at first imagined. And he has put his paper at my disposal if necessity should arise.

MRS. STOCKMANN. Do you think it will?

DR. STOCKMANN. Not for a moment. But at all events it makes me feel proud to know that I have the liberal-minded independent press on my side. Yes, and—just imagine—I have had a visit from the Chairman of the Householders' Association.

MRS. STOCKMANN. Oh! What did he want?

DR. STOCKMANN. To offer me his support, too. They will support me in a body if it should be necessary. Katherine—do you know what I have got behind me?

MRS. STOCKMANN. Behind you? No, what have you got behind you?

DR. STOCKMANN. The compact majority.

MRS. STOCKMANN. Really? Is that a good thing for you, Thomas?

DR. STOCKMANN. I should think it was a good thing. (*Walks up and down rubbing his hands.*) By Jove, it's a fine thing to feel this bond of brotherhood between one's self and one's fellow citizens!

PETRA. And to be able to do so much that is good and useful, Father!

DR. STOCKMANN. And for one's own native town into the bargain, my child!

MRS. STOCKMANN. That was a ring at the bell.

DR. STOCKMANN. It must be he, then. (*A knock is heard at the door.*) Come in!

PETER STOCKMANN. (*Comes in from the hall.*) Good morning.

DR. STOCKMANN. Glad to see you, Peter!

MRS. STOCKMANN. Good morning, Peter. How are you?

PETER STOCKMANN. So so, thank you. (*To* DR. STOCKMANN.) I received from you yesterday, after office hours, a report dealing with the condition of the water at the Baths.

DR. STOCKMANN. Yes. Have you read it?

PETER STOCKMANN. Yes, I have.

DR. STOCKMANN. And what have you to say to it?

PETER STOCKMANN. (*With a sidelong glance.*) Hm!—

MRS. STOCKMANN. Come along, Petra.

(*She and* PETRA *go into the room on the left.*)

PETER STOCKMANN. (*After a pause.*) Was it necessary to make all these investigations behind my back?

DR. STOCKMANN. Yes, because until I was absolutely certain about it—

PETER STOCKMANN.   Then you mean that you are absolutely certain now?

DR. STOCKMANN.   Surely you are convinced of that.

PETER STOCKMANN.   Is it your intention to bring this document before the Baths' Committee as a sort of official communication?

DR. STOCKMANN.   Certainly. Something must be done in the matter —and that quickly.

PETER STOCKMANN.   As usual, you employ violent expressions in your report. You say, among other things, that what we offer visitors in our Baths is a permanent supply of poison.

DR. STOCKMANN.   Well, can you describe it any other way, Peter? Just think—water that is poisonous, whether you drink it or bathe in it! And this we offer to the poor sick folk who come to us trustfully and pay us at an exorbitant [16] rate to be made well again!

PETER STOCKMANN.   And your reasoning leads you to this conclusion, that we must build a sewer to draw off the alleged impurities from Mölledal and must re-lay the water conduits.

DR. STOCKMANN.   Yes. Do you see any other way out of it? I don't.

PETER STOCKMANN.   I made a pretext this morning to go and see the town engineer, and, as if only half seriously, broached the subject of these proposals as a thing we might perhaps have to take under consideration some time later on.

DR. STOCKMANN.   Some time later on!

PETER STOCKMANN.   He smiled at what he considered to be my extravagance, naturally. Have you taken the trouble to consider what your proposed alterations would cost? According to the information I obtained, the expenses would probably mount up to fifteen or twenty thousand pounds.

DR. STOCKMANN.   Would it cost so much?

PETER STOCKMANN.   Yes; and the worst part of it would be that the work would take at least two years.

DR. STOCKMANN.   Two years? Two whole years?

PETER STOCKMANN.   At least. And what are we to do with the Baths in the meantime? Close them? Indeed we should be obliged to. And do you suppose anyone would come near the place after it had got about that the water was dangerous?

DR. STOCKMANN.   Yes, but, Peter, that is what it is.

16. exorbitant: excessive; extravagant; beyond what is just or reasonable.

PETER STOCKMANN.   And all this at this juncture [17]—just as the Baths are beginning to be known. There are other towns in the neighborhood with qualifications to attract visitors for bathing purposes. Don't you suppose they would immediately strain every nerve to divert the entire stream of strangers to themselves? Unquestionably they would; and then where should we be? We should probably have to abandon the whole thing, which has cost us so much money—and then you would have ruined your native town.

DR. STOCKMANN.   I—should have ruined—!

PETER STOCKMANN.   It is simply and solely through the Baths that the town has before it any future worth mentioning. You know that just as well as I.

DR. STOCKMANN.   But what do you think ought to be done, then?

PETER STOCKMANN.   Your report has not convinced me that the condition of the water at the Baths is as bad as you represent it to be.

DR. STOCKMANN.   I tell you it is even worse! Or at all events it will be in summer, when the warm weather comes.

PETER STOCKMANN.   As I said, I believe you exaggerate the matter considerably. A capable physician ought to know what measures to take—he ought to be capable of preventing injurious influences or of remedying them if they become obviously persistent.

DR. STOCKMANN.   Well? What more?

PETER STOCKMANN.   The water supply for the Baths is now an established fact, and in consequence must be treated as such. But probably the Committee, at its discretion,[18] will not be disinclined to consider the question of how far it might be possible to introduce certain improvements consistent with a reasonable expenditure.[19]

DR. STOCKMANN.   And do you suppose that I will have anything to do with such a piece of trickery as that?

PETER STOCKMANN.   Trickery!!

DR. STOCKMANN.   Yes, it would be a trick—a fraud, a lie, a downright crime toward the public, toward the whole community!

PETER STOCKMANN.   I have not, as I remarked before, been able to convince myself that there is actually any imminent [20] danger.

DR. STOCKMANN.   You have not! It is impossible that you should not

17. **juncture:** moment; point in time, especially one at which a critical decision must be made.
18. **discretion:** care or prudence in what is said or done.
19. **expenditure:** amount of money spent.
20. **imminent:** impending; about to happen.

be convinced. I know I have represented the facts absolutely truth-fully and fairly. And you know it very well, Peter, only you won't acknowledge it. It was owing to your action that both the Baths and the water conduits were built where they are; and that is what you won't acknowledge—that damnable blunder of yours. Pooh! Do you suppose I don't see through you?

PETER STOCKMANN.   And even if that were true? If I perhaps guard my reputation somewhat anxiously, it is in the interests of the town. Without moral authority I am powerless to direct public affairs as seems, to my judgment, to be best for the common good. And on that account—and for various other reasons, too—it appears to me to be a matter of importance that your report should not be deliv-ered to the Committee. In the interests of the public, you must withhold it. Then, later on, I will raise the question and we will do our best, privately; but nothing of this unfortunate affair—not a single word of it—must come to the ears of the public.

DR. STOCKMANN.   I am afraid you will not be able to prevent that now, my dear Peter.

PETER STOCKMANN.   It must and shall be prevented.

DR. STOCKMANN.   It is no use, I tell you. There are too many people that know about it.

PETER STOCKMANN.   That know about it? Who? Surely you don't mean those fellows on the *People's Messenger?*

DR. STOCKMANN.   Yes, they know. The liberal-minded independent press is going to see that you do your duty.

PETER STOCKMANN.   (*After a short pause.*)   You are an extraordinarily independent man, Thomas. Have you given no thought to the con-sequences this may have for yourself?

DR. STOCKMANN.   Consequences? For me?

PETER STOCKMANN.   For you and yours, yes.

DR. STOCKMANN.   What the deuce do you mean?

PETER STOCKMANN.   I believe I have always behaved in a brotherly way to you—have always been ready to oblige or to help you?

DR. STOCKMANN.   Yes, you have, and I am grateful to you for it.

PETER STOCKMANN.   There is no need. Indeed, to some extent I was forced to do so—for my own sake. I always hoped that, if I helped to improve your financial position, I should be able to keep some check on you.

DR. STOCKMANN.   What!! Then it was only for your own sake—!

PETER STOCKMANN.   Up to a certain point, yes. It is painful for a man in an official position to have his nearest relative compromising [21] himself time after time.

DR. STOCKMANN.   And do you consider that I do that?

PETER STOCKMANN.   Yes, unfortunately, you do, without even being aware of it. You have a restless, pugnacious,[22] rebellious disposition. And then there is that disastrous propensity [23] of yours to want to write about every sort of possible and impossible thing. The moment an idea comes into your head, you must needs go and write a newspaper article or a whole pamphlet about it.

DR. STOCKMANN.   Well, but is it not the duty of a citizen to let the public share in any new ideas he may have?

PETER STOCKMANN.   Oh, the public doesn't require any new ideas. The public is best served by the good, old-established ideas it already has.

DR. STOCKMANN.   And that is your honest opinion?

PETER STOCKMANN.   Yes, and for once I must talk frankly to you. Hitherto I have tried to avoid doing so, because I know how irritable you are; but now I must tell you the truth, Thomas. You have no concept of what an amount of harm you do yourself by your impetuosity.[24] You complain of the authorities, you even complain of the government—you are always pulling them to pieces; you insist that you have been neglected and persecuted. But what else can such a cantankerous [25] man as you expect?

DR. STOCKMANN.   What next! Cantankerous, am I?

PETER STOCKMANN.   Yes, Thomas, you are an extremely cantankerous man to work with—I know that to my cost. You disregard everything that you ought to have consideration for. You seem completely to forget that it is me you have to thank for your appointment here as medical officer to the Baths—

DR. STOCKMANN.   I was entitled to it as a matter of course!—I and nobody else! I was the first person to see that the town could be made into a flourishing watering place,[26] and I was the only one who saw it at that time. I had to fight single-handed in support of the idea for many years; and I wrote and wrote—

21. **compromising:** laying oneself open to suspicion; imperiling character or reputation.
22. **pugnacious** (pug·nā′shəs): disposed or inclined to fight; quarrelsome.
23. **propensity** (prə·pen′sə·tē): a natural disposition or tendency.
24. **impetuosity:** tendency to act on impulse without forethought.
25. **cantankerous** (kan·tang′kər·əs): bad-tempered; ill-natured.
26. **watering place:** a health resort having mineral springs.

PETER STOCKMANN.   Undoubtedly. But things were not ripe for the scheme then—though, of course, you could not judge of that in your out-of-the-way corner up north. But as soon as the opportune moment came I—and the others—took the matter into our hands—

DR. STOCKMANN.   Yes, and made this mess of all my beautiful plans. It is pretty obvious now what clever fellows you were!

PETER STOCKMANN.   To my mind the whole thing only seems to mean that you are seeking another outlet for your combativeness. You want to pick a quarrel with your superiors—an old habit of yours. You cannot put up with any authority over you. You look askance [27] at anyone who occupies a superior official position; you regard him as a personal enemy, and then any stick is good enough to beat him with. But now I have called your attention to the fact that the town's interests are at stake—and, incidentally, my own, too. And therefore I must tell you, Thomas, that you will find me inexorable [28] with regard to what I am about to require you to do.

DR. STOCKMANN.   And what is that?

PETER STOCKMANN.   As you have been so indiscreet as to speak of this delicate matter to outsiders, despite the fact that you ought to have treated it as entirely official and confidential, it is obviously impossible to hush it up now. All sorts of rumors will get about directly, and everybody who has a grudge against us will take care to embellish [29] these rumors. So it will be necessary for you to refute [30] them publicly.

DR. STOCKMANN.   I! How? I don't understand.

PETER STOCKMANN.   What we shall expect is that, after making further investigations, you will come to the conclusion that the matter is not by any means as dangerous or as critical as you imagined in the first instance.

DR. STOCKMANN.   Oho! So that is what you expect!

PETER STOCKMANN.   And, what is more, we shall expect you to make public profession of your confidence in the Committee and in their readiness to consider fully and conscientiously what steps may be necessary to remedy any possible defects.

DR. STOCKMANN.   But you will never be able to do that by patching and tinkering at it—never! Take my word for it, Peter; I mean what I say, as deliberately and emphatically as possible.

27. **askance** (ə·skans′): distrustfully; disdainfully.
28. **inexorable** (in·ek′sər·ə·bəl): not to be moved by entreaty or persuasion.
29. **embellish**: to heighten or increase interest by adding fictitious details.
30. **refute**: deny.

PETER STOCKMANN.   As an officer under the Committee, you have no right to any individual opinion.

DR. STOCKMANN. (*Amazed.*)   No right?

PETER STOCKMANN.   In your official capacity, no. As a private person, it is quite another matter. But as a subordinate member of the staff of the Baths, you have no right to express any opinion which runs contrary to that of your superiors.

DR. STOCKMANN.   This is too much! I, a doctor, a man of science, have no right to—!

PETER STOCKMANN.   The matter at hand is not simply a scientific one. It is a complicated matter, and has its economic as well as its technical side.

DR. STOCKMANN.   I don't care what it is! I intend to be free to express my opinion on any subject under the sun.

PETER STOCKMANN.   As you please—but not on any subject concerning the Baths. That we forbid.

DR. STOCKMANN. (*Shouting.*)   You forbid—! You! A pack of—

PETER STOCKMANN.   I forbid it—I, your chief; and if I forbid it, you have to obey.

DR. STOCKMANN. (*Controlling himself.*)   Peter—if you were not my brother—

PETRA. (*Throwing open the door.*)   Father, you shan't stand this!

MRS. STOCKMANN. (*Coming in after her.*)   Petra, Petra!

PETER STOCKMANN.   Oh, so you have been eavesdropping.

MRS. STOCKMANN.   You were talking so loud, we couldn't help—

PETRA.   Yes, I was listening.

PETER STOCKMANN.   Well, after all, I am very glad—

DR. STOCKMANN. (*Going up to him.*)   You were saying something about forbidding and obeying?

PETER STOCKMANN.   You obliged me to take that tone with you.

DR. STOCKMANN.   And so I am to give myself the lie, publicly?

PETER STOCKMANN.   We consider it absolutely necessary that you should make some such public statement as I have asked for.

DR. STOCKMANN.   And if I do not—obey?

PETER STOCKMANN.   Then we shall publish a statement ourselves to reassure the public.

DR. STOCKMANN.   Very well; but in that case I shall use my pen against you. I stick to what I have said; I will show that I am right and that you are wrong. And what will you do, then?

PETER STOCKMANN.   Then I shall not be able to prevent your being dismissed.

DR. STOCKMANN. What—?

PETRA. Father—dismissed!

MRS. STOCKMANN. Dismissed!

PETER STOCKMANN. Dismissed from the staff of the Baths. I shall be obliged to propose that you shall immediately be given notice, and shall not be allowed any further participation in the Baths' affairs.

DR. STOCKMANN. You would dare to do that!

PETER STOCKMANN. It is you that are playing the daring game.

PETRA. Uncle, that is a shameful way to treat a man like father!

MRS. STOCKMANN. Do hold your tongue, Petra!

PETER STOCKMANN. (*Looking at* PETRA.) Oh, so we volunteer our opinions already, do we? Of course. (*To* MRS. STOCKMANN.) Katherine, I imagine you are the most sensible person in this house. Use any influence you may have over your husband, and make him see what this will entail for his family as well as—

DR. STOCKMANN. My family is my own concern and nobody else's!

PETER STOCKMANN. —for his own family, as I was saying, as well as for the town he lives in.

DR. STOCKMANN. It is I who have the real good of the town at heart! I want to lay bare the defects that sooner or later must come to the light of day. I will show whether I love my native town.

PETER STOCKMANN. You, who in your blind obstinacy [31] want to cut off the most important source of the town's welfare?

DR. STOCKMANN. The source is poisoned, man! Are you mad? We are making our living by retailing filth and corruption! The whole of our flourishing municipal life derives its sustenance from a lie!

PETER STOCKMANN. All imagination—or something even worse. The man who can throw out such offensive insinuations about his native town must be an enemy of our community.

DR. STOCKMANN. (*Going up to him.*) Do you dare to—!

MRS. STOCKMANN. (*Throwing herself between them.*) Thomas!

PETRA. (*Catching her father by the arm.*) Don't lose your temper, Father!

PETER STOCKMANN. I will not expose myself to violence. Now you have had a warning; so reflect on what you owe to yourself and your family. Good-bye. (*Goes out.*)

DR. STOCKMANN. (*Walking up and down.*) Am I to put up with such treatment as this? In my own house, Katherine! What do you think of that!

31. **obstinacy:** stubbornness.

MRS. STOCKMANN.   Indeed it is both shameful and absurd, Thomas—

PETRA.   If only I could give uncle a piece of my mind—

DR. STOCKMANN.   It is my own fault. I ought to have flown out at him long ago! Shown my teeth! Bitten! To hear him call me an enemy to our community! Me! I shall not take that lying down, upon my soul!

MRS. STOCKMANN.   But, dear Thomas, your brother has power on his side—

DR. STOCKMANN.   Yes, but I have right on mine, I tell you.

MRS. STOCKMANN.   Oh yes, right—right. What is the use of having right on your side if you have not got might?

PETRA.   Oh, Mother, how can you say such a thing!

DR. STOCKMANN.   Do you imagine that in a free country it is no use having right on your side? You are absurd, Katherine. Besides, haven't I got the liberal-minded independent press to lead the way, and the compact majority behind me? That is might enough, I should think!

MRS. STOCKMANN.   But, good heavens, Thomas, you don't mean to—?

DR. STOCKMANN.   Don't mean to what?

MRS. STOCKMANN.   To set yourself up in opposition to your brother.

DR. STOCKMANN.   In God's name, what else do you suppose I should do but take my stand on right and truth?

PETRA.   Yes, I was just going to say that.

MRS. STOCKMANN.   But it won't do you any earthly good. If they won't do it, they won't.

DR. STOCKMANN.   Oho, Katherine! Just give me time, and you will see how I will carry the war into their camp.

MRS. STOCKMANN.   Yes, you carry the war into their camp, and you get your dismissal—that is what you will do.

DR. STOCKMANN.   In any case I shall have done my duty toward the public—toward the community. I, who am called its enemy!

MRS. STOCKMANN.   But toward your family, Thomas? Toward your own home! Do you think that is doing your duty toward those you have to provide for?

PETRA.   Ah, don't think always first of us, Mother.

MRS. STOCKMANN.   Oh, it is easy for you to talk; you are able to shift for yourself, if need be. But remember the boys, Thomas; and think a little, too, of yourself, and of me—

DR. STOCKMANN.   I think you are out of your senses, Katherine! If I were to be such a miserable coward as to go on my knees to Peter and his damned crew, do you suppose I should ever know an hour's peace of mind all my life afterward?

MRS. STOCKMANN.   I don't know anything about that; but God preserve us from the peace of mind we shall have, all the same, if you go on defying him! You will find yourself again without the means of subsistence,[32] with no income to count upon. I should think we had had enough of that in the old days. Remember that, Thomas; think what that means.

DR. STOCKMANN. (*Collecting himself with a struggle and clenching his fists.*)   And this is what this slavery can bring upon a free, honorable man! Isn't it horrible, Katherine?

MRS. STOCKMANN.   Yes, it is sinful to treat you so, it is perfectly true. But, good heavens, one has to put up with so much injustice in this world.—There are the boys, Thomas! Look at them! What is to become of them? Oh, no, no, you can never have the heart—

(EJLIF *and* MORTEN *have come in while she was speaking, with their school books in their hands.*)

DR. STOCKMANN. The boys—! (*Recovers himself suddenly.*) No, even if the whole world goes to pieces, I will never bow my neck to this yoke! (*Goes toward his room.*)

MRS. STOCKMANN. (*Following him.*)   Thomas—what are you going to do!

DR. STOCKMANN. (*At his door.*)   I mean to have the right to look my sons in the face when they are grown men. (*Goes into his room.*)

MRS. STOCKMANN. (*Bursting into tears.*)   God help us all!

PETRA.   Father is splendid! He will not give in.

(*The boys look on in amazement;* PETRA *signals to them not to speak.*)

Curtain.

32. subsistence: support; livelihood.

Meaning and Method: Act II

1. Glance back at the dialogue between Dr. Stockmann and his wife at the beginning of Act II. How do their words help to support the evaluations you made of the Doctor and his brother in Act I? Do Dr. and Mrs. Stockmann reveal themselves in this scene as naive? generous? unrealistic? Explain.

2. In Act I, the Doctor referred to Morten Kiil as "the Badger." Does he live up to the nickname in this scene? Why is he delighted with his son-in-law's discovery? Is he vicious, stupid, or merely uneducated? Explain. How does his assumption regarding Dr. Stockmann's motive serve to heighten the Doctor's sincerity?

3. Hovstad suggests that the polluted Baths are *symbolic*—that is, stand for something else—of a larger evil, "the morass that the whole life of the town is built on and is rotting in." Analyze and explain this metaphor. What does Hovstad say he believes to be the cause of the town's corruption? Does Hovstad have motives different from those of Dr. Stockmann for wishing to expose the pollution of the Baths?

4. Nearly everything Aslaksen says and does must—he reiterates—be done in "moderation." Is Ibsen poking fun at him and his point of view? Decide on your answer by reading aloud speeches in which Aslaksen makes a plea for "moderation." If you were casting the play, how would you costume Aslaksen? What would he look like? Describe his speech and manner. Does he have an ulterior motive in wishing to support Dr. Stockmann?

5. What reaction does Hovstad foresee from the local government—the establishment—that Dr. Stockmann does not see? What limitation in Dr. Stockmann's character does this indicate? Do you think Stockmann is politically naive?

6. To the list of those who oppose him, the Doctor must now add Mrs. Stockmann. Is her attitude in keeping with her character? Does she have any choice? Why do you sympathize or not sympathize with her reasons?

7. List the types of opposition that Dr. Stockmann has encountered. As the scene ends, he is still confident. Why? Is his confidence based on a realistic appraisal of the situation? Do *you* believe he will win?

Act III

The editorial office of the People's Messenger. *The entrance door is on the left-hand side of the back wall; on the right-hand side is another door with glass panels through which the printing room can be seen. Another door in the right-hand wall. In the middle of the room is a large table covered with papers, newspapers, and books. In the foreground on the left a window, before which stand a desk and a high stool. There are a couple of easy chairs by the table, and other chairs standing along the wall. The room is dingy and uncomfortable; the furniture is old, the chairs stained and torn. In the printing room the compositors are seen at work, and a printer is working a handpress.* HOVSTAD *is sitting at the desk, writing.* BILLING *comes in from the right with* DR. STOCKMANN's *manuscript in his hand.*

BILLING. Well, I must say!

HOVSTAD. (*Still writing.*) Have you read it through?

BILLING. (*Laying the manuscript on the desk.*) Yes, indeed I have.

HOVSTAD. Don't you think the Doctor hits them pretty hard?

BILLING. Hard? Bless my soul, he's crushing! Every word falls like—how shall I put it?—like the blow of a sledgehammer.

HOVSTAD. Yes, but they are not the people to throw up the sponge at the first blow.

BILLING. That is true; and for that reason we must strike blow upon blow until the whole of this aristocracy tumbles to pieces. As I sat in there reading this, I almost seemed to see a revolution in being.

HOVSTAD. (*Turning around.*) Hush! Speak so that Aslaksen cannot hear you.

BILLING. (*Lowering his voice.*) Aslaksen is a chicken-hearted chap, a coward; there is nothing of the man in him. But this time you will insist on your own way, won't you? You will put the Doctor's article in?

HOVSTAD. Yes, and if the Mayor doesn't like it—

BILLING. That will be the devil of a nuisance.

HOVSTAD. Well, fortunately we can turn the situation to good account, whatever happens. If the Mayor will not fall in with the Doctor's project, he will have all the small-trades men down on him —the whole of the Householders' Association and the rest of them. And if he does fall in with it, he will fall out with the whole crowd

44

of large shareholders in the Baths, who up to now have been his most valuable supporters—

BILLING. Yes, because they will certainly have to fork out a pretty penny—

HOVSTAD. Yes, you may be sure they will. And in this way the ring will be broken up, you see, and then in every issue of the paper we will enlighten the public on the Mayor's incapability on one point and another, and make it clear that all the positions of trust in the town, the whole control of municipal affairs, ought to be put in the hands of the Liberals.

BILLING. That is perfectly true! I see it coming—I see it coming; we are on the threshold of a revolution!

(*A knock is heard at the door.*)

HOVSTAD. Hush! (*Calls out.*) Come in! (DR. STOCKMANN *comes in by the street door.* HOVSTAD *goes to meet him.*) Ah, it is you, Doctor! Well?

DR. STOCKMANN. You may set to work and print it, Mr. Hovstad!

HOVSTAD. Has it come to that, then?

BILLING. Hurrah!

DR. STOCKMANN. Yes, print away. Undoubtedly it has come to that. Now they must take what they get. There is going to be a fight in the town, Mr. Billing!

BILLING. War to the knife, I hope! We will get our knives to their throats, Doctor!

DR. STOCKMANN. This article is only a beginning. I have already got four or five more sketched out in my head. Where is Aslaksen?

BILLING. (*Calls into the printing room.*) Aslaksen, just come here for a minute!

HOVSTAD. Four or five more articles, did you say? On the same subject?

DR. STOCKMANN. No—far from it, my dear fellow. No, they are about quite another matter. But they all spring from the question of the water supply and the drainage. One thing leads to another, you know. It is like beginning to pull down an old house, exactly.

BILLING. Upon my soul, it's true; you find you are not done till you have pulled all the old rubbish down.

ASLAKSEN. (*Coming in.*) Pulled down? You are not thinking of pulling down the Baths surely, Doctor?

HOVSTAD. Far from it; don't be afraid.

DR. STOCKMANN.   No, we meant something quite different. Well, what do you think of my article, Mr. Hovstad?

HOVSTAD.   I think it is simply a masterpiece—

DR. STOCKMANN.   Do you really think so? Well, I am very pleased, very pleased.

HOVSTAD.   It is so clear and intelligible. One need have no special knowledge to understand the bearing of it. You will have every enlightened man on your side.

ASLAKSEN.   And every prudent [1] man, too, I hope?

BILLING.   The prudent and the imprudent—almost the whole town.

ASLAKSEN.   In that case we may venture to print it.

DR. STOCKMANN.   I should think so!

HOVSTAD.   We will put it in tomorrow morning.

DR. STOCKMANN.   Of course—you must not lose a single day. What I wanted to ask you, Mr. Aslaksen, was if you would supervise the printing of it yourself.

ASLAKSEN.   With pleasure.

DR. STOCKMANN.   Take care of it as if it were a treasure! No misprints —every word is important. I will look in again a little later; perhaps you will be able to let me see a proof. I can't tell you how eager I am to see it in print, and see it burst upon the public—

BILLING.   Burst upon them—yes, like a flash of lightning!

DR. STOCKMANN.   —and to have it submitted to the judgment of my intelligent fellow-townsmen. You cannot imagine what I have gone through today. I have been threatened first with one thing and then with another; they have tried to rob me of my most elementary rights as a man—

BILLING.   What! Your rights as a man!

DR. STOCKMANN.   —they have tried to degrade me, to make a coward of me, to force me to put personal interests before my most sacred convictions—

BILLING.   That is too much—I'm damned if it isn't.

HOVSTAD.   Oh, you mustn't be surprised at anything from that quarter.

DR. STOCKMANN.   Well, they will get the worst of it with me; they may assure themselves of that. I shall consider the *People's Messenger* my sheet anchor [2] now, and every single day I will bombard them with one article after another, like bombshells—

1. prudent: cautious; careful about judgments and actions.
2. sheet anchor: large, emergency anchor; here used figuratively to mean something to rely on in a time of crisis.

ASLAKSEN.   Yes, but—

BILLING.   Hurrah! It is war, it is war!

DR. STOCKMANN.   I shall smite them to the ground—I shall crush them—I shall break down all their defenses, before the eyes of the honest public! That is what I shall do!

ASLAKSEN.   Yes, but in moderation, Doctor—proceed with moderation—

BILLING.   Not a bit of it, not a bit of it! Don't spare the dynamite!

DR. STOCKMANN.   Because it is not merely a question of water supply and drains now, you know. No—it is the whole of our social life that we have got to purify and disinfect—

BILLING.   Spoken like a deliverer!

DR. STOCKMANN.   All the incapables must be turned out, you understand—and that in every walk of life! Endless vistas have opened themselves to my mind's eye today. I cannot see it all quite clearly yet, but I shall in time. Young and vigorous standard-bearers—those are what we need and must seek, my friends; we must have new men in command at all our outposts.

BILLING.   Hear, hear!

DR. STOCKMANN.   We only need to stand by one another, and it will all be perfectly easy. The revolution will be launched like a ship that runs smoothly off the stocks. Don't you think so?

HOVSTAD.   For my part I think we have now a prospect of getting the municipal authority into the hands where it should lie.

ASLAKSEN.   And if only we proceed with moderation, I cannot imagine that there will be any risk.

DR. STOCKMANN.   Who the devil cares whether there is any risk or not? What I am doing, I am doing in the name of truth and for the sake of my conscience.

HOVSTAD.   You are a man who deserves to be supported, Doctor.

ASLAKSEN.   Yes, there is no denying that the Doctor is a true friend to the town—a real friend to the community, that he is.

BILLING.   Take my word for it, Aslaksen, Dr. Stockmann is a friend of the people.

ASLAKSEN.   I fancy the Householders' Association will make use of that expression before long.

DR. STOCKMANN.   (*Affected, grasps their hands.*)   Thank you, thank you, my dear staunch ³ friends. It is very refreshing to me to hear you say that; my brother called me something quite different. By

---

3. staunch: loyal; firm and dependable.

Jove, he shall have it back, with interest! But now I must be off to
see a poor devil—I will come back, as I said. Keep a very careful
eye on the manuscript, Aslaksen, and don't for worlds leave out
any of my notes of exclamation! Rather put one or two more in!
Capital, capital! Well, good-bye for the present—good-bye, good-
bye!

(They show him to the door, and bow him out.)

HOVSTAD.   He may prove an invaluably useful man to us.

ASLAKSEN.   Yes, so long as he confines himself to this matter of the
Baths. But if he goes farther afield, I don't think it would be ad-
visable to follow him.

HOVSTAD.   Hm! That all depends—

BILLING.   You are so infernally timid, Aslaksen!

ASLAKSEN.   Timid? Yes, when it is a question of the local authorities, I am timid, Mr. Billing; it is a lesson I have learned in the
school of experience, let me tell you. But try me in higher politics,
in matters that concern the government itself, and then see if I am
timid.

BILLING.   No, you aren't, I admit. But this is simply contradicting
yourself.

ASLAKSEN.   I am a man with a conscience, and that is the whole
matter. If you attack the government, you don't do the community
any harm, anyway; those fellows pay no attention to attacks, you
see—they go on just as they are, in spite of them. But *local* authorities are different; they *can* be turned out, and then perhaps you may
get an ignorant lot into office who may do irreparable harm to the
householders and everybody else.

HOVSTAD.   But what of the education of citizens by self-government
—don't you attach any importance to that?

ASLAKSEN.   When a man has interests of his own to protect, he cannot think of everything, Mr. Hovstad.

HOVSTAD.   Then I hope I shall never have interests of my own to
protect!

BILLING.   Hear, hear!

ASLAKSEN.   *(With a smile.)*   Hm! *(Points to the desk.)*   Mr. Sheriff
Stensgaard was your predecessor at that editorial desk.

BILLING.   *(Spitting.)*   Bah! That turncoat.[4]

---

4. turncoat: traitor.

HOVSTAD.   I am not a weathercock [5]—and never will be.

ASLAKSEN.   A politician should never be too certain of anything, Mr. Hovstad. And as for you, Mr. Billing, I should think it is time for you to be taking in a reef or two in your sails, seeing that you are applying for the post of secretary to the Bench.

BILLING.   I—!

HOVSTAD.   Are you, Billing?

BILLING.   Well, yes—but you must clearly understand I am doing it only to annoy the bigwigs.

ASLAKSEN.   Anyhow, it is no business of mine. But if I am to be accused of timidity and of inconsistency in my principles, this is what I want to point out: my political past is an open book. I have never changed, except perhaps to become a little more moderate, you see. My heart is still with the people; but I don't deny that my reason has a certain bias toward the authorities—the local ones, I mean. (*Goes into the printing room.*)

BILLING.   Oughtn't we to try and get rid of him, Hovstad?

HOVSTAD.   Do you know anyone else who will advance the money for our paper and printing bill?

BILLING.   It is an infernal [6] nuisance that we don't possess some capital to trade on.

HOVSTAD.   (*Sitting down at his desk.*)   Yes, if we only had that, then—

BILLING.   Suppose you were to apply to Dr. Stockmann?

HOVSTAD.   (*Turning over some papers.*)   What is the use? He has got nothing.

BILLING.   No, but he has got a warm man in the background, old Morten Kiil—"the Badger," as they call him.

HOVSTAD.   (*Writing.*)   Are you so sure *he* has got anything?

BILLING.   Good Lord, of course he has! And some of it must come to the Stockmanns. Most probably he will do something for the children, at all events.

HOVSTAD.   (*Turing half round.*)   Are you counting on that?

BILLING.   Counting on it? Of course I am not counting on anything.

HOVSTAD.   That is right. And I should not count on the secretaryship to the Bench either, if I were you; for I can assure you—you won't get it.

5. **weathercock:** a weather vane, which turns with the wind.
6. **infernal:** hellish.

BILLING. Do you think I am not quite aware of that? My object is precisely *not* to get it. A slight of that kind stimulates a man's fighting power—it is like getting a supply of fresh bile—and I am sure one needs that badly enough in a hole-and-corner place like this, where so seldom anything happens to stir one up.

HOVSTAD. (*Writing.*)   Quite so, quite so.

BILLING. Ah, I shall be heard of yet! Now I shall go and write the appeal to the Householders' Association. (*Goes into the room on the right.*)

HOVSTAD. (*Sitting at his desk, biting his penholder, says slowly.*) Hm! That's it, is it? (*A knock is heard.*) Come in! (PETRA *comes in by the outer door.* HOVSTAD *gets up.*) What, you! Here?

PETRA. Yes, you must forgive me—

HOVSTAD. (*Pulling a chair forward.*)   Won't you sit down?

PETRA. No, thank you; I must go again in a moment.

HOVSTAD. Have you come with a message from your father, by any chance?

PETRA. No, I have come on my own account. (*Takes a book out of her coat pocket.*) Here is the English story.

HOVSTAD. Why have you brought it back?

PETRA. Because I am not going to translate it.

HOVSTAD. But you promised me faithfully—

PETRA. Yes, but then I had not read it. I don't suppose you have read it either?

HOVSTAD. No, you know quite well I don't understand English; but—

PETRA. Quite so. That is why I wanted to tell you that you must find something else. (*Lays the book on the table.*) You can't use this for the *People's Messenger*.

HOVSTAD. Why not?

PETRA. Because it conflicts with all your opinions.

HOVSTAD. Oh, for that matter—

PETRA. You don't understand me. The burden of this story is that there is a supernatural power that looks after the so-called good people in this world and makes everything happen for the best in their case—while all the so-called bad people are punished.

HOVSTAD. Well, but that is all right. That is just what our readers want.

PETRA. And are you going to be the one to give it to them? For myself, I do not believe a word of it. You know quite well that things do not happen so in reality.

HOVSTAD. You are perfectly right, but an editor cannot always act as he would prefer. He is often obliged to bow to the wishes of the public in unimportant matters. Politics are the most important thing in life—for a newspaper, anyway; and if I want to carry my public with me on the path that leads to liberty and progress, I must not frighten them away. If they find a moral tale of this sort in the serial at the bottom of the page, they will be all the more ready to read what is printed above it; they feel more secure, as it were.

PETRA. For shame! You would even go and set a snare like that for your readers; you are not a spider!

HOVSTAD. (*Smiling.*) Thank you for having such a good opinion of me. No; as a matter of fact that is Billing's idea and not mine.

PETRA. Billing's!

HOVSTAD. Yes; anyway he propounded [7] that theory here one day. And it is Billing who is so anxious to have that story in the paper; I don't know anything about the book.

PETRA. But how can Billing, with his emancipated views—

HOVSTAD. Oh, Billing is a many-sided man. He is applying for the post of secretary to the Bench, too, I hear.

PETRA. I don't believe it, Mr. Hovstad. How could he possibly bring himself to do such a thing?

HOVSTAD. Ah, you must ask him that.

PETRA. I should never have thought it of him.

HOVSTAD. (*Looking more closely at her.*)   No? Does it really surprise you so much?

PETRA. Yes. Or perhaps not altogether. Really, I don't quite know—

HOVSTAD. We journalists are not worth much, Miss Stockmann.

PETRA. Do you really mean that?

HOVSTAD. I think so sometimes.

PETRA. Yes, in the ordinary affairs of everyday life, perhaps; I can understand that. But now, when you have taken a weighty matter in hand—

HOVSTAD. This matter of your father's, you mean?

PETRA. Exactly. It seems to me that now you must feel you are a man worth more than most.

HOVSTAD. Yes, today I do feel something of that sort.

PETRA. Of course you do, don't you? It is a splendid vocation you have chosen—to smooth the way for the march of unappreciated truths and new and courageous lines of thought. If it were nothing

7. **propounded:** set forth; explained.

more than because you stand fearlessly in the open and take up the cause of an injured man—

HOVSTAD.   Especially when that injured man is—ahem! I don't rightly know how to—

PETRA.   When that man is so upright and so honest, you mean?

HOVSTAD. (*More gently.*)   Especially when he is your father, I meant.

PETRA. (*Suddenly checked.*)   *That?*

HOVSTAD.   Yes, Petra—Miss Petra.

PETRA.   Is it *that*, that is first and foremost with you? Not the matter itself? Not the truth? Not my father's big generous heart?

HOVSTAD.   Certainly—of course—that, too.

PETRA.   No, thank you; you have betrayed yourself, Mr. Hovstad, and now I shall never trust you again in anything.

HOVSTAD.   Can you really take it so amiss in me that it is mostly for your sake—?

PETRA.   I am angry with you for not having been honest with my father. You talked to him as if the truth and the good of the community were what lay nearest to your heart. You have made fools of both my father and me. You are not the man you made yourself out to be. And that I shall never forgive you—never!

HOVSTAD.   You ought not to speak so bitterly, Miss Petra—least of all now.

PETRA.   Why not now, especially?

HOVSTAD.   Because your father cannot do without my help.

PETRA. (*Looking him up and down.*)   Are you that sort of man, too? For shame!

HOVSTAD.   No, no, I am not. This came upon me so unexpectedly —you must believe that.

PETRA.   I know what to believe. Good-bye.

ASLAKSEN. (*Coming from the printing room, hurriedly and with an air of mystery.*)   Damnation, Hovstad!—(*Sees* PETRA.) Oh, this is awkward—

PETRA.   There is the book; you must give it to someone else. (*Goes toward the door.*)

HOVSTAD. (*Following her.*)   But, Miss Stockmann—

PETRA.   Good-bye. (*Goes out.*)

ASLAKSEN.   I say—Mr. Hovstad—

HOVSTAD.   Well, well! What is it?

ASLAKSEN.   The Mayor is outside in the printing room.

HOVSTAD.   The Mayor, did you say?

ASLAKSEN.   Yes, he wants to speak to you. He came in by the back door—didn't want to be seen, you understand.

HOVSTAD.   What can he want? Wait a bit—I will go myself. (*Goes to the door of the printing room, opens it, bows, and invites* PETER STOCKMANN *in.*) Just see, Aslaksen, that no one—

ASLAKSEN.   Quite so. (*Goes into the printing room.*)

PETER STOCKMANN.   You did not expect to see me here, Mr. Hovstad?

HOVSTAD.   No, I confess I did not.

PETER STOCKMANN.   (*Looking round.*)   You are very snug in here—very nice indeed.

HOVSTAD.   Oh—

PETER STOCKMANN.   And here I come, without any notice, to take up your time!

HOVSTAD.   By all means, Mr. Mayor. I am at your service. But let me relieve you of your— (*Takes* STOCKMANN's *hat and stick and puts them on a chair.*) Won't you sit down?

PETER STOCKMANN.   (*Sitting down by the table.*)   Thank you. (HOVSTAD *sits down.*) I have had an extremely annoying experience today, Mr. Hovstad.

HOVSTAD.   Really? Ah well, I expect with all the various business you have to attend to—

PETER STOCKMANN.   The Medical Officer of the Baths is responsible for what happened today.

HOVSTAD.   Indeed? The Doctor?

PETER STOCKMANN.   He has addressed a kind of report to the Baths' Committee on the subject of certain supposed defects in the Baths.

HOVSTAD.   Has he indeed?

PETER STOCKMANN.   Yes—has he not told you? I thought he said—

HOVSTAD.   Ah, yes—it is true he did mention something about—

ASLAKSEN.   (*Coming from the printing room.*)   I ought to have that copy—

HOVSTAD. (*Angrily.*)   Ahem! There it is on the desk.

ASLAKSEN. (*Taking it.*)   Right.

PETER STOCKMANN.   But look there—that is the thing I was speaking of!

ASLAKSEN.   Yes, that is the Doctor's article, Mr. Mayor.

HOVSTAD.   Oh, is *that* what you were speaking about?

PETER STOCKMANN.   Yes, that is it. What do you think of it?

HOVSTAD.   Oh, I am only a layman—and I have only taken a very cursory [8] glance at it.

PETER STOCKMANN.   But you are going to print it?

HOVSTAD.   I cannot very well refuse a distinguished man—

ASLAKSEN.   I have nothing to do with editing the paper, Mr. Mayor—

PETER STOCKMANN.   I understand.

ASLAKSEN.   I merely print what is put into my hands.

PETER STOCKMANN.   Quite so.

ASLAKSEN.   And so I must— (*Moves off toward the printing room.*)

PETER STOCKMANN.   No, but wait a moment, Mr. Aslaksen. You will allow me, Mr. Hovstad?

HOVSTAD.   If you please, Mr. Mayor.

PETER STOCKMANN.   You are a discreet [9] and thoughtful man, Mr. Aslaksen.

ASLAKSEN.   I am delighted to hear you think so, sir.

PETER STOCKMANN.   And a man of very considerable influence.

ASLAKSEN.   Chiefly among the small-trades men, sir.

PETER STOCKMANN.   The small-tax payers are the majority—here as everywhere else.

ASLAKSEN.   That is true.

PETER STOCKMANN.   And I have no doubt you know the general trend of opinion among them, don't you?

ASLAKSEN.   Yes, I think I may say I do, Mr. Mayor.

PETER STOCKMANN.   Yes. Well, since there is such a praiseworthy spirit of self-sacrifice among the less wealthy citizens of our town—

ASLAKSEN.   What?

HOVSTAD.   Self-sacrifice?

PETER STOCKMANN.   It is pleasing evidence of a public-spirited feeling, extremely pleasing evidence. I might almost say I hardly expected it. But you have a closer knowledge of public opinion than I.

ASLAKSEN.   But, Mr. Mayor—

PETER STOCKMANN.   And indeed it is no small sacrifice that the town is going to make.

HOVSTAD.   The town?

ASLAKSEN.   But I don't understand. Is it the Baths—?

8. **cursory:** quick; hasty.
9. **discreet:** prudent; tactful; careful.

PETER STOCKMANN.   At a provisional [10] estimate, the alterations that the Medical Officer asserts are desirable will cost somewhere about twenty thousand pounds.

ASLAKSEN.   That is a lot of money, but—

PETER STOCKMANN.   Of course it will be necessary to raise a municipal loan.

HOVSTAD.   (*Getting up.*)   Surely you never mean that the town must pay—?

ASLAKSEN.   Do you mean that it must come out of the municipal funds, out of the ill-filled pockets of the small-trades men?

PETER STOCKMANN.   Well, my dear Mr. Aslaksen, where else is the money to come from?

ASLAKSEN.   The gentlemen who own the Baths ought to provide that.

PETER STOCKMANN.   The proprietors [11] of the Baths are not in a position to incur any further expense.

ASLAKSEN.   Is that absolutely certain, Mr. Mayor?

PETER STOCKMANN.   I have satisfied myself that it is so. If the town wants these very extensive alterations, it will have to pay for them.

ASLAKSEN.   But, damn it all—I beg your pardon—this is quite another matter, Mr. Hovstad!

HOVSTAD.   It is, indeed.

PETER STOCKMANN.   The most fatal part of it is that we shall be obliged to shut the Baths for a couple of years.

HOVSTAD.   Shut them? Shut them altogether?

ASLAKSEN.   For two years?

PETER STOCKMANN.   Yes, the work will take as long as that—at least.

ASLAKSEN.   I'm damned if we will stand that, Mr. Mayor! What are we householders to live upon in the meantime?

PETER STOCKMANN.   Unfortunately, that is an extremely difficult question to answer, Mr. Aslaksen. But what would you have us do? Do you suppose we shall have a single visitor in the town, if we go about proclaiming that our water is polluted, that we are living over a plague spot, that the entire town—

ASLAKSEN.   And the whole thing is merely imagination?

PETER STOCKMANN.   With the best will in the world, I have not been able to come to any other conclusion.

10. **provisional:** temporary; tentative.
11. **proprietors:** owners.

ASLAKSEN. Well then, I must say it is absolutely unjustifiable of Dr. Stockmann—I beg your pardon, Mr. Mayor—

PETER STOCKMANN. What you say is lamentably true, Mr. Aslaksen. My brother has, unfortunately, always been a headstrong man.

ASLAKSEN. After this, do you mean to give him your support, Mr. Hovstad?

HOVSTAD. Can you suppose for a moment that I—?

PETER STOCKMANN. I have drawn up a short *résumé* [12] of the situation as it appears from a reasonable man's point of view. In it I have indicated how certain possible defects might suitably be remedied without outrunning the resources of the Baths' Committee.

HOVSTAD. Have you got it with you, Mr. Mayor?

PETER STOCKMANN. (*Fumbling in his pocket.*) Yes, I brought it with me in case you should—

ASLAKSEN. Good Lord, there he is!

PETER STOCKMANN. Who? My brother?

HOVSTAD. Where? Where?

ASLAKSEN. He has just gone through the printing room.

PETER STOCKMANN. How unlucky! I don't want to meet him here, and I had still several things to speak to you about.

HOVSTAD. (*Pointing to the door on the right.*) Go in there for the present.

PETER STOCKMANN. But—?

HOVSTAD. You will only find Billing in there.

ASLAKSEN. Quick, quick, Mr. Mayor—he is just coming.

PETER STOCKMANN. Yes, very well; but see that you get rid of him quickly.

(*Goes out through the door on the right, which* ASLAKSEN *opens for him and shuts after him.*)

HOVSTAD. Pretend to be doing something, Aslaksen.

(*Sits down and writes.* ASLAKSEN *begins foraging* [13] *among a heap of newspapers that are lying on a chair.*)

DR. STOCKMANN. (*Coming in from the printing room.*) Here I am again. (*Puts down his hat and stick.*)

HOVSTAD. (*Writing.*) Already, Doctor? Hurry up with what we were speaking about, Aslaksen. We are very pressed for time today.

12. *résumé* (rez'oŏ·mā') : *French*, summary.
13. **foraging:** searching about.

DR. STOCKMANN. (*To* ASLAKSEN.)   No proof for me to see yet, I hear.

ASLAKSEN. (*Without turning round.*)   You couldn't expect it yet, Doctor.

DR. STOCKMANN.   No, no; but I am impatient, as you can understand. I shall not know a moment's peace of mind till I see it in print.

HOVSTAD.   Hm! It will take a good while yet, won't it, Aslaksen?

ASLAKSEN.   Yes, I am almost afraid it will.

DR. STOCKMANN.   All right, my dear friends; I will come back. I do not mind coming back twice if necessary. A matter of such great importance—the welfare of the town at stake—it is no time to shirk [14] trouble. (*Is just going, but stops and comes back.*) Look here—there is one thing more I want to speak to you about.

HOVSTAD.   Excuse me, but could it not wait till some other time?

DR. STOCKMANN.   I can tell you in half a dozen words. It is only this. When my article is read tomorrow and it is realized that I have been quietly working the whole winter for the welfare of the town—

HOVSTAD.   Yes, but, Doctor—

DR. STOCKMANN.   I know what you are going to say. You don't see how on earth it was any more than my duty—my obvious duty as a citizen. Of course it wasn't; I know that as well as you. But my fellow citizens, you know—! Good Lord, think of all the good souls who think so highly of me—!

ASLAKSEN.   Yes, our townsfolk have had a very high opinion of you so far, Doctor.

DR. STOCKMANN.   Yes, and that is just why I am afraid they— Well, this is the point; when this reaches them, especially the poorer classes, and sounds in their ears like a summons to take the town's affairs into their own hands for the future—

HOVSTAD. (*Getting up.*)   Ahem! Doctor, I won't conceal from you the fact—

DR. STOCKMANN.   Ah!—I knew there was something in the wind! But I won't hear a word of it. If anything of that sort is being set on foot—

HOVSTAD.   Of what sort?

DR. STOCKMANN.   Well, whatever it is—whether it is a demonstration in my honor, or a banquet, or a subscription list for some presentation to me—whatever it is, you must promise me solemnly and faithfully to put a stop to it. You, too, Mr. Aslaksen; do you understand?

14. **shirk:** escape from; evade.

HOVSTAD.   You must forgive me, Doctor, but sooner or later we must tell you the plain truth—

(*He is interrupted by the entrance of* MRS. STOCKMANN, *who comes in from the street door.*)

MRS. STOCKMANN. (*Seeing her husband.*) Just as I thought!

HOVSTAD. (*Going toward her.*) You, too, Mrs. Stockmann?

DR. STOCKMANN.   What on earth do *you* want here, Katherine?

MRS. STOCKMANN.   I should think you know very well what I want.

HOVSTAD.   Won't you sit down? Or perhaps—

MRS. STOCKMANN.   No, thank you; don't trouble. And you must not be offended at my coming to fetch my husband; I am the mother of three children, you know.

DR. STOCKMANN.   Nonsense! We know all about that.

MRS. STOCKMANN.   Well, one would not give you credit for much thought for your wife and children today; if you had had that, you would not have gone and dragged us all into misfortune.

DR. STOCKMANN.   Are you out of your senses, Katherine? Because a man has a wife and children, is he not to be allowed to proclaim the truth—is he not to be allowed to be an actively useful citizen— is he not to be allowed to do a service to his native town?

MRS. STOCKMANN.   Yes, Thomas—in reason.

ASLAKSEN.   Just what I say. Moderation is everything.

MRS. STOCKMANN.   And that is why you wrong us, Mr. Hovstad, in enticing [15] my husband away from his home and making a dupe [16] of him in all this.

HOVSTAD.   I certainly am making a dupe of no one—

DR. STOCKMANN.   Making a dupe of me! Do you suppose *I* should allow myself to be duped?

MRS. STOCKMANN.   It is just what you do. I know quite well you have more brains than anyone in the town, but you are extremely easily duped, Thomas. (*To* HOVSTAD.) Please realize that he loses his post [17] at the Baths if you print what he has written—

ASLAKSEN.   What!

HOVSTAD.   Look here, Doctor—

DR. STOCKMANN. (*Laughing.*) Ha—ha! Just let them try! No, no —they will take good care not to. I have got the compact majority behind me, let me tell you!

15. **enticing**: luring away.
16. **dupe**: one who is deceived or tricked.
17. **post**: job; position.

MRS. STOCKMANN.   Yes, that is just the worst of it—your having any such horrid thing behind you.

DR. STOCKMANN.   Rubbish, Katherine! Go home and look after your house and leave me to look after the community. How can you be so afraid, when I am so confident and happy? (*Walks up and down, rubbing his hands.*) Truth and the People will win the fight, you may be certain! I see the whole of the broad-minded middle class marching like a victorious army—! (*Stops beside a chair.*) What the deuce is that lying there?

ASLAKSEN.   Good Lord!

HOVSTAD.   Ahem!

DR. STOCKMANN.   Here we have the topmost pinnacle [18] of authority!

(*Takes the* MAYOR'S *official hat carefully between his finger tips and holds it up in the air.*)

MRS. STOCKMANN.   The Mayor's hat!

DR. STOCKMANN.   And here is the staff of office, too. How in the name of all that's wonderful—?

HOVSTAD.   Well, you see—

DR. STOCKMANN.   Oh, I understand. He has been here trying to talk you over. Ha—ha! He made rather a mistake there! And as soon as he caught sight of me in the printing room— (*Bursts out laughing.*) Did he run away, Mr. Aslaksen?

ASLAKSEN. (*Hurriedly.*)   Yes, he ran away, Doctor.

DR. STOCKMANN.   Ran away without his stick or his— Fiddlesticks! Peter doesn't run away and leave his belongings behind him. But what the deuce have you done with him? Ah—in there, of course. Now you shall see, Katherine.

MRS. STOCKMANN.   Thomas—please don't—!

ASLAKSEN.   Don't be rash, Doctor.

(DR. STOCKMANN *has put on the* MAYOR'S *hat and taken his stick in his hand. He goes up to the door, opens it and stands with his hand to his hat at the salute.* PETER STOCK-MANN *comes in, red with anger.* BILLING *follows him.*)

PETER STOCKMANN.   What does this tomfoolery [19] mean?

DR. STOCKMANN.   Be respectful, my good Peter. I am the chief authority in the town now. (*Walks up and down.*)

18. **pinnacle:** the highest point or place.
19. **tomfoolery:** foolishness.

MRS. STOCKMANN. (*Almost in tears.*)   Really, Thomas!

PETER STOCKMANN. (*Following him about.*)   Give me my hat and stick.

DR. STOCKMANN. (*In the same tone as before.*)   If you are chief constable,[20] let me tell you that I am the Mayor—I am the master of the whole town, please understand!

PETER STOCKMANN.   Take off my hat, I tell you. Remember it is part of an official uniform.

DR. STOCKMANN.   Pooh! Do you think the newly awakened lion-hearted people are going to be frightened by an official hat? There is going to be a revolution in the town tomorrow, let me tell you. You thought you could turn me out; but now I shall turn you out—turn you out of all your various offices. Do you think I cannot? Listen to me. I have triumphant social forces behind me. Hovstad and Billing will thunder in the *People's Messenger*, and Aslaksen will take the field at the head of the whole Householders' Association—

ASLAKSEN.   That I won't, Doctor.

DR. STOCKMANN.   Of course you will—

PETER STOCKMANN.   Ah! May I ask then if Mr. Hovstad intends to join this agitation?

HOVSTAD.   No, Mr. Mayor.

ASLAKSEN.   No, Mr. Hovstad is not such a fool as to go and ruin his paper and himself for the sake of an imaginary grievance.

DR. STOCKMANN. (*Looking round him.*)   What does this mean?

HOVSTAD.   You have represented your case in a false light, Doctor, and therefore I am unable to give you my support.

BILLING.   And after what the Mayor was so kind as to tell me just now, I—

DR. STOCKMANN.   A false light! Leave that part of it to me. Only print my article; I am quite capable of defending it.

HOVSTAD.   I am not going to print it. I cannot and will not and dare not print it.

DR. STOCKMANN.   You dare not? What nonsense! You are the editor; and an editor controls his paper, I suppose!

ASLAKSEN.   No, it is the subscribers, Doctor.

PETER STOCKMANN.   Fortunately, yes.

ASLAKSEN.   It is public opinion—the enlightened public—householders and people of that kind; they control the newspapers.

20. constable: police officer.

DR. STOCKMANN. (*Composedly.*) And I have all these influences against me?

ASLAKSEN. Yes, you have. It would mean the absolute ruin of the community if your article were to appear.

DR. STOCKMANN. Indeed.

PETER STOCKMANN. My hat and stick, if you please. (DR. STOCKMANN *takes off the hat and lays it on the table with the stick.* PETER STOCKMANN *takes them up.*) Your authority as mayor has come to an untimely end.

DR. STOCKMANN. We have not got to the end yet. (*To* HOVSTAD.) Then it is quite impossible for you to print my article in the *People's Messenger?*

HOVSTAD. Quite impossible—out of regard for your family as well.

MRS. STOCKMANN. You need not concern yourself about his family, thank you, Mr. Hovstad.

PETER STOCKMANN. (*Taking a paper from his pocket.*) It will be sufficient, for the guidance of the public, if this appears. It is an official statement. May I trouble you?

HOVSTAD. (*Taking the paper.*) Certainly; I will see that it is printed.

DR. STOCKMANN. But not mine. Do you imagine that you can silence me and stifle [21] the truth? You will not find it so easy as you suppose. Mr. Aslaksen, kindly take my manuscript at once and print it as a pamphlet—at my expense. l will have four hundred copies—no, five—six hundred.

ASLAKSEN. If you offered me its weight in gold, I could not lend my press for any such purpose, Doctor. It would be flying in the face of public opinion. You will not get it printed anywhere in the town.

DR. STOCKMANN. Then give it back to me.

HOVSTAD. (*Giving him the manuscript.*) Here it is.

DR. STOCKMANN. (*Taking his hat and stick.*) It shall be made public all the same. I will read it out at a mass meeting of the townspeople. All my fellow citizens shall hear the voice of truth!

PETER STOCKMANN. You will not find any public body in the town that will give you the use of their hall for such a purpose.

ASLAKSEN. Not a single one, I am certain.

BILLING. No, I'm damned if you will find one.

MRS. STOCKMANN. But this is too shameful! Why should everyone turn against you like that?

DR. STOCKMANN. (*Angrily.*) I will tell you why. It is because all the

21. **stifle:** hold back; check.

men in this town are old women—like you; they all think of nothing but their families, and never of the community.

MRS. STOCKMANN. (*Putting her arm into his.*)   Then I will show them that an—an old woman can be a man for once. I am going to stand by you, Thomas!

DR. STOCKMANN.   Bravely said, Katherine! It shall be made public— as I am a living soul! If I can't hire a hall, I shall hire a drum, and parade the town with it and read it at every street corner.

PETER STOCKMANN.   You are surely not such an arrant [22] fool as that!

DR. STOCKMANN.   Yes, I am.

ASLAKSEN.   You won't find a single man in the whole town to go with you.

BILLING.   No, I'm damned if you will.

MRS. STOCKMANN.   Don't give in, Thomas. I will tell the boys to go with you.

DR. STOCKMANN.   That is a splendid idea!

MRS. STOCKMANN.   Morten will be delighted; and Ejlif will do whatever he does.

DR. STOCKMANN.   Yes, and Petra! And you too, Katherine!

MRS. STOCKMANN.   No, I won't do that; but I will stand at the window and watch you, that's what I will do.

DR. STOCKMANN. (*Puts his arms round her and kisses her.*)   Thank you, my dear! Now you and I are going to try a fall,[23] my fine gentlemen! I am going to see whether a pack of cowards can succeed in gagging a patriot who wants to purify society!

(*He and his wife go out by the street door.*)

PETER STOCKMANN. (*Shaking his head seriously.*)   Now he has sent *her* out of her senses, too.

Curtain.

22. **arrant** (ar'ənt): complete, confirmed.
23. **try a fall:** come to open struggle.

Meaning and Method: Act III

1. Hovstad and Billing, it can be seen at the beginning of Act III, hope to use Dr. Stockmann's article as a means of accomplishing much more than the cleansing of the Baths. What are their plans? What evidence is there to show that Dr. Stockmann has become their sup-

porter? Would his support be so wholehearted if he knew Hovstad's and Billing's real motives? How do these motives differ from his own?

2. What reason does Aslaksen give Hovstad for moving with caution? What does Aslaksen really mean by "moderation"? What does Aslaksen imply that prompts Hovstad to respond: "I am not a weathercock." Hovstad would like to get rid of Aslaksen. Why doesn't he?

3. How does the dialogue between Petra and Hovstad parallel the conflict between her father and the Mayor? In what ways is Petra's thinking like her father's thinking? How is Hovstad's thinking like the Mayor's? Quote the lines of Hovstad that reveal his true nature to Petra. Why, if you were casting this play, would it be important for Petra to be played by a pretty, young woman?

4. Consider Hovstad's attitude toward Dr. Stockmann, his conduct toward Aslaksen, his conversation with Petra. Then decide what type of man Ibsen is presenting in the character of Hovstad. Explain. Decide on the appearance, voice, and manner you would choose for the actor of the part.

5. By what threat is the Mayor able to take away from Dr. Stockmann the support of the "compact majority"? In what way does this show that each of the characters was acting from motives of self-interest rather than in the name of "truth"?

6. As the act builds toward its climax, do the Doctor's words and actions seem irrational? Or do his reactions seem justified in the light of the betrayal he has just been made aware of?

Act IV

A big old-fashioned room in CAPTAIN HORSTER'S *house. At the back, folding doors, which are open, lead to an anteroom. Three windows are in the left-hand wall. In the middle of the opposite wall a platform has been erected. On this is a small table with two candles, a water bottle and glass, and a bell. The room is lit by lamps placed between the windows. In the foreground on the left there is a table with candles and a chair. To the right is a door and some chairs standing near it. The room is nearly filled with a crowd of townspeople of all sorts, a few women and schoolboys being among them. People are still streaming in from the back, and the room is soon filled.*

FIRST CITIZEN. (*Meeting another.*)   Hullo, Lamstad! You here, too?

SECOND CITIZEN.   I go to every public meeting, I do.

THIRD CITIZEN.   Brought your whistle, too, I expect!

SECOND CITIZEN.   I should think so. Haven't you?

THIRD CITIZEN.   Rather! And old Evensen said he was going to bring a cow-horn, he did.

SECOND CITIZEN.   Good old Evensen!

(*Laughter among the crowd.*)

FOURTH CITIZEN. (*Coming up to them.*)   I say, tell me what is going on here tonight.

SECOND CITIZEN.   Dr. Stockmann is going to deliver an address attacking the Mayor.

FOURTH CITIZEN.   But the Mayor is his brother.

FIRST CITIZEN.   That doesn't matter; Dr. Stockmann's not the chap to be afraid.

THIRD CITIZEN.   But he is in the wrong; it said so in the *People's Messenger.*

SECOND CITIZEN.   Yes, I expect he must be in the wrong this time, because neither the Householders' Association nor the Citizens' Club would lend him their hall for his meeting.

FIRST CITIZEN.   He couldn't even get the loan of the hall at the Baths.

SECOND CITIZEN.   No, I should think not.

A MAN IN ANOTHER PART OF THE CROWD.   I say—who are we to back up in this?

ANOTHER MAN, BESIDE HIM.   Watch Aslaksen, and do as he does.

BILLING. (*Pushing his way through the crowd, with a writing case under his arm.*)   Excuse me, gentlemen—do you mind letting me through? I am reporting for the *People's Messenger*. Thank you very much! (*He sits down at the table on the left.*)

A WORKMAN.   Who was that?

SECOND WORKMAN.   Don't you know him? It's Billing, who writes for Aslaksen's paper.

(CAPTAIN HORSTER *brings in* MRS. STOCKMANN *and* PETRA *through the door on the right.* EJLIF *and* MORTEN *follow them in.*)

HORSTER.   I thought you might all sit here; you can slip out easily from here, if things get too lively.

MRS. STOCKMANN.   Do you think there will be a disturbance?

HORSTER.   One can never tell—with such a crowd. But sit down, and don't be uneasy.

MRS. STOCKMANN. (*Sitting down.*)   It was extremely kind of you to offer my husband the room.

HORSTER.   Well, if nobody else would—

PETRA. (*Who has sat down beside her mother.*)   And it was a plucky [1] thing to do, Captain Horster.

HORSTER.   Oh, it is not such a great matter as all that.

(HOVSTAD *and* ASLAKSEN *make their way through the crowd.*)

ASLAKSEN. (*Going up to* HORSTER.)   Has the Doctor not come yet?

HORSTER.   He is waiting in the next room.

(*Movement in the crowd by the door at the back.*)

HOVSTAD.   Look—here comes the Mayor!

BILLING.   Yes, I'm damned if he hasn't come after all!

(PETER STOCKMANN *makes his way gradually through the crowd, bows courteously, and takes up a position by the wall on the left. Shortly afterward* DR. STOCKMANN *comes in by the right-hand door. He is dressed in a black frockcoat, with a white tie. There is a little feeble applause, which is hushed down. Silence is obtained.*)

DR. STOCKMANN. (*In an undertone.*)   How do you feel, Katherine?

MRS. STOCKMANN.   All right, thank you. (*Lowering her voice.*) Be sure not to lose your temper, Thomas.

DR. STOCKMANN.   Oh, I know how to control myself. (*Looks at his*

1. plucky: brave.

watch, steps on to the platform and bows.) It is a quarter past—
so I will begin. (*Takes his manuscript out of his pocket.*)

ASLAKSEN.   I think we ought to elect a chairman first.

DR. STOCKMANN.   No, it is quite unnecessary.

SOME OF THE CROWD.   Yes—yes!

PETER STOCKMANN.   I certainly think, too, that we ought to have a chairman.

DR. STOCKMANN.   But I have called this meeting to deliver a lecture, Peter.

PETER STOCKMANN.   Dr. Stockmann's lecture may possibly lead to a considerable conflict of opinion.

VOICES IN THE CROWD.   A chairman! A chairman!

HOVSTAD.   The general wish of the meeting seems to be that a chairman shall be elected.

DR. STOCKMANN.   (*Restraining himself.*)   Very well—let the meeting have its way.

ASLAKSEN.   Will the Mayor be good enough to undertake the task?

THREE MEN.   (*Clapping their hands.*)   Bravo! Bravo!

PETER STOCKMANN.   For various reasons, which you will easily understand, I must beg to be excused. But fortunately we have among us a man who I think will be acceptable to you all. I refer to the President of the Householders' Association, Mr. Aslaksen.

SEVERAL VOICES.   Yes—Aslaksen! Bravo, Aslaksen!

>   (DR. STOCKMANN *takes up his manuscript and walks up and down the platform.*)

ASLAKSEN.   Since my fellow-citizens choose to entrust me with this duty, I cannot refuse.

>   (*Loud applause.* ASLAKSEN *mounts the platform.*)

BILLING.   (*Writing.*)   "Mr. Aslaksen was elected with enthusiasm."

ASLAKSEN.   And now, as I am in this position, I should like to say a few brief words. I am a quiet and peaceable man, who believes in discreet moderation, and—and—in moderate discretion. All my friends can bear witness to that.

SEVERAL VOICES.   That's right! That's right, Aslaksen!

ASLAKSEN.   I have learned in the school of life and experience that moderation is the most valuable virtue a citizen can possess—

PETER STOCKMANN.   Hear, hear!

ASLAKSEN.   —And moreover that discretion and moderation are what enable a man to be of most service to the community. I would therefore suggest to our esteemed fellow-citizen, who has called this meeting, that he should strive to keep strictly within the bounds of moderation.

A MAN BY THE DOOR.   Three cheers for the Moderation Society!

A VOICE.   Shame!

SEVERAL VOICES.   Sh!—Sh!

ASLAKSEN.   No interruptions, gentlemen, please! Does anyone wish to make any remarks?

PETER STOCKMANN.   Mr. Chairman.

ASLAKSEN.   The Mayor will address the meeting.

PETER STOCKMANN.   In consideration of the close relationship in which, as you all know, I stand to the present Medical Officer of the Baths, I should have preferred not to speak this evening. But my official position with regard to the Baths and my solicitude [2] for the vital interests of the town compel me to bring forward a motion. I venture to presume that there is not a single one of our citizens present who considers it desirable that unreliable and exaggerated accounts of the sanitary condition of the Baths and the town should be spread abroad.

SEVERAL VOICES.   No, no! Certainly not! We protest against it!

PETER STOCKMANN.   Therefore I should like to propose that the meeting should not permit the Medical Officer either to read or to comment on his proposed lecture.

DR. STOCKMANN.   (*Impatiently.*)   Not permit—! What the devil—!

MRS. STOCKMANN.   (*Coughing.*)   Ahem! Ahem!

DR. STOCKMANN.   (*Collecting himself.*)   Very well. Go ahead!

PETER STOCKMANN.   In my communication to the *People's Messenger*, I have put the essential facts before the public in such a way that every fair-minded citizen can easily form his own opinion. From it you will see that the main result of the Medical Officer's proposals—apart from their constituting [3] a vote of censure on the leading men of the town—would be to saddle the taxpayers with an unnecessary expenditure of at least some thousands of pounds.

(*Sounds of disapproval among the audience, and some catcalls.* [4])

ASLAKSEN.   (*Ringing his bell.*)   Silence, please, gentlemen! I beg to

---

2. **solicitude:** care; concern.
3. **constituting:** forming; making up.
4. **catcalls:** shrill noises denoting mockery or disapproval.

support the Mayor's motion. I quite agree with him that there is something behind this agitation started by the Doctor. He talks about the Baths; but it is a revolution he is aiming at—he wants to get the administration of the town put into new hands. No one doubts the honesty of the Doctor's intentions—no one will suggest that there can be any two opinions as to that. I myself am a believer in self-government for the people, provided it does not fall too heavily on the taxpayers. But that would be the case here; and that is why I will see Dr. Stockmann damned—I beg your pardon —before I go with him in the matter. You can pay too dearly for a thing sometimes; that is my opinion.

(*Loud applause on all sides.*)

HOVSTAD. I, too, feel called upon to explain my position. Dr. Stockmann's agitation appeared to be gaining a certain amount of sympathy at first, so I supported it as impartially [5] as I could. But presently we had reason to suspect that we had allowed ourselves to be misled by misrepresentation of the state of affairs—

DR. STOCKMANN. Misrepresentation—!

HOVSTAD. Well, let us say a not entirely trustworthy representation. The Mayor's statement has proved that. I hope no one here has any doubt as to my liberal principles; the attitude of the *People's Messenger* toward important political questions is well known to everyone. But the advice of experienced and thoughtful men has convinced me that in purely local matters a newspaper ought to proceed with a certain caution.

ASLAKSEN. I entirely agree with the speaker.

HOVSTAD. And, in the matter before us, it is now an undoubted fact that Dr. Stockmann has public opinion against him. Now, what is an editor's first and most obvious duty, gentlemen? Is it not to work in harmony with his readers? Has he not received a sort of tacit [6] mandate [7] to work persistently and assiduously [8] for the welfare of those whose opinions he represents? Or is it possible I am mistaken in that?

VOICES FROM THE CROWD. No, no! You are quite right!

HOVSTAD. It has cost me a severe struggle to break with a man in whose house I have been lately a frequent guest—a man who till

---

5. **impartially:** justly; fairly.
6. **tacit:** unspoken.
7. **mandate:** instruction; command.
8. **assiduously** (ə·sij′o͞o·əs·lē) : diligently; industriously.

today has been able to pride himself on the undivided goodwill of his fellow-citizens—a man whose only, or at all events whose essential, failing is that he is swayed by his heart rather than his head.

A FEW SCATTERED VOICES.   That is true! Bravo, Stockmann!

HOVSTAD.   But my duty to the community obliged me to break with him. And there is another consideration that impels me to oppose him, and, as far as possible, to arrest him on the perilous course he has adopted; that is, consideration for his family—

DR. STOCKMANN.   Please stick to the water supply and drainage!

HOVSTAD.   —consideration, I repeat, for his wife and his children for whom he has made no provision.

MORTEN.   Is that us, Mother?

MRS. STOCKMANN.   Hush!

ASLAKSEN.   I will now put the Mayor's proposition to the vote.

DR. STOCKMANN.   There is no necessity! Tonight I have no intention of dealing with all that filth down at the Baths. No; I have something quite different to say to you.

PETER STOCKMANN.   (*Aside.*)   What is coming now?

A DRUNKEN MAN.   (*By the entrance door.*)   I am a taxpayer! And therefore I have a right to speak too! And my entire—firm—inconceivable opinion is—

A NUMBER OF VOICES.   Be quiet back there!

OTHERS.   He is drunk! Turn him out!

(*They turn him out.*)

DR. STOCKMANN.   Am I allowed to speak?

ASLAKSEN.   (*Ringing his bell.*)   Dr. Stockmann will address the meeting.

DR. STOCKMANN.   I should like to have seen anyone, a few days ago, dare to attempt to silence me as has been done tonight! I would have defended my sacred rights as a man, like a lion! But now it is all one to me; I have something of even weightier importance to say to you.

(*The crowd presses nearer to him,* MORTEN KIIL *conspicuous among them.*)

I have thought and pondered a great deal, these last few days—pondered over such a variety of things that in the end my head seemed too full to hold them—

PETER STOCKMANN.   (*With a cough.*)   Ahem!

DR. STOCKMANN.   —but I got them clear in my mind at last, and then I saw the whole situation lucidly.[9] And that is why I am standing here tonight. I have a great revelation to make to you, my fellow-citizens! I will impart to you a discovery of a far wider scope than the trifling matter that our water supply is poisoned and our medicinal Baths are standing on pestiferous [10] soil.

A NUMBER OF VOICES. (*Shouting.*)   Don't talk about the Baths! We won't hear you! None of that!

DR. STOCKMANN.   I have already told you that what I want to speak about is the great discovery I have made lately—the discovery that all the sources of our *moral* life are poisoned and that the whole fabric [11] of our civic community is founded on the pestiferous soil of falsehood.

VOICES OF DISCONCERTED CITIZENS.   What is that he says?

PETER STOCKMANN.   Such an insinuation—!

ASLAKSEN. (*With his hand on his bell.*)   I call upon the speaker to moderate his language.

DR. STOCKMANN.   I have always loved my native town as a man only can love the home of his youthful days. I was not old when I went away from here; and exile, longing, and memories cast, as it were, an additional halo over both the town and its inhabitants. (*Some clapping and applause.*) And there I stayed, for many years, in a horrible hole far away up north. When I came into contact with some of the people that lived scattered about among the rocks, I often thought it would have been more service to the poor half-starved creatures if a veterinary doctor had been sent up there, instead of a man like me.

(*Murmurs among the crowd.*)

BILLING. (*Laying down his pen.*)   I'm damned if I have ever heard—!

HOVSTAD.   It is an insult to a respectable population!

DR. STOCKMANN.   Wait a bit! I do not think anyone will charge me with having forgotten my native town up there. I was like one of the eider ducks [12] brooding on its nest, and what I hatched was— the plans for these Baths. (*Applause and protests.*) And then when fate at last decreed for me the great happiness of coming home again—I assure you, gentlemen, I thought I had nothing more in

9. **lucidly**: clearly.
10. **pestiferous**: infected; diseased.
11. **fabric**: framework; structure.
12. **eider** (ī′dər) **ducks**: large northern sea ducks, whose down is used for making bedding.

the world to wish for. Or rather, there was one thing I wished for—eagerly, untiringly, ardently—and that was to be able to be of service to my native town and the good of the community.

PETER STOCKMANN. (*Looking at the ceiling.*) You chose a strange way of doing it—ahem!

DR. STOCKMANN. And so, with my eyes blinded to the real facts, I reveled [13] in happiness. But yesterday morning—no, to be precise, it was yesterday afternoon—the eyes of my mind were opened wide, and the first thing I realized was the colossal stupidity of the authorities—

(*Uproar, shouts, and laughter.* MRS. STOCKMANN *coughs persistenty.*)

PETER STOCKMANN. Mr. Chairman!

ASLAKSEN. (*Ringing his bell.*) By virtue of my authority—!

DR. STOCKMANN. It is a petty thing to catch me up on a word, Mr. Aslaksen. What I mean is only that I got scent of the unbelievable piggishness our leading men had been responsible for down at the Baths. I can't stand leading men at any price!—I have had enough of such people in my time. They are like billy goats in a young plantation; they do mischief everywhere. They stand in a free man's way, whichever way he turns, and what I should like best would be to see them exterminated like any other vermin [14]—

(*Uproar.*)

PETER STOCKMANN. Mr. Chairman, can we allow such expressions to pass?

ASLAKSEN. (*With his hand on his bell.*) Doctor—!

DR. STOCKMANN. I cannot understand how it is that I have only now acquired a clear conception of what these gentry are, when I had almost daily before my eyes in this town such an excellent specimen of them—my brother Peter—slowwitted and hidebound in prejudice—

(*Laughter, uproar, and hisses.* MRS. STOCKMANN *sits coughing assiduously.* ASLAKSEN *rings his bell violently.*)

THE DRUNKEN MAN. (*Who has got in again.*) Is it me he is talking about? My name's Petersen, all right—but devil take me if I—

13. **reveled:** took great delight, indulged freely.
14. **vermin:** filthy and destructive animals, such as flies, lice, rats, and weasels.

ANGRY VOICES.   Turn out that drunken man! Turn him out. (*He is turned out again.*)

PETER STOCKMANN.   Who was that person?

FIRST CITIZEN.   I don't know who he is, Mr. Mayor.

SECOND CITIZEN.   He doesn't belong here.

THIRD CITIZEN.   I expect he is a lumberman from over at (*The rest is inaudible.*)

ASLAKSEN.   He had obviously had too much beer. Proceed, Doctor; but please strive to be moderate in your language.

DR. STOCKMANN.   Very well, gentlemen, I will say no more about our leading men. And if anyone imagines, from what I have just said, that my object is to attack these people this evening, he is wrong—absolutely wide of the mark. For I cherish the comforting conviction that these parasites [15]—all these venerable [16] relics of a dying school of thought—are most admirably paving the way for their own extinction; they need no doctor's help to hasten their end. Nor is it folk of that kind who constitute the most pressing danger to the community. It is not they who are most instrumental in poisoning the sources of our moral life and infecting the ground on which we stand. It is not they who are the most dangerous enemies of truth and freedom among us.

SHOUTS FROM ALL SIDES.   Who then? Who is it? Name! Name!

DR. STOCKMANN.   You may depend upon it I shall name them! That is precisely the great discovery I made yesterday. (*Raises his voice.*) The most dangerous enemy of truth and freedom among us is the compact majority—yes, the damned compact Liberal majority—that is it! Now you know!

> (*Tremendous uproar. Most of the crowd are shouting, stamping, and hissing. Some of the older men among them exchange stolen glances and seem to be enjoying themselves.* MRS. STOCKMANN *gets up, looking anxious.* EJLIF *and* MORTEN *advance threateningly upon some schoolboys who are playing pranks.* ASLAKSEN *rings his bell and begs for silence.* HOVSTAD *and* BILLING *both talk at once, but are inaudible. At last quiet is restored.*)

ASLAKSEN.   As chairman, I call upon the speaker to withdraw the ill-considered expressions he has just used.

15. **parasites:** those who live at the expense of others, without making any contribution of their own.
16. **venerable:** deserving respect, usually because of age.

DR. STOCKMANN. Never, Mr. Aslaksen! It is the majority in our community that denies me my freedom and seeks to prevent my speaking the truth.

HOVSTAD. The majority always has right on its side.

BILLING. And truth, too, by God!

DR. STOCKMANN. The majority *never* has right on its side. Never, I say! That is one of these social lies against which an independent, intelligent man must wage war. Who constitutes the majority of the population in a country? Is it the clever folk or the stupid? I don't imagine you will dispute [17] the fact that at present the stupid people are in an absolutely overwhelming majority all the world over. But, good Lord, you can never pretend that it is right that the stupid folk should govern the clever ones! (*Uproar and cries.*) Oh, yes—you can shout me down, I know! But you cannot answer me. The majority has *might* on its side—unfortunately; but *right* it has *not*. I am in the right—I and a few other scattered individuals. The minority is always in the right.

(*Renewed uproar.*)

HOVSTAD. Aha! So Dr. Stockmann has become an aristocrat since the day before yesterday!

DR. STOCKMANN. I have already said that I don't intend to waste a word on the puny, narrow-chested, short-winded crew whom we are leaving astern.[18] Pulsating [19] life no longer concerns itself with them. I am thinking of the few, the scattered few amongst us, who have absorbed new and vigorous truths. Such men stand, as it were, at the outposts, so far ahead that the compact majority has not yet been able to come up with them; and there they are fighting for truths that are too newly born into the world of consciousness to have any considerable number of people on their side as yet.

HOVSTAD. So the Doctor is a revolutionary now!

DR. STOCKMANN. Good heavens—of course I am, Mr. Hovstad! I propose to raise a revolution against the lie that the majority has the monopoly of the truth. What sort of truth are they that the majority usually supports? They are truths that are of such advanced age that they are beginning to break up. And if a truth is as old as that, it is also in a fair way to become a lie, gentlemen. (*Laughter and mocking cries.*) Yes, believe me or not, as you like;

17. **dispute:** question or resist the truth of.
18. **astern:** at the back of, or behind, a ship; hence, in the rear.
19. **Pulsating:** beating strongly; throbbing.

but truths are by no means as long-lived as Methuselah [20]—as some
folk imagine. A normally constituted truth lives, let us say, as a
rule seventeen or eighteen, or at most twenty years; seldom longer.
But truths as aged as that are always worn frightfully thin, and
nevertheless it is only then that the majority recognizes them
and recommends them to the community as wholesome moral
nourishment. There is no great nutritive [21] value in that sort of
fare, I can assure you; and, as a doctor, I ought to know. These
"majority truths" are like last year's cured meat—like rancid,[22]
tainted ham; and they are the origin of the moral scurvy that is
rampant [23] in our communities.

ASLAKSEN.   It appears to me that the speaker is wandering a long way
from his subject.

PETER STOCKMANN.   I quite agree with the Chairman.

DR. STOCKMANN.   Have you gone clean out of your senses, Peter? I
am sticking as closely to my subject as I can; for my subject is precisely this, that it is the masses, the majority—this infernal compact majority—that poisons the sources of our moral life and in-
fects the ground we stand on.

HOVSTAD.   And all this because the great, broad-minded majority of
the people is prudent enough to show deference only to well-
ascertained [24] and well-approved truths?

DR. STOCKMANN.   Ah, my good Mr. Hovstad, don't talk nonsense
about well-ascertained truths! The truths of which the masses now
approve are the very truths that the fighters at the outposts held to
in the days of our grandfathers. We fighters at the outposts now-
adays no longer approve of them; and I do not believe there is any
other well-ascertained truth except this, that no community can
live a healthy life if it is nourished only on such old marrowless [25]
truths.

HOVSTAD.   But instead of standing there using vague generalities, it
would be interesting if you would tell us what these old marrowless truths are, that we are nourished on.

(*Applause from many quarters.*)

20. **Methuselah** (mə·thōō′zə·lə) : one of the Old Testament patriarchs, supposed
to have lived for nearly a thousand years (*see* Genesis 5:27).
21. **nutritive:** nourishing; strengthening.
22. **rancid:** spoiled.
23. **rampant:** widespread; uncontrolled.
24. **well-ascertained:** worked out with great certainty.
25. **marrowless:** lacking inner substance; without vitality or strength.

DR. STOCKMANN.   Oh, I could give you a whole string of such abominations; [26] but to begin with I will confine myself to one well-approved truth, which at bottom is a foul lie, but upon which nevertheless Mr. Hovstad and the *People's Messenger* and all the *Messenger's* supporters are nourished.

HOVSTAD.   And that is—?

DR. STOCKMANN.   That is, the doctrine you have inherited from your forefathers and proclaim thoughtlessly far and wide—the doctrine that the public, the crowd, the masses are the essential part of the population—that they constitute the People—that the common folk, the ignorant and incomplete element in the community, have the same right to pronounce judgment and to approve, to direct, and to govern, as the isolated, intellectually superior personalities in it.

BILLING.   Well, damn me if ever I—

HOVSTAD.   (*At the same time, shouting out.*)   Fellow-citizens, take good note of that!

A NUMBER OF VOICES.   (*Angrily.*)   Oho! We are not the People! Only the superior folks are to govern, are they?

A WORKMAN.   Turn the fellow out, for talking such rubbish!

ANOTHER.   Out with him!

ANOTHER.   (*Calling out.*)   Blow your horn, Evensen!

(*A horn is blown loudly, amid hisses and an angry uproar.*)

DR. STOCKMANN.   (*When the noise has somewhat abated.*)   Be reasonable! Can't you stand hearing the voice of truth for once! I don't in the least expect you to agree with me all at once; but I must say I did expect Mr. Hovstad to admit I was right, when he had recovered his composure [27] a little. He claims to be a freethinker [28]—

VOICES.   (*In murmurs of astonishment.*)   Freethinker, did he say? Is Hovstad a freethinker?

HOVSTAD.   (*Shouting.*)   Prove it, Dr. Stockmann! When have I said so in print?

DR. STOCKMANN.   (*Reflecting.*)   No, confound it, you are right! You have never had the courage to. Well, I won't put you in a hole,

26. **abominations:** deplorable facts or realities.
27. **composure:** calmness.
28. **freethinker:** an independent thinker; especially, one who forms his own religious opinions without regard to religious authority.

Mr. Hovstad. Let us say it is I that am the freethinker, then. I am going to prove to you, scientifically, that the *People's Messenger* leads you by the nose in a shameful manner when it tells you that you—that the common people, the crowd, the masses are the real essence of the People. That is only a newspaper lie, I tell you! The common people are nothing more than the raw material of which a People is made. (*Groans, laughter, and uproar.*) Well, isn't that the case? Isn't there an enormous difference between a well-bred and an ill-bred strain of animals? Take, for instance, a common barn-door hen. What sort of eating do you get from a shriveled-up old scrag of a fowl like that? Not much, do you? And what sort of eggs does it lay? A fairly good crow or a raven can lay pretty nearly as good an egg. But take a well-bred Spanish or Japanese hen, or a good pheasant or a turkey—then you will see the difference. Or take the case of dogs, with whom we humans are on such intimate terms. Think first of an ordinary common cur—I mean one of the horrible, coarse-haired, low-bred curs that do nothing but run about the streets and befoul the walls of the houses. Compare one of these curs with a poodle whose sires for many generations have been bred in a gentleman's house, where they have had the best of food and had the opportunity of hearing soft voices and music. Do you not think that the poodle's brain is developed to quite a different degree from that of the cur? Of course it is. It is puppies of well-bred poodles like that that showmen train to do incredibly clever tricks—things that a common cur could never learn to do even if it stood on its head.

(Uproar and mocking cries.)

A CITIZEN. (*Calls out.*)   Are you going to make out we are dogs, now?

ANOTHER CITIZEN.   We are not animals, Doctor!

DR. STOCKMANN.   Yes, but, bless my soul, we *are*, my friend! It is true we are the finest animals anyone could wish for; but, even among us, exceptionally fine animals are rare. There is a tremendous difference between poodle-men and cur-men. And the amusing part of it is that Mr. Hovstad quite agrees with me as long as it is a question of four-footed animals—

HOVSTAD.   Yes, it is true enough as far as they are concerned.

DR. STOCKMANN.   Very well. But as soon as I extend the principle and apply it to two-legged animals, Mr. Hovstad stops short. He no longer dares to think independently, or to pursue his ideas to their logical conclusion; so he turns the whole theory upside down and proclaims in the *People's Messenger* that it is the barn-door hens and street curs that are the finest specimens in the menagerie. But that is always the way, as long as a man retains the traces of common origin and has not worked his way up to intellectual distinction.

HOVSTAD. I lay no claim to any sort of distinction. I am the son of humble countryfolk, and I am proud that the stock I come from is rooted deep among the common people he insults.

VOICES. Bravo, Hovstad! Bravo! Bravo!

DR. STOCKMANN. The kind of common people I mean are not only to be found low down in the social scale; they crawl and swarm all around us—even in the highest social positions. You have only to look at your own fine, distinguished Mayor! My brother Peter is every bit as plebeian [29] as anyone that walks in two shoes—

(Laughter and hisses.)

PETER STOCKMANN. I protest against personal allusions [30] of this kind.

DR. STOCKMANN. (*Imperturbably.*) —and that, not because he is, like myself, descended from some old rascal of a pirate from Pomerania or thereabouts—because that is who we are descended from—

PETER STOCKMANN. An absurd legend. I deny it!

DR. STOCKMANN. —but because he thinks what his superiors think and holds the same opinions as they. People who do that are, intellectually speaking, common people; and that is why my magnificent brother Peter is in reality so very far from any distinction—and consequently also so far from being liberal-minded.

PETER STOCKMANN. Mr. Chairman—!

HOVSTAD. So it is only the distinguished men that are liberal-minded in this country? We are learning something quite new!

(Laughter.)

DR. STOCKMANN. Yes, that is part of my new discovery too. And another part of it is that broad-mindedness is almost precisely the same thing as morality. That is why I maintain that it is absolutely inexcusable in the *People's Messenger* to proclaim, day in and day

29. **plebeian** (plĭ·bē′ən) : common; from the Latin *plebeius,* the common people. *Plebeian* may also mean coarse and vulgar.
30. **allusions:** references.

out, the false doctrine that the masses, the crowd, the compact majority have the monopoly of broad-mindedness and morality—and that vice and corruption and every kind of intellectual depravity [31] are the result of culture, just as all the filth that is draining into our Baths is the result of the tanneries up at Mölledal! (*Uproar and interruptions.* DR. STOCKMANN *is undisturbed, and goes on, carried away by his ardor, with a smile.*) And yet this same *People's Messenger* can go on preaching that the masses ought to be elevated to higher conditions of life! But, bless my soul, if the *Messenger's* teaching is to be depended upon, this very raising up the masses would mean nothing more or less than setting them straightway upon the paths of depravity! Happily the theory that culture demoralizes is only an old falsehood that our forefathers believed in and we have inherited. No, it is ignorance, poverty, ugly conditions of life that do the devil's work! In a house which does not get aired and swept every day—my wife Katherine maintains that the floor ought to be scrubbed as well, but that is a debatable question—in such a house, let me tell you, people will lose within two or three years the power of thinking or acting in a moral manner. Lack of oxygen weakens the conscience. And there must be a plentiful lack of oxygen in very many houses in this town, I should think, judging from the fact that the whole compact majority can be unconscientious enough to wish to build the town's prosperity on a quagmire [32] of falsehood and deceit.

ASLAKSEN. We cannot allow such a grave accusation to be flung at a citizen community.

A CITIZEN. I move that the Chairman direct the speaker to sit down.

VOICES. (*Angrily.*) Hear, hear! Quite right! Make him sit down!

DR. STOCKMANN. (*Losing his self-control.*) Then I will go and shout the truth at every street corner! I will write it in other towns' newspapers! The whole country shall know what is going on here!

HOVSTAD. It almost seems as if Dr. Stockmann's intention were to ruin the town.

DR. STOCKMANN. Yes, my native town is so dear to me that I would rather ruin it than see it flourishing upon a lie.

ASLAKSEN. This is really serious.

(*Uproar and catcalls.* MRS. STOCKMANN *coughs, but to no purpose; her husband does not listen to her any longer.*)

31. **depravity:** moral corruption or wickedness.
32. **quagmire:** marshy ground that gives way under foot.

HOVSTAD. (*Shouting above the din.*)   A man must be a public enemy to wish to ruin a whole community!

DR. STOCKMANN. (*With growing fervor.*)   What does the destruction of a community matter, if it lives on lies! It ought to be razed [33] to the ground, I tell you! All who live by lies ought to be exterminated like vermin! You will end by infecting the whole country; you will bring about such a state of things that the whole country will deserve to be ruined. And if things come to that pass, I shall say from the bottom of my heart: Let the whole country perish, let all these people be exterminated!

VOICES FROM THE CROWD.   That is talking like an out-and-out enemy of the people!

BILLING.   There sounded the voice of the people, by all that's holy!

THE WHOLE CROWD. (*Shouting.*)   Yes, yes! He is an enemy of the people! He hates his country! He hates his own people!

ASLAKSEN.   Both as a citizen and as an individual, I am profoundly disturbed by what we have had to listen to. Dr. Stockmann has shown himself in a light I should never have dreamed of. I am un-happily obliged to subscribe to the opinion which I have just heard my estimable [34] fellow-citizens utter; and I propose that we should give expression to that opinion in a resolution. I propose a resolu-tion as follows: "This meeting declares that it considers Dr. Thomas Stockmann, Medical Officer of the Baths, to be an enemy of the people."

(*A storm of cheers and applause. A number of men surround the* DOCTOR *and hiss him.* MRS. STOCKMANN *and* PETRA *have got up from their seats.* MORTEN *and* EJLIF *are fighting the other schoolboys for hissing; some of their elders separate them.*)

DR. STOCKMANN. (*To the men who are hissing him.*)   Oh, you fools! I tell you that—

ASLAKSEN. (*Ringing his bell.*)   We cannot hear you now, Doctor. A formal vote is about to be taken; but, out of regard for personal feelings, it shall be by ballot and not verbal. Have you any clean paper, Mr. Billing?

BILLING.   I have both blue and white here.

ASLAKSEN. (*Going to him.*)   That will do nicely; we shall get on

33. **razed:** torn down completely.
34. **estimable** (es′tə·mə·bəl) : well-thought-of; respected.

more quickly that way. Cut it up into small strips—yes, that's it. (*To the meeting.*) Blue means no; white means yes. I will come round myself and collect votes.

(PETER STOCKMANN *leaves the hall.* ASLAKSEN *and one or two others go round the room with the slips of paper in their hats.*)

FIRST CITIZEN. (*To* HOVSTAD.)   I say, what has come to the Doctor? What are we to think of it?

HOVSTAD.   Oh, you know how headstrong he is.

SECOND CITIZEN. (*To* BILLING.)   Billing, you go to their house—have you ever noticed if the fellow drinks?

BILLING.   Well, I'm hanged if I know what to say. There are always spirits on the table when you go.

THIRD CITIZEN.   I rather think he goes quite off his head sometimes.

FIRST CITIZEN.   I wonder if there is any madness in his family?

BILLING.   I shouldn't wonder if there were.

FOURTH CITIZEN.   No, it is nothing more than sheer malice; he wants to get even with somebody for something or other.

BILLING.   Well, certainly he suggested a raise in his salary on one occasion lately, and did not get it.

THE CITIZENS. (*Together.*)   Ah! Then it is easy to understand how it is!

THE DRUNKEN MAN. (*Who has got among the audience again.*)   I want a blue one, I do! And I want a white one too!

VOICES.   It's that drunken chap again! Turn him out!

MORTEN KIIL. (*Going up to* DR. STOCKMANN.)   Well, Stockmann, do you see what these monkey tricks of yours lead to?

DR. STOCKMANN.   I have done my duty.

MORTEN KIIL.   What was that you said about the tanneries at Mölledal?

DR. STOCKMANN.   You heard well enough. I said they were the source of all the filth.

MORTEN KIIL.   My tannery, too?

DR. STOCKMANN.   Unfortunately, your tannery is by far the worst.

MORTEN KIIL.   Are you going to put that in the papers?

DR. STOCKMANN.   I shall conceal nothing.

MORTEN KIIL.   That may cost you dear, Stockmann. (*Goes out.*)

A STOUT MAN. (*Going up to* CAPTAIN HORSTER, *without taking any notice of the ladies.*)   Well, Captain, so you lend your house to enemies of the people?

HORSTER.   I imagine I can do what I like with my own possessions, Mr. Vik.

THE STOUT MAN.   Then you can have no objection to my doing the same with mine.

HORSTER.   What do you mean, sir?

THE STOUT MAN.   You shall hear from me in the morning. (*Turns his back on him and moves off.*)

PETRA.   Was that not your owner, Captain Horster?

HORSTER.   Yes, that was Mr. Vik, the shipowner.

ASLAKSEN. (*With the voting papers in his hands, gets up on to the platform and rings his bell.*)   Gentlemen, allow me to announce the result. By the votes of everyone here except one person—

A YOUNG MAN.   That is the drunk chap!

ASLAKSEN.   By the votes of everyone here except a tipsy man, this meeting of citizens declares Dr. Thomas Stockmann to be an enemy of the people. (*Shouts and applause.*) Three cheers for our ancient and honorable citizen community! (*Renewed applause.*) Three cheers for our able and energetic Mayor, who has so loyally suppressed the promptings of family feeling! (*Cheers.*) The meeting is dissolved. (*Gets down.*)

BILLING.   Three cheers for the Chairman!

THE WHOLE CROWD.   Three cheers for Aslaksen! Hurrah!

DR. STOCKMANN.   My hat and coat, Petra! Captain, have you room on your ship for passengers to the New World?

HORSTER.   For you and yours we will make room, Doctor.

DR. STOCKMANN. (*As PETRA helps him into his coat.*)   Good. Come, Katherine! Come, boys!

MRS. STOCKMANN. (*In an undertone.*)   Thomas, dear, let us go out by the back way.

DR. STOCKMANN.   No back ways for me, Katherine. (*Raising his voice.*) You will hear more of this enemy of the people, before he shakes the dust off his shoes upon you! I am not so forgiving as a certain Person; I do not say: "I forgive you, for ye know not what ye do." [35]

ASLAKSEN. (*Shouting.*)   That is a blasphemous comparison, Dr. Stockmann!

BILLING.   It is, by God! It's dreadful for an earnest man to listen to.

A COARSE VOICE.   Threatens us now, does he?

35. "**I forgive . . . do**": Dr. Stockmann is here echoing the words of Christ on the cross: "Father, forgive them; for they know not what they do" (Luke, 23:34).

OTHER VOICES. (*Excitedly.*)   Let's go and break his windows! Duck him in the fiord! [36]

ANOTHER VOICE.   Blow your horn, Evensen! Pip, pip!

(*Horn-blowing, hisses, and wild cries.* DR. STOCKMANN *goes out through the hall with his family,* HORSTER *elbowing a way for them.*)

THE WHOLE CROWD. (*Howling after them as they go.*)   Enemy of the People! Enemy of the People!

BILLING. (*As he puts his papers together.*)   Well, I'm damned if I go and drink toddy with the Stockmanns tonight!

(*The crowd presses toward the exit. The uproar continues outside; shouts of* "Enemy of the People!" *are heard from without.*)

Curtain.

36. fiord (fyôrd): a narrow inlet of the sea between high cliffs.

Meaning and Method: Act IV

1. What lines spoken by the people (page 64) show that they are not truly prepared to seek the truth for themselves? What are the sources of their opinions? From the individual examples he has created for this scene, what does Ibsen's attitude toward the common people seem to be?

2. The Mayor claims to have a feeling of "solicitude for the vital interests of the town" (page 67). Why might this statement be true in one sense, false in another? Point out the ways in which money seems to be the overriding "vital interest" of the town.

3. After the Mayor's introductory remarks, Aslaksen agrees that Dr. Stockmann should be denied the right to speak. What reasons does he give? Does anyone other than Dr. Stockmann actually have a right to speak at the meeting? Why or why not?

4. Hovstad says that Dr. Stockmann's greatest fault is that "he is swayed by his heart rather than his head" (page 69). In what way is this remark a clever move by Hovstad? To what extent is it true?

5. Why is the "compact majority," according to Dr. Stockmann, the greatest enemy of truth and freedom? Would *the masses* be a suitable synonym for the *compact majority? the common people?* Why or why

not? Suggest other terms that might be used to describe the people about whom Dr. Stockmann is speaking, but try to select words that clarify but do not change the implications of the original term. What examples does the Doctor use to prove that "the majority never has right on its side" (page 73)?

6. In the context of the small-town, nineteenth-century society in which the play is set, how decisive a factor is Dr. Stockmann's admission of "freethinking" in the town's animosity? Point out the lines that show that Petra has religious views similar to those of her father. What do you think would be the reaction of the "compact majority" in a small town in the United States today to similar "freethinking" views?

7. Why do you suppose Ibsen used a drunken man in this Act? Does he provide a necessary bit of comedy? Why does Ibsen have him wanting to vote both ways?

8. One critic has said that "Ibsen . . . was not really a revolutionary. He was not proposing any overthrow of his wrong-headed majority." Why, then, does Ibsen have Dr. Stockmann—interpreted by many as a direct representative of Ibsen's views—attack the people and the officials elected by the people? Is he not thereby attacking the democratic process? If you had been in the audience, would you have found parts of his speech offensive? Why or why not? Are there sentiments with which you would have agreed? Quote passages to support your answer.

Act V

DR. STOCKMANN's *study. Bookcases and cabinets containing speci-mens line the walls. At the back is a door leading to the hall; in the foreground on the left, a door leading to the sitting room. In the right-hand wall are two windows, of which all the panes are broken. The* DOCTOR's *desk, littered with books and papers, stands in the middle of the room, which is in disorder. It is morning.* DR. STOCK-MANN, *in dressing gown and slippers, is bending down and raking with an umbrella under one of the cabinets. After a little while he rakes out a stone.*

DR. STOCKMANN. (*Calling through the open sitting-room door.*) Katherine, I have found another one.

MRS. STOCKMANN. (*From the sitting room.*) Oh, you will find a lot more yet, I expect.

DR. STOCKMANN. (*Adding the stone to a heap of others on the table.*) I shall treasure these stones as relics. Ejlif and Morten shall look at them every day, and when they are grown up they shall inherit them as heirlooms. (*Rakes about under a bookcase.*) Hasn't—what the deuce is her name? The girl, you know—hasn't she been to fetch the glazier [1] yet?

MRS. STOCKMANN. (*Coming in.*) Yes, but he said he didn't know if he would be able to come today.

DR. STOCKMANN. You will see he won't dare to come.

MRS. STOCKMANN. Well, that is just what Randine thought—that he didn't dare to, on account of the neighbors. (*Calls into the sitting room.*) What is it you want, Randine? Give it to me. (*Goes in, and comes out again directly.*) Here is a letter for you, Thomas.

DR. STOCKMANN. Let me see it. (*Opens and reads it.*) Ah! Of course.

MRS. STOCKMANN. Who is it from?

DR. STOCKMANN. From the landlord. Notice to quit.

MRS. STOCKMANN. Is it possible? Such a nice man—

DR. STOCKMANN. (*Looking at the letter.*) Does not dare do other-wise, he says. Doesn't like doing it, but dare not do otherwise—on account of his fellow-citizens—out of regard for public opinion. Is in a dependent position—dare not offend certain influential men—

1. **glazier:** one who fits windows and doors with glass.

MRS. STOCKMANN. There, you see, Thomas!

DR. STOCKMANN. Yes, yes, I see well enough; the whole lot of them in the town are cowards; not a man among them dares do anything for fear of the others. (*Throws the letter onto the table.*) But it doesn't matter to us, Katherine. We are going to sail away to the New World, and—

MRS. STOCKMANN. But, Thomas, are you sure we are well advised to take this step?

DR. STOCKMANN. Are you suggesting that I should stay here, where they have pilloried me as an enemy of the people—branded me—broken my windows! And just look here, Katherine—they have torn a great rent in my black trousers too!

MRS. STOCKMANN. Oh, dear! And they are the best pair you have got!

DR. STOCKMANN. You should never wear your best trousers when you go out to fight for freedom and truth. It is not that I care so much about the trousers, you know; you can always sew them up again for me. But that the common herd should dare to make this attack on me, as if they were my equals—that is what I cannot, for the life of me, swallow!

MRS. STOCKMANN. There is no doubt they have behaved very ill to you, Thomas; but is that sufficient reason for our leaving our native country for good and all?

DR. STOCKMANN. If we went to another town, do you suppose we should not find the common people just as insolent as they are here? Depend upon it, there is not much to choose between them. Oh, well, let the curs snap—that is not the worst part of it. The worst is that, from one end of this country to the other, every man is the slave of his Party. Although, as far as that goes, I daresay it is not much better in the free West either; the compact majority, and liberal public opinion, and all that infernal old bag of tricks are probably rampant there too. But there things are done on a larger scale, you see. They may kill you, but they won't put you to death by slow torture. They don't squeeze a free man's soul in a vice, as they do here. And, if need be, one can live in solitude. (*Walks up and down.*) If only I knew where there was a virgin forest or a small South Sea island for sale, cheap—

MRS. STOCKMANN. But think of the boys, Thomas.

DR. STOCKMANN. (*Standing still.*) What a strange woman you are, Katherine! Would you prefer to have the boys grow up in a society like this? You saw for yourself last night that half the population are out of their minds; and if the other half have not lost their senses, it is because they are mere brutes, with no sense to lose.

MRS. STOCKMANN. But, Thomas dear, the imprudent things you said had something to do with it, you know.

DR. STOCKMANN. Well, isn't what I said perfectly true? Don't they turn every idea topsy-turvy? Don't they make a regular hotch potch of right and wrong? Don't they say that the things I know are true are lies? The craziest part of it all is the fact of these "liberals," men of full age, going about in crowds imagining that they are the broad-minded party! Did you ever hear anything like it, Katherine?

MRS. STOCKMANN. Yes, yes, it's mad enough of them, certainly; but— (PETRA *comes in from the sitting room.*) Back from school already?

PETRA. Yes. I have been given notice of dismissal.

MRS. STOCKMANN. Dismissal?

DR. STOCKMANN. You, too?

PETRA. Mrs. Busk gave me my notice; so I thought it was best to go at once.

DR. STOCKMANN. You were perfectly right, too!

MRS. STOCKMANN. Who would have thought Mrs. Busk was a woman like that?

PETRA. Mrs. Busk isn't a bit like that, Mother; I saw quite plainly how it hurt her to do it. But she didn't dare do otherwise, she said; and so I got my notice.

DR. STOCKMANN. (*Laughing and rubbing his hands.*) She didn't dare do otherwise, either! It's delicious!

MRS. STOCKMANN. Well, after the dreadful scenes last night—

PETRA. It was not only that. Just listen to this, Father!

DR. STOCKMANN. Well?

PETRA. Mrs. Busk showed me no less than three letters she received this morning—

DR. STOCKMANN. Anonymous, I suppose?

PETRA. Yes.

DR. STOCKMANN. Yes, because they didn't dare to risk signing their names, Katherine!

PETRA. And two of them were to the effect that a man, who has been our guest here, was declaring last night at the Club that my views on various subjects are extremely emancipated—

DR. STOCKMANN. You did not deny that, I hope?

PETRA. No, you know I wouldn't. Mrs. Busk's own views are toler-
ably emancipated, when we are alone together; but now that this
report about me is being spread, she dare not keep me on any
longer.

MRS. STOCKMANN. And someone who had been a guest of ours!
That shows you the return you get for your hospitality, Thomas!

DR. STOCKMANN. We won't live in such a disgusting hole any longer.
Pack up as quickly as you can, Katherine; the sooner we can get
away the better.

MRS. STOCKMANN. Be quiet—I think I hear someone in the hall.
See who it is, Petra.

PETRA. (*Opening the door.*) Oh, it's you, Captain Horster! Do
come in.

HORSTER. (*Coming in.*) Good morning. I thought I would just
come in and see how you were.

DR. STOCKMANN. (*Shaking his hand.*) Thanks—that is really kind
of you.

MRS. STOCKMANN. And thank you, too, for helping us through the
crowd, Captain Horster.

PETRA. How did you manage to get home again?

HORSTER. Oh, somehow or other. I am fairly strong, and there is
more sound than fury about these folk.

DR. STOCKMANN. Yes, isn't their swinish cowardice astonishing?
Look here, I will show you something! There are all the stones
they have thrown through my windows. Just look at them! I'm
hanged if there are more than two decently large bits of hardstone
in the whole heap; the rest are nothing but gravel—wretched little
things. And yet they stood out there bawling and swearing that
they would do me some violence; but as for *doing* anything—you
don't see much of that in this town.

HORSTER. Just as well for you this time, Doctor!

DR. STOCKMANN. True enough. But it makes one angry all the same;
because if some day it should be a question of a national fight in real
earnest, you will see that public opinion will be in favor of taking
to one's heels, and the compact majority will turn tail like a flock
of sheep, Captain Horster. That is what is so mournful to think of;
it gives me so much concern, that— No, devil take it, it is ridiculous to care about it! They have called me an enemy of the people,
so an enemy of the people let me be!

MRS. STOCKMANN.   You will never be that, Thomas.

DR. STOCKMANN.   Don't swear to that, Katherine. To be called an ugly name may have the same effect as a pin scratch in the lung. And that hateful name—I can't get quit of it. It is sticking here in the pit of my stomach, eating into me like a corrosive acid. And no magnesia will remove it.

PETRA.   Bah! You should only laugh at them, Father.

HORSTER.   They will change their minds some day, Doctor.

MRS. STOCKMANN.   Yes, Thomas, as sure as you are standing here.

DR. STOCKMANN.   Perhaps, when it is too late. Much good may it do them! They may wallow [2] in their filth then and rue [3] the day when they drove a patriot into exile. When do you sail, Captain Horster?

HORSTER.   Hm! That was just what I had come to speak about—

DR. STOCKMANN.   Why, has anything gone wrong with the ship?

HORSTER.   No; but what has happened is that I am not to sail in it.

PETRA.   Do you mean that you have been dismissed from your command?

HORSTER. (*Smiling.*)   Yes, that's just it.

PETRA.   You, too.

MRS. STOCKMANN.   There, you see, Thomas!

DR. STOCKMANN.   And that for the truth's sake! Oh, if I had thought such a thing possible—

HORSTER.   You mustn't take it to heart; I shall be sure to find a job with some shipowner or other, elsewhere.

DR. STOCKMANN.   And that is this man Vik—a wealthy man, independent of everyone and everything—! Shame on him!

HORSTER.   He is quite an excellent fellow otherwise; he told me himself he would willingly have kept me on, if only he had dared—

DR. STOCKMANN.   But he didn't dare? No, of course not.

HORSTER.   It is not such an easy matter, he said, for a party man [4]—

DR. STOCKMANN.   The worthy man spoke the truth. A party is like a sausage machine; it mashes up all sorts of heads together into the same mincemeat—fatheads and blockheads, all in one mash!

MRS. STOCKMANN.   Come, come, Thomas dear!

PETRA. (*To* HORSTER.)   If only you had not come home with us, things might not have come to this pass.

2. **wallow:** roll about, like pigs in mud.
3. **rue:** regret.
4. **party man:** a consistent follower of one political party.

HORSTER.   I do not regret it.

PETRA.   (*Holding out her hand to him.*)   Thank you for that!

HORSTER.   (*To* DR. STOCKMANN.)   And so what I came to say was that if you are determined to go away, I have thought of another plan—

DR. STOCKMANN.   That's splendid! If only we can get away at once.

MRS. STOCKMANN.   Hush! Wasn't that someone knocking?

PETRA.   That is uncle, surely.

DR. STOCKMANN.   Aha! (*Calls out.*) Come in!

MRS. STOCKMANN.   Dear Thomas, promise me definitely—

(PETER STOCKMANN *comes in from the hall.*)

PETER STOCKMANN.   Oh, you are engaged. In that case, I will—

DR. STOCKMANN.   No, no, come in.

PETER STOCKMANN.   But I wanted to speak to you alone.

MRS. STOCKMANN.   We will go into the sitting room in the meanwhile.

HORSTER.   And I will look in again later.

DR. STOCKMANN.   No, go in there with them, Captain Horster; I want to hear more about—

HORSTER.   Very well, I will wait, then.

(*He follows* MRS. STOCKMANN *and* PETRA *into the sitting room.*)

DR. STOCKMANN.   I daresay you find it rather drafty here today. Put your hat on.

PETER STOCKMANN.   Thank you, if I may. (*Does so.*) I think I caught cold last night; I stood and shivered—

DR. STOCKMANN.   Really? I found it warm enough.

PETER STOCKMANN.   I regret that it was not in my power to prevent those excesses last night.

DR. STOCKMANN.   Have you anything particular to say to me besides that?

PETER STOCKMANN.   (*Taking a big letter from his pocket.*)   I have this document for you, from the Baths' Committee.

DR. STOCKMANN.   My dismissal?

PETER STOCKMANN.   Yes, dating from today. (*Lays the letter on the able.*) It gives us pain to do it; but, to speak frankly, we dared not do otherwise on account of public opinion.

DR. STOCKMANN.   (*Smiling.*)   Dared not? I seem to have heard that word before, today.

PETER STOCKMANN. I must beg you to understand your position clearly. For the future you must not count on any practice whatever in the town.

DR. STOCKMANN. Devil take the practice! But why are you so sure of that?

PETER. STOCKMANN. The Householders' Association is circulating a list from house to house. All right-minded citizens are being called upon to give up employing you; and I can assure you that not a single head of a family will risk refusing his signature. They simply dare not.

DR. STOCKMANN. No, no; I don't doubt it. But what then?

PETER STOCKMANN. If I might advise you, it would be best to leave the place for a little while—

DR. STOCKMANN. Yes, the propriety [5] of leaving the place *has* occurred to me.

PETER STOCKMANN. Good. And then, when you have had six months to think things over, if, after mature consideration, you can persuade yourself to write a few words of regret, acknowledging your error—

DR. STOCKMANN. I might have my appointment restored to me, do you mean?

PETER STOCKMANN. Perhaps. It is not at all impossible.

DR. STOCKMANN. But what about public opinion, then? Surely you would not dare to do it on account of public feeling.

PETER STOCKMANN. Public opinion is an extremely mutable [6] thing. And, to be quite candid with you, it is a matter of great importance to us to have some admission of that sort from you in writing.

DR. STOCKMANN. Oh, that's what you are after, is it? I will just trouble you to remember what I said to you lately about foxy tricks of that sort!

PETER STOCKMANN. Your position was quite different then. At that time you had reason to suppose you had the whole town at your back—

DR. STOCKMANN. Yes, and now I feel I have the whole town *on* my back— (*Flaring up.*) I would not do it if I had the devil and his dam [7] on my back—! Never—never, I tell you!

PETER STOCKMANN. A man with a family has no right to behave as you do. You have no right to do it, Thomas.

5. **propriety** (prə·prī′ə·tē) : the quality of being proper; correctness.
6. **mutable:** capable of change.
7. **dam:** a female parent—usually used in reference to animals.

DR. STOCKMANN. I have no right! There is only one single thing in the world a free man has no right to do. Do you know what that is?

PETER STOCKMANN. No.

DR. STOCKMANN. Of course you don't, but I will tell you. A free man has no right to soil himself with filth; he has no right to behave in a way that would justify his spitting in his own face.

PETER STOCKMANN. This sort of thing sounds extremely plausible, of course; and if there were no other explanation for your obstinacy— But as it happens there is.

DR. STOCKMANN. What do you mean?

PETER STOCKMANN. You understand very well what I mean. But, as your brother and as a man of discretion, I advise you not to build too much upon expectations and prospects that may so very easily fail you.

DR. STOCKMANN. What in the world is all this about?

PETER STOCKMANN. Do you really ask me to believe that you are ignorant of the terms of Mr. Kiil's will?

DR. STOCKMANN. I know that the small amount he possesses is to go to an institution for indigent old workpeople. How does that concern me?

PETER STOCKMANN. In the first place, it is by no means a small amount that is in question. Mr. Kiil is a fairly wealthy man.

DR. STOCKMANN. I had no notion of that!

PETER STOCKMANN. Hm! Hadn't you really? Then I suppose you had no notion, either, that a considerable portion of his wealth will come to your children, you and your wife having a life income from the capital. Has he never told you so?

DR. STOCKMANN. Never, on my honor! Quite the reverse; he has consistently done nothing but fume at being so unconscionably [8] heavily taxed. But are you perfectly certain of this, Peter?

PETER STOCKMANN. I have it from an absolutely reliable source.

DR. STOCKMANN. Then, thank God, Katherine is provided for—and the children, too! I must tell her this at once— (*Calls out.*) Katherine, Katherine!

PETER STOCKMANN. (*Restraining him.*) Hush, don't say a word yet!

MRS. STOCKMANN. (*Opening the door.*) What is the matter?

DR. STOCKMANN. Oh, nothing, nothing; you can go back. (*She shuts the door.* DR. STOCKMANN *walks up and down in his excitement.*)

8. **unconscionably:** unjustifiably.

Provided for!—Just think of it, we are all provided for! And for life! What a blessed feeling it is to know one is provided for!

PETER STOCKMANN.   Yes, but that is just exactly what you are not. Mr. Kiil can alter his will any day he likes.

DR. STOCKMANN.   But he won't do that, my dear Peter. The "Badger" is much too delighted at my attack on you and your wise friends.

PETER STOCKMANN. (*Starts and looks intently at him.*)   Ah, that throws a light on various things.

DR. STOCKMANN.   What things?

PETER STOCKMANN.   I see that the whole thing was a combined maneuver on your part and his. These violent, reckless attacks that you have made against the leading men of the town, under the pretense that it was in the name of truth—

DR. STOCKMANN.   What about them?

PETER STOCKMANN.   I see that they were nothing else than the stipulated [9] price for that vindictive [10] old man's will.

DR. STOCKMANN. (*Almost speechless.*)   Peter—you are the most disgusting plebeian I have ever met in all my life.

PETER STOCKMANN.   All is over between us. Your dismissal is irrevocable—we have a weapon against you now. (*Goes out.*)

DR. STOCKMANN.   For shame! For shame! (*Calls out.*) Katherine, you must have the floor scrubbed after him! Let—what's her name—devil take it, the girl who has always got soot on her nose—

MRS. STOCKMANN. (*In the sitting room.*)   Hush, Thomas, be quiet!

PETRA. (*Coming to the door.*)   Father, grandfather is here, asking if he may speak to you alone.

DR. STOCKMANN.   Certainly he may. (*Going to the door.*) Come in, Mr. Kiil. (MORTEN KIIL *comes in.* DR. STOCKMANN *shuts the door after him.*) What can I do for you? Won't you sit down?

MORTEN KIIL.   I won't sit. (*Looks around.*) You look very comfortable here today, Thomas.

DR. STOCKMANN.   Yes, don't we?

MORTEN KIIL.   Very comfortable—plenty of fresh air. I should think you have got enough today of that oxygen you were talking about yesterday. Your conscience must be in splendid order today, I should think.

DR. STOCKMANN.   It is.

MORTEN KIIL.   So I should think. (*Taps his chest.*) Do you know what I have got here?

---

9. **stipulated:** required; specified.
10. **vindictive:** revengeful.

DR. STOCKMANN. A good conscience, too, I hope.

MORTEN KIIL. Bah!—No, it is something better than that.

(*He takes a thick pocketbook from his breast-pocket, opens it, and displays a packet of papers.*)

DR. STOCKMANN. (*Looking at him in astonishment.*) Shares in the Baths?

MORTEN KIIL. They were not difficult to get today.

DR. STOCKMANN. And you have been buying—?

MORTEN KIIL. As many as I could pay for.

DR. STOCKMANN. But, my dear Mr. Kiil—consider the state of the Baths' affairs!

MORTEN KIIL. If you behave like a reasonable man, you can soon set the Baths on their feet again.

DR. STOCKMANN. Well, you can see for yourself that I have done all I can, but— They are all mad in this town!

MORTEN KIIL. You said yesterday that the worst of this pollution came from my tannery. If that is true, then my grandfather and my father before me, and I myself, for many years past, have been poisoning the town like three destroying angels. Do you think I am going to sit quiet under that reproach?

DR. STOCKMANN. Unfortunately, I am afraid you will have to.

MORTEN KIIL. No, thank you. I am jealous of my name and reputation. They call me "the Badger," I am told. A badger is a kind of pig, I believe; but I am not going to give them the right to call me that. I mean to live and die a clean man.

DR. STOCKMANN. And how are you going to set about it?

MORTEN KIIL. You shall cleanse me, Thomas.

DR. STOCKMANN. I!

MORTEN KIIL. Do you know what money I have bought these shares with? No, of course you can't know—but I will tell you. It is the money that Katherine and Petra and the boys will have when I am gone. Because I have been able to save a little bit after all, you know.

DR. STOCKMANN. (*Flaring up.*) And you have gone and taken Katherine's money for *this!*

MORTEN KIIL. Yes, the whole of the money is invested in the Baths now. And now I just want to see whether you are quite stark, staring mad, Thomas! If you still make out that these animals and other nasty things of that sort come from my tannery, it will be exactly as if you were to flay broad strips of skin from Katherine's

body, and Petra's, and the boys'; and no decent man would do that
—unless he were mad.

DR. STOCKMANN. (*Walking up and down.*)   Yes, but I *am* mad; I
am mad!

MORTEN KIIL.   You cannot be so absurdly mad as all that, when it
is a question of your wife and children.

DR. STOCKMANN. (*Standing still in front of him.*)   Why couldn't you
consult me about it, before you went and bought all that trash?

MORTEN KIIL.   What is done cannot be undone.

DR. STOCKMANN. (*Walks about uneasily.*)   If only I were not so certain about it—! But I am absolutely convinced that I am right.

MORTEN KIIL. (*Weighing the pocketbook in his hand.*)   If you stick
to your mad idea, this won't be worth much, you know. (*Puts
the pocketbook in his pocket.*)

DR. STOCKMANN.   But, hang it all! It might be possible for science
to discover some prophylactic,[11] I should think—or some antidote
of some kind—

MORTEN KIIL.   To kill these animals, do you mean?

DR. STOCKMANN.   Yes, or to make them innocuous.[12]

MORTEN KIIL.   Couldn't you try some ratsbane? [13]

DR. STOCKMANN.   Don't talk nonsense! They all say it is only imagination, you know. Well, let it go at that! Let them have their own
way about it! Haven't the ignorant, narrow-minded curs reviled [14]
me as an enemy of the people? And haven't they been ready to
tear the clothes off my back too?

MORTEN KIIL.   And broken all your windows to pieces!

DR. STOCKMANN.   And then there is my duty to my family. I must
talk it over with Katherine; she is great on those things.

MORTEN KIIL.   That is right; be guided by a reasonable woman's advice.

DR. STOCKMANN. (*Advancing toward him.*)   To think you could do
such a preposterous thing! Risking Katherine's money in this way,
and putting me in such a horribly painful dilemma! [15] When I
look at you, I think I see the devil himself—

11. **prophylactic** (prō'fə·lak'tik) : preventive; tending to ward off something, as
disease.
12. **innocuous** (i·nok'yōō·əs) : harmless.
13. **ratsbane**: rat poison.
14. **reviled** (ri·vīld') : used abusive or contemptuous language.
15. **dilemma**: a situation or problem requiring a choice between equally undesire-
able alternatives.

MORTEN KIIL.   Then I had better go. But I must have an answer from you before two o'clock—yes or no. If it is no, the shares go to a charity, and that this very day.

DR. STOCKMANN.   And what does Katherine get?

MORTEN KIIL.   Not a halfpenny. (*The door leading to the hall opens, and* HOVSTAD *and* ASLAKSEN *make their appearance.*) Look at those two!

DR. STOCKMANN.   (*Staring at them.*)   What the devil! Have *you* actually the face to come into my house?

HOVSTAD.   Certainly.

ASLAKSEN.   We have something to say to you, you see.

MORTEN KIIL.   (*In a whisper.*)   Yes or no—before two o'clock.

ASLAKSEN.   (*Glancing at* HOVSTAD.)   Aha!

(MORTEN KIIL *goes out.*)

DR. STOCKMANN.   Well, what do you want with me? Be brief.

HOVSTAD.   I can quite understand that you are annoyed with us for our attitude at the meeting yesterday—

DR. STOCKMANN.   Attitude, do you call it? Yes, it was a charming attitude! I call it weak, womanish—damnably shameful!

HOVSTAD.   Call it what you like; we could not do otherwise.

DR. STOCKMANN.   You *dared* not do otherwise—isn't that it?

HOVSTAD.   Well, if you like to put it that way.

ASLAKSEN.   But why did you not let us have word of it beforehand —just a hint to Mr. Hovstad or to me?

DR. STOCKMANN.   A hint? Of what?

ASLAKSEN.   Of what was behind it all.

DR. STOCKMANN.   I don't understand you in the least.

ASLAKSEN.   (*With a confidential nod.*)   Oh, yes, you do, Dr. Stockmann.

HOVSTAD.   It is no good making a mystery of it any longer.

DR. STOCKMANN.   (*Looking first at one of them and then at the other.*) What the devil do you both mean?

ASLAKSEN.   May I ask if your father-in-law is not going round the town buying up all the shares in the Baths?

DR. STOCKMANN.   Yes, he has been buying Baths' shares today; but—

ASLAKSEN.   It would have been more prudent to get someone else to do it—someone less nearly related to you.

HOVSTAD.   And you should not have let your name appear in the affair. There was no need for anyone to know that the attack on the Baths came from you. You ought to have consulted me, Dr. Stockmann.

DR. STOCKMANN. (*Looks in front of him; then a light seems to dawn on him and he says in amazement.*) Are such things conceivable? Are such things possible?

ASLAKSEN. (*With a smile.*)   Evidently they are. But it is better to use a little finesse,[16] you know.

HOVSTAD.   And it is much better to have several persons in a thing of that sort, because the responsibility of each individual is lessened, when there are others with him.

DR. STOCKMANN. (*Composedly.*)   Come to the point, gentlemen. What do you want?

ASLAKSEN.   Perhaps Mr. Hovstad had better—

HOVSTAD.   No, you tell him, Aslaksen.

ASLAKSEN.   Well, the fact is that, now we know the bearings of the whole affair, we think we might venture to put the *People's Messenger* at your disposal.

DR. STOCKMANN.   Do you dare do that now? What about public opinion? Are you not afraid of a storm breaking upon our heads?

HOVSTAD.   We will try to weather it.

ASLAKSEN.   And you must be ready to go off quickly on a new tack, Doctor. As soon as your invective [17] has done its work—

DR. STOCKMANN.   Do you mean, as soon as my father-in-law and I have got hold of the shares at a low figure?

HOVSTAD.   Your reasons for wishing to get the control of the Baths are mainly scientific, I take it.

DR. STOCKMANN.   Of course; it was for scientific reasons that I persuaded the old "Badger" to stand in with me in the matter. So we will tinker at the conduit pipes a little, and dig up a little bit of the shore, and it shan't cost the town a sixpence. That will be all right—eh?

HOVSTAD.   I think so—if you have the *People's Messenger* behind you.

ASLAKSEN.   The Press is a power in a free community, Doctor.

DR. STOCKMANN.   Quite so. And so is public opinion. And you, Mr. Aslaksen—I suppose you will be answerable for the Householders' Association?

16. **finesse:** skill; cunning.
17. **invective:** strong verbal attack.

ASLAKSEN.   Yes, and for the Temperance Society. You may rely on that.

DR. STOCKMANN.   But, gentlemen—I really am ashamed to ask the question—but, what return do you—?

HOVSTAD.   We should prefer to help you without any return whatever, believe me. But the *People's Messenger* is in rather a shaky condition; it doesn't go really well; and I should be very unwilling to suspend the paper now, when there is so much work to do here in the political way.

DR. STOCKMANN.   Quite so; that would be a great trial to such a friend of the people as you are. (*Flares up.*) But I am an enemy of the people, remember! (*Walks about the room.*) Where have I put my stick? Where the devil is my stick?

HOVSTAD.   What's that?

ASLAKSEN.   Surely you never mean—?

DR. STOCKMANN.   (*Standing still.*)   And suppose I don't give you a single penny of all I get out of it? Money is not very easy to get out of us rich folk, please to remember!

HOVSTAD.   And you please to remember that this affair of the shares can be represented in two ways!

DR. STOCKMANN.   Yes, and you are just the man to do it. If I don't come to the rescue of the *People's Messenger*, you will certainly take an evil view of the affair; you will hunt me down, I can well imagine—pursue me—try to throttle me as a dog does a hare.

HOVSTAD.   It is a natural law; every animal must fight for its own livelihood.

ASLAKSEN.   And get its food where it can, you know.

DR. STOCKMANN.   (*Walking about the room.*)   Then you go and look for yours in the gutter, because I am going to show you which is the strongest animal of us three! (*Finds an umbrella and brandishes it above his head.*) Ah, now—!

HOVSTAD.   You are surely not going to use violence!

ASLAKSEN.   Take care what you are doing with that umbrella.

DR. STOCKMANN.   Out of the window with you, Mr. Hovstad!

HOVSTAD.   (*Edging to the door.*)   Are you quite mad?

DR. STOCKMANN.   Out of the window, Mr. Aslaksen! Jump, I tell you! You will have to do it, sooner or later.

ASLAKSEN.   (*Running round the writing table.*)   Moderation, Doctor —I am a delicate man—I can stand so little—(*Calls out.*) Help, help!

(MRS. STOCKMANN, PETRA, *and* HORSTER *come in from the sitting room.*)

MRS. STOCKMANN.   Good gracious, Thomas! What is happening?

DR. STOCKMANN.   (*Brandishing the umbrella.*) Jump out, I tell you! Out into the gutter!

HOVSTAD.   An assault on an unoffending man! I call you to witness, Captain Horster. (*Hurries out through the hall.*)

ASLAKSEN.   (*Irresolutely.*) If only I knew the way about here— (*Steals out through the sitting room.*)

MRS. STOCKMANN.   (*Holding her husband back.*) Control yourself, Thomas!

DR. STOCKMANN.   (*Throwing down the umbrella.*) Upon my soul, they have escaped after all.

MRS. STOCKMANN.   What did they want you to do?

DR. STOCKMANN.   I will tell you later on; I have something else to think about now. (*Goes to the table and writes something on a calling card.*) Look there, Katherine; what is written there?

MRS. STOCKMANN.   Three big No's; what does that mean?

DR. STOCKMANN.   I will tell you that too, later on. (*Holds out the card to* PETRA.) There, Petra; tell sooty-face to run over to the "Badger's" with that as quickly as she can. Hurry up!

(PETRA *takes the card and goes out to the hall.*)

DR. STOCKMANN.   Well, I think I have had a visit from every one of the devil's messengers today! But now I am going to sharpen my pen till they can feel its point; I shall dip it in venom and gall; [18] I shall hurl my ink-pot at their heads!

MRS. STOCKMANN.   Yes, but we are going away, you know, Thomas.

(PETRA *comes back.*)

DR. STOCKMANN.   Well?

PETRA.   She has gone with it.

DR. STOCKMANN.   Good. Going away, did you say? No, I'll be hanged if we are going away! We're going to say where we are, Katherine!

PETRA.   Stay here?

MRS. STOCKMANN.   Here, in the town?

DR. STOCKMANN.   Yes, here. This is the field of battle—this is where

---

18. **venom and gall:** poisonous and bitter liquids; *that is,* he will write with bitterness and malice.

the fight will be. This is where I shall triumph! As soon as I have had my trousers sewn up I shall go out and look for another house. We must have a roof over our heads for the winter.

HORSTER. That you shall have in my house.

DR. STOCKMANN. Can I?

HORSTER. Yes, quite well. I have plenty of room, and I am almost never at home.

MRS. STOCKMANN. How good of you, Captain Horster!

PETRA. Thank you!

DR. STOCKMANN. (*Grasping his hand.*) Thank you, thank you! That is one trouble over! Now I can set to work in earnest at once. There is an endless amount of things to look through here, Katherine! Luckily I shall have all my time at my disposal, because I have been dismissed from the Baths, you know.

MRS. STOCKMANN. (*With a sigh.*) Oh, yes, I expected that.

DR. STOCKMANN. And they want to take my practice away from me, too. Let them! I have got the poor people to fall back upon, any-way—those that don't pay anything; and, after all, they need me most, too. But, by Jove, they will have to listen to me; I shall preach to them in season and out of season, as it says somewhere.

MRS. STOCKMANN. But, dear Thomas, I should have thought events had showed you what use it is to preach.

DR. STOCKMANN. You are really ridiculous, Katherine. Do you want me to let myself be beaten off the field by public opinion and the compact majority and all that devilry? No, thank you! And what I want to do is so simple and clear and straightforward. I only want to drum into the heads of these curs the fact that the liberals are the most insidious enemies of freedom—that party programs stran-gle every young and vigorous truth—that considerations of expedi-ency [19] turn morality and justice upside down—and that they will end by making life here unbearable. Don't you think, Captain Horster, that I ought to be able to make people understand that?

HORSTER. Very likely; I don't know much about such things myself.

DR. STOCKMANN. Well, look here—I will explain! It is the party leaders that must be exterminated. A party leader is like a wolf, you see—like a voracious wolf. He requires a certain number of smaller victims to prey upon every year, if he is to live. Just look at Hovstad and Aslaksen! How many smaller victims have they not put an end to—or at any rate maimed and mangled until they are

19. **expediency:** consideration for what is politic, not for what is right.

fit for nothing except to be householders or subscribers to the *People's Messenger!* (*Sits down on the edge of the table.*) Come here, Katherine—look how beautifully the sun shines today! And this lovely spring air I am drinking in!

MRS. STOCKMANN.   Yes, if only we could live on sunshine and spring air, Thomas.

DR. STOCKMANN.   Oh, you will have to pinch and save a bit—then we shall get along. That gives me very little concern. What is much worse is that I know of no one who is liberal-minded and high-minded enough to venture to take up my work after me.

PETRA.   Don't think about that, Father; you have plenty of time before you. Hullo, here are the boys already!

(EJLIF *and* MORTEN *come in from the sitting room.*)

MRS. STOCKMANN.   Have you got a holiday?

MORTEN.   No; but we were fighting with the other boys between lessons—

EJLIF.   That isn't true; it was the other boys were fighting with us.

MORTEN.   Well, and then Mr. Rörlund said we had better stay at home for a day or two.

DR. STOCKMANN. (*Snapping his fingers and getting up from the table.*) I have it! I have it, by Jove! You shall never set foot in the school again!

THE BOYS.   No more school!

MRS. STOCKMANN.   But, Thomas—

DR. STOCKMANN.   Never, I say. I will educate you myself; that is to say, you shan't learn a blessed thing—

MORTEN.   Hooray!

DR. STOCKMANN.   —but I will make liberal-minded and high-minded men of you. You must help me with that, Petra.

PETRA.   Yes, Father, you may be sure I will.

DR. STOCKMANN.   And my school shall be in the room where they insulted me and called me an enemy of the people. But we are too few as we are; I must have at least twelve boys to begin with.

MRS. STOCKMANN.   You will certainly never get them in this town.

DR. STOCKMANN.   We shall. (*To the boys.*) Don't you know any street urchins—regular ragamuffins—?

MORTEN.   Yes, Father, I know lots!

DR. STOCKMANN.   That's capital! Bring me some specimens of them. I am going to experiment with curs, just for once; there may be some exceptional heads among them.

MORTEN.   And what are we going to do, when you have made liberal-minded and high-minded men of us?

DR. STOCKMANN.   Then you shall drive all the wolves out of the country, my boys!

(EJLIF *looks rather doubtful about it;* MORTEN *jumps about crying "Hurrah!"*)

MRS. STOCKMANN.   Let us hope it won't be the wolves that will drive you out of the country, Thomas.

DR. STOCKMANN.   Are you out of your mind, Katherine? Drive me out! Now—when I am the strongest man in the town!

MRS. STOCKMANN.   The strongest—now?

DR. STOCKMANN.   Yes, and I will go so far as to say that now I am the strongest man in the whole world.

MORTEN.   I say!

DR. STOCKMANN.   (*Lowering his voice.*)   Hush! You mustn't say anything about it yet, but I have made a great discovery.

MRS. STOCKMANN.   Another one?

DR. STOCKMANN.   Yes. (*Gathers them round him, and says confidentially.*) It is this, let me tell you—that the strongest man in the world is he who stands most alone.

MRS. STOCKMANN.   (*Smiling and shaking her head.*)   Oh, Thomas, Thomas!

PETRA.   (*Encouragingly, as she grasps her father's hands.*)   Father!

Curtain.

Meaning and Method: Act V

1. In this last act there is a rising crescendo of people who "dare not" act against public opinion. Note all the characters who "dare not," from first through last. What is the dramatic effect of the repetition of these words? Note, too, that Ibsen presents an array of forces which a man must consider: "public opinion," "consequences," "family," "party demands," etc.

   Cite examples from recent history of those who "dare not" express or act upon unpopular opinion.

2. The Mayor always sees selfish personal motives behind his brother's actions. What does this indicate about the Mayor? What "weapon" does the Mayor think he has discovered in relation to Morten Kiil's will? Why does Morten Kiil attempt to get the Doctor to withdraw

his criticisms of the Baths? Both Kiil and Peter Stockmann test the Doctor. What makes you think he is ready to give in at this point? What stops him? Quote passages from the play to prove your answer.

3. Why is Hovstad's belief that the Doctor and his father-in-law were partners in a dishonest and unprincipled money-making scheme typical of the town? In what way is Hovstad's hope to benefit from his "discovery" a form of blackmail? In what sense is the press free in Hovstad's and Stockmann's town? In what sense is the press free in a democracy such as ours?

4. Why does Dr. Stockmann not leave town as he had originally planned? What do you think of his plan to educate the common "curs" whom he has previously condemned? In what way is this in keeping or not in keeping with his character?

5. Examine the following similes used by Dr. Stockmann. Do the comparisons make the meanings clearer and more effective? Are the statements true, untrue, debatable?

   (a) "It is sticking here in the pit of my stomach, eating into me like a corrosive acid. And no magnesia will remove it." (On being called an enemy of the people.)

   (b) "A party is like a sausage machine; it mashes up all sorts of heads together into the same mincemeat—fatheads and blockheads, all in one mash!" (On party politics.)

6. At the end of the play Dr. Stockmann declares that "the strongest man in the world is he who stands most alone," and that he is "now the strongest man in the world." In what sense is the statement true and untrue? Does the play support or contradict the Doctor's self-evaluation?

Meaning and Method: On the Play as a Whole

1. *An Enemy of the People* is a *problem play*. That is, it is a drama in which a social problem is illustrated. Usually, in such problem or *thesis* plays, a solution to the problem is suggested or implied. But the best problem plays often ask questions of wider meaning than is immediately apparent.

   Ibsen, in *An Enemy of the People*, moves from the concrete to the abstract, from the specific to the general, by presenting a particular problem and then giving the larger implications of it. In this play, what is the immediate problem? What is the conflict that arises? What is the larger problem Ibsen is attacking? How do the Doctor and the Mayor represent both the concrete problem and its larger implications? Give specific evidence from the text.

2. On page 99, Dr. Stockmann insists that "considerations of expediency turn morality and justice upside down." Just what does this mean? Can you give examples from contemporary life?

May the statement just quoted be considered the theme of the play?

3. Is Dr. Stockmann a success or a failure? Is he the hero of the play or merely the protagonist? In what sense is he really an "enemy of the people"? In what way a friend? Is the title ironic? What qualities does Dr. Stockmann have other than those of the crusader or reformer? Why have these characteristics been introduced by the playwright? Why do none of the other characters in the play have such a variety of facets revealed?

4. What function does Captain Horster serve in the play? Is he there as a possible love interest for Petra? some other reason? Discuss.

5. Although An Enemy of the People is approaching its hundredth anniversary, it still seems topical. What political and social problems that Ibsen raises are still with us today? Give examples. Does Ibsen offer any solutions? What solutions would you offer? Ibsen said of himself as a dramatist that his purpose was "to raise questions, not to answer them." Is An Enemy of the People an example of this policy?

Composition and Discussion

1. Write a character sketch of Petra or of Dr. Stockmann.

2. Write two newspaper accounts of the meeting in Act IV, emphasizing Dr. Stockmann's speech. In a biased account, report the meeting as Hovstad might write it; in the second account, write as straightforward and objective an account of events as you are able.

3. At the height of his public address, Dr. Stockmann states that public opinion and the will of the majority have never done anything right. In an expository essay, describe and analyze some recent event that either affirms or contradicts the Doctor's point of view.

4. Ibsen believed that his mission was not to answer social questions, but to raise them. One such question is whether a man's primary responsibility is to his family or to his community. Be prepared to take part in a panel discussion weighing man's responsibility to his family versus the need to act upon his convictions and beliefs.

ARMS AND THE MAN

George Bernard Shaw

[1856–1950]

George Bernard Shaw was born in Dublin, of English stock. He left school at fourteen, and the next five years worked in a real-estate office. He received little attention from his preoccupied parents—his father a drinker scarcely earning a living, and his talented mother busy studying and teaching music.

At twenty Shaw moved to London, where he was an early member of the Fabian Society, a British organization devoted to the gradual introduction of socialism. During the following years he wrote five novels, each rejected by publishers. In order to earn a living he began to do criticism for various British publications, eventually writing music criticism for *The Star*, drama criticism for *The Saturday Review*, and art criticism for *The World*.

During this period Shaw developed his great interest in the theater, and he soon began to offer plays of his own to London audiences. The first two plays produced were not accepted by the public, but with the production of *Arms and the Man* in 1894, Shaw was well on the way to becoming the leading playwright in England. In 1925 he was awarded the Nobel prize for literature. A prolific writer throughout his life, by the end of his career Shaw had written more than fifty dramatic pieces. His complete works (to that time) were published in the early 1930's in thirty volumes.

As a result of seeing and studying so many plays, Shaw learned a great many things about the traditional construction of drama. Yet his plays were entirely new for his time, quite different from those of his predecessors. Unlike Shakespeare, Shaw did not write tragedies, and only one of his plays, *Saint Joan*, can possibly be considered a history play. His plays are witty, yet they deal with serious social and moral problems. Theater audiences rarely enjoy plays that teach too obviously, but Shaw had the unique talent of being able to present a problem or a lesson to an audience in such a way that it was unaware that it was being instructed. This he accomplished by skillful use of comedy and satire.

Shaw's prefaces to his plays often described their purpose. "I must warn my readers," he wrote, "that my attacks are directed against themselves, not against my stage figures." The following excerpt from the Preface of *Arms and the Man* summarizes the main ideas underlying not only this play but also many of his other crusading plays.

> I can no longer be satisfied with fictitious morals and fictitious good conduct, shedding fictitious glory on overcrowding, disease, crime, drink, war, cruelty, infant mortality, and all the other commonplaces of civilization which drive men to the theater to make foolish pretenses that such things are progress, science, morals, religion, patriotism, imperial supremacy, national greatness, and all the other names the newspapers call them. . . . And with that hint as to what I am driving at, I withdraw and ring up the curtain. (Preface to *Plays Pleasant and Unpleasant*, the collection in which *Arms and the Man* first appeared.)

Shaw was interested in economics, politics, philosophy, religion, and—curiously—spelling reform. In fact, his will left most of his substantial estate for the establishment of a new phonetic method that would simplify and standardize the spelling of the English language.

CHARACTERS

Major Paul Petkoff	**Nicola**, their manservant
Catherine, his wife	**Major Sergius Saranoff**
Raina, his daughter	**Captain Bluntschli**
Louka, their maid	**An officer**

Act I

Night. A lady's bedchamber in Bulgaria, in a small town near the Dragoman Pass. It is late in November in the year 1885, and through an open window with a little balcony on the left can be seen a peak of the Balkans, wonderfully white and beautiful in the starlit snow. The interior of the room is not like anything to be seen in the east of Europe. It is half rich Bulgarian, half cheap Viennese. The counterpane [1] and hangings of the bed, the window curtains, the little carpet, and all the ornamental textile fabrics in the room are oriental [2] and gorgeous: the paper on the walls is occidental [3] and paltry. Above the head of the bed, which stands against a little wall cutting off the right-hand corner of the room diagonally, is a painted wooden shrine, blue and gold, with an ivory image of Christ, and a light hanging before it in a pierced metal ball suspended by three chains. On the left, further forward, is an ottoman.[4] The washstand, against the wall on the left, consists of an enameled iron basin with a pail beneath it in a painted metal frame, and a single towel on the rail at the side. A chair near it is Austrian bent wood, with cane seat. The dressing table, between the bed and the window, is an ordinary pine table, covered with a cloth of many colors, but with an expensive toilet mirror on it. The door is on the right; and there is a chest of drawers between the door and the bed. This chest of drawers is also covered by a variegated [5] native cloth, and on it there are a pile of paperbacked novels, a box of chocolate creams, and a miniature easel, on which is a large photograph of an extremely handsome officer, whose lofty bearing and magnetic glance can be felt even from the portrait. The

1. **counterpane:** bedspread.
2. **oriental:** eastern; from the countries east of Europe.
3. **occidental:** western; in contrast to oriental, the countries of Europe.
4. **ottoman:** an upholstered, armless seat or sofa, usually without a back.
5. **variegated:** striped or streaked with many colors.

room is lighted by a candle on the chest of drawers, and another on the dressing table, with a box of matches beside it.

The window is hinged doorwise and stands wide open, folding back to the left. Outside, a pair of wooden shutters, opening outward, also stand open. On the balcony, a young lady, intensely conscious of the romantic beauty of the night, and of the fact that her own youth and beauty are a part of it, is gazing at the snowy Balkans. She is covered by a long mantle of furs, worth, on a moderate estimate, about three times the furniture of her room.

Her reverie is interrupted by her mother, CATHERINE PETKOFF, *a woman over forty, imperiously energetic, with magnificent black hair and eyes, who might be a very splendid specimen of the wife of a mountain farmer, but is determined to be a Viennese lady, and to that end wears a fashionable tea gown on all occasions.*

CATHERINE. (*Entering hastily, full of good news.*) Raina— (*She pronounces it Rah-eena, with the stress on the ee.*) Raina— (*She goes to the bed, expecting to find* RAINA *there.*) Why, where— (RAINA *looks into the room.*) Heavens, child, are you out in the night air instead of in your bed? You'll catch your death. Louka told me you were asleep.

RAINA. (*Coming in.*) I sent her away. I wanted to be alone. The stars are so beautiful! What is the matter?

CATHERINE. Such news. There has been a battle!

RAINA. (*Her eyes dilating.*) Ah! (*She throws the cloak on the ottoman, and comes eagerly to Catherine in her nightgown, a pretty garment, but evidently the only one she has on.*)

CATHERINE. A great battle at Slivnitza![6] A victory! And it was won by Sergius.

RAINA. (*With a cry of delight.*) Ah! (*Rapturously.*) Oh, Mother! (*Then, with sudden anxiety.*) Is father safe?

CATHERINE. Of course; he sent me the news. Sergius is the hero of the hour, the idol of the regiment.

RAINA. Tell me, tell me. How was it! (*Ecstatically.*) Oh, Mother, Mother, Mother! (RAINA *pulls her mother down on the ottoman; and they kiss one another frantically.*)

CATHERINE. (*With surging enthusiasm.*) You can't guess how splendid it is. A cavalry charge—think of that! He defied our Russian

6. **Slivnitza** (Slĭv′nĭ·tsä): a small town near the Bulgarian capital of Sofia, where the Serbian invasion of Bulgaria was halted in 1885.

commanders—acted without orders—led a charge on his own responsibility—headed it himself—was the first man to sweep through their guns. Can't you see it, Raina; our gallant splendid Bulgarians with their swords and eyes flashing, thundering down like an avalanche and scattering the wretched Serbian dandies like chaff.[7] And you—you kept Sergius waiting a year before you would be betrothed to him. Oh, if you have a drop of Bulgarian blood in your veins, you will worship him when he comes back.

RAINA.   What will he care for my poor little worship after the acclamations [8] of a whole army of heroes? But no matter; I am so happy —so proud! (*She rises and walks about excitedly.*) It proves that all our ideas were real after all.

CATHERINE. (*Indignantly.*)   Our ideas real! What do you mean?

RAINA.   Our ideas of what Sergius would do—our patriotism—our heroic ideals. Oh, what faithless little creatures girls are!—I sometimes used to doubt whether they were anything but dreams. When I buckled on Sergius's sword he looked so noble; it was treason to think of disillusion or humiliation or failure. And yet—and yet— (*Quickly.*) Promise me you'll never tell him.

CATHERINE.   Don't ask me for promises until I know what I am promising.

RAINA.   Well, it came into my head just as he was holding me in his arms and looking into my eyes, that perhaps we only had our heroic ideas because we are so fond of reading Byron and Pushkin,[9] and because we were so delighted with the opera that season at Bucharest. Real life is so seldom like that—indeed never, as far as I knew it then. (*Remorsefully.*) Only think, Mother, I doubted him. I wondered whether all his heroic qualities and his soldiership might not prove mere imagination when he went into a real battle. I had an uneasy fear that he might cut a poor figure there beside all those clever Russian officers.

CATHERINE.   A poor figure! Shame on you! The Serbians have Austrian officers who are just as clever as our Russians; but we have beaten them in every battle for all that.

7. **chaff**: the external envelopes or husks of grain; hence, something trival and worthless.
8. **acclamations**: shouts of approval; applause.
9. **Byron and Pushkin**: George Gordon, Lord Byron (1788–1824), one of England's foremost Romantic poets; he died of fever in Greece while working for Greek independence. His outlook on life, characterized in the "Byronic hero," is described vividly by Shaw in the stage directions on page 130. Aleksander Sergeyevich Pushkin (1799–1837), a Russian poet and novelist, greatly admired the poetry of Byron, and his earlier works reflect the style and ideas of the English poet.

RAINA. (*Laughing and sitting down again.*)   Yes, I was only a prosaic [10] little coward. Oh, to think that it was all true—that Sergius is just as splendid and noble as he looks—that the world is really a glorious world for women who can see its glory and men who can act its romance! What happiness! What unspeakable fulfilment! Ah! (*She throws herself on her knees beside her mother and flings her arms passionately round her. They are interrupted by the entry of* LOUKA, *a handsome, proud girl in a pretty Bulgarian peasant's dress with double apron, so defiant that her servility [11] to* RAINA *is almost insolent. She is afraid of* CATHERINE, *but even with her goes as far as she dares. She is just now excited like the others; but she has no sympathy for* RAINA'S *raptures and looks contemptuously at the ecstasies of the two before she addresses them.*)

LOUKA.   If you please, madam, all the windows are to be closed and the shutters made fast. They say there may be shooting in the streets. (RAINA *and* CATHERINE *rise together, alarmed.*) The Serbians are being chased right back through the pass; and they say they may run into the town. Our cavalry will be after them; and our people will be ready for them you may be sure, now that they are running away. (*She goes out on the balcony and pulls the outside shutters to; then steps back into the room.*)

RAINA.   I wish our people were not so cruel. What glory is there in killing wretched fugitives?

CATHERINE. (*Businesslike, her housekeeping instincts aroused.*) I must see that everything is made safe downstairs.

RAINA. (*To* LOUKA.)   Leave the shutters so that I can just close them if I hear any noise.

CATHERINE. (*Authoritatively, turning on her way to the door.*)   Oh, no, dear, you must keep them fastened. You would be sure to drop off to sleep and leave them open. Make them fast, Louka.

LOUKA.   Yes, madam. (*She fastens them.*)

RAINA.   Don't be anxious about me. The moment I hear a shot, I shall blow out the candles and roll myself up in bed with my ears well covered.

CATHERINE.   Quite the wisest thing you can do, my love. Good night.

RAINA.   Good night. (*They kiss one another, and* RAINA'S *emotion comes back for a moment.*) Wish me joy of the happiest night of my life—if only there are no fugitives.

10. **prosaic** (prō·zā′ik) : dull; commonplace.
11. **servility:** submissiveness, usually suggesting something slavelike.

CATHERINE. Go to bed, dear; and don't think of them. (*She goes out.*)

LOUKA. (*Secretly, to* RAINA.) If you would like the shutters open, just give them a push like this. (*She pushes them: they open: she pulls them to again.*) One of them ought to be bolted at the bottom; but the bolt's gone.

RAINA. (*With dignity, reproving her.*) Thanks, Louka; but we must do what we are told. (LOUKA *makes a grimace.*[12]) Good night.

LOUKA. (*Carelessly.*) Good night. (*She goes out, swaggering.*[13])

(RAINA, *left alone, goes to the chest of drawers, and adores the portrait there with feelings that are beyond all expression. She does not kiss it or press it to her breast, or show it any mark of bodily affection; but she takes it in her hands and elevates it like a priestess.*)

RAINA. (*Looking up at the picture with worship.*) Oh, I shall never be unworthy of you any more, my hero—never, never, never. (*She replaces it reverently, and selects a novel from the little pile of books. She turns over the leaves dreamily; finds her page; turns the book inside out at it; and then, with a happy sigh, gets into bed and prepares to read herself to sleep. But before abandoning herself to fiction, she raises her eyes once more, thinking of the blessed reality and murmurs.*) My hero! my hero! (*A distant shot breaks the quiet of the night outside. She starts, listening; and two more shots, much nearer, follow, startling her so that she scrambles out of bed, and hastily blows out the candle on the chest of drawers. Then, putting her fingers in her ears, she runs to the dressing table and blows out the light there, and hurries back to bed. The room is now in darkness; nothing is visible but the glimmer of the light in the pierced ball before the image, and the starlight seen through the slits at the top of the shutters. The firing breaks out again; there is a startling fusillade*[14] *quite close at hand. Whilst it is still echoing, the shutters disappear, pulled open from without, and for an instant the rectangle of snowy starlight flashes out with the figure of a man in black upon it. The shutters close immediately and the room is dark again. But the silence is now broken by the*

12. **grimace** (gri·mās′) : distorted facial expression.
13. **swaggering**: walking boldly so as to show off.
14. **fusillade** (fyo͞o′zə·lād′) : rapid and continual shooting of several guns at once. The word is from French *fusiller*, to shoot, from *fusil*, musket.

sound of panting. Then there is a scrape; and the flame of a match is seen in the middle of the room.)

RAINA. (*Crouching on the bed.*)   Who's there? (*The match is out instantly.*) Who's there? Who is that?

A MAN'S VOICE. (*In the darkness, subduedly, but threateningly.*) Sh—sh! Don't call out or you'll be shot. Be good; and no harm will happen to you. (*She is heard leaving her bed, and making for the door.*) Take care, there's no use in trying to run away. Remember, if you raise your voice my pistol will go off. (*Commandingly.*) Strike a light and let me see you. Do you hear? (*Another moment of silence and darkness. Then she is heard retreating to the dressing table. She lights a candle, and the mystery is at an end. A man of about 35, in a deplorable plight, bespattered with mud and blood and snow, his belt and the strap of his revolver case keeping together the torn ruins of the blue coat of a Serbian artillery officer. As far as the candlelight and his unwashed, unkempt [15] condition make it possible to judge, he is a man of middling stature and undistinguished appearance, with strong neck and shoulders, a roundish, obstinate-looking head covered with short, crisp, bronze curls, clear, quick blue eyes and good brows and mouth, a hopelessly prosaic nose like that of a strong-minded baby, trim soldierlike carriage and energetic manner, and with all his wits about him in spite of his desperate predicament—even with a sense of humor of it, without, however, the least intention of trifling with it or throwing away a chance. He reckons up what he can guess about RAINA—her age, her social position, her character, the extent to which she is frightened—at a glance, and continues, more politely but still most determinedly.*) Excuse my disturbing you; but you recognize my uniform—Serbian. If I'm caught I shall be killed. (*Determinedly.*) Do you understand that?

RAINA.   Yes.

MAN.   Well, I don't intend to get killed if I can help it. (*Still more determinedly.*) Do you understand that? (*He locks the door with a snap.*)

RAINA. (*Disdainfully.*)   I suppose not. (*She draws herself up superbly, and looks him straight in the face, saying with emphasis.*) Some soldiers, I know, are afraid of death.

MAN. (*With grim good humor.*)   All of them, dear lady, all of them,

15. **unkempt:** untidy; messy.

believe me. It is our duty to live as long as we can, and kill as many of the enemy as we can. Now if you raise an alarm—

RAINA. (*Cutting him short.*)   You will shoot me. How do you know that I am afraid to die?

MAN. (*Cunningly.*)   Ah; but suppose I don't shoot you, what will happen then? Why, a lot of your cavalry—the greatest black-guards [16] in your army—will burst into this pretty room of yours and slaughter me here like a pig; for I'll fight like a demon; they shan't get me into the street to amuse themselves with; I know what they are. Are you prepared to receive that sort of company in your present undress? (RAINA, *suddenly conscious of her nightgown, instinctively shrinks and gathers it more closely about her. He watches her, and adds, pitilessly.*) It's rather scanty, eh? (*She turns to the ottoman. He raises his pistol instantly, and cries.*) Stop! (*She stops.*) Where are you going?

RAINA. (*With dignified patience.*)   Only to get my cloak.

MAN. (*Darting to the ottoman and snatching the cloak.*)   A good idea. No; I'll keep the cloak; and you will take care that nobody comes in and sees you without it. This is a better weapon than the pistol. (*He throws the pistol down on the ottoman.*)

RAINA. (*Revolted.*)   It is not the weapon of a gentleman!

MAN.   It's good enough for a man with only you to stand between him and death. (*As they look at one another for a moment,* RAINA *hardly able to believe that even a Serbian officer can be so cynically and selfishly unchivalrous, they are startled by a sharp fusillade in the street. The chill of imminent death hushes the man's voice as he adds.*) Do you hear? If you are going to bring those scoundrels in on me you shall receive them as you are. (RAINA *meets his eye with unflinching scorn. Suddenly he starts, listening. There is a step outside. Someone tries the door, and then knocks hurriedly and urgently at it.* RAINA *looks at the man, breathless. He throws up his head with the gesture of a man who sees that it is all over with him, and, dropping the manner which he has been assuming to intimidate her, flings the cloak to her, exclaiming, sincerely and kindly.*) No use; I'm done for. Quick! Wrap yourself up; they're coming!

RAINA. (*Catching the cloak eagerly.*)   Oh, thank you. (*She wraps herself up with great relief. He draws his saber [17] and turns to the door, waiting.*)

16. **blackguards:** scoundrels.
17. **saber:** heavy cavalry sword with curved blade.

LOUKA. (*Outside, knocking.*) My lady, my lady! Get up, quick, and open the door.

RAINA. (*Anxiously.*) What will you do?

MAN. (*Grimly.*) Never mind. Keep out of the way. It will not last long.

RAINA. (*Impulsively.*) I'll help you. Hide yourself, oh, hide yourself, quick, behind the curtain. (*She seizes him by a torn strip of his sleeve, and pulls him toward the window.*)

MAN. (*Yielding to her.*) There is just half a chance, if you keep your head. Remember, nine soldiers out of ten are born fools. (*He hides behind the curtain, looking out for a moment to say, finally.*) If they find me, I promise you a fight—a devil of a fight! (*He disappears.* RAINA *takes off the cloak and throws it across the foot of the bed. Then with a sleepy, disturbed air, she opens the door.* LOUKA *enters excitedly.*)

LOUKA. A man has been seen climbing up the water pipe to your balcony—a Serbian. The soldiers want to search for him; and they are so wild and drunk and furious. My lady says you are to dress at once.

RAINA. (*As if annoyed at being disturbed.*) They shall not search here. Why have they been let in?

CATHERINE. (*Coming in hastily.*) Raina, darling, are you safe? Have you seen anyone or heard anything?

RAINA. I heard the shooting. Surely the soldiers will not dare come in here?

CATHERINE. I have found a Russian officer, thank Heaven. He knows Sergius. (*Speaking through the door to someone outside.*) Sir, will you come in now! My daughter is ready.

> (*A young Russian officer, in Bulgarian uniform, enters, sword in hand.*)

THE OFFICER. (*With soft, feline* [18] *politeness and stiff military carriage.*) Good evening, gracious lady. I am sorry to intrude, but there is a fugitive hiding on the balcony. Will you and the gracious lady your mother please to withdraw whilst we search?

RAINA. (*Petulantly.*) Nonsense, sir, you can see that there is no one on the balcony. (*She throws the shutters wide open and stands with her back to the curtain where the man is hidden, pointing to the moonlit balcony. A couple of shots are fired right under the*

18. **feline** (fē′lĭn): sly; catlike, from Latin *felis*, cat.

window, and a bullet shatters the glass opposite RAINA, who winks and gasps, but stands her ground, whilst CATHERINE screams, and the officer rushes to the balcony.)

THE OFFICER. (On the balcony, shouting savagely down to the street.) Cease firing there, you fools; do you hear? Cease firing, damn you. (He glares down for a moment; then turns to RAINA, trying to resume his polite manner.) Could anyone have got in without your knowledge? Were you asleep?

RAINA.   No, I have not been to bed.

THE OFFICER. (Impatiently, coming back into the room.) Your neighbors have their heads so full of run-away Serbians that they see them everywhere. (Politely.) Gracious lady, a thousand pardons. Good night. (Military bow, which RAINA returns coldly. Another to CATHERINE, who follows him out. RAINA closes the shutters. She turns and sees LOUKA, who has been watching the scene curiously.)

RAINA.   Don't leave my mother, Louka, whilst the soldiers are here. (LOUKA glances at RAINA, at the ottoman, at the curtain; then purses her lips secretively, laughs to herself, and goes out. RAINA follows her to the door, shuts it behind her with a slam, and locks it violently. The man immediately steps out from behind the curtain, sheathing his saber, and dismissing the danger from his mind in a businesslike way.)

MAN.   A narrow shave; but a miss is as good as a mile. Dear young lady, your servant until death. I wish for your sake I had joined the Bulgarian army instead of the Serbian. I am not a native Serbian.

RAINA. (Haughtily.[19]) No, you are one of the Austrians who set the Serbians on to rob us of our national liberty, and who officer their army for them. We hate them!

MAN.   Austrian! Not I. Don't hate me, dear young lady. I am only a Swiss, fighting merely as a professional soldier. I joined Serbia because it was nearest to me. Be generous; you've beaten us hollow.

RAINA.   Have I not been generous?

MAN.   Noble! Heroic! But I'm not saved yet. This particular rush will soon pass through; but the pursuit will go on all night by fits and starts. I must take my chance to get off during a quiet interval. You don't mind my waiting just a minute or two, do you?

RAINA.   Oh, no. I am sorry you will have to go into danger again.

19. **Haughtily** (hô′tə·lē) : proudly; scornfully; from Old French haut, high.

(*Motioning toward ottoman.*) Won't you sit— (*She breaks off with an irrepressible cry of alarm as she catches sight of the pistol. The man, all nerves, shies like a frightened horse.*)

MAN. (*Irritably.*)   Don't frighten me like that. What is it?

RAINA.   Your pistol! It was staring that officer in the face all the time. What an escape!

MAN. (*Vexed at being unnecessarily terrified.*)   Oh, is that all?

RAINA. (*Staring at him rather superciliously,*[20] *conceiving a poorer and poorer opinion of him, and feeling proportionately more and more at her ease with him.*)   I am sorry I frightened you. (*She takes up the pistol and hands it to him.*) Pray take it to protect yourself against me.

MAN. (*Grinning wearily at the sarcasm as he takes the pistol.*)   No use, dear young lady; there's nothing in it. It's not loaded. (*He makes a grimace at it, and drops it disparagingly* [21] *into his revolver case.*)

RAINA.   Load it by all means.

MAN.   I've no ammunition. What use are cartridges in battle? I always carry chocolate instead; and I finished the last cake of that yesterday.

RAINA. (*Outraged in her most cherished ideals of manhood.*)   Chocolate! Do you stuff your pockets with sweets—like a schoolboy—even in the field?

MAN.   Yes. Isn't it contemptible?

(RAINA *stares at him, unable to utter her feelings. Then she sails away scornfully to the chest of drawers, and returns with the box of confectionery in her hand.*)

RAINA.   Allow me. I am sorry I have eaten them all except these. (*She offers him the box.*)

MAN. (*Ravenously.*)   You're an angel! (*He gobbles the comfits.*[22]) Creams! Delicious! (*He looks anxiously to see whether there are any more. There are none. He accepts the inevitable with pathetic good humor, and says, with grateful emotion.*) Bless you, dear lady. You can always tell an old soldier by the inside of his holsters and cartridge boxes. The young ones carry pistols and cartridges; the

---

20. superciliously (soō′pər·sil′ē·əs·lē) : arrogantly; in a superior manner.
21. disparagingly (dis·par′ij·ing·lē) : contemptuously; disrespectfully.
22. comfits: sweets; candies.

old one, grub. Thank you. (*He hands back the box. She snatches it contemptuously from him and throws it away. This impatient action is so sudden that he shies again.*) Ugh! Don't do things so suddenly, gracious lady. Don't revenge yourself because I frightened you just now.

RAINA. (*Superbly.*)   Frighten me! Do you know, sir, that though I am only a woman, I think I am at heart as brave as you.

MAN.   I should think so. You haven't been under fire for three days as I have. I can stand two days without showing it much; but no man can stand three days. I'm as nervous as a mouse. (*He sits down on the ottoman, and takes his head in his hands.*) Would you like to see me cry?

RAINA. (*Quickly.*)   No.

MAN.   If you would, all you have to do is to scold me just as if I were a little boy and you my nurse. If I were in camp now they'd play all sorts of tricks on me.

RAINA. (*A little moved.*)   I'm sorry. I won't scold you. (*Touched by the sympathy in her tone, he raises his head and looks gratefully at her; she immediately draws back and says stiffly.*) You must excuse me; our soldiers are not like that. (*She moves away from the ottoman.*)

MAN.   Oh, yes, they are. There are only two sorts of soldiers: old ones and young ones. I've served fourteen years; half of your fellows never smelled powder before. Why, how is it that you've just beaten us? Sheer ignorance of the art of war, nothing else. (*Indignantly.*) I never saw anything so unprofessional.

RAINA. (*Ironically.*)   Oh, was it unprofessional to beat you?

MAN.   Well, come, is it professional to throw a regiment of cavalry on a battery of machine guns, with the dead certainty that if the guns go off not a horse or man will ever get within fifty yards of the fire? I couldn't believe my eyes when I saw it.

RAINA. (*Eagerly turning to him, as all her enthusiasm and her dream of glory rush back on her.*)   Did you see the great cavalry charge? Oh, tell me about it. Describe it to me.

MAN.   You never saw a cavalry charge, did you?

RAINA.   How could I?

MAN.   Ah, perhaps not—of course. Well, it's a funny sight. It's like slinging a handful of peas against a window pane; first one comes; then two or three close behind him; and then all the rest in a lump.

RAINA. (*Her eyes dilating* [23] *as she raises her clasped hand ecstatically.*) Yes, first One!—The bravest of the brave!

MAN. (*Prosaically.*) Hm! You should see the poor devil pulling at his horse.

RAINA. Why should he pull at his horse?

MAN. (*Impatient of so stupid a question.*) It's running away with him, of course. Do you suppose the fellow wants to get there before the others and be killed? Then they all come. You can tell the young ones by their wildness and their slashing. The old ones come bunched up under the number one guard; they know that they are mere projectiles,[24] and that it's no use trying to fight. The wounds are mostly broken knees, from the horses cannoning [25] together.

RAINA. Ugh! But I don't believe the first man is a coward. I believe he is a hero!

MAN. (*Good-humoredly.*) That's what you'd have said if you'd seen the first man in the charge today.

RAINA. (*Breathless.*) Ah, I knew it! Tell me—tell me about him.

MAN. He did it like an operatic tenor—a regular handsome fellow, with flashing eyes and lovely moustache, shouting a war cry and charging like Don Quixote [26] at the windmills. We nearly burst with laughter at him; but when the sergeant ran up as white as a sheet, and told us they'd sent us the wrong cartridges, and that we couldn't fire a shot for the next ten minutes, we laughed at the other side of our mouths. I never felt so sick in my life, though I've been in one or two very tight places. And I hadn't even a revolver cartridge—nothing but chocolate. We'd no bayonets— nothing. Of course, they just cut us to bits. And there was Don Quixote flourishing like a drum major, thinking he'd done the cleverest thing ever known, whereas he ought to be courtmartialed for it. Of all the fools ever let loose on a field of battle, that man must be the very maddest. He and his regiment simply committed suicide—only the pistol missed fire, that's all.

---

23. dilating: growing larger; from Latin *dilatare,* to spread out, from *dis-*, apart, plus *latus,* wide.
24. projectiles (prə·jek′təls): objects intended to be hurled or thrown.
25. cannoning: knocking against each other and rebounding.
26. Don Quixote (don kē·hō′tē; kwik′sət): hero of the novel *Don Quixote de La Mancha* (1615) by the Spanish author Cervantes; the name usually refers to a man marked by rash, impractical ideals or foolish chivalry. In the novel Don Quixote does battle with a windmill, thinking it to be an enormous giant.

.

RAINA. (*Deeply wounded, but steadfastly loyal to her ideals.*) Indeed! Would you know him again if you saw him?

MAN. Shall I ever forget him. (*She again goes to the chest of drawers. He watches her with a vague hope that she may have something else for him to eat. She takes the portrait from its stand and brings it to him.*)

RAINA. That is a photograph of the gentleman—the patriot and hero —to whom I am betrothed.

MAN. (*Looking at it.*) I'm really very sorry. (*Looking at her.*) Was it fair to lead me on? (*He looks at the portrait again.*) Yes, that's him; not a doubt of it. (*He stifles a laugh.*)

RAINA. (*Quickly.*) Why do you laugh?

MAN. (*Shamefacedly, but still greatly tickled.*) I didn't laugh, I assure you. At least I didn't mean to. But when I think of him charging the windmills and thinking he was doing the finest thing— (*Chokes with suppressed laughter.*)

RAINA. (*Sternly.*) Give me back the portrait, sir.

MAN. (*With sincere remorse.*) Of course. Certainly. I'm really very sorry. (*She deliberately kisses it, and looks him straight in the face, before returning to the chest of drawers to replace it. He follows her, apologizing.*) Perhaps I'm quite wrong, you know; no doubt I am. Most likely he had got wind of the cartridge business some- how, and knew it was a safe job.

RAINA. That is to say, he was a pretender and a coward! You did not dare say that before.

MAN. (*With a comic gesture of despair.*) It's no use, dear lady; I can't make you see it from the professional point of view. (*As he turns away to get back to the ottoman, the firing begins again in the distance.*)

RAINA. (*Sternly, as she sees him listening to the shots.*) So much the better for you.

MAN. (*Turning.*) How?

RAINA. You are my enemy; and you are at my mercy. What would I do if I were a professional soldier?

MAN. Ah, true, dear young lady; you're always right. I know how good you have been to me; to my last hour I shall remember those three chocolate creams. It was unsoldierly; but it was angelic.

RAINA. (*Coldly.*) Thank you. And now I will do a soldierly thing. You cannot stay here after what you have just said about my future husband; but I will go out on the balcony and see whether it is safe for you to climb down into the street. (*She turns to the window.*)

MAN. (*Changing countenance.*)   Down that water pipe! Stop! Wait! I can't! I daren't! The very thought of it makes me giddy. I came up it fast enough with death behind me. But to face it now in cold blood!—(*He sinks on the ottoman.*) It's no use; I give up; I'm beaten. Give the alarm. (*He drops his head on his hands in the deepest dejection.*)

RAINA. (*Disarmed by pity.*)   Come, don't be disheartened. (*She stoops over him almost maternally; he shakes his head.*) Oh, you are a very poor soldier—a chocolate-cream soldier. Come, cheer up; it takes less courage to climb down than to face capture—remember that.

MAN. (*Dreamily, lulled by her voice.*)   No, capture only means death; and death is sleep—oh, sleep, sleep, sleep, undisturbed sleep! Climbing down the pipe means doing something—exerting myself —thinking! Death ten times over first.

RAINA. (*Softly and wonderingly, catching the rhythm of his weariness.*)   Are you so sleepy as that?

MAN.   I've not had two hours undisturbed sleep since the war began. I'm on the staff; you don't know what that means. I haven't closed my eyes for thirty-six hours.

RAINA. (*Desperately.*)   But what am I to do with you.

MAN. (*Staggering up.*)   Of course I must do something. (*He shakes himself; pulls himself together; and speaks with rallied vigor and courage.*) You see, sleep or no sleep, hunger or no hunger, tired or not tired, you can always do a thing when you know it must be done. Well, that pipe must be got down—(*He hits himself on the chest, and adds.*)—Do you hear that, you chocolate-cream soldier? (*He turns to the window.*)

RAINA. (*Anxiously.*)   But if you fall?

MAN.   I shall sleep as if the stones were a feather bed. Good-bye. (*He makes boldly for the window, and his hand is on the shutter when there is a terrible burst of firing in the street beneath.*)

RAINA. (*Rushing to him.*)   Stop! (*She catches him by the shoulder, and turns him quite round.*) They'll kill you.

MAN. (*Coolly, but attentively.*)   Never mind; this sort of thing is all in my day's work. I'm bound to take my chance. (*Decisively.*) Now do what I tell you. Put out the candles, so that they shan't see the light when I open the shutters. And keep away from the window, whatever you do. If they see me, they're sure to have a shot at me.

RAINA. (*Clinging to him.*)   They're sure to see you; it's bright moonlight. I'll save you—oh, how can you be so indifferent? You want me to save you, don't you?

MAN.   I really don't want to be troublesome. (*She shakes him in her impatience.*) I am not indifferent, dear young lady, I assure you. But how is it to be done?

RAINA.   Come away from the window—please. (*She coaxes him back to the middle of the room. He submits humbly. She releases him, and addresses him patronizingly.*[27]) Now listen. You must trust to our hospitality. You do not yet know in whose house you are. I am a Petkoff.

MAN.   What's that?

RAINA.   (*Rather indignantly.*)   I mean that I belong to the family of the Petkoffs, the richest and best known in our country.

MAN.   Oh, yes, of course. I beg your pardon. The Petkoffs, to be sure. How stupid of me!

RAINA.   You know you never heard of them until this minute. How can you stoop to pretend?

MAN.   Forgive me; I'm too tired to think; and the change of subject was too much for me. Don't scold me.

RAINA.   I forgot. It might make you cry. (*He nods, quite seriously. She pouts and then resumes her patronizing tone.*) I must tell you that my father holds the highest command of any Bulgarian in our army. He is (*Proudly.*) a Major.

MAN.   (*Pretending to be deeply impressed.*)   A Major! Bless me! Think of that!

RAINA.   You showed great ignorance in thinking that it was necessary to climb up to the balcony, because ours is the only private house that has two rows of windows. There is a flight of stairs inside to get up and down by.

MAN.   Stairs! How grand! You live in great luxury indeed, dear young lady.

RAINA.   Do you know what a library is?

MAN.   A library? A roomful of books.

RAINA.   Yes, we have one, the only one in Bulgaria.

MAN.   Actually a real library! I should like to see that.

27. **patronizingly:** condescendingly.

RAINA. (*Affectedly.*)   I tell you these things to show you that you are not in the house of ignorant country folk who would kill you the moment they saw your Serbian uniform, but among civilized people. We go to Bucharest every year for the opera season; and I have spent a whole month in Vienna.

MAN.   I saw that, dear young lady. I saw at once that you knew the world.

RAINA.   Have you ever seen the opera of Ernani?

MAN.   Is that the one with the devil in it in red velvet, and a soldier's chorus?

RAINA. (*Contemptuously.*)   NO!

MAN. (*Stifling a heavy sigh of weariness.*)   Then I don't know it.

RAINA.   I thought you might have remembered the great scene where Ernani, flying from his foes just as you are tonight, takes refuge in the castle of his bitterest enemy, an old Castilian noble. The noble refuses to give him up. His guest is sacred to him.

MAN. (*Quickly waking up a little.*)   Have your people got that notion?

RAINA. (*With dignity.*)   My mother and I can understand that notion, as you call it. And if instead of threatening me with your pistol as you did, you had simply thrown yourself as a fugitive on our hospitality, you would have been as safe as in your father's house.

MAN.   Quite sure?

RAINA. (*Turning her back on him in disgust.*)   Oh, it is useless to try and make you understand.

MAN.   Don't be angry; you see how awkward it would be for me if there was any mistake. My father is a very hospitable man; he keeps six hotels; but I couldn't trust him as far as that. What about your father?

RAINA.   He is away at Slivnitza fighting for his country. I answer for your safety. There is my hand in pledge of it. Will that reassure you? (*She offers him her hand.*)

MAN. (*Looking dubiously at his own hand.*)   Better not touch my hand, dear young lady. I must have a wash first.

RAINA. (*Touched.*)   That is very nice of you. I see that you are a gentleman.

MAN. (*Puzzled.*)   Eh?

RAINA.   You must not think I am surprised. Bulgarians of really good standing—people in our position—wash their hands nearly every day. But I appreciate your delicacy. You may take my hand. (*She offers it again.*)

MAN. (*Kissing it with his hands behind his back.*)   Thanks, gracious young lady; I feel safe at last. And now would you mind breaking the news to your mother? I had better not stay here secretly longer than is necessary.

RAINA.   If you will be so good as to keep perfectly still whilst I am away.

MAN.   Certainly. (*He sits down on the ottoman.*)

(RAINA *goes to the bed and wraps herself in the fur cloak. His eyes close. She goes to the door, but on turning for a last look at him, sees that he is dropping off to sleep.*)

RAINA. (*At the door.*)   You are not going asleep, are you? (*He murmurs inarticulately:* [28] *she runs to him and shakes him.*)   Do you hear? Wake up; you are falling asleep.

MAN.   Eh? Falling aslee—? Oh, no, not the least in the world; I was only thinking. It's all right; I'm wide awake.

RAINA. (*Severely.*)   Will you please stand up while I am away. (*He rises reluctantly.*) All the time, mind.

MAN. (*Standing unsteadily.*)   Certainly—certainly; you may depend on me.

(RAINA *looks doubtfully at him. He smiles foolishly. She goes reluctantly, turning again at the door, and almost catching him in the act of yawning. She goes out.*)

MAN. (*Drowsily.*)   Sleep, sleep, sleep, sleep, slee— (*The words trail off into a murmur. He wakes again with a shock on the point of falling.*) Where am I? That's what I want to know; where am I? Must keep awake. Nothing keeps me awake except danger—remember that—(*Intently.*) danger, danger, danger, dan— Where's danger? Must find it. (*He starts off vaguely around the room in search of it.*) What am I looking for? Sleep—danger—don't know. (*He stumbles against the bed.*) Ah, yes; now I know. All right now. I'm to go to bed, but not to sleep—be sure not to sleep—because of danger. Not to lie down, either, only sit down. (*He sits on the bed. A blissful expression comes into his face.*) Ah! (*With a happy sigh he sinks back at full length; lifts his boots into the bed with a final effort; and falls fast asleep instantly.*)

28. **inarticulately:** incoherently.

(CATHERINE *comes in, followed by* RAINA.)

RAINA. (*Looking at the ottoman.*)   He's gone! I left him here.

CATHERINE.   Here! Then he must have climbed down from the—

RAINA. (*Seeing him.*)   Oh! (*She points.*)

CATHERINE. (*Scandalized.*) Well! (*She strides to the left side of the bed,* RAINA *following and standing opposite her on the right.*) He's fast asleep. The brute!

RAINA. (*Anxiously.*)   Sh!

CATHERINE. (*Shaking him.*)   Sir! (*Shaking him again, harder.*) Sir!! (*Vehemently shaking very hard.*) Sir!!!

RAINA. (*Catching her arm.*)   Don't, Mamma; the poor dear is worn out. Let him sleep.

CATHERINE. (*Letting him go and turning amazed to* RAINA.)   The poor dear! Raina!!! (*She looks sternly at her daughter. The man sleeps profoundly.*)

Curtain.

Meaning and Method: Act I

1. What do we learn about the Petkoff family by Shaw's description of Raina's bedroom as "half rich Bulgarian, half cheap Viennese"? What descriptions and actions in the stage directions help characterize Raina as a very romantic girl?

2. In the dialogue between Raina and Catherine about Sergius's heroism at the battle of Slivnitza, Shaw introduces the subject of "heroic ideals" (pages 107–09). State the attitude of each of these two women toward war. What is Shaw's attitude toward these women? Consider the use, in his stage directions, of such adverbs as *rapturously, ecstatically,* and *frantically.*

3. How does Louka's announcement about the fighting in the streets (page 109) show a realistic and common-sense approach in contrast to the previous dialogue between Raina and her mother? What other evidence in this episode indicates that Louka is more realistic and practical than Raina? How does her behavior differ from what you would expect of most servants?

4. What is the truth about Sergius's "heroic" calvary charge? According to The Man, what is the difference between an old soldier and a young one? How does the soldier respond to Raina's outrage at his carrying chocolates instead of ammunition? How else are soldiers, war, and weapons made fun of?

5. The principal conflict of the play is a tug of war between the claims of romanticism and those of realism. How do the "chocolate-cream soldier" and Raina represent this conflict? How does the soldier's appearance contrast with the image given of Sergius through his photograph and Raina's comments?

6. How does Shaw further establish the pretentiousness of Raina and the Petkoff family? What is indicated by The Man's rejoinder, "I saw at once that you knew the world"?

7. An example of foreshadowing, so far as setting the stage for the entrance of The Man and preparing the reader for Raina's subsequent actions, is her remark, "What glory is there in killing wretched fugitives?" Nevertheless, the scene is filled with suspense as well as humor.

   How does Shaw use sound and lighting to establish suspense? Give examples from the play. What actions and props also add to the suspense?

Act II

The sixth of March, 1886. In the garden of MAJOR PETKOFF'S *house. It is a fine spring morning; and the garden looks fresh and pretty. Beyond the paling* [1] *the tops of a couple of minarets* [2] *can be seen, showing that there is a valley there, with the little town in it. A few miles further the Balkan mountains rise and shut in the view. Within the garden the side of the house is seen on the right, with a garden door reached by a little flight of steps. On the left the stable yard, with its gateway, encroaches on the garden. There are fruit bushes along the paling and house, covered with washing hung out to dry. A path runs by the house, and rises by two steps at the corner where it turns out of the sight along the front. In the middle a small table, with two bent wood chairs at it, is laid for breakfast with a Turkish coffee pot, cups, rolls, etc.; but the cups have been used and the bread broken. There is a wooden garden seat against the wall on the left.*

LOUKA, *smoking a cigarette, is standing between the table and the house, turning her back with angry disdain on a manservant who is lecturing her. He is a middle-aged man of cool temperament and low but clear and keen intelligence, with the complacency* [3] *of the servant who values himself on his rank in servility, and the imperturbability* [4] *of the accurate calculator* [5] *who has no illusions.* [6] *He wears a white Bulgarian costume jacket with decorated border, sash, wide knicker-bockers,* [7] *and decorated gaiters. His head is shaved up to the crown, giving him a high Japanese forehead. His name is* NICOLA.

NICOLA.   Be warned in time, Louka; mend your manners. I know the mistress. She is so grand that she never dreams that any servant could dare to be disrespectful to her; but if she once suspects that you are defying her, out you go.

LOUKA.   I do defy her. I will defy her. What do I care for her?

NICOLA.   If you quarrel with the family, I never can marry you. It's the same as if you quarrelled with me!

1. **paling:** fence made of narrow pointed stakes.
2. **minaret:** a high, slender tower attached to a Moslem mosque.
3. **complacency:** a feeling of self-satisfaction.
4. **imperturbability** (im'pər·tûrb'ə·bil'i·tē) : ability to remain undisturbed.
5. **calculator:** shrewd person; schemer.
6. **illusions:** overly optimistic ideas.
7. **knickerbockers:** short loose trousers gathered in at the knees; knickers.

LOUKA. You take her part against me, do you?

NICOLA. (*Sedately.*)   I shall always be dependent on the good will of the family. When I leave their service and start a shop in Sofia, their custom will be half my capital; their bad word would ruin me.

LOUKA. You have no spirit. I should like to see them dare say a word against me!

NICOLA. (*Pityingly.*)   I should have expected more sense from you, Louka. But you're young, you're young!

LOUKA. Yes; and you like me the better for it, don't you? But I know some family secrets they wouldn't care to have told, young as I am. Let them quarrel with me if they dare!

NICOLA. (*With compassionate superiority.*)   Do you know what they would do if they heard you talk like that?

LOUKA. What could they do?

NICOLA. Discharge you for untruthfulness. Who would believe any stories you told after that? Who would give you another situation? Who in this house would dare be seen speaking to you ever again? How long would your father be left on his little farm? (*She impatiently throws away the end of her cigarette, and stamps on it.*) Child, you don't know the power such high people have over the likes of you and me when we try to rise out of our poverty against them. (*He goes close to her and lowers his voice.*) Look at me, ten years in their service. Do you think I know no secrets? I know things about the mistress that she wouldn't have the master know for a thousand levas.[8] I know things about him that she wouldn't let him hear the last of for six months if I blabbed them to her. I know things about Raina that would break off her match with Sergius if—

LOUKA. (*Turning on him quickly.*)   How do you know? I never told you!

NICOLA. (*Opening his eyes cunningly.*)   So that's your little secret, is it? I thought it might be something like that. Well, you take my advice, and be respectful; and make the mistress feel that no matter what you know or don't know, they can depend on you to hold your tongue and serve the family faithfully. That's what they like; and that's how you'll make most out of them.

LOUKA. (*With searching scorn.*)   You have the soul of a servant, Nicola.

NICOLA. (*Complacently.*)   Yes; that's the secret of success in service.

8. **thousand levas:** approximately two hundred dollars.

(*A loud knocking with a whip handle on a wooden door, outside on the left, is heard.*)

MALE VOICE OUTSIDE.   Hello! Hello there! Nicola!

LOUKA.   Master! Back from the war!

NICOLA. (*Quickly.*)   My word for it, Louka, the war's over. Off with you and get some fresh coffee. (*He runs out into the stable yard.*)

LOUKA. (*As she puts the coffee pot and the cups upon the tray, and carries it into the house.*)   You'll never put the soul of a servant into me.

(MAJOR PETKOFF *comes from the stable yard, followed by* NICOLA. *He is a cheerful, excitable, insignificant, unpolished man of about fifty, naturally unambitious except as to his income and his importance in local society, but just now greatly pleased with the military rank which the war has thrust on him as a man of consequence in his town. The fever of plucky patriotism which the Serbian attack roused in all the Bulgarians has pulled him through the war; but he is obviously glad to be home again.*)

PETKOFF. (*Pointing to the table with his whip.*)   Breakfast out here, eh?

NICOLA.   Yes sir. The mistress and Miss Raina have just gone in.

PETKOFF. (*Sitting down and taking a roll.*)   Go in and say I've come; and get me some fresh coffee.

NICOLA.   It's coming, sir. (*He goes to the house door.* LOUKA, *with fresh coffee, a clean cup, and a brandy bottle on her tray meets him.*) Have you told the mistress?

LOUKA.   Yes; she's coming.

(NICOLA *goes into the house.* LOUKA *brings the coffee to the table.*)

PETKOFF.   Well, the Serbians haven't run away with you, have they?

LOUKA.   No, sir.

PETKOFF.   That's right. Have you brought me some cognac?

LOUKA. (*Putting the bottle on the table.*)   Here, sir.

PETKOFF.   That's right. (*He pours some into his coffee.*)

(CATHERINE, *who has at this early hour made only a very perfunctory toilet,[9] and wears a Bulgarian apron over a once*

9. **perfunctory toilet:** hasty and rather careless effort to dress and groom properly.

brilliant, but now half-worn-out red dressing gown, and a colored handkerchief tied over her thick black hair, with Turkish slippers on her bare feet, comes from the house, looking astonishingly handsome and stately under all the circumstances. LOUKA *goes into the house.*)

CATHERINE.   My dear Paul, what a surprise for us. (*She stoops over the back of his chair to kiss him.*) Have they brought you fresh coffee?

PETKOFF.   Yes, Louka's been looking after me. The war's over. The treaty was signed three days ago at Bucharest; and the decree for our army to demobilize was issued yesterday.

CATHERINE.   (*Springing erect, with flashing eyes.*)   The war over! Paul; have you let the Austrians force you to make peace?

PETKOFF.   (*Submissively.*)   My dear, they didn't consult me. What could I do? (*She sits down and turns away from him.*) But of course we saw to it that the treaty was an honorable one. It declares peace—

CATHERINE.   (*Outraged.*)   Peace!

PETKOFF.   (*Appeasing her.*)   —but not friendly relations; remember that. They wanted to put that in; but I insisted on its being struck out. What more could I do?

CATHERINE.   You could have annexed Serbia and made Prince Alexander Emperor of the Balkans. That's what I would have done.

PETKOFF.   I don't doubt it in the least, my dear. But I should have had to subdue the whole Austrian Empire first; and that would have kept me too long away from you. I missed you greatly.

CATHERINE.   (*Relenting.*)   Ah! (*Stretches her hand affectionately across the table to squeeze his.*)

PETKOFF.   And how have you been, my dear?

CATHERINE.   Oh, my usual sore throats, that's all.

PETKOFF.   (*With conviction.*)   That comes from washing your neck every day. I've often told you so.

CATHERINE.   Nonsense, Paul!

PETKOFF.   (*Over his coffee and cigarette.*)   I don't believe in going too far with these modern customs. All this washing can't be good for the health; it's not natural. There was an Englishman at Phillipopolis who used to wet himself all over with cold water every morning when he got up. Disgusting! It all comes from the English; their climate makes them so dirty that they have to be perpetually washing themselves. Look at my father; he never had a bath in his life; and he lived to be ninety-eight, the healthiest man in Bulgaria. I don't mind a good wash once a week to keep up my position; but once a day is carrying the thing to a ridiculous extreme.

CATHERINE.   You are a barbarian [10] at heart still, Paul. I hope you behaved yourself before all those Russian officers.

PETKOFF.   I did my best. I took care to let them know that we had a library.

CATHERINE.   Ah; but you didn't tell them that we have an electric bell in it? I have had one put up.

PETKOFF.   What's an electric bell?

CATHERINE.   You touch a button; something tinkles in the kitchen; and then Nicola comes up.

PETKOFF.   Why not shout for him?

CATHERINE.   Civilized people never shout for their servants. I've learned that while you were away.

PETKOFF.   Well, I'll tell you something I've learned, too. Civilized people don't hang out their washing to dry where visitors can see it; so you'd better have all that (*Indicating the clothes on the bushes.*), put somewhere else.

CATHERINE.   Oh, that's absurd, Paul. I don't believe really refined people notice such things.

(*Someone is heard knocking at the stable gates.*)

PETKOFF.   There's Sergius. (*Shouting.*) Hello, Nicola!

CATHERINE.   Oh, don't shout, Paul; it really isn't nice.

PETKOFF.   Bosh! (*He shouts louder than before.*) Nicola!

NICOLA. (*Appearing at the house door.*)   Yes, sir.

PETKOFF.   If that is Major Saranoff, bring him round this way. (*He pronounces the name with the stress on the second syllable— Sar·ah'noff.*)

NICOLA.   Yes, sir. (*He goes into the stable yard.*)

PETKOFF.   You must talk to him, my dear, until Raina takes him off our hands. He bores my life out about our not promoting him— over my head, mind you.

CATHERINE.   He certainly ought to be promoted when he marries Raina. Besides, the country should insist on having at least one native general.

10. barbarian: savage, uncivilized person.

PETKOFF. Yes, so that he could throw away whole brigades instead of regiments. It's no use, my dear; he has not the slightest chance of promotion until we are quite sure that the peace will be a lasting one.

NICOLA. (At the gate, announcing.)   Major Sergius Saranoff! (He goes into the house and returns presently with a third chair, which he places at the table. He then withdraws.)

(MAJOR SERGIUS SARANOFF, the original of the portrait in RAINA'S room, is a tall, romantically handsome man, with the physical hardihood, the high spirit, and the susceptible imagination of an untamed mountaineer chieftain. But his remarkable personal distinction is of a characteristically civilized type. The ridges of his eyebrows, curving with a ram's-horn twist round the marked projections at the outer corners, his jealously observant eye, his nose, thin, keen, and apprehensive in spite of the pugnacious high bridge and large nostril, his assertive [11] chin, would not be out of place in a Paris salon.[12] In short, the clever, imaginative barbarian has an acute [13] critical faculty which has been thrown into intense activity by the arrival of western civilization in the Balkans; and the result is precisely what the advent [14] of nineteenth-century thought first produced in England: to wit, Byronism. By his brooding on the perpetual failure, not only of others, but of himself, to live up to his imaginative ideals, his consequent cynical scorn for humanity, the jejune [15] credulity as to the absolute validity of his ideals and the unworthiness of the world in disregarding them, his wincings [16] and mockeries under the sting of the petty disillusions which every hour spent among men brings to his infallibly [17] quick observation, he has acquired the half-tragic, half-ironic air, the mysterious moodiness, the suggestion of a strange and terrible history that has left him

11. **assertive:** very bold and self-confident; aggressive.
12. **salon:** gathering of artists or writers in the home of a prominent person. *Salon* can also mean drawing room, or room in which guests are received.
13. **acute:** keen; sensitive.
14. **advent:** coming; arrival.
15. **jejune** (jə·jōōn′) : lacking in substance or interest; insipid; naive; from the Latin *jejunus,* hungry.
16. **wincings:** shrinkings back, as from pain.
17. **infallibly:** reliably. *Infallible* means free from fallacy or error.

nothing but undying remorse, by which Childe Harold [18] *fascinated the grandmothers of his English contemporaries. Altogether it is clear that here or nowhere is* RAINA's *ideal hero.* CATHERINE *is hardly less enthusiastic, and much less reserved in showing her enthusiasm. As he enters from the stable gate, she rises effusively* [19] *to greet him.* PETKOFF *is distinctly less disposed to make a fuss about him.*)

PETKOFF.   Here already, Sergius. Glad to see you!

CATHERINE.   My dear Sergius! (*She holds out both her hands.*)

SERGIUS.   (*Kissing them with scrupulous* [20] *gallantry.*)   My dear mother, if I may call you so.

PETKOFF. (*Drily.*)   Mother-in-law, Sergius; mother-in-law! Sit down, and have some coffee.

SERGIUS.   Thank you, none for me. (*He gets away from the table with a certain distaste for* PETKOFF's *enjoyment of it, and posts himself with conscious grace against the rail of the steps leading to the house.*)

CATHERINE.   You look superb—splendid. The campaign has improved you. Everybody here is mad about you. We were all wild with enthusiasm about that magnificent cavalry charge.

SERGIUS.   (*With grave irony.*)   Madam, it was the cradle and the grave of my military reputation.

CATHERINE.   How so?

SERGIUS.   I won the battle the wrong way when our worthy Russian generals were losing it the right way. That upset their plans, and wounded their self-esteem. Two of their colonels got their regiments driven back on the correct principles of scientific warfare. Two major-generals got killed strictly according to military etiquette. Those two colonels are now major-generals; and I am still a simple Major.

CATHERINE.   You shall not remain so, Sergius. The women are on your side; and they will see that justice is done you.

SERGIUS.   It is too late. I have only waited for the peace to send in my resignation.

PETKOFF. (*Dropping his cup in his amazement.*)   Your resignation!

CATHERINE.   Oh, you must withdraw it!

18. **Childe Harold:** self-conscious melancholy hero in a Romantic poem by Byron.
19. **effusively** (i·fy$\overline{oo}$′siv·lē) : demonstratively; gushingly.
20. **scrupulous:** exact; careful.

SERGIUS. (*With resolute, measured emphasis, folding his arms.*)   I never withdraw!

PETKOFF. (*Vexed.*)   Now who could have supposed you were going to do such a thing?

SERGIUS. (*With fire.*)   Everyone that knew me. But enough of myself and my affairs. How is Raina; and where is Raina?

RAINA. (*Suddenly coming round the corner of the house and standing at the top of the steps in the path.*)   Raina is here. (*She makes a charming picture as they all turn to look at her. She wears an underdress of pale green silk, draped with an overdress of thin ecru [21] canvas embroidered with gold. On her head she wears a pretty Phrygian cap [22] of gold tinsel. SERGIUS, with an exclamation of pleasure, goes impulsively to meet her. She stretches out her hand; he drops chivalrously on one knee and kisses it.*)

PETKOFF. (*Aside to CATHERINE, beaming with parental pride.*)   Pretty, isn't it? She always appears at the right moment.

CATHERINE. (*Impatiently.*)   Yes, she listens for it. It is an abominable habit.

(*SERGIUS leads RAINA forward with splendid gallantry, as if she were a queen. When they come to the table, she turns to him with a bend of the head; he bows; and thus they separate, he coming to his place, and she going behind her father's chair.*)

RAINA. (*Stooping and kissing her father.*)   Dear Father! Welcome home!

PETKOFF. (*Patting her cheek.*)   My little pet girl. (*He kisses her; she goes to the chair left by NICOLA for SERGIUS, and sits down.*)

CATHERINE.   And so you're no longer a soldier, Sergius.

SERGIUS.   I am no longer a soldier. Soldiering, my dear madam, is the coward's art of attacking mercilessly when you are strong, and keeping out of harm's way when you are weak. That is the whole secret of successful fighting. Get your enemy at a disadvantage; and never, on any account, fight him on equal terms. Eh, Major!

PETKOFF.   They wouldn't let us make a fair stand-up fight of it. However, I suppose soldiering has to be a trade like any other trade.

---

21. ecru (ek'rōō): light tan color.
22. Phrygian cap: fitted, soft, brimless cap with the crown loosely folded over; also called "liberty cap." This cap was adopted during the French Revolution as a symbol of liberty.

SERGIUS. Precisely. But I have no ambition to succeed as a trades-
man; so I have taken the advice of that bagman [23] of a captain
that settled the exchange of prisoners with us at Peerot, and given
it up.

PETKOFF. What, that Swiss fellow? Sergius, I've often thought of
that exchange since. He over-reached [24] us about those horses.

SERGIUS. Of course he over-reached us. His father was a hotel and
livery-stable keeper; and he owed his first step to his knowledge of
horse-dealing. (*With mock enthusiasm.*) Ah, he was a soldier—
every inch a soldier! If only I had bought the horses for my regiment instead of foolishly leading it into danger, I should have
been a field-marshal now!

CATHERINE. A Swiss? What was he doing in the Serbian army?

PETKOFF. A volunteer, of course—keen on picking up his profession.
(*Chuckling.*) We shouldn't have been able to begin fighting if
these foreigners hadn't shown us how to do it; we knew nothing
about it; and neither did the Serbians. Egad, there'd have been no
war without them.

RAINA. Are there many Swiss officers in the Serbian army?

PETKOFF. No—all Austrians, just as our officers were all Russians.
This was the only Swiss I came across. I'll never trust a Swiss again.
He cheated us—humbugged us into giving him fifty able-bodied
men for two hundred confounded worn out chargers. They weren't
even eatable!

SERGIUS. We were two children in the hands of that consummate [25]
soldier, Major, simply two innocent little children.

RAINA. What was he like?

CATHERINE. Oh, Raina, what a silly question!

SERGIUS. He was like a commercial traveler in uniform. Bourgeois [26]
to his boots.

PETKOFF. (*Grinning.*) Sergius, tell Catherine that queer story his
friend told us about him—how he escaped after Slivnitza. You remember—about his being hid by two women?

SERGIUS. (*With bitter irony.*) Oh, yes, quite a romance. He was serv-
ing in the very battery I so unprofessionally charged. Being a thorough soldier, he ran away like the rest of them, with our cavalry at

23. **bagman**: swindler.
24. **over-reached**: outwitted.
25. **consummate** (kən·sum'it): perfect; complete.
26. **Bourgeois** (boor'zhwä): middle class; hence, engrossed in material things;
from the French for "town," related to Germanic *burgess*.

his heels. To escape their attentions, he had the good taste to take refuge in the chamber of some patriotic young Bulgarian lady. The young lady was enchanted by his persuasive commercial traveler's manners. She very modestly entertained him for an hour or so and then called in her mother lest her conduct should appear unmaidenly. The old lady was equally fascinated; and the fugitive was sent on his way in the morning, disguised in an old coat belonging to the master of the house, who was away at the war.

RAINA. (*Rising with marked stateliness.*)   Your life in the camp has made you coarse, Sergius. I did not think you would have repeated such a story before me. (*She turns away coldly.*)

CATHERINE. (*Also rising.*)   She is right, Sergius. If such women exist, we should be spared the knowledge of them.

PETKOFF.   Pooh! Nonsense! What does it matter?

SERGIUS. (*Ashamed.*)   No, Petkoff; I was wrong. (*To* RAINA, *with earnest humility.*) I beg your pardon. I have behaved abominably. Forgive me, Raina. (*She bows reservedly.*) And you, too, madam. (CATHERINE *bows graciously and sits down. He proceeds solemnly, again addressing* RAINA.) The glimpses I have had of the seamy side of life during the last few months have made me cynical; but I should not have brought my cynicism here—least of all into your presence, Raina. I—(*Here, turning to the others, he is evidently about to begin a long speech when the Major interrupts him.*)

PETKOFF.   Stuff and nonsense, Sergius. That's quite enough fuss about nothing; a soldier's daughter should be able to stand up without flinching to a little strong conversation. (*He rises.*) Come, it's time for us to get to business. We have to make up our minds how those three regiments are to get back to Phillipopolis; there's no forage [27] for them on the Sofia route. (*He goes toward the house.*) Come along. (SERGIUS *is about to follow him when* CATHERINE *rises and intervenes.*[28])

CATHERINE.   Oh, Paul, can't you spare Sergius for a few moments? Raina has hardly seen him yet. Perhaps I can help you to settle about the regiments.

SERGIUS. (*Protesting.*)   My dear madam, impossible; you—

CATHERINE. (*Stopping him playfully.*)   You stay here, my dear Sergius; there's no hurry. I have a word or two to say to Paul. (SERGIUS

27. **forage** (for′ij) : food suitable for horses or cattle. *Forage* may also be used as a verb, meaning "to search about" or "to rummage."
28. **intervenes**: interferes.

instantly bows and steps back.) Now, dear (*Taking* PETKOFF's *arm.*), come and see the electric bell.

PETKOFF. Oh, very well, very well. (*They go into the house together affectionately.* SERGIUS, *left alone with* RAINA, *looks anxiously at her, fearing that she may be still offended. She smiles, and stretches out her arms to him.*)

SERGIUS. (*Hastening to her, but refraining from touching her without express permission.*) Am I forgiven?

RAINA. (*Placing her hands on his shoulder as she looks up at him with admiration and worship.*) My hero! My king.

SERGIUS. My queen! (*He kisses her on the forehead with holy awe.*)

RAINA. How I have envied you, Sergius! You have been out in the world, on the field of battle, able to prove yourself there worthy of any woman in the world; whilst I have had to sit at home inactive —dreaming—useless—doing nothing that could give me the right to call myself worthy of any man.

SERGIUS. Dearest, all my deeds have been yours. You inspired me. I have gone through the war like a knight in a tournament with his lady looking on at him!

RAINA. And you have never been absent from my thoughts for a moment. (*Very solemnly.*) Sergius, I think we two have found the higher love. When I think of you, I feel that I could never do a base deed, or think an ignoble thought.

SERGIUS. My lady, and my saint! (*Clasping her reverently.*)

RAINA. (*Returning his embrace.*) My lord and my g—

SERGIUS. Sh—sh! Let me be the worshipper, dear. You little know how unworthy even the best man is of a girl's pure passion!

RAINA. I trust you. I love you. You will never disappoint me, Sergius. (LOUKA *is heard singing within the house. They quickly release each other.*) Hush! I can't pretend to talk indifferently before her; my heart is too full. (LOUKA *comes from the house with her tray. She goes to the table, and begins to clear it, with her back turned to them.*) I will go and get my hat; and then we can go out until lunch time. Wouldn't you like that?

SERGIUS. Be quick. If you are away five minutes, it will seem five hours. (RAINA *runs to the top of the steps and turns there to exchange a look with him and wave him a kiss with both hands. He looks after her with emotion for a moment, then turns slowly away, his face radiant with the exultation* [29] *of the scene which has just*

29. **exultation:** jubilation; great rejoicing; triumph.

passed. The movement shifts his field of vision, into the corner of which there now comes the tail of LOUKA's *double apron. His eye gleams at once. He takes a stealthy* [30] *look at her, and begins to twirl his moustache nervously, with his left hand akimbo* [31] *on his hip. Finally, striking the ground with his heels in something of a cavalry swagger, he strolls over to the left of the table, opposite her, and says:*) Louka, do you know what the higher love is?

LOUKA. (*Astonished.*)   No, sir.

SERGIUS.   Very fatiguing thing to keep up for any length of time, Louka. One feels the need of some relief after it.

LOUKA. (*Innocently.*)   Perhaps you would like some coffee, sir? (*She stretches her hand across the table for the coffee pot.*)

SERGIUS. (*Taking her hand.*)   Thank you, Louka.

LOUKA. (*Pretending to pull.*)   Oh, sir, you know I didn't mean that. I'm surprised at you!

SERGIUS. (*Coming clear of the table and drawing her with him.*)   I am surprised at myself, Louka. What would Sergius, the hero of Slivnitza, say if he saw me now. What would Sergius, the apostle of the higher love, say if he saw me now? What would the half dozen Sergiuses who keep popping in and out of this handsome figure of mine say if they caught us here? (*Letting go her hand and slipping his arm dexterously* [32] *round her waist.*) Do you consider my figure handsome, Louka?

LOUKA.   Let me go, sir. I shall be disgraced. (*She struggles; he holds her inexorably.* [33]) Oh, will you let go?

SERGIUS. (*Looking straight into her eyes.*)   No.

LOUKA.   Then stand back where we can't be seen. Have you no common sense?

SERGIUS.   Ah, that's reasonable. (*He takes her into the stableyard gateway, where they are hidden from the house.*)

LOUKA. (*Complaining.*)   I may have been seen from the windows; Miss Raina is sure to be spying about after you.

SERGIUS. (*Stung—letting her go.*)   Take care, Louka. I may be worthless enough to betray the higher love; but do not you insult it.

LOUKA. (*Demurely.* [34])   Not for the world, sir, I'm sure. May I go on with my work please, now?

30. **stealthy:** furtive; sly.
31. **akimbo:** arm position with hand on hip and elbow bent outward; from Middle English *in kenebowe,* in a sharp bow.
32. **dexterously:** skillfully; easily.
33. **inexorably** (in·ek′sər·ə·blē) : firmly; relentlessly; unyieldingly.
34. **demurely:** gravely; sedately.

SERGIUS. (*Again putting his arm round her.*)   You are a provoking little witch, Louka. If you were in love with me, would you spy out of windows on me?

LOUKA.   Well, you see, sir, since you say you are half a dozen different gentlemen all at once, I should have a great deal to look after.

SERGIUS. (*Charmed.*)   Witty as well as pretty. (*He tries to kiss her.*)

LOUKA. (*Avoiding him.*)   No, I don't want your kisses. Gentlefolk are all alike—you making love to me behind Miss Raina's back, and she doing the same behind yours.

SERGIUS. (*Recoiling*[35] *a step.*)   Louka!

LOUKA.   It shows how little you really care!

SERGIUS. (*Dropping his familiarity and speaking with freezing politeness.*)   If our conversation is to continue, Louka, you will please remember that a gentleman does not discuss the conduct of the lady he is engaged to with her maid.

LOUKA.   It's so hard to know what a gentleman considers right. I thought from your trying to kiss me that you had given up being so particular.

SERGIUS. (*Turning from her and striking his forehead as he comes back into the garden from the gateway.*)   Devil! Devil!

LOUKA.   Ha! Ha! I expect one of the six of you is very like me, sir, though I am only Miss Raina's maid. (*She goes back to her work at the table, taking no further notice of him.*)

SERGIUS. (*Speaking to himself.*)   Which of the six is the real man? That's the question that torments me. One of them is a hero, another a buffoon,[36] another a humbug, another perhaps a bit of a blackguard. (*He pauses and looks furtively*[37] *at* LOUKA, *as he adds with deep bitterness.*) And one, at least, is a coward—jealous, like all cowards. (*He goes to the table.*) Louka.

LOUKA.   Yes?

SERGIUS.   Who is my rival?

LOUKA.   You shall never get that out of me, for love or money.

SERGIUS   Why?

LOUKA.   Never mind why. Besides, you would tell that I told you; and I should lose my place.

SERGIUS. (*Holding out his right hand in affirmation.*[38])   No; on the honor of a—(*He checks himself, and his hand drops nerveless as he*

---

35. Recoiling: falling or shrinking back from.
36. buffoon: clown.
37. furtively: cautiously; secretly; derived from Latin *fur*, thief.
38. affirmation: solemn declaration; assertion.

concludes sardonically.[39])—of a man capable of behaving as I have been behaving for the last five minutes. Who is he?

LOUKA.   I don't know. I never saw him. I only heard his voice through the door of her room.

SERGIUS.   Damnation! How dare you?

LOUKA.   (*Retreating.*)   Oh, I mean no harm; you've no right to take up my words like that. The mistress knows all about it. And I tell you that if that gentleman ever comes here again, Miss Raina will marry him, whether he likes it or not. I know the difference between the sort of manner you and she put on before one another and the real manner. (SERGIUS *shivers as if she had stabbed him. Then, setting his face like iron, he strides grimly to her, and grips her above the elbows with both hands.*)

SERGIUS.   Now you listen to me!

LOUKA.   (*Wincing.*)   Not so tight; you're hurting me!

SERGIUS.   That doesn't matter. You have stained my honor by making me a party to your eavesdropping. And you have betrayed your mistress—

LOUKA.   (*Writhing.*)   Please—

SERGIUS.   That shows that you are an abominable little clod of common clay, with the soul of a servant. (*He lets her go as if she were an unclean thing, and turns away, dusting his hands of her, to the bench by the wall, where he sits down with averted*[40] *head, meditating gloomily.*)

LOUKA.   (*Whimpering angrily with her hands up her sleeves, feeling her bruised arms.*)   You know how to hurt with your tongue as well as with your hands. But I don't care, now I've found out that whatever clay I'm made of, you're made of the same. As for her, she's a liar; and her fine airs are a cheat; and I'm worth six of her. (*She shakes the pain off hardily; tosses her head; and sets to work to put the things on the tray. He looks doubtfully at her once or twice. She finishes packing the tray, and laps the cloth over the edges, so as to carry all out together. As she stoops to lift it, he rises.*)

SERGIUS.   Louka! (*She stops and looks defiantly at him with the tray in her hands.*) A gentleman has no right to hurt a woman under any circumstances. (*With profound humility, uncovering his head.*) I beg your pardon.

39. **sardonically:** bitterly; scornfully.
40. **averted:** turned aside.

LOUKA.   That sort of apology may satisfy a lady. Of what use is it to a servant?

SERGIUS.   (*Thus rudely crossed in his chivalry, throws it off with a bitter laugh and says slightingly.*)   Oh, you wish to be paid for the hurt? (*He puts on his shako,*[41] *and takes some money from his pocket.*)

LOUKA.   (*Her eyes filling with tears in spite of herself.*)   No, I want my hurt made well.

SERGIUS.   (*Sobered by her tone.*)   How?

(*She rolls up her left sleeve; clasps her arm with the thumb and fingers of her right hand; and looks down at the bruise. Then she raises her head and looks straight at him. Finally, with a superb gesture she presents her arm to be kissed. Amazed, he looks at her; at the arm; at her again; hesitates; and then, with shuddering intensity, exclaims:*) Never! (*And gets away as far as possible from her.*)

(*Her arm drops. Without a word, and with unaffected dignity, she takes her tray, and is approaching the house when* RAINA *returns wearing a hat and jacket in the height of the Vienna fashion of the previous year, 1885. Louka makes way proudly for her, and then goes into the house.*)

RAINA.   I'm ready! What's the matter? (*Gaily.*) Have you been flirting with Louka?

SERGIUS.   (*Hastily.*)   No, no. How can you think such a thing?

RAINA.   (*Ashamed of herself.*)   Forgive me, dear; it was only a jest. I am so happy today.

(*He goes quickly to her, and kisses her hand remorsefully.* CATHERINE *comes out and calls to them from the top of the steps.*)

CATHERINE.   (*Coming down to them.*)   I am sorry to disturb you, children; but Paul is distracted over those three regiments. He does not know how to get them to Phillipopolis; and he objects to every suggestion of mine. You must go and help him, Sergius. He is in the library.

RAINA.   (*Disappointed.*)   But we are just going out for a walk.

SERGIUS.   I shall not be long. Wait for me just five minutes. (*He runs up the steps to the door.*)

41. shako: military dress hat with a plume.

RAINA. (*Following him to the foot of the steps and looking up at him with timid coquetry.*[42]) I shall go round and wait in full view of the library windows. Be sure you draw father's attention to me. If you are a moment longer than five minutes, I shall go in and fetch you, regiments or no regiments.

SERGIUS. (*Laughing.*) Very well. (*He goes in.* RAINA *watches him until he is out of her sight. Then, with a perceptible relaxation of manner, she begins to pace up and down about the garden in a brown study.*[43])

CATHERINE.   Imagine their meeting that Swiss and hearing the whole story! The very first thing your father asked for was the old coat we sent him off in. A nice mess you have got us into!

RAINA. (*Gazing thoughtfully at the gravel as she walks.*)   The little beast!

CATHERINE.   Little beast! What little beast?

RAINA.   To go and tell. Oh, if I had him here, I'd stuff him with chocolate creams till he couldn't ever speak again!

CATHERINE.   Don't talk nonsense. Tell me the truth, Raina. How long was he in your room before you came to me?

RAINA. (*Whisking round and recommencing her march in the opposite direction.*)   Oh, I forget.

CATHERINE.   You cannot forget! Did he really climb up after the soldiers were gone, or was he there when that officer searched the room?

RAINA.   No. Yes, I think he must have been there then.

CATHERINE.   You think! Oh, Raina, Raina! Will anything ever make you straightforward? If Sergius finds out, it is all over between you.

RAINA. (*With cool impertinence.*[44])   Oh, I know Sergius is your pet. I sometimes wish you could marry him instead of me. You would just suit him. You would pet him, and spoil him, and mother him to perfection.

CATHERINE. (*Opening her eyes very widely indeed.*)   Well, upon my word!

RAINA. (*Capriciously*[45]—*half to herself.*)   I always feel a longing to do or say something dreadful to him—to shock his propriety[46]—to

42. **coquetry:** flirting.
43. **brown study:** state of being completely absorbed in thought. *Brown* once denoted "gloomy."
44. **impertinence** (im·pûr′tə·nəns): impudence; boldness.
45. **Capriciously:** whimsically; flightily.
46. **propriety:** proper behavior; decorum.

scandalize the five senses out of him! (*To Catherine perversely.*[47]) I don't care whether he finds out about the chocolate-cream soldier or not. I half hope he may. (*She again turns flippantly away and strolls up the path to the corner of the house.*)

CATHERINE.   And what should I be able to say to your father, pray?

RAINA. (*Over her shoulder, from the top of the two steps.*)   Oh, poor father! As if he could help himself! (*She turns the corner and passes out of sight.*)

CATHERINE. (*Looking after her, her fingers itching.*) Oh, if you were only ten years younger! (*Louka comes from the house with a salver,*[48] *which she carries hanging down by her side.*) Well?

LOUKA.   There's a gentleman just called, madam—a Serbian officer—

CATHERINE. (*Flaming.*)   A Serbian! How dare he—(*Checking herself bitterly.*) Oh, I forgot. We are at peace now. I suppose we shall have them calling every day to pay their compliments. Well, if he is an officer why don't you tell your master? He is in the library with Major Saranoff. Why do you come to me?

LOUKA.   But he asks for you, madam. And I don't think he knows who you are; he said the lady of the house. He gave me this little ticket for you. (*She takes a card out of her bosom; puts it on the salver and offers it to* CATHERINE.[49])

CATHERINE. (*Reading.*)   "Captain Bluntschli!" That's a German name.

LOUKA.   Swiss, madam, I think.

CATHERINE. (*With a bound that makes* LOUKA *jump back.*)   Swiss! What is he like?

LOUKA. (*Timidly.*)   He has a big carpet bag, madam.

CATHERINE.   Oh, heavens, he's come to return the coat! Send him away—say we're not at home—ask him to leave his address and I'll write to him. Oh, stop; that will never do. Wait! (*She throws herself into a chair to think it out.* LOUKA *waits.*) The master and Major Saranoff are busy in the library, aren't they?

LOUKA.   Yes, madam.

CATHERINE. (*Decisively.*)   Bring the gentleman out here at once. (*Imperatively.*) And be very polite to him. Don't delay. Here (*Impatiently snatching the salver from her.*), leave that here, and go straight back to him.

47. **perversely:** in a deliberately disagreeable manner.
48. **salver:** tray on which letters or visiting cards are presented.
49. **little ticket . . . Catherine:** The "little ticket" is a calling card, the fashionable thing to present in 1885; but the joke is that Louka, and probably her mistress, are ignorant of its use.

LOUKA. Yes, madam. (*Going.*)

CATHERINE. Louka!

LOUKA. (*Stopping.*)   Yes, madam.

CATHERINE. Is the library door shut?

LOUKA. I think so, madam.

CATHERINE. If not, shut it as you pass through.

LOUKA. Yes, madam. (*Going.*)

CATHERINE. Stop! (LOUKA *stops.*) He will have to go out that way. (*Indicating the gate of the stable yard.*) Tell Nicola to bring his bag here after him. Don't forget.

LOUKA. (*Surprised.*) His bag?

CATHERINE. Yes, here, as soon as possible. (*Vehemently.*) Be quick! (LOUKA *runs into the house.* CATHERINE *snatches her apron off and throws it behind a bush. She then takes up the salver and uses it as a mirror, with the result that the handkerchief tied round her head follows the apron. A touch to her hair and a shake to her dressing gown makes her presentable.*) Oh, how—how—how can a man be such a fool! Such a moment to select! (LOUKA *appears at the door of the house, announcing* "Captain Bluntschli" *and stands aside at the top of the steps to let him pass before she goes in again. He is the man of the adventure in* RAINA's *room. He is now clean, well brushed, smartly uniformed, and out of trouble, but still unmistakably, the same man. The moment* LOUKA's *back is turned,* CATHERINE *swoops on him with hurried, urgent, coaxing appeal.*) Captain Bluntschli, I am very glad to see you; but you must leave this house at once. (*He raises his eyebrows.*) My husband has just returned, with my future son-in-law; and they know nothing. If they did, the consequences would be terrible. You are a foreigner; you do not feel our national animosities [50] as we do. We still hate the Serbians; the only effect of the peace on my husband is to make him feel like a lion balked of [51] his prey. If he discovered our secret, he would never forgive me; and my daughter's life would hardly be safe. Will you, like the chivalrous gentleman and soldier you are, leave at once before he finds you here?

BLUNTSCHLI. (*Disappointed, but philosophical.*)   At once, gracious lady. I only came to thank you and return the coat you lent me. If you will allow me to take it out of my bag and leave it with

---

50. **animosities:** resentments; hatreds.
51. **balked of:** thwarted from; blocked from.

your servant as I pass out, I need detain you no further. (*He turns to go into the house.*)

CATHERINE. (*Catching him by the sleeve.*)   Oh, you must not think of going back that way. (*Coaxing him across to the stable gates.*) This is the shortest way out. Many thanks. So glad to have been of service to you. Good-bye.

BLUNTSCHLI.   But my bag?

CATHERINE.   It will be sent on. You will leave me your address.

BLUNTSCHLI.   True. Allow me. (*He takes out his cardcase, and stops to write his address, keeping* CATHERINE *in an agony of impatience. As he hands her the card,* PETKOFF, *hatless, rushes from the house in a fluster of hospitality, followed by* SERGIUS.)

PETKOFF. (*As he hurries down the steps.*)   My dear Captain Bluntschli—

CATHERINE.   Oh, heavens! (*She sinks on the seat against the wall.*)

PETKOFF. (*Too preoccupied to notice her as he shakes* BLUNTSCHLI'S *hand heartily.*)   Those stupid people of mine thought I was out here, instead of in the—hum—library. (*He cannot mention the library without betraying how proud he is of it.*) I saw you through the window. I was wondering why you didn't come in. Saranoff is with me; you remember him, don't you?

SERGIUS. (*Saluting humorously, and then offering his hand with great charm of manner.*)   Welcome, our friend the enemy!

PETKOFF.   No longer the enemy, happily. (*Rather anxiously.*)   I hope you've come as a friend, and not on business.

CATHERINE.   Oh, quite as a friend, Paul. I was just asking Captain Bluntschli to stay to lunch; but he declares he must go at once.

SERGIUS. (*Sardonically.*)   Impossible, Bluntschli. We want you here badly. We have to send on three cavalry regiments to Phillipopolis; and we don't in the least know how to do it.

BLUNTSCHLI. (*Suddenly attentive and businesslike.*)   Phillipopolis! The forage is the trouble, eh?

PETKOFF. (*Eagerly.*)   Yes, that's it. (*To* SERGIUS.) He sees the whole thing at once.

BLUNTSCHLI.   I think I can show you how to manage that.

SERGIUS.   Invaluable man! Come along! (*Towering over* BLUNTSCHLI, *he puts his hand on his shoulder and takes him to the steps,* PETKOFF *following. As* BLUNTSCHLI *puts his foot on the first step,* RAINA *comes out of the house.*)

RAINA. (*Completely losing her presence of mind.*)   Oh, the chocolate-cream soldier!

(BLUNTSCHLI *stands rigid.* SERGIUS, *amazed, looks at* RAINA, *then at* PETKOFF, *who looks back at him and then at his wife.*)

CATHERINE. (*With commanding presence of mind.*) My dear Raina, don't you see that we have a guest here—Captain Bluntschli, one of our new Serbian friends?

(RAINA *bows;* BLUNTSCHLI *bows.*)

RAINA. How silly of me! (*She comes down into the center of the group, between* BLUNTSCHLI *and* PETKOFF.) I made a beautiful ornament this morning for the ice pudding; and that stupid Nicola has just put down a pile of plates on it and spoiled it. (*To* BLUNTSCHLI, *winningly.*) I hope you didn't think that you were the chocolate-cream soldier, Captain Bluntschli.

BLUNTSCHLI. (*Laughing.*) I assure you I did. (*Stealing a whimsical glance at her.*) Your explanation was a relief.

PETKOFF. (*Suspiciously, to* RAINA.) And since when, pray, have you taken to cooking?

CATHERINE. Oh, whilst you were away. It is her latest fancy.

PETKOFF. (*Testily.*) And has Nicola taken to drinking? He used to be careful enough. First he shows Captain Bluntschli out here when he knew quite well I was in the—hum—library; and then he goes downstairs and breaks Raina's chocolate soldier. He must— (*At this moment* NICOLA *appears at the top of the steps right, with a carpet bag. He descends; places it respectfully before* BLUNTSCHLI; *and waits for further orders. General amazement.* NICOLA, *unconscious of the effect he is producing, looks perfectly satisfied with himself. When* PETKOFF *recovers his power of speech, he breaks out at him with:*) Are you mad, Nicola?

NICOLA. (*Taken aback.*) Sir?

PETKOFF. What have you brought that for?

NICOLA. My lady's orders, sir. Louka told me that—

CATHERINE. (*Interrupting him.*) My orders! Why should I order you to bring Captain Bluntschli's luggage out here? What are you thinking of, Nicola?

NICOLA. (*After a moment's bewilderment, picking up the bag as he addresses* BLUNTSCHLI *with the very perfection of servile discretion.*) I beg your pardon, sir, I am sure. (*To* CATHERINE.) My fault, madam! I hope you'll overlook it! (*He bows, and is going to the steps with the bag, when* PETKOFF *addresses him angrily.*)

PETKOFF. You'd better go and slam that bag, too, down on Miss Raina's ice pudding! (*This is too much for* NICOLA. *The bag drops from his hands on* PETKOFF's *corns, eliciting* [52] *a roar of anguish from him.*) Begone, you butter-fingered donkey.

NICOLA. (*Snatching up the bag, and escaping into the house.*) Yes, sir.

CATHERINE. Oh, never mind, Paul. Don't be angry!

PETKOFF. (*Muttering.*) Scoundrel. He's got out of hand while I was away. I'll teach him. (*Recollecting his guest.*) Oh, well, never mind. Come Bluntschli, let's have no more nonsense about you having to go away. You know very well you're not going back to Switzerland yet. Until you do go back you'll stay with us.

RAINA. Oh, do, Captain Bluntschli.

PETKOFF. (*To* CATHERINE.) Now, Catherine, it's of you that he's afraid. Press him and he'll stay.

CATHERINE. Of course I shall be only too delighted if (*Appealingly.*) Captain Bluntschli really wishes to stay. He knows my wishes.

BLUNTSCHLI. (*In his driest military manner.*) I am at madam's orders.

SERGIUS. (*Cordially.*) That settles it!

PETKOFF. (*Heartily.*) Of course!

RAINA. You see, you must stay!

BLUNTSCHLI. (*Smiling.*) Well, if I must, I must!

(*Gesture of despair from* CATHERINE.)

Curtain.

52. **eliciting:** drawing forth; from Latin *e-*, out, plus *lacere*, to entice.

Meaning and Method: Act II

1. The opening dialogue between Louka and Nicola, like the dialogue between Raina and the escaped soldier in Act I, reveals that their values are different. Why does Louka say "You have the soul of a servant, Nicola." (page (126) when she herself is a servant? How does she differ from Nicola?

2. How does the dialogue between Catherine and her husband, Major Petkoff, provide another example of a contrast between realistic and unrealistic views of life and war? Which specific parts of their speeches further advance Shaw's satirical treatment of these members of the ruling class?

3. Reread the long stage direction in which Major Sergius Saranoff is characterized (page 130–31). Is Shaw making fun of Sergius? Give reasons for your answer.

4. Sergius's description of the cavalry charge which he led at Slivnitza is the third account of it so far in the play. Compare Sergius's account of it with (a) Catherine's and (b) Captain Bluntschli's in Act I. How is it different from each of these? In comparing Sergius's views of the charge with Captain Bluntschli's, which of the two do you think is the more experienced fighting man? Which of the two thinks he is?

5. What is the tone or quality of the relationship between Sergius and Raina? Compare the dialogue and actions between Sergius and Raina and between Sergius and Louka. How do they differ? How does Sergius explain these differences?

   Why does Louka tell Sergius about Raina and another man? Do you think the scene between Louka and Sergius is the beginning of a subplot? Why or why not?

   How can these differences between Sergius and Raina and Sergius and Louka be said to be still another of Shaw's examples of the conflict between realism and romanticism? How can this scene also be interpreted as a criticism of the pretenses of the upper class?

6. Why do Raina and her mother pretend to object to Sergius's story of the escape of the Swiss soldier? By what incident does Shaw dramatize the fact that Sergius, like Raina, is also a pretender?

7. In Act II although Captain Bluntschli does not make his appearance until almost the end of this act, he nevertheless remains the protagonist or the hero of the play. How has Shaw kept us aware of him before his appearance?

8. How do the changes and developments in the plot heighten the suspense? What situations or problems remain to be solved or resolved in Act III?

Act III

In the library after lunch. It is not much of a library, its literary equipment consisting of a single fixed shelf stocked with old paper covered novels, broken-backed, coffee-stained, torn and thumbed, and a couple of little hanging shelves with a few gift books on them, the rest of the wall space being occupied by trophies of war and the chase. But it is a most comfortable sitting room. A row of three large windows in the front of the house show a mountain panorama,[1] which is just now seen in one of its softest aspects in the mellowing afternoon light. In the left-hand corner, a square earthenware stove, a perfect tower of colored pottery, rises nearly to the ceiling and guarantees plenty of warmth. The ottoman in the middle is a circular bank of decorated cushions, and the window seats are well upholstered divans. Little Turkish tables, one of them with an elaborate hookah [2] on it, and a screen to match them, complete the handsome effect of the furnishing. There is one object, however, which is hopelessly out of keeping with its surroundings. This is a small kitchen table, much the worse for wear, fitted as a writing table with an old canister full of pens, an eggcup filled with ink, and a deplorable scrap of severely used pink blotting paper.

At the side of this table, which stands on the right, BLUNTSCHLI *is hard at work, with a couple of maps before him, writing orders. At the head of it sits* SERGIUS, *who is also supposed to be at work, but who is actually gnawing the feather of a pen, and contemplating* BLUNT-SCHLI'S *quick, sure, businesslike progress with a mixture of envious irritation at his own incapacity, and awestruck wonder at an ability which seems to him almost miraculous, though its prosaic character forbids him to esteem it. The* MAJOR *is comfortably established on the ottoman, with a newspaper in his hand and the tube of the hookah within his reach.* CATHERINE *sits at the stove, with her back to them, embroidering.* RAINA, *reclining on the divan under the left-hand window, is gazing in a daydream out at the Balkan landscape, with a neglected novel in her lap.*

The door is on the left. The button of the electric bell is between the door and the fireplace.

1. **panorama:** a complete, unobstructed view.
2. **hookah** (hŏŏk′ə) : an oriental pipe with a long coil or stem that passes through a jar of water, which thus cools the smoke.

PETKOFF. (*Looking up from his paper to watch how they are getting on at the table.*)   Are you sure I can't help you in any way, Bluntschli?

BLUNTSCHLI. (*Without interrupting his writing or looking up.*) Quite sure, thank you. Saranoff and I will manage it.

SERGIUS. (*Grimly.*)   Yes; we'll manage it. He finds out what to do; draws up the orders; and I sign 'em. Division of labor, Major. (BLUNTSCHLI *passes him a paper.*) Another one? Thank you. (*He plants the papers squarely before him; sets his chair carefully parallel to them; and signs with the air of a man resolutely performing a difficult and dangerous feat.*) This hand is more accustomed to the sword than to the pen.

PETKOFF.   It's very good of you, Bluntschli, it is indeed, to let yourself be put upon in this way. Now are you quite sure I can do nothing?

CATHERINE. (*In a low, warning tone.*)   You can stop interrupting, Paul.

PETKOFF. (*Starting and looking round at her.*)   Eh? Oh! Quite right, my love, quite right. (*He takes his newspaper up; but lets it drop again.*) Ah, you haven't been campaigning, Catherine; you don't know how pleasant it is for us to sit here, after a good lunch, with nothing to do but enjoy ourselves. There's only one thing I want to make me thoroughly comfortable.

CATHERINE.   What is that?

PETKOFF.   My old coat. I'm not at home in this one; I feel as if I were on parade.

CATHERINE.   My dear Paul, how absurd you are about that old coat! It must be hanging in the blue closet where you left it.

PETKOFF.   My dear Catherine, I tell you I've looked there. Am I to believe my own eyes or not? (CATHERINE *quietly rises and presses the button of the electric bell by the fireplace.*) What are you showing off that bell for? (*She looks at him majestically, and silently resumes her chair and her needlework.*) My dear, if you think the obstinacy of your sex can make a coat out of two old dressing gowns of Raina's, your waterproof, and my mackintosh,[3] you're mistaken. That's exactly what the blue closet contains at present. (NICOLA *presents himself.*)

CATHERINE. (*Unmoved by* PETKOFF's *sally.*[4]) Nicola, go to the blue

3. waterproof . . . mackintosh: raincoats.
4. sally: a bantering remark.

closet and bring your master's old coat here—the braided one he usually wears in the house.

NICOLA.   Yes, madam. (NICOLA *goes out.*)

PETKOFF.   Catherine.

CATHERINE.   Yes, Paul?

PETKOFF.   I bet you any piece of jewelry you like to order from Sofia, against a week's housekeeping money, that the coat isn't there.

CATHERINE.   Done, Paul.

PETKOFF. (*Excited by the prospect of a gamble.*) Come, here's an opportunity for some sport. Who'll bet on it? Bluntschli, I'll give you six to one.

BLUNTSCHLI. (*Imperturbably.*)   It would be robbing you, Major. Madam is sure to be right. (*Without looking up, he passes another batch of papers to* SERGIUS.)

SERGIUS. (*Also excited.*)   Bravo, Switzerland! Major, I bet my best charger against an Arab mare for Raina that Nicola finds the coat in the blue closet.

PETKOFF. (*Eagerly.*)   Your best char—

CATHERINE. (*Hastily interrupting him.*)   Don't be foolish, Paul. An Arabian mare will cost you 50,000 levas.

RAINA. (*Suddenly coming out of her picturesque reverie.*)   Really, Mother, if you are going to take the jewelry, I don't see why you should grudge me my Arab.

(NICOLA *comes back with the coat and brings it to* PETKOFF, *who can hardly believe his eyes.*)

CATHERINE.   Where was it, Nicola?

NICOLA.   Hanging in the blue closet, madam.

PETKOFF.   Well, I am d—

CATHERINE. (*Stopping him.*)   Paul!

PETKOFF.   I could have sworn it wasn't there. Age is beginning to tell on me. I'm getting hallucinations. (*To* NICOLA.) Here, help me to change. Excuse me, Bluntschli. (*He begins changing coats,* NICOLA *acting as valet.*) Remember, I didn't take that bet of yours, Sergius. You'd better give Raina that Arab steed yourself, since you've roused her expectations. Eh, Raina? (*He looks round at her; but she is again rapt in the landscape. With a little gush of paternal affection and pride, he points her out to them and says:*) She's dreaming, as usual.

SERGIUS. Assuredly she shall not be the loser.

PETKOFF. So much the better for her. I shan't come off so cheap, I expect. (*The change is now complete.* NICOLA *goes out with the discarded coat.*) Ah, now I feel at home at last. (*He sits down and takes his newspaper with a grunt of relief.*)

BLUNTSCHLI. (*To* SERGIUS, *handing a paper.*) That's the last order.

PETKOFF. (*Jumping up.*) What! Finished?

BLUNTSCHLI. Finished.

PETKOFF. (*Goes beside* SERGIUS; *looks curiously over his left shoulder as he signs; and says with childlike envy:*) Haven't you anything for me to sign?

BLUNTSCHLI. Not necessary. His signature will do.

PETKOFF. Ah, well, I think we've done a thundering good day's work. (*He goes away from the table.*) Can I do anything more?

BLUNTSCHLI. You had better both see the fellows that are to take these. (*To* SERGIUS.) Pack them off at once; and show them that I've marked on the orders the time they should hand them in by. Tell them that if they stop to drink or tell stories—if they're five minutes late, they'll have the skin taken off their backs.

SERGIUS. (*Rising indignantly.*) I'll say so. And if one of them is man enough to spit in my face for insulting him, I'll buy his discharge and give him a pension. (*He strides out, his humanity deeply outraged.*)

BLUNTSCHLI. (*Confidentially.*) Just see that he talks to them properly, Major, will you?

PETKOFF. (*Officiously.*[5]) Quite right, Bluntschli, quite right. I'll see to it. (*He goes to the door importantly, but hesitates on the threshold.*) By the bye, Catherine, you may as well come, too. They'll be far more frightened of you than of me.

CATHERINE. (*Putting down her embroidery.*) I daresay I had better. You will only splutter at them. (*She goes out,* PETKOFF *holding the door for her and following her.*)

BLUNTSCHLI. What a country! They make cannons out of cherry trees; and the officers send for their wives to keep discipline! (*He begins to fold and docket*[6] *the papers.* RAINA, *who has risen from the divan, strolls down the room with her hands clasped behind her, and looks mischievously at him.*)

---

5. **Officiously:** in a self-important manner.
6. **docket:** to label.

RAINA. You look ever so much nicer than when we last met. (*He looks up, surprised.*) What have you done to yourself?

BLUNTSCHLI. Washed; brushed; good night's sleep and breakfast. That's all.

RAINA. Did you get back safely that morning?

BLUNTSCHLI. Quite, thanks.

RAINA. Were they angry with you for running away from Sergius's charge?

BLUNTSCHLI. No, they were glad; because they'd all just run away themselves.

RAINA. (*Going to the table, and leaning over it toward him.*) It must have made a lovely story for them—all that about me and my room.

BLUNTSCHLI. Capital story. But I only told it to one of them—a particular friend.

RAINA. On whose discretion you could absolutely rely?

BLUNTSCHLI. Absolutely.

RAINA. Hm! He told it all to my father and Sergius the day you exchanged the prisoners. (*She turns away and strolls carelessly across to the other side of the room.*)

BLUNTSCHLI. (*Deeply concerned and half incredulous.*) No! You don't mean that, do you?

RAINA. (*Turning, with sudden earnestness.*) I do, indeed. But they don't know that it was in this house that you hid. If Sergius knew, he would challenge you and kill you in a duel.

BLUNTSCHLI. Bless me! Then don't tell him.

RAINA. (*Full of reproach for his levity.*) Can you realize what it is to me to deceive him? I want to be quite perfect with Sergius—no meanness, no smallness, no deceit. My relation to him is the one really beautiful and noble part of my life. I hope you can understand that.

BLUNTSCHLI. (*Skeptically.*) You mean that you wouldn't like him to find out that the story about the ice pudding was a—a—a— You know.

RAINA. (*Wincing.*) Ah, don't talk of it in that flippant way. I lied; I know it. But I did it to save your life. He would have killed you. That was the second time I ever uttered a falsehood. (BLUNTSCHLI *rises quickly and looks doubtfully and somewhat severely at her.*) Do you remember the first time?

BLUNTSCHLI. I! No. Was I present?

RAINA. Yes; and I told the officer who was searching for you that you were not present.

BLUNTSCHLI. True. I should have remembered it.

RAINA. (*Greatly encouraged.*)   Ah, it is natural that you should forget it first. It cost you nothing. It cost me a lie, a lie!! (*She sits down on the ottoman, looking straight before her with her hands clasped on her knee.* BLUNTSCHLI, *quite touched, goes to the ottoman with a particularly reassuring and considerate air, and sits down beside her.*)

BLUNTSCHLI. My dear young lady, don't let this worry you. Remember, I'm a soldier. Now what are the two things that happen to a soldier so often that he comes to think nothing of them? One is hearing people tell lies (RAINA *recoils.*); the other is getting his life saved in all sorts of ways by all sorts of people.

RAINA. (*Rising in indignant protest.*)   And so he becomes a creature incapable of faith and of gratitude.

BLUNTSCHLI. (*Making a wry face.*[7])   Do you like gratitude? I don't. If pity is akin to love, gratitude is akin to the other thing.

RAINA. Gratitude! (*Turning on him.*) If you are incapable of gratitude you are incapable of any noble sentiment. Even animals are grateful. Oh, I see now exactly what you think of me! You were not surprised to hear me lie. To you it was something I probably did every day—every hour. That is how men think of women. (*She walks up the room melodramatically.*)

BLUNTSCHLI. (*Dubiously.*)   There's reason in everything. You said you'd told only two lies in your whole life. Dear young lady, isn't that rather a short allowance? I'm quite a straightforward man myself; but it wouldn't last me a whole morning.

RAINA. (*Staring haughtily at him.*)   Do you know, sir, that you are insulting me?

BLUNTSCHLI. I can't help it. When you get into that noble attitude and speak in that thrilling voice, I admire you; but I find it impossible to believe a single word you say.

RAINA. (*Superbly.*)   Captain Bluntschli!

BLUNTSCHLI. (*Unmoved.*)   Yes?

RAINA. (*Coming a little toward him, as if she could not believe her senses.*)   Do you mean what you said just now? Do you know what you said just now?

---

7. **Making a wry face:** twisting the features out of shape. *Wry* means contorted; askew.

BLUNTSCHLI. I do.

RAINA. (*Gasping.*) I! I!!! (*She points to herself incredulously, meaning "I, Raina Petkoff, tell lies!" He meets her gaze unflinchingly. She suddenly sits down beside him, and adds, with a complete change of manner from the heroic to the familiar.*) How did you find me out?

BLUNTSCHLI. (*Promptly.*) Instinct, dear young lady. Instinct, and experience of the world.

RAINA. (*Wonderingly.*) Do you know, you are the first man I ever met who did not take me seriously?

BLUNTSCHLI. You mean, don't you, that I am the first man that has ever taken you quite seriously?

RAINA. Yes, I suppose I do mean that. (*Cosily, quite at her ease with him.*) How strange it is to be talked to in such a way! You know, I've always gone on like that—I mean the noble attitude and the thrilling voice. I did it when I was a tiny child to my nurse. She believed in it. I do it before my parents. They believe in it. I do it before Sergius. He believes in it.

BLUNTSCHLI. Yes. He's a little in that line himself, isn't he?

RAINA. (*Startled.*) Do you think so?

BLUNTSCHLI. You know him better than I do.

RAINA. I wonder—I wonder is he? If I thought that—! (*Discouraged.*) Ah, well, what does it matter? I suppose, now that you've found me out, you despise me.

BLUNTSCHLI. (*Warmly, rising.*) No, my dear young lady, no, no, no a thousand times. It's part of your youth—part of your charm. I'm like all the rest of them—the nurse—your parents—Sergius; I'm your infatuated [8] admirer.

RAINA. (*Pleased.*) Really?

BLUNTSCHLI. (*Slapping his breast smartly with his hand, German fashion.*) Hand aufs Herz! [9] Really and truly.

RAINA. (*Very happy.*) But what did you think of me for giving you my portrait?

BLUNTSCHLI. (*Astonished.*) Your portrait! You never gave me your portrait.

RAINA. (*Quickly.*) Do you mean to say you never got it?

BLUNTSCHLI. No. (*He sits down beside her, with renewed interest, and says, with some complacency.*) When did you send it to me?

---

8. **infatuated**: inspired with a foolish and exaggerated love.
9. **Hand aufs Herz**: German, "hand on heart." "Cross my heart" is the American expression.

RAINA. (*Indignantly.*) I did not send it to you. (*She turns her head away, and adds, reluctantly.*) It was in the pocket of that coat.

BLUNTSCHLI. (*Pursing his lips and rounding his eyes.*) Oh-o-oh! I never found it. It must be there still.

RAINA. (*Springing up.*) There still; for my father to find the first time he puts his hand in his pocket! Oh, how could you be so stupid?

BLUNTSCHLI. (*Rising also.*) It doesn't matter; it's only a photograph. How can he tell who it was intended for? Tell him he put it there himself.

RAINA. (*Impatiently.*) Yes, that is so clever—so clever! What shall I do?

BLUNTSCHLI. Ah, I see. You wrote something on it. That was rash!

RAINA. (*Annoyed almost to tears.*) Oh, to have done such a thing for you, who care no more—except to laugh at me—oh! Are you sure nobody has touched it?

BLUNTSCHLI. Well, I can't be quite sure. You see I couldn't carry it about with me all the time; one can't take much luggage on active service.

RAINA. What did you do with it?

BLUNTSCHLI. When I got through to Peerot I had to put it in safe keeping somehow. I thought of the railway cloak room; but that's the surest place to get looted in modern warfare. So I pawned it.

RAINA. Pawned it!!!

BLUNTSCHLI. I know it doesn't sound nice; but it was much the safest plan. I redeemed it the day before yesterday. Heaven only knows whether the pawnbroker cleared out the pockets or not.

RAINA. (*Furious—throwing the words right into his face.*) You have a low, shopkeeping mind. You think of things that would never come into a gentleman's head.

BLUNTSCHLI. (*Phlegmatically.[10]*) That's the Swiss national character, dear lady.

RAINA. Oh, I wish I had never met you. (*She flounces away and sits at the window fuming.*)

(LOUKA *comes in with a heap of letters and telegrams on her salver, and crosses, with her bold, free gait, to the table. Her left sleeve is looped up to the shoulder with a brooch,[11]*

10. **Phlegmatically:** calmly; indifferently.
11. **brooch:** an ornamental pin.

*showing her naked arm, with a broad gilt bracelet covering
the bruise.*)

LOUKA. (*To* BLUNTSCHLI.) For you. (*She empties the salver reck-
lessly on the table.*) The messenger is waiting. (*She is determined
not to be civil to a Serbian, even if she must bring him his letters.*)

BLUNTSCHLI. (*To* RAINA.) Will you excuse me? The last postal de-
livery that reached me was three weeks ago. These are the subsequent accumulations. Four telegrams—a week old. (*He opens one.*)
Oho! Bad news!

RAINA. (*Rising and advancing a little remorsefully.*) Bad news?

BLUNTSCHLI. My father's dead. (*He looks at the telegram with his
lips pursed, musing on the unexpected change in his arrangements.*)

RAINA. Oh, how very sad!

BLUNTSCHLI. Yes, I shall have to start for home in an hour. He has
left a lot of big hotels behind him to be looked after. (*Takes up a
heavy letter in a long, blue envelope.*) Here's a whacking letter
from the family solicitor. (*He pulls out the enclosures and glances
over them.*) Great heavens! Seventy! Two hundred! (*In a crescendo of dismay.*) Four hundred! Four thousand!! Nine thousand
six hundred!!! What on earth shall I do with them all?

RAINA. (*Timidly.*) Nine thousand hotels?

BLUNTSCHLI. Hotels! Nonsense. If you only knew!—Oh, it's too
ridiculous! Excuse me, I must give my fellow orders about starting.
(*He leaves the room hastily, with the documents in his hand.*)

LOUKA. (*Tauntingly.*) He has not much heart, that Swiss, though
he is so fond of the Serbians. He has not a word of grief for his
poor father.

RAINA. (*Bitterly.*) Grief! A man who has been doing nothing but
killing people for years! What does he care? What does any soldier
care? (*She goes to the door, evidently restraining her tears with
difficulty.*)

LOUKA. Major Saranoff has been fighting, too; and he has plenty of
heart left. (RAINA, *at the door, looks haughtily at her and goes out.*)
Aha! I thought you wouldn't get much feeling out of your soldier.
(*She is following* RAINA *when* NICOLA *enters with an armful of logs
for the fire.*)

NICOLA. (*Grinning amorously at her.*) I've been trying all the afternoon to get a minute alone with you, my girl. (*His countenance
changes as he notices her arm.*) Why, what fashion is that of wearing your sleeve, child?

LOUKA. (*Proudly.*)   My own fashion.

NICOLA.   Indeed! If the mistress catches you, she'll talk to you. (*He throws the logs down on the ottoman, and sits comfortably beside them.*)

LOUKA.   Is that any reason why you should take it on yourself to talk to me?

NICOLA.   Come, don't be so contrary with me. I've some good news for you. (*He takes out some paper money.* LOUKA, *with an eager gleam in her eyes, comes close to look at it.*) See, a twenty leva bill! Sergius gave me that out of pure swagger. A fool and his money are soon parted. There's ten levas more. The Swiss gave me that for backing up the mistress's and Raina's lies about him. He's no fool, he isn't. You should have heard old Catherine downstairs as polite as you please to me, telling me not to mind the Major being a little impatient; for they knew what a good servant I was —after making a fool and a liar of me before them all! The twenty will go to our savings; and you shall have the ten to spend if you'll only talk to me so as to remind me I'm a human being. I get tired of being a servant occasionally.

LOUKA. (*Scornfully.*)   Yes, sell your manhood for thirty levas, and buy me for ten! Keep your money. You were born to be a servant. I was not. When you set up your shop you will only be everybody's servant instead of somebody's servant.

NICOLA. (*Picking up his logs, and going to the stove.*)   Ah, wait till you see. We shall have our evenings to ourselves; and I shall be master in my own house, I promise you. (*He throws the logs down and kneels at the stove.*)

LOUKA.   You shall never be master in mine. (*She sits down on* SERGIUS's *chair.*)

NICOLA. (*Turning, still on his knees, and squatting down rather forlornly, on his calves, daunted* [12] *by her implacable* [13] *disdain.* [14]) You have a great ambition in you, Louka. Remember, if any luck comes to you, it was I that made a woman of you.

LOUKA.   You!

NICOLA. (*With dogged self-assertion.*)   Yes, me. Who was it made you give up wearing a couple of pounds of false black hair on your head and reddening your lips and cheeks like any other Bulgarian girl? I did. Who taught you to trim your nails, and keep your hands

12. **daunted:** dismayed; defeated.
13. **implacable:** relentless; impossible to ease.
14. **disdain:** contempt.

clean, and be dainty about yourself, like a fine Russian lady? Me!
Do you hear that? Me! (*She tosses her head defiantly; and he rises,
ill-humoredly, adding more coolly:*) I've often thought that if
Raina were out of the way, and you just a little less of a fool and
Sergius just a little more of one, you might come to be one of my
grandest customers, instead of only being my wife and costing me
money.

LOUKA.   I believe you would rather be my servant than my husband.
You would make more out of me. Oh, I know that soul of yours.

NICOLA. (*Going up close to her for greater emphasis.*)   Never you
mind my soul; but just listen to my advice. If you want to be a lady,
your present behavior to me won't do at all, unless when we're
alone. It's too sharp and impudent; and impudence is a sort of
familiarity; it shows affection for me. And don't you try being high
and mighty with me either. You're like all country girls; you think
it's genteel [15] to treat a servant the way I treat a stableboy.
That's only your ignorance; and don't you forget it. And don't be
so ready to defy everybody. Act as if you expected to have your own
way, not as if you expected to be ordered about. The way to get
on as a lady is the same as the way to get on as a servant; you've
got to know your place; that's the secret of it. And you may depend
on me to know my place if you get promoted. Think over it, my
girl. I'll stand by you; one servant should always stand by another.

LOUKA. (*Rising impatiently.*)   Oh, I must behave in my own way.
You take all the courage out of me with your cold-blooded wisdom.
Go and put those logs on the fire; that's the sort of thing you understand. (*Before* NICOLA *can retort,* SERGIUS *comes in. He checks
himself a moment on seeing* LOUKA; *then goes to the stove.*)

SERGIUS. (*To* NICOLA.)   I am not in the way of your work, I hope.

NICOLA. (*In a smooth, elderly manner.*)   Oh, no, sir, thank you
kindly. I was only speaking to this foolish girl about her habit of
running up here to the library whenever she gets a chance, to look
at the books. That's the worst of her education, sir; it gives her
habits above her station. (*To* LOUKA.) Make that table tidy, Louka,
for the Major. (*He goes out sedately.*[16])

(LOUKA, *without looking at* SERGIUS, *begins to arrange the
papers on the table. He crosses slowly to her, and studies the
arrangement of her sleeve reflectively.*)

---

15. **genteel** (jen·tēl′) : well-bred or refined; elegant.
16. **sedately**: calmly; gravely.

SERGIUS. Let me see; is there a mark there? (*He turns up the brace-let and sees the bruise made by his grasp. She stands motionless, not looking at him; fascinated, but on her guard.*) Ff ff! Does it hurt?

LOUKA. Yes.

SERGIUS. Shall I cure it?

LOUKA. (*Instantly withdrawing herself proudly, but still not looking at him.*) No. You cannot cure it now.

SERGIUS. (*Masterfully.*) Quite sure? (*He makes a movement as if to take her in his arms.*)

LOUKA. Don't trifle with me, please. An officer should not trifle with a servant.

SERGIUS. (*Touching the arm with a merciless stroke of his forefinger.*) That was no trifle, Louka.

LOUKA. No. (*Looking at him for the first time.*) Are you sorry?

SERGIUS. (*With measured emphasis, folding his arms.*) I am never sorry.

LOUKA. (*Wistfully.*) I wish I could believe a man could be so unlike a woman as that. I wonder are you really a brave man?

SERGIUS. (*Unaffectedly, relaxing his attitude.*) Yes, I am a brave man. My heart jumped like a woman's at the first shot; but in the charge I found that I was brave. Yes, that at least is real about me.

LOUKA. Did you find in the charge that the men whose fathers are poor like mine were any less brave than the men who are rich like you?

SERGIUS. (*With bitter levity.*[17]) Not a bit. They all slashed and cursed and yelled like heroes. Psha! The courage to rage and kill is cheap. I have an English bull terrier who has as much of that sort of courage as the whole Bulgarian nation, and the whole Russian nation at its back. But he lets my groom thrash him, all the same. That's your soldier all over! No, Louka, your poor men can cut throats; but they are afraid of their officers; they put up with insults and blows; they stand by and see one another punished like children—aye, and help to do it when they are ordered. And the officers!—Well (*With a short, bitter laugh.*) I am an officer. Oh, (*Fervently.*) give me the man who will defy to the death any power on earth or in heaven that sets itself up against his own will and conscience; he alone is the brave man.

LOUKA. How easy it is to talk! Men never seem to me to grow up;

17. **levity:** gaiety.

they all have schoolboy's ideas. You don't know what true courage is.

SERGIUS. (*Ironically.*)   Indeed! I am willing to be instructed.

LOUKA.   Look at me! How much am I allowed to have my own will? I have to get your room ready for you—to sweep and dust, to fetch and carry. How could that degrade me if it did not degrade you to have it done for you? But (*With subdued* [18] *passion.*), if I were Empress of Russia, above everyone in the world, then—ah, then, though according to you I could show no courage at all, you should see, you should see.

SERGIUS.   What would you do, most noble Empress?

LOUKA.   I would marry the man I loved, which no other queen in Europe has the courage to do. If I loved you, though you would be as far beneath me as I am beneath you, I would dare to be the equal of my inferior. Would you dare as much if you loved me? No, if you felt the beginnings of love for me you would not let it grow. You dare not, you would marry a rich man's daughter because you would be afraid of what other people would say of you.

SERGIUS. (*Carried away.*)   You lie, it is not so, by all the stars! If I loved you, and I were the Czar himself, I would set you on the throne by my side. You know that I love another woman, a woman as high above you as heaven as above earth. And you are jealous of her.

LOUKA.   I have no reason to be. She will never marry you now. The man I told you of has come back. She will marry the Swiss.

SERGIUS. (*Recoiling.*)   The Swiss!

LOUKA.   A man worth ten of you. Then you can come to me, and I will refuse you. You are not good enough for me. (*She turns to the door.*)

SERGIUS. (*Springing after her and catching her fiercely on his arms.*) I will kill the Swiss; and afterward I will do as I please with you.

LOUKA. (*In his arms, passive and steadfast.*)   The Swiss will kill you, perhaps. He has beaten you in love. He may beat you in war.

SERGIUS. (*Tormentedly.*)   Do you think I believe that she—she whose worst thoughts are higher than your best ones, is capable of trifling with another man behind my back?

LOUKA.   Do you think she would believe the Swiss if he told her now that I am in your arms?

SERGIUS. (*Releasing her in despair.*)   Damnation! Oh, damnation!

18. **subdued:** softened; diminished.

Mockery, mockery everywhere; everything I think is mocked by everything I do. (*He strikes himself frantically on the breast.*) Coward, liar, fool! Shall I kill myself like a man, or live and pretend to laugh at myself? (*She again turns to go.*) Louka! (*She stops near the door.*) Remember, you belong to me.

LOUKA. (*Quietly.*)   What does that mean—an insult?

SERGIUS. (*Commandingly.*)   It means that you love me, and that I have had you here in my arms, and will perhaps have you there again. Whether that is an insult I neither know nor care; take it as you please. But (*Vehemently.*), I will not be a coward and a trifler. If I choose to love you, I dare marry you, in spite of all Bulgaria. If these hands ever touch you again, they shall touch my affianced [19] bride.

LOUKA.   We shall see whether you dare keep your word. But take care. I will not wait long.

SERGIUS. (*Again folding his arms and standing motionless in the middle of the room.*)   Yes, we shall see. And you shall wait my pleasure.

(BLUNTSCHLI, *much preoccupied, with his papers still in his hand, enters, leaving the door open for* LOUKA *to go out. He goes across to the table, glancing at her as he passes.* SERGIUS, *without altering his resolute attitude, watches him steadily.* LOUKA *goes out, leaving the door open.*)

BLUNTSCHLI. (*Absently, sitting at the table as before, and putting down his papers.*)   That's a remarkable-looking young woman.

SERGIUS. (*Gravely, without moving.*)   Captain Bluntschli.

BLUNTSCHLI.   Eh?

SERGIUS.   You have deceived me. You are my rival. I brook no rivals. At six o'clock I shall be in the drilling ground on the Klissoura road, alone, on horseback, with my saber. Do you understand?

BLUNTSCHLI. (*Staring, but sitting quite at his ease.*)   Oh, thank you; that's a cavalry man's proposal. I'm in the artillery; and I have the choice of weapons. If I go, I shall take a machine gun. And there shall be no mistake about the cartridges this time.

SERGIUS. (*Flushing, but with deadly coldness.*)   Take care, sir. It is not our custom in Bulgaria to allow invitations of that kind to be trifled with.

BLUNTSCHLI. (*Warmly.*)   Pooh! Don't talk to me about Bulgaria.

19. affianced: pledged; engaged.

You don't know what fighting is. But have it your own way. Bring your saber along. I'll meet you.

SERGIUS. (*Fiercely delighted to find his opponent a man of spirit.*) Well said, Switzer. Shall I lend you my best horse?

BLUNTSCHLI.   No, damn your horse! Thank you all the same, my dear fellow. (RAINA *comes in, and hears the next sentence.*) I shall fight you on foot. Horseback's too dangerous; I don't want to kill you if I can help it.

RAINA. (*Hurrying forward anxiously.*)   I have heard what Captain Bluntschli said, Sergius. You are going to fight. Why? (SERGIUS *turns away in silence, and goes to the stove, where he stands watching her as she continues, to* BLUNTSCHLI.) What about?

BLUNTSCHLI.   I don't know; he hasn't told me. Better not interfere, dear young lady. No harm will be done; I've often acted as sword instructor. He won't be able to touch me; and I'll not hurt him. It will save explanations. In the morning I shall be off home; and you'll never see me or hear of me again. You and he will then make it up and live happily ever after.

RAINA. (*Turning away deeply hurt, almost with a sob in her voice.*) I never said I wanted to see you again.

SERGIUS. (*Striding forward.*)   Ha! That is a confession.

RAINA. (*Haughtily.*)   What do you mean?

SERGIUS.   You love that man!

RAINA. (*Scandalized.*)   Sergius!

SERGIUS.   You allow him to make love to you behind my back, just as you accept me as your affianced husband behind his. Bluntschli, you know our relations; and you deceived me. It is for that that I call you to account, not for having received favors that I never enjoyed.

BLUNTSCHLI. (*Jumping up indignantly.*)   Stuff! Rubbish! I have received no favors. Why, the young lady doesn't even know whether I'm married or not.

RAINA. (*Forgetting herself.*)   Oh! (*Collapsing on the ottoman.*) Are you?

SERGIUS.   You see the young lady's concern, Captain Bluntschli. Denial is useless. You have enjoyed the privilege of being received in her own room, late at night—

BLUNTSCHLI. (*Interrupting him pepperily.*)   Yes; you blockhead! She received me with a pistol at her head. Your cavalry were at my heels. I'd have blown out her brains if she'd uttered a cry.

SERGIUS. (*Taken aback.*)   Bluntschli! Raina, is this true?

RAINA. (*Rising in wrathful majesty.*)   Oh, how dare you, how dare you?

BLUNTSCHLI.   Apologize, man, apologize! (*He resumes his seat at the table.*)

SERGIUS. (*With the old, measured emphasis, folding his arms.*)   I never apologize.

RAINA. (*Passionately.*)   This is the doing of that friend of yours, Captain Bluntschli. It is he who is spreading this horrible story about me. (*She walks about excitedly.*)

BLUNTSCHLI.   No, he's dead—burned alive.

RAINA. (*Stopping, shocked.*)   Burned alive!

BLUNTSCHLI.   Shot in the hip in a wood yard. Couldn't drag himself out. Your fellows' shells set the timber on fire and burned him, with half a dozen other poor devils in the same predicament.

RAINA.   How horrible!

SERGIUS.   And how ridiculous! Oh, war! War! The dream of patriots and heroes! A fraud, Bluntschli, a hollow sham, like love.

RAINA. (*Outraged.*)   Like love! You say that before me.

BLUNTSCHLI.   Come, Saranoff, that matter is explained.

SERGIUS.   A hollow sham, I say. Would you have come back here if nothing had passed between you, except at the muzzle of your pistol? Raina is mistaken about our friend who was burned. He was not my informant.

RAINA.   Who then? (*Suddenly guessing the truth.*) Ah, Louka! My maid, my servant! You were with her this morning all that time after—after— oh, what sort of god is this I have been worshipping! (*He meets her gaze with sardonic enjoyment of her disenchantment. Angered all the more, she goes closer to him, and says, in a lower, intenser tone.*)   Do you know that I looked out of the window as I went upstairs, to have another sight of my hero; and I saw something that I did not understand then. I know now that you were making love to her.

SERGIUS. (*With grim humor.*)   You saw that?

RAINA.   Only too well. (*She turns away, and throws herself on the divan under the center window, quite overcome.*)

SERGIUS. (*Cynically.*)   Raina, our romance is shattered. Life's a farce.

BLUNTSCHLI. (*To* RAINA, *good-humoredly.*)   You see, he's found himself out now.

SERGIUS.   Bluntschli, I have allowed you to call me a blockhead. You may now call me a coward as well. I refuse to fight you. Do you know why?

BLUNTSCHLI.   No; but it doesn't matter. I didn't ask the reason when you cried on; and I don't ask the reason now that you cry off. I'm a professional soldier. I fight when I have to, and am very glad to get out of it when I haven't to. You're only an amateur; you think fighting's an amusement.

SERGIUS.   You shall hear the reason all the same, my professional. The reason is that it takes two men—real men—men of heart, blood, and honor—to make a genuine combat. I could no more fight with you than I could make love to an ugly woman. You've no magnetism; you're not a man, you're a machine.

BLUNTSCHLI. (*Apologetically.*)   Quite true, quite true. I always was that sort of chap. I'm very sorry. But now that you've found that life isn't a farce, but something quite sensible and serious, what further obstacle is there to your happiness?

RAINA. (*Rising.*)   You are very solicitous about my happiness and his. Do you forget his new love—Louka? It is not you that he must fight now, but his rival, Nicola.

SERGIUS.   Rival!! (*Striking his forehead.*)

RAINA.   Did you not know that they are engaged?

SERGIUS.   Nicola! Are fresh abysses [20] opening! Nicola!!

RAINA. (*Sarcastically.*)   A shocking sacrifice, isn't it? Such beauty, such intellect, such modesty, wasted on a middle-aged servant man! Really, Sergius, you cannot stand by and allow such a thing. It would be unworthy of your chivalry.

SERGIUS. (*Losing all self-control.*)   Viper! [21] Viper! (*He rushes to and fro, raging.*)

BLUNTSCHLI.   Look here, Saranoff; you're getting the worst of this.

RAINA. (*Getting angrier.*)   Do you realize what he has done, Captain Bluntschli? He has set this girl as a spy on us; and her reward is that he makes love to her.

SERGIUS.   False! Monstrous!

RAINA.   Monstrous! (*Confronting him.*)   Do you deny that she told you about Captain Bluntschli being in my room?

SERGIUS.   No, but—

RAINA. (*Interrupting.*)   Do you deny that you were making love to her when she told you?

20. **abyss:** a bottomless gulf; a void; from Greek *a-*, without, plus *byssos*, bottom.
21. **Viper:** *literally*, a poisonous snake; here, a treacherous or spiteful person.

SERGIUS.   No; but I tell you—

RAINA.   (*Cutting him short contemptuously.*)   It is unnecessary to tell us anything more. That is quite enough for us. (*She turns her back on him and sweeps majestically back to the window.*)

BLUNTSCHLI.   (*Quietly, as* SERGIUS, *in an agony of mortification,*[22] *sinks on the ottoman, clutching his averted head between his fists.*)   I told you you were getting the worst of it, Saranoff.

SERGIUS.   Tiger cat!

RAINA.   (*Running excitedly to* BLUNTSCHLI.)   You hear this man calling me names, Captain Bluntschli?

BLUNTSCHLI.   What else can he do, dear lady? He must defend himself somehow. Come (*Very persuasively.*), don't quarrel. What good does it do?

> (RAINA, *with a gasp, sits down on the ottoman, and after a vain effort to look vexedly at* BLUNTSCHLI, *she falls a victim to her sense of humor, and is attacked with a disposition to laugh.*)

SERGIUS.   Engaged to Nicola! (*He rises.*) Ha! ha! (*Going to the stove and standing with his back to it.*) Ah, well, Bluntschli, you are right to take this huge imposture [23] of a world coolly.

RAINA.   (*To* BLUNTSCHLI *with an intuitive* [24] *guess at his state of mind.*) I daresay you think us a couple of grown-up babies, don't you?

SERGIUS.   (*Grinning a little.*)   He does, he does. Swiss civilization nursetending Bulgarian barbarism, eh?

BLUNTSCHLI.   (*Blushing.*)   Not at all, I assure you. I'm only very glad to get you two quieted. There now, let's be pleasant and talk it over in a friendly way. Where is this other young lady?

RAINA.   Listening at the door, probably.

SERGIUS.   (*Shivering as if a bullet had struck him, and speaking with quiet but deep indignation.*)   I will prove that that, at least, is a calumny.[25] (*He goes with dignity to the door and opens it. A yell of fury bursts from him as he looks out. He darts into the passage, and returns dragging in* LOUKA, *whom he flings against the table, as he cries:*) Judge her, Bluntschli—you, the moderate, cautious man, judge the eavesdropper.

22. **mortfication:** humiliation; shame.
23. **imposture:** deception.
24. **intuitive:** instinctive.
25. **calumny** (kal′əm·nē) : lie.

(LOUKA *stands her ground, proud and silent.*)

BLUNTSCHLI. (*Shaking his head.*)   I mustn't judge her. I once listened myself outside a tent when there was a mutiny brewing. It's all a question of the degree of provocation. My life was at stake.

LOUKA.   My love was at stake. (SERGIUS *flinches, ashamed of her in spite of himself.*) I am not ashamed.

RAINA. (*Contemptuously.*)   Your love! Your curiosity, you mean.

LOUKA. (*Facing her and returning her contempt with interest.*)   My love, stronger than anything you can feel, even for your chocolate-cream soldier.

SERGIUS. (*With quick suspicion—to* LOUKA.)   What does that mean?

LOUKA. (*Fiercely.*)   It means—

SERGIUS. (*Interrupting her slightingly.*)   Oh, I remember, the ice pudding. A paltry [26] taunt, girl.

(MAJOR PETKOFF *enters, in his shirtsleeves.*)

PETKOFF.   Excuse my shirtsleeves, gentlemen. Raina, somebody has been wearing that coat of mine, I'll swear it—somebody with bigger shoulders than mine. It's all burst open at the back. Your mother is mending it. I wish she'd make haste. I shall catch cold. (*He looks more attentively at them.*) Is anything the matter?

RAINA.   No. (*She sits down at the stove with a tranquil air.*)

SERGIUS.   Oh, no! (*He sits down at the end of the table, as at first.*)

BLUNTSCHLI. (*Who is already seated.*)   Nothing, nothing.

PETKOFF. (*Sitting down on the ottoman in his old place.*)   That's all right. (*He notices* LOUKA.) Anything the matter, Louka?

LOUKA.   No, sir.

PETKOFF. (*Genially.*)   That's all right. (*He sneezes.*) Go and ask your mistress for my coat, like a good girl, will you? (*She turns to obey; but* NICOLA *enters with the coat; and she makes a pretense of having business in the room by taking the little table with the hookah away to the wall near the windows.*)

RAINA. (*Rising quickly, as she sees the coat on* NICOLA's *arm.*)   Here it is, Papa. Give it to me, Nicola; and do you put some more wood on the fire. (*She takes the coat, and brings it to the* MAJOR, *who stands up to put it on.* NICOLA *attends to the fire.*)

PETKOFF. (*To* RAINA, *teasing her affectionately.*)   Aha! Going to be very good to poor old papa just for one day after his return from the wars, eh?

26. **paltry:** trivial; petty.

RAINA. (*With solemn reproach.*)   Ah, how can you say that to me, Father?

PETKOFF.   Well, well, only a joke, little one. Come, give me a kiss. (*She kisses him.*) Now give me the coat.

RAINA.   Now, I am going to put it on for you. Turn your back. (*He turns his back and feels behind him with his arms for the sleeves. She dexterously takes the photograph from the pocket and throws it on the table before* BLUNTSCHLI, *who covers it with a sheet of paper under the very nose of* SERGIUS, *who looks on amazed, with his suspicions roused in the highest degree. She then helps* PETKOFF *on with his coat.*) There, dear! Now are you comfortable?

PETKOFF.   Quite, little love. Thanks. (*He sits down; and* RAINA *returns to her seat near the stove.*) Oh, by the bye, I've found something funny. What's the meaning of this? (*He puts his hand into the picked pocket.*) Eh? Hello! (*He tries the other pocket.*) Well, I could have sworn— (*Much puzzled, he tries the breast pocket.*) I wonder— (*Tries the original pocket.*) where can it— (*A light flashes on him; he rises, exclaiming.*) Your mother's taken it.

RAINA. (*Very red.*)   Taken what?

PETKOFF.   Your photograph, with the inscription: "Raina, to her Chocolate-Cream Soldier—a souvenir." Now you know there's something more in this than meets the eye; and I'm going to find it out. (*Shouting.*) Nicola!

NICOLA. (*Dropping a log, and turning.*)   Sir!

PETKOFF.   Did you spoil any pastry of Miss Raina's this morning?

NICOLA.   You heard Miss Raina say that I did, sir.

PETKOFF.   I know that, you idiot. Was it true?

NICOLA.   I am sure Miss Raina is incapable of saying anything that is not true, sir.

PETKOFF.   Are you? Then I'm not. (*Turning to the others.*) Come, do you think I don't see it all? (*Goes to* SERGIUS, *and slaps him on the shoulder.*) Sergius, you're the chocolate-cream soldier, aren't you?

SERGIUS. (*Starting up.*)   I! A chocolate-cream soldier! Certainly not.

PETKOFF.   Not! (*He looks at them. They are all very serious and very conscious.*) Do you mean to tell me that Raina sends photographic souvenirs to other men?

SERGIUS. (*Enigmatically.*[27])   The world is not such an innocent place as we used to think, Petkoff.

---

27. **Enigmatically** (en'·ig·mat'i·kəl·lē): mysteriously; intending to puzzle.

BLUNTSCHLI. (*Rising.*)   It's all right, Major. I'm the chocolate-cream soldier. (PETKOFF *and* SERGIUS *are equally astonished.*) The gracious young lady saved my life by giving me chocolate creams when I was starving—shall I ever forget their flavor! My late friend Stolz told you the story at Peerot. I was the fugitive.

PETKOFF.   You! (*He gasps.*) Sergius, do you remember how those two women went on this morning when we mentioned it? (SERGIUS *smiles cynically.* PETKOFF *confronts* RAINA *severely.*) You're a nice young woman, aren't you?

RAINA. (*Bitterly.*)   Major Saranoff has changed his mind. And when I wrote that on the photograph, I did not know that Captain Bluntschli was married.

BLUNTSCHLI. (*Much startled, protesting vehemently.*)   I'm not married.

RAINA. (*With deep reproach.*)   You said you were.

BLUNTSCHLI.   I did not. I positively did not. I never was married in my life.

PETKOFF. (*Exasperated.*)   Raina, will you kindly inform me, if I am not asking too much, which gentleman you are engaged to?

RAINA.   To neither of them. This young lady (*Introducing Louka, who faces them all proudly.*), is the object of Major Saranoff's affections at present.

PETKOFF.   Louka! Are you mad, Sergius? Why this girl's engaged to Nicola.

NICOLA. (*Coming forward.*)   I beg your pardon, sir. There is a mistake. Louka is not engaged to me.

PETKOFF.   Not engaged to you, you scoundrel! Why, you had twenty-five levas from me on the day of your betrothal; and she had that gilt bracelet from Miss Raina.

NICOLA. (*With cool unction.*[28])   We gave it out so, sir. But it was only to give Louka protection. She had a soul above her station; and I have been no more than her confidential servant. I intend, as you know, sir, to set up a shop later on in Sofia; and I look forward to her custom and recommendation should she marry into the nobility. (*He goes out with impressive discretion, leaving them all staring after him.*)

PETKOFF. (*Breaking the silence.*)   Well, I am—hm!

SERGIUS.   This is either the finest heroism or the most crawling baseness. Which is it, Bluntschli?

28. **With . . . unction:** oily-tongued. *Unction* denotes smug pretense of moral fervor.

BLUNTSCHLI.   Never mind whether it's heroism or baseness. Nicola's the ablest man I've met in Bulgaria. I'll make him manager of a hotel if he can speak French and German.

LOUKA. (*Suddenly breaking out at* SERGIUS.)   I have been insulted by everyone here. You set them the example. You owe me an apology. (SERGIUS *immediately, like a repeating clock of which the spring has been touched, begins to fold his arms.*)

BLUNTSCHLI. (*Before he can speak.*)   It's no use. He never apologizes.

LOUKA.   Not to you, his equal and his enemy. To me, his poor servant, he will not refuse to apologize.

SERGIUS. (*Approvingly.*)   You are right. (*He bends his knee in his grandest manner.*) Forgive me!

LOUKA.   I forgive you. (*She timidly gives him her hand, which he kisses.*) That touch makes me your affianced wife.

SERGIUS. (*Springing up.*)   Ah, I forgot that!

LOUKA. (*Coldly.*)   You can withdraw if you like.

SERGIUS.   Withdraw! Never! You belong to me! (*He puts his arm about her and draws her to him.*)

(CATHERINE *comes in and finds* LOUKA *in* SERGIUS's *arms, and all the rest gazing at them in bewildered astonishment.*)

CATHERINE.   What does this mean? (SERGIUS *releases* LOUKA.)

PETKOFF.   Well, my dear, it appears that Sergius is going to marry Louka instead of Raina. (*She is about to break out indignantly at him; he stops her by exclaiming testily.*) Don't blame me; I've nothing to do with it. (*He retreats to the stove.*)

CATHERINE.   Marry Louka! Sergius, you are bound by your word to us!

SERGIUS. (*Folding his arms.*)   Nothing binds me.

BLUNTSCHLI. (*Much pleased by this piece of common sense.*)   Saranoff, your hand. My congratulations. These heroics of yours have their practical side after all. (*To* LOUKA.) Gracious young lady, the best wishes of a good Republican! [29] (*He kisses her hand, to* RAINA's *great disgust.*)

CATHERINE. (*Threateningly.*)   Louka, you have been telling stories.

LOUKA.   I have done Raina no harm.

CATHERINE. (*Haughtily.*)   Raina! (RAINA *is equally indignant at the liberty.*)

---

29. **Republican:** *here*, one who believes in government by the people.

LOUKA.   I have a right to call her Raina; she calls me Louka. I told Major Saranoff she would never marry him if the Swiss gentleman came back.

BLUNTSCHLI. (*Surprised.*)   Hello!

LOUKA. (*Turning to* RAINA.)   I thought you were fonder of him than of Sergius. You know best whether I was right.

BLUNTSCHLI.   What nonsense! I assure you, my dear Major, my dear Madam, the gracious young lady simply saved my life, nothing else. She never cared two straws for me. Why, bless my heart and soul, look at the young lady and look at me. She, rich, young, beautiful, with her imagination full of fairy princes and noble natures and cavalry charges and goodness knows what! And I, a commonplace Swiss soldier who hardly knows what a decent life is after fifteen years of barracks and battles—a vagabond—a man who has spoiled all his chances in life through an incurably romantic disposition—a man—

SERGIUS. (*Starting as if a needle has pricked him and interrupting* BLUNTSCHLI *in incredulous amazement.*)   Excuse me, Bluntschli, what did you say had spoiled your chances in life?

BLUNTSCHLI. (*Promptly.*)   An incurably romantic disposition. I ran away from home twice when I was a boy. I went into the army instead of into my father's business. I climbed the balcony of this house when a man of sense would have dived into the nearest cellar. I came sneaking back here to have another look at the young lady when any other man of my age would have sent the coat back—

PETKOFF.   My coat!

BLUNTSCHLI.   —Yes, that's the coat I mean—would have sent it back and gone quietly home. Do you suppose I am the sort of fellow a young girl falls in love with? Why, look at our ages! I'm thirty-four; I don't suppose the young lady is much over seventeen. (*This estimate produces a marked sensation, all the rest turning and staring at one another. He proceeds innocently.*) All that adventure which was life or death to me, was only a schoolgirl's game to her—chocolate creams and hide and seek. Here's the proof! (*He takes the photograph from the table.*) Now, I ask you, would a woman who took the affair seriously have sent me this and written on it: "Raina, to her Chocolate-Cream soldier—a souvenir"? (*He exhibits the photograph triumphantly, as if it settled the matter beyond all possibility of refutation.*)

PETKOFF.   That's what I was looking for. How the deuce did it get there?

BLUNTSCHLI.   (*To* RAINA *complacently*.)   I have put everything right, I hope, gracious young lady!

RAINA.   (*In uncontrollable vexation.*)   I quite agree with your account of yourself. You are a romantic idiot. (BLUNTSCHLI *is unspeakably taken aback.*) Next time I hope you will know the difference between a schoolgirl of seventeen and a woman of twenty-three.

BLUNTSCHLI.   (*Stupefied.*)   Twenty-three! (*She snaps the photograph contemptuously from his hand; tears it across; and throws the pieces at his feet.*)

SERGIUS.   (*With grim enjoyment of* BLUNTSCHLI's *discomfiture.*) Bluntschli, my one last belief is gone. Your sagacity [30] is a fraud, like all the other things. You have less sense than even I have.

BLUNTSCHLI.   (*Overwhelmed.*)   Twenty-three! Twenty-three!! (*He considers.*) Hm! (*Swiftly making up his mind.*) In that case, Major Petkoff, I beg to propose formally to become a suitor for your daughter's hand, in place of Major Saranoff retired.

RAINA.   You dare!

BLUNTSCHLI.   If you were twenty-three when you said those things to me this afternoon, I shall take them seriously.

CATHERINE.   (*Loftily polite.*)   I doubt, sir, whether you quite realize either my daughter's position or that of Major Sergius Saranoff, whose place you propose to take. The Petkoffs and the Saranoffs are known as the richest and most important families in the country. Our position is almost historical; we can go back for nearly twenty years.

PETKOFF.   Oh, never mind that, Catherine. (*To* BLUNTSCHLI.) We should be most happy, Bluntschli, if it were only a question of your position; but hang it, you know, Raina is accustomed to a very comfortable establishment. Sergius keeps twenty horses.

BLUNTSCHLI.   But what on earth is the use of twenty horses? Why, it's a circus.

CATHERINE.   (*Severely.*)   My daughter, sir, is accustomed to a first-rate stable.

RAINA.   Hush, Mother, you're making me ridiculous.

BLUNTSCHLI.   Oh, well, if it comes to a question of an establishment,

30. **sagacity:** wisdom.

here goes! (*He goes impetuously to the table and seizes the papers in the blue envelope.*) How many horses did you say?

SERGIUS.   Twenty, noble Switzer!

BLUNTSCHLI.   I have two hundred horses. (*They are amazed.*) How many carriages?

SERGIUS.   Three.

BLUNTSCHLI.   I have seventy. Twenty-four of them will hold twelve inside, besides two on the box, without counting the driver and conductor. How many tablecloths have you?

SERGIUS.   How the deuce do I know?

BLUNTSCHLI.   Have you four thousand?

SERGIUS.   No.

BLUNTSCHLI.   I have. I have nine thousand, six hundred pairs of sheets and blankets, with two thousand, four hundred eiderdown quilts. I have ten thousand knives and forks, and the same quantity of dessert spoons. I have six hundred servants. I have six palatial establishments, besides two livery stables, a tea garden and a private house. I have four medals for distinguished services; I have the rank of an officer and the standing of a gentleman; and I have three native languages. Show me any man in Bulgaria that can offer as much.

PETKOFF. (*With childish awe.*)   Are you Emperor of Switzerland?

BLUNTSCHLI.   My rank is the highest known in Switzerland. I'm a free citizen.

CATHERINE.   Then Captain Bluntschli, since you are my daughter's choice, I shall not stand in the way of her happiness. (PETKOFF *is about to speak.*) That is Major Petkoff's feeling also.

PETKOFF.   Oh, I shall be only too glad. Two hundred horses! Whew!

SERGIUS.   What says the lady?

RAINA. (*Pretending to sulk.*)   The lady says that he can keep his tablecloths and his omnibuses. I am not here to be sold to the highest bidder.

BLUNTSCHLI.   I won't take that answer. I appealed to you as a fugitive, a beggar, and a starving man. You accepted me. You gave me your hand to kiss, your bed to sleep in, and your roof to shelter me—

RAINA. (*Interrupting him.*)   I did not give them to the Emperor of Switzerland!

BLUNTSCHLI.   That's just what I say. (*He catches her hand quickly and looks her straight in the face as he adds, with confident mastery.*) Now tell us who you did give them to.

RAINA. (*Succumbing with a shy smile.*)   To my chocolate-cream soldier!

BLUNTSCHLI. (*With a boyish laugh of delight.*)   That'll do. Thank you. (*Looks at his watch and suddenly becomes businesslike.*) Time's up, Major. You've managed those regiments so well that you are sure to be asked to get rid of some of the Infantry of the Teemok division. Send them home by way of Lom Palanka. Saranoff, don't get married until I come back. I shall be here punctually at five in the evening on Tuesday fortnight.[31] Gracious ladies, —good evening. (*He makes them a military bow, and goes.*)

SERGIUS.   What a man! What a man!

Curtain.

31. **Tuesday fortnight:** two weeks from next Tuesday.

Meaning and Method: Act III

1. Act III opens with Bluntschli and Sergius working together. What is their relationship? What does this show about the difference between a professional soldier and the "heroic" one? How do the position and behavior of the other characters in the room reflect their personalities?
2. When Raina and Bluntschli are alone, the conversation turns to the subject of lying. In what way does Bluntschli once again prove himself a "realist" in his opinions? How does Raina continue to play a false role? When she finally shows her true self to Bluntschli, how does he react? What quality does their relationship finally have that Raina's and Sergius's does not?
3. Each scene between Sergius and Louka has emphasized the superior physical strength of Sergius. In Act III, how does Louka show that in the art of love it is she who is stronger in the sense that she is the superior strategist?
4. After challenging Bluntschli to a duel, Sergius withdraws, telling him: "You're not a man; you're a machine" (page 163). In what way might this statement be more applicable to Sergius himself than to Bluntschli?
5. How can Bluntschli be said to be outwardly a realist and inwardly a romantic? In what way is the name *Bluntschli* a clue to his character?
6. What do we learn of Raina in this act? Does she have a sense of humor? Is she honest in her self-discovery? Is she merely a product of her breeding and environment? Have you changed your opinion of her? Why or why not?

7. How do Petkoff's coat, Raina's photograph, and the threat of a duel add to the humor of Act III? What purpose is served by these props and devices? Could they be omitted from the play?

8. Some critics have said that Louka is typical of Shaw's designing women. Do you think Louka is "a designing woman"? Or is she an honest, straightforward girl who falls in love with someone from a higher class?

9. Instead of ending the play with Bluntschli's statement, "That'll do. Thank you," after Raina says she had given the candy to her chocolate-cream soldier, Shaw gives Bluntschli some additional dialogue. How is this additional dialogue in keeping with Bluntschli's character? What would have been the effect had Shaw ended the play with "That'll do. Thank you."?

Meaning and Method: On the Play as a Whole

1. Shaw called his play a "romantic comedy." He used the word *romantic* in the sense that boy meets girl, they fall in love, and they live happily ever after. After reading the play, would you call it romantic in this sense, or are there more elements in it that might be termed anti-romantic or realistic? Explain.

2. What is the setting of the play? Would you say that it is romantic or realistic? In what way do the sets contribute to the comedy?

3. Are the hero and the villain clearly identified in *Arms and the Man*? May Bluntschli, who is the key figure in the play, be considered the hero, and Sergius the villain? Why or why not? Or is this a play in which one must refer to the protagonist and the antagonist because there are neither heroes nor villains? Explain.

4. Point out the exposition, the rising action, the climax, and the falling or resulting action (or dénouement) in the play. In giving your answers, make specific references to the text.

5. What do Nicola and Bluntschli have in common? What do Louka and Raina have in common? In what way does the relationship of the two servants to each other form the basis of the subplot? How does this subplot also serve to intensify a clash of ideals in the play? What do the relationships among these four show about Shaw's attitude toward the class system? What is the climax of the subplot? Does this climax correspond to the climax of the main plot? Explain.

6. The title of the play is a translation of the first two words of the *Aeneid* (i·nē′id), a Latin epic poem written between the years 30 to 19 B.C., in which the author, Vergil, celebrates Rome from the founding of the city to the full expansion of the Empire. The epic glorifies martial exploits and military heroes. Shaw, in taking his title from this epic, is mocking and satirizing war and the heroism and resulting romanticism usually associated with war. Point out as many passages

as you can find in the play that show Shaw's point of view. Is this an anti-war play? Could it influence an individual to fight or not to fight? Is it still timely today?

7. In Act III, Sergius sums up Bluntschli's relationship to the rest of the characters in the play with the sentiment "Swiss civilization nursetending Bulgarian barbarism" (page 164). What are the so-called signs of civilization that Shaw satirizes in the play? How does Shaw also make fun of the Petkoffs as typical of the *nouveaux riches*? What signs of the modern era does Shaw seem to look favorably upon? In giving your answers, make specific references to the text.

8. Which of the two major strains or motifs—romanticism or realism—seem to prevail in the play? Which traits of character does Shaw use to distinguish the romantics from the realists? What is the theme of the play?

9. Shaw has written elaborate and detailed stage directions for *Arms and the Man*. What do you think his purpose was in doing so? What help are they to the reader of the play? What value do they have for the director of a production of the play? Are there ways in which they could be a hindrance to an actor or director? Explain.

10. One definition of comedy is that it deals with the actions of men insofar as they fall short of what they should or could be. In what way does the comedy of *Arms and the Man* conform to this definition? The author of comedy often demonstrates that he is a realist by his awareness of the actual and by his unwillingness to deceive himself, even when striving for the ideal or the perfect society. In what way does Shaw seem to be this kind of realist? What specific contrasts between the ideal and the actual does Shaw set up? On the basis of this play, what do you think would be Shaw's perfect society?

11. Is the play realistic in terms of the events that occur? In answering this question, consider Bluntschli's escape into Raina's room, the officer's search for him, his return of the coat, the picture in its pocket, and so forth. Does the plot rely too much on coincidence? Would one realistically expect Sergius to marry the maid and Bluntschli to marry Raina?

Comedy often involves exaggeration of types and qualities with which the audience is already familiar. How much exaggeration is there in the play? Can exaggeration and realism go hand in hand? Can there be comedy without exaggeration? Discuss.

Composition and Discussion

1. You are the casting director for *Arms and the Man*. Write a "Help Wanted" paragraph for your school newspaper designed to attract potential actors and actresses to try out for parts. Include physical descriptions of the characters in the play, but place the greatest emphasis on the types of personalities your eight future actors must create in order to portray the roles as Shaw intended them.

2. Write a character sketch of Major Petkoff or Catherine. Review the methods of characterization (*see* "Character and Characterization" in the Glossary), and then base your sketch on details from the play.

3. Write a composition in which you compare and contrast the attitudes of Raina and Bluntschli toward heroism, war, business, education, manners, and love.

4. Some critics have pointed out that in many of his plays Shaw has made his women characters stronger than his men. Does this seem to be true in *Arms and the Man?* Do Raina, Catherine, and Louka have stronger, more decisive personalities than Sergius, Petkoff, and Nicola? State your reasons in a composition in which you compare and contrast each of the three sets of characters. Use a separate paragraph for each pair of characters.

5. Shaw, in one of his essays, defines an *ideal* as "a fancy picture" invented "as a mask for reality." Is Shaw's definition the only meaning of *idealism?* First consult a dictionary. Then discuss, giving examples of events or persons demonstrating a different meaning of idealism.

6. *The characters in* Arms and the Man *and their "unrealistic" attitude toward war, love, and social position do actually exist, even today.* Using this as a topic sentence, write a composition agreeing or disagreeing with this statement. Support your opinion with examples from newspaper stories, magazine accounts, biographies, personal friends, and acquaintances.

7. Some critics have objected that Shaw's characters are not individuals but rather stereotyped instruments through which Shaw gives his political, religious, and social beliefs. Do you think this is true of *Arms and the Man?*

8. Another criticism of Shaw is that his ideas and suggestions were always destructive. Must a play have a constructive solution, either explicit or implied, for a problem? How could constructive suggestions have been made in *Arms and the Man?*

9. In 1908 a musical comedy was made from *Arms and the Man.* It was called *The Chocolate Soldier,* with music by Oscar Straus.

Which episodes or situations do you think lend themselves to musical interpretations? For example, would you have Raina sing a song at the beginning or at the end of Act I? Why or why not? If yes, what kind of song?

10. Shaw's references to Russian and Austrian officers concern the practice then of the training of officers and troops of Bulgaria and Serbia by Russia and Austria. What are some parallels with the present? What are the reasons—honorable and/or dishonorable—for such practices? What are the benefits and the dangers?

JULIUS CAESAR

William Shakespeare

[1564–1616]

> *How many ages hence*
> *Shall this our lofty scene be acted over*
> *In states unborn and accents yet unknown!*

When William Shakespeare wrote these lines for *Julius Caesar* in 1599, he could not have realized how prophetic they would turn out to be. They represent an accurate prediction of the future, not only of the "lofty scene" in *Julius Caesar,* but of most of Shakespeare's other plays as well. Whether it's the history play *Richard III* in London, the Russian film version of the tragedy of *Hamlet* in Moscow, or the comedy *A Midsummer Night's Dream* on television in the United States, audiences around the world—by now truly "many ages hence" from the year 1599 and speaking in many "accents yet unknown" to Shakespeare—are still fascinated, delighted, and moved by the works of England's greatest playwright.

Although Shakespeare was a popular writer during his lifetime, only a few small nuggets of hard fact about his life have come down to us, for biography was then limited to the aristocracy and those who had made their names in affairs of state. But gradually over the past three hundred years numerous small scraps of information have been gathered from legal documents and diaries that have been found in dusty files, and from records of churches, libraries, and municipal buildings. From these bits and pieces, scholars have put together an adequate, although partial, account of Shakespeare's life.

William Shakespeare was born in April, 1564, in the small village of Stratford-on-Avon, about eighty miles north of London. His father,

John Shakespeare, was a middle-class merchant in the glove-making trade. At the age of eighteen, Shakespeare married Anne Hathaway, the daughter of a neighboring farmer. Church records show that they had three children.

Of Shakespeare's life between 1585, three years after his marriage, and the early 1590's when he is noticed as an actor and playwright in London, there is no clear record. It is these years for which scholars have been unable to account, and which have given rise, therefore, to the greatest amount of speculation. Exactly when Shakespeare left Stratford, for instance, is a mystery—and why he left is a matter equally dark. All that is clearly known is that the young man, who probably had no more formal education than elementary school, is the same man who, by 1594, was recognized and admired as a new talent in the London theater. By the late 1590's Shakespeare was part owner of the *Globe*, the theater built in cooperation with fellow shareholders in the acting company. His share of the profits of the company was evidently financially rewarding, for the record of those years shows that he made substantial real-estate purchases in Stratford.

The following years, from 1599 to 1606, are those during which Shakespeare wrote his greatest tragedies—*Hamlet, Othello, Macbeth*, and *King Lear*. During those same years Shakespeare's company was appointed the King's Men, personal favorites of King James I. Like Queen Elizabeth, Queen of England from 1558 to 1603, James enjoyed the theater. The love these two successive monarchs had for the theater protected and nurtured the development of Shakespeare and that of other talented contemporaries.

After 1606, Shakespeare gradually began to retire from the theater. By about 1610 he had settled once again into a comfortable house in Stratford, to live there quietly the rest of his days. The register of the Stratford church shows that "Will. Shakespeare, gent" was buried on April 25, 1616, while the small monument in the church has inscribed on it the date April 23. Still preserved in all its detail, Shakespeare's will carefully divides his money and possessions, including such homely items as his "second-best bed," among his family and friends. His will does not mention, however, the most valuable legacy he left behind—37 plays, 154 sonnets, several long poems, and a number of short, beautiful songs.

In 1623 two surviving members of the King's Men—John Heminges and Henry Condell—gathered thirty-six of Shakespeare's plays, many of which had not before been printed, and published them in a collection now known as the *First Folio*. Were it not for the desire of these two friends to see Shakespeare's plays all together in print, more than half of the dramas might have been lost entirely.

Included in the *First Folio* is a short poem of tribute by Ben Jonson, a friend and also a leading playwright of his day. The opening line of his poem was prophetic: "He was not of an age, but for all time."

Elizabethan Theaters

The company of which Shakespeare was a prosperous working member had its own theater, the *Globe.* (*See* illustration opposite.) Since the kinds of plays that are written at any time or place are directly related to the audience and the kind of place in which they are performed, a few comments about the typical theater of the Elizabethan Period will be helpful.

The theaters were small. No spectator was more than fifty or sixty feet from the stage. It is easy to see that this would lead to acting styles quite different, for example, from the style used in a large school auditorium, in which it may be hard to hear all the way in the back, or in vast hall or opera house seating two thousand persons. In turn, in writing a play the Elizabethan playwright would, consciously or unconsciously, take into consideration the physical relationship between the actors and the audience. He would know that the audience could hear every word, that it could see every nuance of facial expression.

The platform stage of the Elizabethans was quite different from the stage most of us have become accustomed to today. The most common stage in this country right now is a rather boxlike affair with a curtain that can be lowered to separate the audience from the stage. In most of our theaters, the stage is somewhat like a framed picture, frequently with a painted canvas flat on the back wall—the *backdrop.*

The Elizabethan stage, in contrast, was essentially a simple platform that came out into the audience. Theater buildings themselves were either octagonal or round, not rectangular as most of ours are. Tiers of covered galleries (or balconies) went around the inner walls of the building, except for the portion where the stage, or platform, jutted out. Those who paid the least stood on the ground on all three sides of the platform. (One can see why these playgoers were called *groundlings.*) For an extra fee, one could sit in the balconies.

A sketch of The Globe Theater, where most of Shakespeare's plays were probably produced at one time or another.

On the back wall, behind the platform on which the actors performed, were one, two, or even three balconies. Scenes could be played on any one of them, or one character on a balcony could speak down to another on the main platform. Thus was played the *Romeo and Juliet* scenes in which Juliet—on the balcony—speaks to Romeo, in the garden.

Also along the back wall, under the center balcony, was an *inner stage*, which had a curtain that could be opened or closed. Early stage directions show us that this inner stage represented, in *Romeo and Juliet*, Juliet's bedroom, Friar Laurence's cell, the ballroom where Capulet's guests are dancing, as well as several other places.

The most important thing to note about the physical characteristics of the Elizabethan stage is that they did not change, no matter what play was performed. There was no backdrop. There was no attempt at all to make one place look like a garden and another like a battlefield, or to give to one the characteristics of a street and to another those of a ballroom. The only light was daylight, and all atmosphere came from the dialogue and not from clever lighting.

The second important difference to notice is that there was no curtain separating the audience from the stage and the actors on it. Acts and scenes flowed into one another, with no breaks or intermissions. The actors moved onto or left the platform by means of doors that were also set along the back wall.

But if there were no *sets* used to give an illusion of a specific place, there were quite elaborate costumes and stage properties, or *props*. Chairs or stools suggested a tavern. A tree could represent a forest. The props of one company in 1598 included a cage, three tombs, a bed, a lion's skin, a coffin, a dragon, a horse, a black dog, and a realistic device for beheading. Costumes were magnificent and beautiful, with a large wardrobe kept on hand and at least a few new costumes added for each production.

Acting Companies

The Elizabethan acting companies were permanent companies, what we today would call "repertory" companies. Unlike the majority of our stage, television, or movie groups, which hire new actors and actresses, new directors, and new backstage people for each new play, the group of people in an acting company in Shakespeare's day usually stayed together for many years. Shakespeare was a member of an acting company, wrote plays for them, and probably acted in and directed his own plays and those of others.

One advantage of such permanent companies is that they have constant practice in performing, and members can help one another improve in craft. Members can also earn a regular living, as Shakespeare did. Hits can absorb flops, and therefore many more plays can be tried. The playwright, in turn, with a ready market for his work, is likely to write more plays. And an additional effect of permanent companies was that parts were often written with the physical appearance and talents of particular actors in mind. Thus, in three romantic comedies written within a few months of one another—*Much Ado About Nothing*, *As You Like It*, and *Twelfth Night*—one of the women is always small. In *As You Like It*, it is Celia who is "low and browner than her brother."

There were no women in Shakespeare's company—nor in any other company of the time. Young boys whose voices had not yet changed were costumed and wigged for the parts of girls and women. Although we may be skeptical, the evidence is that contemporary audiences found their performances convincing.

The Tragedy of Julius Caesar

By the time Shakespeare wrote *The Tragedy of Julius Caesar*, he had already created his famous history plays based on the lives of English monarchs. Like *Julius Caesar*, these plays grew from actual events. To take a plot from historical chronicle was common practice at the time. Indeed, the whole idea of "original" stories, so dear to the twentieth century, was entirely foreign to the sixteenth and seventeenth centuries.

The story of Julius Caesar had often been repeated in poem, story, and play, but Shakespeare's basic source was primarily an English translation of a Latin work called *The Lives of the Noble Grecians and Romans by that eminent historiographer and philosopher, Plutarch of Chaeronea*. Better known as Plutarch's *Lives*, it contains a series of biographical and psychological studies of great men of the ancient world. Plutarch's studies of Julius Caesar, Marcus Brutus, and Marcus Antonius—key figures in the tragedy—provided Shakespeare with a rich source of information and interpretation. Shakespeare's task was to transform this data into drama—that is, into words and actions to be performed by actors on a stage. Complex historical events that had occurred over a period of many months had to be selected and compressed into a play of a few hours length. A point of view interpreting the reasons behind the actions had to be established.

Modern historians attempt to be objective and unbiased, although in varying degrees all history is interpretation. The dramatist, on the other hand, often is valued insofar as he *has* a bias, a point of view. When Shakespeare chose to add an incident, omit another, and change a third in *Julius Caesar*, he did so. A comparison, for example, of Plutarch's account of Mark Antony's funeral oration with that written by Shakespeare shows that Plutarch mentions only that Antony spoke to the common people and made them violent. From this brief clue Shakespeare created the powerful speech beginning, "Friends, Romans, countrymen, lend me your ears. I come to bury

Caesar, not to praise him." So authentic a political speech does it sound, and so famous has it become, that many people have come to believe that it was one actually made by Mark Antony. Such insights serve Shakespeare well. Some historians have seen Caesar as a vicious Hitler-type dictator; others as a great military and political hero. Shakespeare's interpretation—one of many that have come down to us—is still valuable and convincing because he saw behind the historical event to the hearts and motivations of his characters.

CHARACTERS

Julius Caesar

Octavius Caesar
Marcus Antonius } triumvirs after Caesar's death
M. Aemilius Lepidus

Cicero
Publius } Senators
Popilius Lena

Marcus Brutus
Cassius
Casca
Trebonius conspirators against Julius Caesar
Ligarius
Decius Brutus
Metellus Cimber
Cinna

Flavius } tribunes of
Marullus } the people

Artemidorus of Cnidos,
a teacher of rhetoric

A Soothsayer

Cinna,
a poet

Another Poet

Lucilius
Titinius friends of
Messala } Brutus and
Young Cato Cassius
Volumnius

Varro
Clitus
Claudius } servants of Brutus
Strato
Lucius
Dardanius

Pindarus,
servant of Cassius

Calpurnia,
wife of Caesar

Portia,
wife of Brutus

Senators, Citizens, Guards, and **Attendants**

Place.   During a great part of the play, at Rome; afterward at Sardis, in Asia Minor, and near Philippi, in Macedonia.

Act I

(*Enter* FLAVIUS, MARULLUS, *and certain* COMMONERS.)

FLAVIUS.   Hence! Home, you idle creatures, get you home!
    Is this a holiday? What! Know you not,
    Being mechanical,° you ought not walk
    Upon a laboring day without the sign°
    Of your profession? Speak, what trade art thou?   5
CARPENTER.   Why, sir, a carpenter.
MARULLUS.   Where is thy leather apron and thy rule?
    What dost thou with the best apparel on?
    You, sir, what trade are you?
COBBLER.   Truly, sir, in respect of a fine workman,° I am but,   10
    as you would say, a cobbler°
MARULLUS.   But what trade art thou? Answer me directly.
COBBLER.   A trade, sir, that I hope I may use with a safe con-
    science; which is, indeed, sir, a mender of bad soles.°
MARULLUS.   What trade, thou knave? Thou naughty knave,   15
    what trade?
COBBLER.   Nay, I beseech you, sir, be not out with me. Yet if
    you be out,° sir, I can mend you.
MARULLUS.   What mean'st thou by that? Mend me, thou saucy
    fellow!   20
COBBLER.   Why, sir, cobble you.
FLAVIUS.   Thou art a cobbler, art thou?
COBBLER.   Truly, sir, all that I live by is with the awl.° I meddle
    with no tradesman's matters, nor women's matters, but
    with awl. I am, indeed, sir, a surgeon to old shoes. When   25
    they are in great danger, I recover them. As proper° men as
    ever trod upon neat's leather° have gone upon my handi-
    work.

---

3. mechanical: workingmen. **4. sign:** tools and working clothes. **10. in respect
. . . workman:** so far as fine work is concerned. **11. cobbler:** a shoemaker. It may
also mean a bungler. **14. soles:** a pun on "sole" and "soul." **17–18. out . . . out:**
The first meaning of *out* is "angry," or "put out." The second *out*, a pun, is
used in the sense that one says a sleeve is "out" at the elbow, or the bridge is
"out." **23. awl:** a tool for piercing small holes in leather. The cobbler is having
fun punning at the expense of Marullus and Flavius. **26. proper:** handsome.
27. neat's leather: oxhide.

FLAVIUS.   But wherefore art not in thy shop today?
    Why dost thou lead these men about the streets?   30

COBBLER.   Truly, sir, to wear out their shoes, to get myself into
    more work. But, indeed, sir, we make holiday, to see Caesar
    and to rejoice in his triumph.°

MARULLUS.   Wherefore rejoice? What conquest brings he
    home?
    What tributaries° follow him to Rome,   35
    To grace in captive bonds his chariot wheels?
    You blocks, you stones, you worse than senseless things!
    O you hard hearts, you cruel men of Rome,
    Knew you not Pompey? Many a time and oft
    Have you climbed up to walls and battlements,   40
    To towers and windows, yea, to chimney tops,°
    Your infants in your arms, and there have sat
    The livelong day, with patient expectation,
    To see great Pompey pass the streets of Rome.
    And when you saw his chariot but appear,   45
    Have you not made a universal shout,
    That Tiber° trembled underneath her banks
    To hear the replication° of your sounds
    Made in her concave shores?
    And do you now put on your best attire?   50
    And do you now cull out° a holiday?
    And do you now strew flowers in his way
    That comes in triumph over Pompey's blood?
    Be gone!
    Run to your houses, fall upon your knees,   55
    Pray to the gods to intermit° the plague
    That needs must light on this ingratitude.

FLAVIUS.   Go, go, good countrymen, and for this fault
    Assemble all the poor men of your sort.
    Draw them to Tiber banks and weep your tears   60
    Into the channel till the lowest stream
    Do kiss the most exalted shores of all.

---

33. triumph: Roman generals, after a victorious campaign, entered Rome in a triumphal procession. Caesar's triumph, however, was over a fellow Roman, Pompey. **35. tributaries:** captives. **41. chimney tops:** Throughout the play Shakespeare had in mind his own London rather than ancient Rome, where chimney tops did not exist. **47. Tiber:** The Tiber River runs through Rome. **48. replication:** echo. **51. cull out:** choose to take. **56. intermit:** omit; leave out.

(*Exeunt all the* COMMONERS.)

See whether their basest metal° be not moved;
They vanish tongue-tied in their guiltiness.
Go you down that way toward the Capitol;   65
This way will I. Disrobe the images,°
If you do find them decked with ceremonies.°
MARULLUS.   May we do so?
You know it is the feast of Lupercal.°
FLAVIUS.   It is no matter. Let no images   70
Be hung with Caesar's trophies. I'll about,
And drive away the vulgar from the streets.
So do you too, where you perceive them thick.
These growing feathers plucked from Caesar's wing
Will make him fly an ordinary pitch,°   75
Who else would soar above the view of men
And keep us all in servile fearfulness.   (*Exeunt.*)

63. metal: material or stuff of which they are made; "metal" and "mettle," considered as two different words today, were used as the same word in Shakespeare's day. **66. Disrobe the images:** Strip the statues. **67. ceremonies:** decorations. **69. Lupercal:** the festival of the Lupercalia, celebrated by the Romans on February fifteenth in honor of Lupercus, the patron god of agriculture. Part of the festivities included a ceremony in which young noblemen raced through the city, gently striking with leather thongs all women they encountered. This ritual was believed to ensure that Roman women would be able to bear children. **75. pitch:** flight (of a soaring hawk); a term used in falconry.

Meaning and Method: Act I, Scene 1

1. The first scene opens with lively comic word play and teasing between the tribunes and the workingmen. Yet there are serious undertones. What are they? Why have the workingmen taken the day off? Why are the tribunes, Flavius and Marullus, angry at them? What do the tribunes order them to do? How do the tribunes and the commoners seem to differ regarding Caesar and Pompey?

2. The plot of *Julius Caesar* is based on actual historical events. No historian, however, has recorded that a few workingmen met a couple of tribunes and punned and pretended to misunderstand them on the night Caesar reentered Rome. Such an opening, designed to give the audience the basic background information it needs to know, is called the *exposition*.

  If you recall the information the playwright has managed to impart in this scene, you will understand why it was invented. What is the information you have been given about the time and place in history in which the play is located and the attitudes of different classes toward Caesar and toward each other?

3. Throughout the play Shakespeare presents the characters as though they were Elizabethans, and Rome seems very much like London. At least one example of this appears in the constant punning in Scene 1, for punning and word play were a much-admired Elizabethan form of humor. Explain any one of the puns made by the Cobbler, showing exactly what the meanings are (*see* lines 17–18, 23).

4. When a writer—either intentionally or unintentionally—puts a person, place, or event into a wrong, especially into an earlier, time period, he has used what is known as an *anachronism*. The reference in line 41 to the existence of chimney tops in ancient Rome is an example of an anachronism. Notice others as you find them throughout the rest of the play.

SCENE 2. *A public place.*

(*A public square near the Forum. A flourish of trumpets announces the approach of* CAESAR. *A crowd of* COMMONERS *gathers quickly, among them a* SOOTH-SAYER.* *Enter* CAESAR, *his wife* CALPURNIA, PORTIA, DECIUS, CICERO, BRUTUS, CASSIUS, CASCA, *and* ANTONY, *stripped for running in the games.*)

CAESAR.   Calpurnia!
CASCA.   Peace, ho! Caesar speaks.

(*Music ceases.*)

CAESAR.   Calpurnia!
CALPURNIA.   Here, my lord.
CAESAR.   Stand you directly in Antonius' way,   5
      When he doth run his course. Antonius!
ANTONY.   Caesar, my lord?
CAESAR.   Forget not, in your speed, Antonius,
      To touch Calpurnia; for our elders say,
      The barren, touchèd in this holy chase,   10
      Shake off their sterile curse.
ANTONY.   I shall remember:
      When Caesar says "Do this," it is performed.

* **Soothsayer:** one who foretells the future.

CAESAR.   Set on; and leave no ceremony out.   (*Music.*)
SOOTHSAYER.   Caesar!
CAESAR.   Ha! Who calls?   15
CASCA.   Bid every noise be still; peace yet again!

(*Music ceases. The whole procession comes to a halt.*)

CAESAR.   Who is it in the press° that calls on me?
   I hear a tongue, shriller than all the music,
   Cry "Caesar!" Speak. Caesar is turned to hear.
SOOTHSAYER.   Beware the ides of March.°
CAESAR.   What man is that?   20
BRUTUS.   A soothsayer bids you beware the ides of March.
CAESAR.   Set him before me. Let me see his face.
CASSIUS.   Fellow, come from the throng. Look upon Caesar.
CAESAR.   What say'st thou to me now? Speak once again.
SOOTHSAYER.   Beware the ides of March.   25
CAESAR.   He is a dreamer. Let us leave him. Pass.

(*Sennet.† Exeunt all but* BRUTUS *and* CASSIUS.)

CASSIUS.   Will you go see the order of the course?
BRUTUS.   Not I.
CASSIUS.   I pray you, do.
BRUTUS.   I am not gamesome. I do lack some part   30
   Of that quick spirit that is in Antony.
   Let me not hinder, Cassius, your desires.
   I'll leave you.
CASSIUS.   Brutus, I do observe you now of late.
   I have not from your eyes that gentleness   35
   And show of love as I was wont to have.
   You bear too stubborn and too strange a hand
   Over your friend that loves you.
BRUTUS.   Cassius,
   Be not deceived. If I have veiled my look,
   I turn the trouble of my countenance   40
   Merely upon myself. Vexèd I am
   Of late with passions of some difference,°
   Conceptions only proper to myself,
   Which give some soil° perhaps to my behaviors.
   But let not therefore my good friends be grieved—   45

17. **press:** crowd. 20. **ides of March:** March 15. † **Sennet:** trumpet call. 42. **passions of some difference:** conflicting emotions. 44. **soil:** blemish.

Among which number, Cassius, be you one—
Nor construe° any further my neglect,
Than that poor Brutus, with himself at war,
Forgets the shows of love to other men.

CASSIUS.   Then, Brutus, I have much mistook your passion,   50
By means whereof this breast of mine hath buried
Thoughts of great value, worthy cogitations.°
Tell me, good Brutus, can you see your face?

BRUTUS.   No, Cassius; for the eye sees not itself
But by reflection, by some other things.   55

CASSIUS.   'Tis just.
And it is very much lamented, Brutus,
That you have no such mirrors as will turn
Your hidden worthiness into your eye,
That you might see your shadow.° I have heard   60
Where many of the best respect in Rome—
Except immortal Caesar°—speaking of Brutus
And groaning underneath this age's yoke,°
Have wished that noble Brutus had his eyes.

BRUTUS.   Into what dangers would you lead me, Cassius,   65
That you would have me seek into myself
For that which is not in me?

CASSIUS.   Therefore, good Brutus, be prepared to hear.
And since you know you cannot see yourself
So well as by reflection, I, your glass,°   70
Will modestly discover to yourself
That of yourself which you yet know not of.
And be not jealous on° me, gentle Brutus.
Were I a common laugher,° or did use
To stale° with ordinary oaths my love   75
To every new protester;° if you know
That I do fawn on men and hug them hard,
And after scandal° them; or if you know
That I profess° myself in banqueting
To all the rout,° then hold me dangerous.   80

47. construe: interpret. 52. cogitations: important thoughts. 60. shadow: reflection. 62. Except immortal Caesar: This phrase is spoken with great bitterness. Cassius does not mean to praise Caesar when he calls him immortal. 63. ages yoke: burdens of these times. 70. glass: looking glass; mirror. 73. jealous on: suspicious of. 74. laugher: jester. 75. stale: make common. 76. protester: one who solemnly professes friendship. 78. scandal: slander. 79. profess: publicize. 80. rout: rabble.

(*Flourish and shout.*)

BRUTUS.   What means this shouting? I do fear the people
Choose Caesar for their king.

CASSIUS.   Aye, do you fear it?
Then must I think you would not have it so.

BRUTUS.   I would not, Cassius; yet I love him well.
But wherefore do you hold me here so long?   85
What is it that you would impart to me?
If it be aught toward the general good,
Set honor in one eye and death i' the other,
And I will look on both indifferently;
For let the gods so speed° me as I love   90
The name of honor more than I fear death.

CASSIUS.   I know that virtue to be in you, Brutus,
As well as I do know your outward favor.°
Well, honor is the subject of my story.
I cannot tell what you and other men   95
Think of this life, but for my single self
I had as lief° not be as live to be
In awe of such a thing as I myself.°
I was born free as Caesar; so were you.
We both have fed as well, and we can both   100
Endure the winter's cold as well as he.
For once, upon a raw and gusty day,
The troubled Tiber chafing with her shores,
Caesar said to me, "Darest thou, Cassius, now
Leap in with me into this angry flood,   105
And swim to yonder point?" Upon the word,
Accoutered° as I was, I plungèd in
And bade him follow. So indeed he did.
The torrent roared, and we did buffet it
With lusty sinews,° throwing it aside   110
And stemming it with hearts of controversy,°
But ere we could arrive the point proposed,
Caesar cried, "Help me, Cassius, or I sink!"
I, as Aeneas, our great ancestor,

---

90. speed: give good fortune to. **93.** favor: face. **97.** lief: soon. **98. In . . . my-self:** afraid of a mere mortal like myself. **107. Accoutered** (ə·koo′tərd): fully armed; dressed in armor. **110.** sinews: muscles. **111. hearts of controversy:** eager rivalry.

Did from the flames of Troy upon his shoulder   115
The old Anchises° bear, so from the waves of Tiber
Did I the tired Caesar—and this man
Is now become a god, and Cassius is
A wretched creature, and must bend his body,
If Caesar carelessly but nod on him.   120
He had a fever when he was in Spain,
And when the fit was on him, I did mark
How he did shake. 'Tis true, this god did shake.
His coward lips did from their color fly,
And that same eye whose bend° doth awe the world   125
Did lose his luster. I did hear him groan.
Aye, and that tongue of his that bade the Romans
Mark him and write his speeches in their books,
Alas, it cried, "Give me some drink, Titinius,"
As a sick girl. Ye gods! It doth amaze me   130
A man of such a feeble temper should
So get the start° of the majestic world
And bear the palm° alone.

(*Shout. Flourish.*)

BRUTUS.   Another general shout!   135
I do believe that these applauses are
For some new honors that are heaped on Caesar.
CASSIUS.   Why, man, he doth bestride the narrow world
Like a Colossus,° and we petty men
Walk under his huge legs and peep about
To find ourselves dishonorable graves.   140
Men at some time are masters of their fates.
The fault, dear Brutus, is not in our stars,°
But in ourselves, that we are underlings.
"Brutus" and "Caesar." What should be in that "Caesar"?
Why should that name be sounded more than yours?   145

114–116. Aeneas . . . Anchises: According to the *Aeneid,* a long epic poem by
the Roman poet Vergil, Aeneas was one of the few Trojans who escaped the
destruction of Troy by the Greeks. He bore his old father Anchises from the flaming city, and later in the poem he becomes founder of the city of Rome. 125.
bend: glance. 132. get the start: become the leader. 133. palm: prize; sign
of victory. 138. Colossus: The Colossus of Rhodes was one of the seven wonders
of the ancient world. It was a giant bronze statue straddling the entrance to the
harbor, beneath which ships passed. 142. stars: This is a reference to astrology,
which holds that the movement and position of the stars determine the events in
a man's life.

Write them together, yours is as fair a name;
Sound them, it doth become the mouth as well;
Weigh them, it is as heavy. Conjure° with 'em,
"Brutus" will start a spirit as soon as "Caesar."
Now, in the names of all the gods at once,   150
Upon what meat doth this our Caesar feed,
That he is grown so great? Age, thou art shamed!
Rome, thou hast lost the breed of noble bloods!
When went there by an age, since the great flood,
But it was famed with more than with one man?   155
When could they say till now, that talked of Rome,
That her wide walls encompassed but one man?
Now is it Rome indeed and room° enough,
When there is in it but one only man.
Oh, you and I have heard our fathers say,   160
There was a Brutus° once that would have brooked°
The eternal devil to keep his state in Rome
As easily as a king.
BRUTUS.   That you do love me, I am nothing jealous.
What you would work me to, I have some aim.   165
How I have thought of this and of these times,
I shall recount hereafter; for this present,
I would not, so with love I might entreat you,
Be any further moved. What you have said
I will consider. What you have to say   170
I will with patience hear, and find a time
Both meet° to hear and answer such high things.
Till then, my noble friend, chew upon this:
Brutus had rather be a villager
Than to repute himself a son of Rome   175
Under these hard conditions as this time
Is like to lay upon us.
CASSIUS.   I am glad that my weak words
Have struck but thus much show of fire from Brutus.
BRUTUS.   The games are done, and Caesar is returning.   180
CASSIUS.   As they pass by, pluck Casca by the sleeve,

148. **Conjure:** summon evil spirits. 158. **Rome . . . room:** a·common pun, here expressing contempt. Both words were pronounced alike. 161. **Brutus:** Lucius Junius Brutus, from whom Marcus Brutus claimed descent, was chiefly responsible for the expulsion of Tarquin, the last King of Rome (sixth-century B.C.). **brooked:** endured. 172. **meet:** fit.

And he will, after his sour fashion, tell you
What hath proceeded worthy note today.

(*Reenter* CAESAR *and his train.*)

BRUTUS.   I will do so. But look you, Cassius,
          The angry spot doth glow on Caesar's brow,   185
          And all the rest look like a chidden train.°
          Calpurnia's cheek is pale, and Cicero
          Looks with such ferret° and such fiery eyes
          As we have seen him in the Capitol,
          Being crossed in conference by some Senators.   190
CASSIUS.   Casca will tell us what the matter is.
CAESAR.   Antonius!
ANTONY.   Caesar?
CAESAR.   Let me have men about me that are fat,
          Sleek-headed men and such as sleep o' nights.   195
          Yond Cassius has a lean and hungry look.
          He thinks too much; such men are dangerous.
ANTONY.   Fear him not, Caesar. He's not dangerous;
          He is a noble Roman and well given.°
CAESAR.   Would he were fatter! But I fear him not.   200
          Yet, if my name were liable to fear,
          I do not know the man I should avoid
          So soon as that spare Cassius. He reads much.
          He is a great observer, and he looks
          Quite through the deeds of men; he loves no plays,   205
          As thou dost, Antony; he hears no music.
          Seldom he smiles, and smiles in such a sort
          As if he mocked himself and scorned his spirit
          That could be moved to smile at anything.
          Such men as he be never at heart's ease   210
          While they behold a greater than themselves,
          And therefore are they very dangerous.
          I rather tell thee what is to be feared
          Than what I fear; for always I am Caesar.
          Come on my right hand, for this ear is deaf,°   215
          And tell me truly what thou think'st of him.

186. **chidden train:** scolded followers. 188. **ferret:** a small weasel-like animal
with little red eyes; here, sharp, nervous. 199. **well given:** well disposed. 215. **ear
is deaf:** History does not record any such defect in Caesar's hearing. Perhaps the
reference is to being "deafened" by shouts of popular acclaim.

(Sennet. Exeunt CAESAR *and all his train but* CASCA.*)*

CASCA.   You pulled me by the cloak. Would you speak with me?
BRUTUS.   Aye, Casca. Tell us what hath chanced today,
That Caesar looks so sad.
CASCA.   Why, you were with him, were you not?   220
BRUTUS.   I should not then ask Casca what had chanced.
CASCA.   Why, there was a crown offered him; and being offered
him, he put it by with the back of his hand, thus. And then
the people fell a-shouting.
BRUTUS.   What was the second noise for?   225
CASCA.   Why, for that too.
CASSIUS.   They shouted thrice. What was the last cry for?
CASCA.   Why, for that too.
BRUTUS.   Was the crown offered him thrice?
CASCA.   Aye, marry,° was 't, and he put it by thrice, every time 230
gentler than other. And at every putting-by mine honest
neighbors shouted.
CASSIUS.   Who offered him the crown?
CASCA.   Why, Antony.
BRUTUS.   Tell us the manner of it, gentle Casca.   235
CASCA.   I can as well be hanged as tell the manner of it. It was
mere foolery—I did not mark it. I saw Mark Antony offer
him a crown—yet 'twas not a crown neither, 'twas one of
these coronets°—and, as I told you, he put it by once. But,
for all that, to my thinking, he would fain° have had it.   240
Then he offered it to him again; then he put it by again.
But, to my thinking, he was very loath to lay fingers off it.
And then he offered it the third time; he put it the third
time by. And still as he refused it, the rabblement hooted
and clapped their chapped hands and threw up their sweaty   245
nightcaps and uttered such a deal of stinking breath because Caesar refused the crown that it had almost choked
Caesar; for he swounded° and fell down at it. And for mine
own part, I durst not laugh, for fear of opening my lips and
receiving the bad air.   250
CASSIUS.   But, soft, I pray you. What! Did Caesar swound?

---

230. **marry:** an Elizabethan oath meaning "by the Virgin Mary." Notice the anachronism—the oath is being used before the birth of Christ. 239. **coronets:** little
crowns worn by those of lesser rank than king. 240. **fain:** gladly. 248. **swounded:**
swooned, fainted.

CASCA.   He fell down in the market place, and foamed at mouth
and was speechless.

BRUTUS.   'Tis very like—he hath the falling sickness.°

CASSIUS.   No, Caesar hath it not. But you, and I,   255
And honest Casca, we have the falling sickness.

CASCA.   I know not what you mean by that, but I am sure
Caesar fell down. If the tagrag people did not clap him and
hiss him according as he pleased and displeased them, as
they used to do the players in the theater, I am no true man.   260

BRUTUS.   What said he when he came unto himself?

CASCA.   Marry, before he fell down, when he perceived the common herd was glad he refused the crown, he plucked me
ope his doublet° and offered them his throat to cut. An° I
had been a man of any occupation,° if I would not have   265
taken him at a word, I would I might go to hell among the
rogues. And so he fell. When he came to himself again, he
said if he had done or said anything amiss, he desired Their
Worships to think it was his infirmity. Three or four
wenches, where I stood, cried, "Alas, good soul!" and for-   270
gave him with all their hearts. But there's no heed to be
taken of them. If Caesar had stabbed their mothers, they
would have done no less.

BRUTUS.   And after that, he came, thus sad, away?

CASCA.   Aye.   275

CASSIUS.   Did Cicero say anything?

CASCA.   Aye, he spoke Greek.

CASSIUS.   To what effect?

CASCA.   Nay, an I tell you that, I'll ne'er look you i' the face
again. But those that understood him smiled at one another   280
and shook their heads; but, for mine own part, it was Greek
to me. I could tell you more news too. Marullus and Flavius, for pulling scarfs off Caesar's images, are put to silence.° Fare you well. There was more foolery yet, if I could
remember it.   285

CASSIUS.   Will you sup with me tonight, Casca?

CASCA.   No, I am promised forth.

254. falling sickness: epilepsy. 264. doublet: short coat worn in Shakespeare's
time. An: if. 265. occupation: trade, and therefore provided with tools. 283–84.
put to silence: imprisoned.

CASSIUS.   Will you dine with me tomorrow?

CASCA.   Aye, if I be alive, and your mind hold, and your dinner
    worth the eating.   290

CASSIUS.   Good; I will expect you.

CASCA.   Do so. Farewell, both. (*Exit.*)

BRUTUS.   What a blunt fellow is this grown to be!
    He was quick mettle when he went to school.

CASSIUS.   So is he now in execution   295
    Of any bold or noble enterprise,
    However he puts on this tardy form.°
    This rudeness is a sauce to his good wit,
    Which gives men stomach to digest his words
    With better appetite.   300

BRUTUS.   And so it is. For this time I will leave you.
    Tomorrow, if you please to speak with me,
    I will come home to you, or, if you will,
    Come home to me, and I will wait for you.

CASSIUS.   I will do so. Till then, think of the world.   305

(*Exit* BRUTUS.)

Well, Brutus, thou art noble. Yet, I see,
Thy honorable mettle may be wrought
From that it is disposed.° Therefore it is meet
That noble minds keep ever with their likes,
For who so firm that cannot be seduced?   310
Caesar doth bear me hard; but he loves Brutus.
If I were Brutus now and he were Cassius,
He should not humor° me. I will this night,
In several hands,° in at his windows throw,
As if they came from several citizens,   315
Writings, all tending to the great opinion
That Rome holds of his name; wherein obscurely
Caesar's ambition° shall be glancèd at.°
And after this let Caesar seat him° sure,
For we will shake him, or worse days endure.   (*Exit.*) 320

297. **tardy form:** appearance of stupidity. 308. **From . . . disposed:** from its
natural quality. 313. **humor:** influence. 314. **several hands:** different handwrit-
ings. 318. **ambition:** *here,* greed for power. **glancèd at:** hinted at. 319. **him:**
himself.

Meaning and Method: Act I, Scene 2

1. Two short episodes at the beginning of Scene 2 (lines 1–26) show Caesar for the first time in the play. What characteristics of Caesar do the episodes convey? For example, what is revealed by Antony's statement, "When Caesar says 'Do this,' it is performed"? And by Caesar's dismissal of the Soothsayer as a "dreamer"?

2. Cassius is not satisfied with Brutus's answer that he is "with himself at war." In what way does he attempt to flatter Brutus into revealing himself? What are Brutus's first reactions (*see* lines 65–67 and lines 84–91)?

3. In lines 92–163 Cassius reveals his reasons for hating Caesar. What are they? Are they personal or political or both?

4. Reread lines 127–43. What does Cassius mean when he says, "The fault, dear Brutus, is not in our stars, / But in ourselves"? How does this statement help to characterize him and to show how he feels about a man's destiny?

5. Throughout the dialogue between Cassius and Brutus, shouts and trumpet calls are heard off-stage. Elizabethans loved noise in the theater for its own sake, yet these sound effects are necessary, and the dialogue and action on stage rely upon them. For example, how do they provide a contrast to the conversation between Cassius and Brutus? How do they add excitement and immediacy to the scene?

6. Beginning with line 194, both Caesar and Mark Antony comment on Cassius. What kind of judgments do they make about Cassius's character? Do their evaluations seem to be based on superficial evidence? When, if ever, can character be judged by appearance?

7. Why did Caesar faint when Antony offered him the crown? What was the reaction of the crowd? Why had Caesar "offered them his throat to cut" (line 264)? It was no secret to Shakespeare's original audience, any more than it is to us today, that Caesar must be murdered in the play as he was in life. In what way could his offer serve as a foreshadowing of that event? In what way can such foreshadowing increase the tension, and hence the interest, of the audience?

8. Cassius' last speech (lines 306–20) in Scene 2 is a *soliloquy*, an extended speech in which a character alone on stage expresses his thoughts. What parts of this soliloquy suggest that Cassius' intention may be to corrupt an honorable man? Is the action Cassius proposes to take with letters honest or dishonest? Why? Is it justified by his political views?

SCENE 3. *Late evening on the fourteenth of March. A street.*

(*Thunder and lightning. Enter, from opposite sides,* CASCA, *with his sword drawn, and* CICERO.)

CICERO.   Good even, Casca. Brought you Caesar home?
    Why are you breathless, and why stare you so?
CASCA.   Are not you moved, when all the sway° of earth
    Shakes like a thing unfirm? O Cicero,
    I have seen tempests when the scolding winds   •   5
    Have rived° the knotty oaks, and I have seen
    The ambitious ocean swell, and rage, and foam,
    To be exalted with° the threatening clouds.
    But never till tonight, never till now,
    Did I go through a tempest dropping fire.   10
    Either there is a civil strife in heaven,
    Or else the world, too saucy with the gods,
    Incenses them to send destruction.
CICERO.   Why, saw you anything more wonderful?
CASCA.   A common slave—you know him well by sight—   15
    Held up his left hand, which did flame and burn
    Like twenty torches joined, and yet his hand,
    Not sensible of° fire, remained unscorched.
    Besides—I have not since put up my sword—
    Against° the Capitol I met a lion,°   20
    Who glazed upon me and went surly by
    Without annoying me. And there were drawn
    Upon a heap a hundred ghastly women
    Transformèd with their fear, who swore they saw
    Men all in fire walk up and down the streets.   25
    And yesterday the bird of night° did sit
    Even at noonday upon the market place,
    Hooting and shrieking. When these prodigies
    Do so conjointly meet, let not men say
    "These are their reasons, they are natural."°   30

---

3. sway: settled order. **6.** rived: split. **8. exalted with:** raised to the level of. **18. sensible of:** sensitive to. **20. Against:** beside. **Capitol . . . lion:** Shakespeare thought of the Capitol as if it were the Tower of London. Here were kept the lions which were among the sights of London. **26. bird of night:** screech owl, an omen of evil. This bird's appearance "at noonday" is an event against the laws of nature. **30. "These . . . natural":** There is a scientific explanation for this.

For I believe they are portentous things
Unto the climate that they point upon.°

CICERO.   Indeed, it is a strange-disposèd time.
But men may construe things after their fashion,
Clean from the purpose of the things themselves.   35
Comes Caesar to the Capitol tomorrow?

CASCA.   He doth, for he did bid Antonius
Send word to you he would be there tomorrow.

CICERO.   Good night then, Casca. This disturbèd sky
Is not to walk in.

CASCA.   Farewell, Cicero.   40

(*Exit* CICERO. *Enter* CASSIUS.)

CASSIUS.   Who's there?

CASCA.   A Roman.

CASSIUS.   Casca, by your voice.

CASCA.   Your ear is good. Cassius, what night is this!

CASSIUS.   A very pleasing night to honest men.

CASCA.   Who ever knew the heavens menace so?

CASSIUS.   Those that have known the earth so full of faults.   45
For my part, I have walked about the streets,
Submitting me unto the perilous night,
And thus unbraced,° Casca, as you see,
Have bared my bosom to the thunder stone.°
And when the cross° blue lightning seemed to open   50
The breast of heaven, I did present myself
Even in the aim and very flash of it.

CASCA.   But wherefore did you so much tempt the heavens?
It is the part of men to fear and tremble
When the most mighty gods by tokens send   55
Such dreadful heralds to astonish us.

CASSIUS.   You are dull, Casca, and those sparks of life
That should be in a Roman you do want,°
Or else you use not. You look pale and gaze
And put on fear and cast yourself in wonder,   60
To see the strange impatience of the heavens.
But if you would consider the true cause
Why all these fires, why all these gliding ghosts,

31–32. portentous . . . upon: They are evil omens for the country in which they occur. 48. unbraced: with the doublet loose; carefree. 49. thunder stone: thunderbolt. 50. cross: zigzag. 58. want: lack.

Why birds and beasts from quality and kind,°
Why old men fool and children calculate,°   65
Why all these things change from their ordinance,°
Their natures and preformèd faculties,
To monstrous quality, why, you shall find
That heaven hath infused them with these spirits
To make them instruments of fear and warning   70
Unto some monstrous state.
Now could I, Casca, name to thee a man
Most like this dreadful night,
That thunders, lightens, opens graves, and roars
As doth the lion in the Capitol—   75
A man no mightier than thyself or me
In personal action, yet prodigious grown
And fearful, as these strange eruptions are.

CASCA.   'Tis Caesar that you mean, is it not, Cassius?
CASSIUS.   Let it be who it is. For Romans now   80
    Have thews° and limbs like to their ancestors;
    But, woe the while! Our fathers' minds are dead,
    And we are governed with our mothers' spirits.
    Our yoke and sufferance show us womanish.
CASCA.   Indeed, they say the Senators tomorrow   85
    Mean to establish Caesar as a king,
    And he shall wear his crown by sea and land
    In every place, save here in Italy.
CASSIUS.   I know where I will wear this dagger then;
    Cassius from bondage will deliver Cassius.   90
    Therein, ye gods, you make the weak most strong.
    Therein, ye gods, you tyrants do defeat.
    Nor stony tower, nor walls of beaten brass,
    Nor airless dungeon, nor strong links of iron,
    Can be retentive to the strength of spirit;   95
    But life, being weary of these wordly bars,
    Never lacks power to dismiss itself.
    If I know this, know all the world besides,
    That part of tyranny that I do bear
    I can shake off at pleasure.

(*Thunder still.*)

64. from . . . kind: contrary to their natural behavior. **65. calculate:** prophesize.
66. ordinance: natural order. **81. thews** (thyōōz): sinews; strength.

CASCA.   So can I: 100
    So every bondman in his own hand bears
    The power to cancel his capitivity.
CASSIUS.   And why should Caesar be a tyrant, then?
    Poor man! I know he would not be a wolf,
    But that he sees the Romans are but sheep.   105
    He were no lion were not Romans hinds.°
    Those that with haste will make a mighty fire
    Begin it with weak straws. What trash is Rome,
    What rubbish and what offal,° when it serves
    For the base matter to illuminate   110
    So vile a thing as Caesar! But, O Grief,
    Where hast thou led me? I perhaps speak this
    Before a willing bondman; then I know,
    My answer must be made. But I am armed,
    And dangers are to me indifferent.   115
CASCA.   You speak to Casca, and to such a man
    That is no fleering° telltale. Hold, my hand,
    Be factious for redress° of all these griefs,
    And I will set this foot of mine as far
    As who goes farthest.
CASSIUS.   There's a bargain made.   120
    Now know you, Casca, I have moved already
    Some certain of the noblest-minded Romans
    To undergo with me an enterprise
    Of honorable-dangerous consequence.
    And I do know, by this they stay for me   125
    In Pompey's porch;° for now, this fearful night,
    There is no stir or walking in the streets,
    And the complexion of the element°
    In favor's like the work we have in hand,
    Most bloody, fiery, and most terrible.   130
CASCA.   Stand close awhile, for here comes one in haste.
CASSIUS.   'Tis Cinna; I do know him by his gait;
    He is a friend.   (*Enter* CINNA.)
        Cinna, where haste you so?

---

106. **hinds:** female deer. 109. **offal:** the waste parts of a butchered animal. 117.
fleering: sneering. 118. **factious for redress:** active in righting the wrongs. 126.
Pompey's porch: the covered entrance of the theater built by Pompey. 128. **ele-**
ment: sky.

CINNA. To find out you. Who's that? Metellus Cimber?

CASSIUS. No, it is Casca, one incorporate   135
   To our attempts.° Am I not stayed for, Cinna?

CINNA. I am glad on 't. What a fearful night is this!
   There's two or three of us have seen strange sights.

CASSIUS. Am I not stayed for? Tell me.

CINNA.   Yes, you are.
   O Cassius, if you could   140
   But win the noble Brutus to our party—

CASSIUS. Be you content. Good Cinna, take this paper,
   And look you lay it in the praetor's° chair,
   Where Brutus may but find it, and throw this
   In at his window; set this up with wax°   145
   Upon old Brutus'° statue. All this done,
   Repair to Pompey's porch, where you shall find us.
   Is Decius Brutus and Trebonius there?

CINNA. All but Metellus Cimber, and he's gone
   To seek you at your house. Well, I will hie,   150
   And so bestow these papers as you bade me.

CASSIUS. That done, repair to Pompey's theater.

(*Exit* CINNA.)

   Come, Casca, you and I will yet ere day
   See Brutus at his house. There parts of him
   Is ours already, and the man entire   155
   Upon the next encounter yields him ours.

CASCA. Oh, he sits high in all the people's hearts,
   And that which would appear offense in us,
   His countenance, like richest alchemy,°
   Will change to virtue and to worthiness.   160

CASSIUS. Him and his worth and our great need of him
   You have right well conceited.° Let us go,
   For it is after midnight, and ere day
   We will awake him and be sure of him.   (*Exeunt.*)

135–36. one . . . attempts: one of our conspiracy. 143. praetor: a Roman official next in rank to the consul. The consul was the highest official in Rome. Brutus was praetor at this time. 145. wax: attach this by means of melted wax. 146. old Brutus': Brutus's ancestor, Lucius Julius Brutus. 159. alchemy: a form of chemistry that was practiced in medieval times. 162. conceited: perceived; understood.

Meaning and Method: Act I, Scene 3

1. Elizabethans believed that weird events and extremes in nature—such as violent storms—were products or foreshadowings of dire happenings. In what way, then, would Shakespeare's audience have interpreted the dialogue between Cassius and Casca? Are our reactions in any way similar? How would you stage this scene? Describe the sound effects and lighting you would use.

   What is Cassius' purpose in commenting on these signs or manifestations? Is he contradicting himself, in light of his having told Brutus in Scene 2 that "The fault, dear Brutus, is not in our stars, / But in ourselves, that we are underlings"?

2. Notice that the playwright consistently returns to the matter of Brutus's character. What judgment about him does Casca make at the end of Scene 3? In what way, if any, is Cassius' attitude in this scene different from what it was in the earlier scene with Brutus?

3. Describe Cassius. Is he ruled by emotion or reason? What is his attitude toward the common people?

Act II

Rome. BRUTUS's *orchard.*

(Enter BRUTUS.*)*

BRUTUS.   What, Lucius, ho!
   I cannot, by the progress of the stars,
   Give guess how near to day. Lucius, I say!
   I would it were my fault to sleep so soundly.
   When, Lucius, when? Awake, I say! What, Lucius!   5

(Enter LUCIUS.*)*

LUCIUS.   Called you, my lord?
BRUTUS.   Get me a taper° in my study, Lucius.
   When it is lighted, come and call me here.
LUCIUS.   I will, my lord. *(Exit.)*
BRUTUS.   It must be by his death;° and for my part,   10
   I know no personal cause to spurn at him
   But for the general.° He would be crowned.
   How that might change his nature, there's the question.
   It is the bright day that brings forth the adder,
   And that craves wary walking. Crown him?—That!—   15
   And then, I grant, we put a sting in him,
   That at his will he may do danger with.
   The abuse of greatness is when it disjoins
   Remorse from power; and to speak truth of Caesar,
   I have not known when his affections swayed   20
   More than his reason. But 'tis a common proof
   That lowliness is young ambition's ladder,
   Whereto the climber-upward turns his face.
   But when he once attains the upmost round,
   He then unto the ladder turns his back,   25
   Looks in the clouds, scorning the base degrees°
   By which he did ascend. So Caesar may.
   Then, lest he may, prevent. And since the quarrel

7. **taper**: candle. 10. **his death**: Caesar's. 12. **general**: general good. 26. **degrees**: steps.

Will bear no color° for the thing he is,
Fashion it thus:° that what he is, augmented,   30
Would run to these and these extremities.
And therefore think him as a serpent's egg
Which hatched would, as his kind, grow mischievous,
And kill him in the shell.

(*Reenter* LUCIUS.)

LUCIUS.   The taper burneth in your closet,° sir.   35
Searching the window for a flint, I found
This paper thus sealed up; and I am sure
It did not lie there when I went to bed.

Forged note appears here

(*Gives him the letter.*)

BRUTUS.   Get you to bed again. It is not day.
Is not tomorrow, boy, the ides of March?   40
LUCIUS.   I know not, sir.
BRUTUS.   Look in the calendar and bring me word.
LUCIUS.   I will, sir. (*Exit.*)
BRUTUS.   The exhalations° whizzing in the air
Give so much light that I may read by them.   45

(*Opens the letter and reads.*)

> *Brutus, thou sleep'st. Awake, and see thyself.*
> *Shall Rome, etc. Speak, strike, redress.*

"Brutus, thou sleep'st. Awake."
Such instigations have been often dropped
Where I have took them up.   50
"Shall Rome, etc." Thus must I piece it out ——
Shall Rome stand under one man's awe? What, Rome?
My ancestors did from the streets of Rome
The Tarquin drive, when he was called a king.
"Speak, strike, redress." Am I entreated   55
To speak and strike? O Rome, I made thee promise,
If the redress will follow, thou receivest
Thy full petition at the hand of Brutus!

(*Reenter* LUCIUS.)

LUCIUS.   Sir, March is wasted fifteen days.

---

29. bear no color: cannot be justified. **30. Fashion it thus:** Look at it this way.
35. closet: small private room. **44. exhalations:** meteors.

(*Knocking within.*)

BRUTUS.   'Tis good. Go to the gate. Somebody knocks.   60

(*Exit* LUCIUS.)

Since Cassius first did whet me again Caesar,
I have not slept.
Between the acting of a dreadful thing
And the first motion, all the interim is
Like a phantasma, or a hideous dream.   65
The Genius and the mortal instruments
Are then in council, and the state of man,
Like to a little kingdom, suffers then
The nature of an insurrection.°

(*Reenter* LUCIUS.)

LUCIUS.   Sir, 'tis your brother° Cassius at the door,   70
   Who doth desire to see you.
BRUTUS.   Is he alone?
LUCIUS.   No sir, there are more with him.
BRUTUS.   Do you know them?
LUCIUS.   No, sir. Their hats are plucked about their ears,
   And half their faces buried in their cloaks,
   That by no means I may discover them   75
   By any mark of favor.
BRUTUS.   Let 'em enter.

(*Exit* LUCIUS.)

They are the faction.° O Conspiracy,
Shamest thou to show thy dangerous brow by night,
When evils are most free? Oh, then by day
Where wilt thou find a cavern dark enough   80
To mask thy monstrous visage? Seek none, Conspiracy—
Hide it in smiles and affability.
For if thou path thy native semblance on,°
Not Erebus° itself were dim enough
To hide thee from prevention.°   85

66–69. Genius . . . insurrection: The mind (*Genius*) and body (*mortal instruments*) and a man's whole nature are then like a nation in a state of civil war.
70. brother: brother-in-law. 77. faction: of the party. 83. path . . . on: walk openly without disguising your face or feelings. 84. Erebus: in Greek mythology, a dark passage to hell. 85. prevention: premature discovery.

(*Enter the conspirators,* CASSIUS, CASCA, DECIUS, CINNA,
METELLUS CIMBER, *and* TREBONIUS.)

CASSIUS.   I think we are too bold upon your rest.
Good morrow, Brutus. Do we trouble you?

BRUTUS.   I have been up this hour—awake all night.
Know I these men that come along with you?

CASSIUS.   Yes, every man of them; and no man here   90
But honors you; and every one doth wish
You had but that opinion of yourself
Which every noble Roman bears of you.
This is Trebonius.

BRUTUS.   He is welcome hither.

CASSIUS.   This, Decius Brutus.

BRUTUS.   He is welcome too.   95

CASSIUS.   This, Casca; this, Cinna; and this, Metellus Cimber.

BRUTUS.   They are all welcome.
What watchful cares do interpose themselves
Betwixt your eyes and night?

CASSIUS.   Shall I entreat a word?   100

(BRUTUS *and* CASSIUS *whisper.*)

DECIUS.   Here lies the east. Doth not the day break here?

CASCA.   No.

CINNA.   Oh, pardon, sir, it doth; and yon gray lines
That fret° the clouds are messengers of day.

CASCA.   You shall confess that you are both deceived.   105
Here, as I point my sword, the sun arises,
Which is a great way growing on the south,
Weighing the youthful season of the year.
Some two months hence up higher toward the north
He first presents his fire, and the high east   110
Stands, as the Capitol, directly here.

BRUTUS.   Give me your hands all over, one by one.

CASSIUS.   And let us swear our resolution.

BRUTUS.   No, not an oath. If not the face of men,
The sufferance of our souls, the time's abuse—   115
If these be motives weak, break off betimes,°

---

104. fret: ornament. 114–16. If not . . . betimes: If honor (*face*), the suffering of our souls, and the abuses of this time are not sufficient motives and
bonds for conspiracy, it will end in good time (*betimes*).

And every man hence to his idle bed.
So let high-sighted tyranny range on,
Till each man drop by lottery. But if these,
As I am sure they do, bear fire enough   120
To kindle cowards and to steel with valor
The melting spirits of women, then, countrymen,
What need we any spur but our own cause
To prick° us to redress? What other bond
Than secret Romans that have spoke the word,   125
And will not palter?° And what other oath
Than honesty to honesty engaged,
That this shall be, or we will fall for it?
Swear priests and cowards and men cautelous,°
Old feeble carrions° and such suffering souls   130
That welcome wrongs; unto bad causes swear
Such creatures as men doubt; but do not stain
The even° virtue of our enterprise,
Nor the insuppressive mettle of our spirits,
To think that or our cause or° our performance   135
Did need an oath when every drop of blood
That every Roman bears, and nobly bears,
Is guilty of a several bastardy
If he do break the smallest particle
Of any promise that hath passed from him.   140
CASSIUS.   But what of Cicero? Shall we sound him?
   I think he will stand very strong with us.
CASCA.   Let us not leave him out.
CINNA.   No, by no means.
METELLUS.   Oh, let us have him, for his silver hairs
   Will purchase us a good opinion   145
   And buy men's voices to commend our deeds.
   It shall be said his judgment ruled our hands.
   Our youths and wildness shall no whit appear,
   But all be buried in his gravity.
BRUTUS.   Oh, name him not. Let us not break with him,°   150
   For he will never follow anything
   That other men begin.
CASSIUS.   Then leave him out.

124. prick: spur. 126. palter: play false. 129. cautelous: crafty. 130. carrions:
carcasses. 133. even: firm, unchanging. 135. or . . . or: either . . . or. 150. not
break with him: not disclose our plans to him.

CASCA.   Indeed he is not fit.

DECIUS.   Shall no man else be touched but only Caesar?

CASSIUS.   Decius, well urged. I think it is not meet   155
   Mark Antony, so well beloved of Caesar,
   Should outlive Caesar. We shall find of him
   A shrewd contriver; and you know his means,
   If he improve them, may well stretch so far
   As to annoy° us all. Which to prevent,   160
   Let Antony and Caesar fall together.

BRUTUS.   Our course shall seem too bloody, Caius Cassius,
   To cut the head off and then hack the limbs,
   Like wrath in death and envy afterward.
   For Antony is but a limb of Caesar.   165
   Let us be sacrificers, but not butchers, Caius.
   We all stand up against the spirit of Caesar,
   And in the spirit of men there is no blood.
   Oh, that we then could come by Caesar's spirit,
   And not dismember Caesar! But, alas,   170
   Caesar must bleed for it! And, gentle friends,
   Let's kill him boldly, but not wrathfully.
   Let's carve him as a dish fit for the gods,
   Not hew him as a carcass fit for hounds.
   And let our hearts, as subtle masters do,   175
   Stir up their servants to an act of rage,
   And after seem to chide 'em. This shall make
   Our purpose necessary and not envious,
   Which so appearing to the common eyes,
   We shall be called purgers,° not murderers.   180
   And for Mark Antony, think not of him;
   For he can do no more than Caesar's arm
   When Caesar's head is off.

CASSIUS.   Yet I fear him;
   For in the ingrafted love he bears to Caesar—

BRUTUS.   Alas, good Cassius, do not think of him.   185
   If he love Caesar, all that he can do
   Is to himself, take thought and die for Caesar.
   And that were much he should, for he is given
   To sports, to wildness and much company.

160. **annoy:** *here,* harm. 180. **purgers:** those who clean or purify.

TREBONIUS.   There is no fear in him. Let him not die,   190
    For he will live, and laugh at this hereafter.

                  (*Clock strikes.*)

BRUTUS.   Peace! Count the clock.
CASSIUS.   The clock hath stricken three.
TREBONIUS.   'Tis time to part.
CASSIUS.   But it is doubtful yet
    Whether Caesar will come forth today or no;   195
    For he is superstitious grown of late,
    Quite from the main opinion he held once
    Of fantasy, of dreams and ceremonies.
    It may be these apparent prodigies,°
    The unaccustomed terror of this night,   200
    And the persuasion of his augurers°
    May hold him from the Capitol today.
DECIUS.   Never fear that. If he be so resolved,
    I can o'ersway him. For he loves to hear
    That unicorns may be betrayed with trees,   205
    And bears with glasses, elephants with holes,
    Lions with toils,° and men with flatterers;
    But when I tell him he hates flatterers,
    He says he does, being then most flattered.
    Let me work,   210
    For I can give his humor the true bent,
    And I will bring him to the Capitol.
CASSIUS.   Nay, we will all of us be there to fetch him.
BRUTUS.   By the eighth hour. Is that the uttermost?
CINNA.   Be that the uttermost, and fail not then.   215
METELLUS.   Caius Ligarius doth bear Caesar hard,
    Who rated° him for speaking well of Pompey.
    I wonder none of you have thought of him.
BRUTUS.   Now, good Metellus, go along by him.
    He loves me well, and I have given him reasons.   220
    Send him but hither and I'll fashion him.°

---

199. prodigies: signs of disaster. **201. augurers:** professional interpreters of omens.
205–07. unicorns . . . toils: It was believed that unicorns could be trapped by
having a hunter stand in front of a tree, provoke the unicorn into charging, and
then step quickly aside. Bears were supposed to be very vain and easily lured by
mirrors. Elephants can still be caught in pits and lions in snares (toils). **217.
rated:** rebuked; berated. **221. fashion him:** mold his opinions.

CASSIUS.   The morning comes upon 's. We'll leave you, Brutus.
   And friends, disperse yourselves; but all remember
   What you have said, and show yourselves true Romans.
BRUTUS.   Good gentlemen, look fresh and merrily;   225
   Let not our looks put on our purposes,
   But bear it as our Roman actors do,
   With untired spirits and formal constancy.°
   And so, good morrow to you every one.

(Exeunt all but BRUTUS.*)*

Boy! Lucius! Fast asleep? It is no matter.   230
Enjoy the honey-heavy dew of slumber.
Thou hast no figures° nor no fantasies
Which busy care draws in the brains of men;
Therefore thou sleep'st so sound.

(Enter PORTIA.*)*

PORTIA.   Brutus, my lord!
BRUTUS.   Portia, what mean you? Wherefore rise you now?   235
   It is not for your health thus to commit
   Your weak condition to the raw cold morning.
PORTIA.   Nor for yours neither. You've ungently, Brutus,
   Stole from my bed. And yesternight at supper
   You suddenly arose, and walked about,   240
   Musing and sighing, with your arms across,
   And when I asked you what the matter was,
   You stared upon me with ungentle looks.
   I urged you further, then you scratched your head,
   And too impatiently stamped with your foot.   245
   Yet I insisted, yet you answered not,
   But, with an angry wafture° of your hand
   Gave sign for me to leave you. So I did,
   Fearing to strengthen that impatience
   Which seemed too much enkindled, and withal   250
   Hoping it was but an effect of humor,°

---

228. constancy: outward appearance of steadfastness. **232. figures:** visions, as in a dream. **247. wafture:** wave. **251. humor:** moodiness. In Shakespeare's day, it was believed by many that bodily health and human behavior were influenced by four principal fluids in the body. These four fluids, called *humors*, were blood, phlegm, yellow bile, and black bile.

Which sometime hath his hour with every man.
It will not let you eat, nor talk, nor sleep,
And, could it work so much upon your shape
As it hath much prevailed on your condition,   255
I should not know you, Brutus. Dear my lord,
Make me acquainted with your cause of grief.

BRUTUS.   I am not well in heath, and that is all.

PORTIA.   Brutus is wise, and were he not in health,
He would embrace the means to come by it.   260

BRUTUS.   Why, so I do. Good Portia, go to bed.

PORTIA.   Is Brutus sick? And is it physical°
To walk unbraced and suck up the humors
Of the dank morning? What, is Brutus sick,
And will he steal out of his wholesome bed,   265
To dare the vile contagion of the night,
And tempt the rheumy° and unpurgèd air
To add unto his sickness? No, my Brutus;
You have some sick offense within your mind,
Which by the right and virtue of my place   270
I ought to know of. And, upon my knees,
I charm° you, by my once commended beauty,
By all your vows of love and that great vow
Which did incorporate and make us one,
That you unfold to me, yourself, your half,   275
Why you are heavy, and what men tonight
Have had resort to you; for here have been
Some six or seven who did hide their faces
Even from darkness.

BRUTUS.   Kneel not, gentle Portia.

PORTIA.   I should not need if you were gentle Brutus.   280
Within the bond of marriage, tell me, Brutus,
Is it excepted I should know no secrets
That appertain to you? Am I your self,
But, as it were, in sort or limitation?
To keep with you at meals, comfort your bed,   285
And talk to you sometimes? Dwell I but in the suburbs
Of your good pleasure? If it be no more,
Portia is Brutus' harlot, not his wife.

262. physical: good for your health. 267. rheumy: likely to cause rheumatism.
272. charm: adjure.

BRUTUS.   You are my true and honorable wife,
  As dear to me as the ruddy drops°   290
  That visit my sad heart.
PORTIA.   If this were true, then should I know this secret.
  I grant I am a woman; but withal,
  A woman that Lord Brutus took to wife.
  I grant I am a woman; but withal,   295
  A woman well reputed—Cato's° daughter.
  Think you I am no stronger than my sex,
  Being so fathered, and so husbanded?
  Tell me your counsels, I will not disclose 'em.
  I have made strong proof of my constancy,   300
  Giving myself a voluntary wound
  Here in the thigh. Can I bear that with patience
  And not my husband's secrets?
BRUTUS.   O ye gods!
  Render me worthy of this noble wife!

                      (*Knocking within.*)

  Hark, hark! One knocks. Portia, go in awhile,   305
  And by and by thy bosom shall partake
  The secrets of my heart.
  All my engagements I will construe to thee,
  All the charactery of my sad brows.°
  Leave me with haste.

                      (*Exit* PORTIA.)

                      Lucius, who's that knocks?   310

              (*Reenter* LUCIUS *with* LIGARIUS.)

LUCIUS.   Here is a sick man that would speak with you.
BRUTUS.   Caius Ligarius, that Metellus spake of.
  Boy, stand aside. Caius Ligarius! How?
LIGARIUS.   Vouchsafe good morrow from a feeble tongue.
BRUTUS.   Oh, what a time have you chose out, brave Caius,   315
  To wear a kerchief! Would you were not sick!

290. **ruddy drops:** blood. 296. **Cato** (kā'to): Marcus Porcius Cato (the Younger),
a man of notable political honesty and a strong opponent of Caesar. When the
armies of Pompey were finally defeated, Cato killed himself rather than live under
Caesar's rule. 309. **charactery . . . brows:** that which is written in my face.

LIGARIUS.   I am not sick, if Brutus have in hand
  Any exploit worthy the name of honor.
BRUTUS.   Such an exploit have I in hand, Ligarius,
  Had you a healthful ear to hear of it.   320
LIGARIUS.   By all the gods that Romans bow before,
  I here discard my sickness! Soul of Rome!
  Brave son, derived from honorable loins!
  Thou, like an exorcist,° hast conjured up
  My mortified spirit. Now bid me run,   325
  And I will strive with things impossible
  Yea, get the better of them. What's to do?
BRUTUS.   A piece of work that will make sick men whole.
LIGARIUS.   But are not some whole that we must make sick?
BRUTUS.   That must we also. What it is, my Caius,   330
  I shall unfold to thee, as we are going
  To whom it must be done.
LIGARIUS.   Set on your foot,
  And with a heart new-fired I follow you,
  To do I know not what; but it sufficeth
  That Brutus leads me on.
BRUTUS.   Follow me, then.   (*Exeunt.*)   335

324. **exorcist:** one who summons the spirits of the dead.

Meaning and Method: Act II, Scene 1

1. The soliloquy of Brutus at the beginning of Act II (lines 10–34) shows that his fear is for what Caesar may do in the future rather than for what he has done in the past. What, specifically, is he afraid Caesar may do? Does he seem to think his fears justify joining a plot to kill Caesar? Quote the lines that support your answer.
2. Compare and contrast the characters of Cassius and Brutus as shown by their views about (a) taking an oath (lines 113–40), and (b) the fate of Mark Antony (lines 155–89). Which man is more realistic? Which is more idealistic? Which quality is more valuable in a political conspiracy? Neither? Both?
3. Cassius reports Caesar to have grown "suspicious of late." What possibilities might this suggest to the audience?
4. What reasoning allows Portia to know that something is on Brutus's mind? What does this show about her qualities as a wife? How would you contrast Portia's appeal to Brutus with Cassius' appeal to him (lines 90–93)? What does Brutus's response to his wife show about

his character and personality? What do you learn about the status of women from her speech?

5. What is appropriate about the fact that so much of the plot occurs at night?

SCENE 2. CAESAR's *house.*

(*Thunder and lightning. Enter* CAESAR *in his nightgown.*)

CAESAR.   Nor heaven nor earth have been at peace tonight.
Thrice hath Calpurnia in her sleep cried out,
"Help, ho! They murder Caesar!" Who's within?

(*Enter a* SERVANT.)

SERVANT.   My lord?
CAESAR.   Go bid the priests do present° sacrifice,   5
And bring me their opinions of success.
SERVANT.   I will, my lord. (*Exit.*)

(*Enter* CALPURNIA.)

CALPURNIA.   What mean you, Caesar? Think you to walk forth?
You shall not stir out of your house today.
CAESAR.   Caesar shall forth. The things that threatened me   10
Ne'er looked but on my back. When they shall see
The face of Caesar, they are vanishèd.
CALPURNIA.   Caesar, I never stood on ceremonies,°
Yet now the fright me. There is one within,
Besides the things that we have heard and seen,   15
Recounts most horrid sights seen by the watch.°
A lioness had whelpèd° in the streets;
And graves have yawned and yielded up their dead.
Fierce fiery warriors fight upon the clouds,
In ranks and squadrons and right form of war,   20
Which drizzled blood upon the Capitol.
The noise of battle hurtled in the air,
Horses did neigh and dying men did groan,
And ghosts did shriek and squeal about the streets.
O Caesar! These things are beyond all use,°   25
And I do fear them.

5. **present:** immediate. 13. **stood on ceremonies:** believed much in omens or auguries. 16. **watch:** soldiers on guard. 17. **whelpèd:** given birth to its young. 25. **use:** custom; habit.

CAESAR.   What can be avoided
   Whose end is purposed by the mighty gods?
   Yet Caesar shall go forth, for these predictions
   Are to the world in general as to Caesar.
CALPURNIA.   When beggars die, there are no comets seen;   30
   The heavens themselves blaze forth the death of princes.
CAESAR.   Cowards die many times before their deaths;
   The valiant never taste of death but once.
   Of all the wonders that I yet have heard,
   It seems to me most strange that men should fear,   35
   Seeing that death, a necessary end,
   Will come when it will come.

                    (*Reenter* SERVANT.)

                    What say the augurers?
SERVANT.   They would not have you stir forth today.
   Plucking the entrails of an offering forth,
   They could not find a heart within the beast.°   40
CAESAR.   The gods do this in shame of cowardice.
   Caesar should be a beast without a heart
   If he should stay at home today for fear.
   No, Caesar shall not. Danger knows full well
   That Caesar is more dangerous than he.   45
   We are two lions littered in one day,
   And I the elder and more terrible
   And Caesar shall go forth.
CALPURNIA.   Alas, my lord,
   Your wisdom is consumed in confidence.
   Do not go forth today. Call it my fear   50
   That keeps you in the house, and not your own.
   We'll send Mark Antony to the Senate House;
   And he shall say you are not well today.
   Let me, upon my knee, prevail in this.
CAESAR.   Mark Antony shall say I am not well,   55
   And for thy humor,° I will stay at home.

                    (*Enter* DECIUS.)

   Here's Decius Brutus. He shall tell them so.

39–40. Plucking . . . beast: The augurers have killed an animal as a sacrifice
(*offering*) to the gods; the absence of the animal's heart (or any other abnor-
mality in the body) was a bad omen. 56. thy humor: your whim.

DECIUS.   Caesar, all hail! Good morrow, worthy Caesar;
    I come to fetch you to the Senate House.
CAESAR.   And you are come in very happy time   60
    To bear my greetings to the Senators
    And tell them that I will not come today.
    Cannot, is false, and that I dare not, falser—
    I will not come today. Tell them so, Decius.
CALPURNIA.   Say he is sick.
CAESAR.   Shall Caesar send a lie?   65
    Have I in conquest stretched mine arm so far,
    To be afeared to tell graybeards the truth?
    Decius, go tell them Caesar will not come.
DECIUS.   Most mighty Caesar, let me know some cause,
    Lest I be laughed at when I tell them so.   70
CAESAR.   The cause is in my will—I will not come.
    That is enough to satisfy the Senate,
    But for your private satisfaction,
    Because I love you, I will let you know.
    Calpurnia here, my wife, stays me at home.   75
    She dreamed tonight she saw my statuë,°
    Which, like a fountain with a hundred spouts,
    Did run pure blood; and many lusty Romans
    Came smiling, and did bathe their hands in it.
    And these does she apply for warnings, and portents,   80
    And evils imminent; and on her knee
    Hath begged that I will stay at home today.
DECIUS.   This dream is all amiss interpreted.   *Flattery*
    It was a vision fair and fortunate.
    Your statue spouting blood in many pipes,   85
    In which so many smiling Romans bathed,
    Signifies that from you great Rome shall suck
    Reviving blood, and that great men shall press
    For tinctures, stains, relics, and cognizance.°
    This by Calpurnia's dream is signified.   90

76. statuë: *here*, pronounced as three syllables. 88–89. great . . . cognizance:
Decius interprets the dream in a double sense. To Caesar he implies that men
shall seek honors from him in the form of coats of arms and badges signifying that
they are his personal servants. To the audience the meaning of his speech is that
men will preserve relics of his death. It was a custom to dip handkerchiefs in the
blood of those executed for their religious principles. These relics were highly
valued.

CAESAR.   And this way have you well expounded it.

DECIUS.   I have, when you have heard what I can say.
And know it now. The Senate have concluded
To give this day a crown to mighty Caesar.   95
If you shall send them word you will not come,
Their minds may change. Besides, it were a mock
Apt to be rendered, for someone to say,
"Break up the Senate till another time,
When Caesar's wife shall meet with better dreams!"
If Caesar hide himself, shall they not whisper,   100
"Lo, Caesar is afraid"?
Pardon me, Caesar, for my dear dear love
To your proceeding bids me tell you this,
And reason to my love is liable.

CAESAR.   How foolish do your fears seem now, Calpurnia!   105
I am ashamèd I did yield to them.
Give me my robe, for I will go.

(*Enter* PUBLIUS, BRUTUS, LIGARIUS, METELLUS, CASCA,
TREBONIUS, *and* CINNA.)

And look where Publius is come to fetch me.

PUBLIUS.   Good morrow, Caesar.

CAESAR.   Welcome, Publius.
What, Brutus, are you stirred so early too?   110
Good morrow, Casca. Caius Ligarius,
Caesar was ne'er so much your enemy
As that same ague which hath made you lean.
What is 't o'clock?

BRUTUS.   Caesar, 'tis strucken eight.

CAESAR.   I thank you for your pains and courtesy.   115

(*Enter* ANTONY.)

See! Antony, that revels long o' nights,
Is notwithstanding up. Good morrow, Antony.

ANTONY.   So to most noble Caesar.

CAESAR.   Bid them prepare within.
I am to blame to be thus waited for.
Now, Cinna; now, Metellus; what, Trebonius!   120
I have an hour's talk in store for you.
Remember that you call on me today.
Be near me, that I may remember you.

TREBONIUS. Caesar, I will. (*Aside.*) And so near will I be,
  That your best friends shall wish I had been further.   125
CAESAR. Good friends, go in and taste some wine with me,
  And we, like friends, will straightway go together.
BRUTUS. (*Aside.*) That every like is not the same, O Caesar,
  The heart of Brutus yearns° to think upon!   (*Exeunt.*)

129. yearns: grieves.

Meaning and Method: Act II, Scene 2

1. Two scenes follow each other in which wives show great concern for
   their husbands. In what specific ways are the scenes parallel? What
   might be the dramatist's purpose in introducing the wives in such
   similar ways? What is the point of contrasting the "public" man and
   the "private" man?
2. What are the signs that could prevent Caesar from going out on this
   day? What does he mean, in lines 32–33, when he says, "Cowards die
   many times before their deaths; / The valiant never taste of death but
   once"?
3. What weaknesses in Caesar does Decius play upon in order to get
   Caesar to go to the Capitol? What do you think is an audience's
   reaction to Caesar at the end of this scene? Why?

SCENE 3. A *street near the Capitol.*

level

  (*Enter* ARTEMIDORUS, *reading a paper.*)

Warning of Caesar's fate

ARTEMIDORUS. "Caesar, beware of Brutus; take heed of Cassius;
  come not near Casca; have an eye to Cinna; trust not
  Trebonius; mark well Metellus Cimber; Decius Brutus
  loves thee not; thou hast wronged Caius Ligarius. There is
  but one mind in all these men, and it is bent against   5
  Caesar. If thou beest not immortal, look about you.
  Security° gives away to conspiracy. The mighty gods de-
  fend thee!
                                 Thy lover, ARTEMIDORUS."
  Here will I stand till Caesar pass along,   10
  And as a suitor° will I give him this.

7. Security: carelessness. 11. suitor: petitioner.

My heart laments that virtue cannot live
Out of the teeth of emulation.°
If thou read this, O Caesar, thou mayest live;
If not, the Fates with traitors do contrive.   (*Exit.*)   15

12–13. virtue . . . emulation: goodness cannot survive in the teeth of envy (*emulation*).

SCENE 4.   *Rome. Before* BRUTUS's *house.*

(*Enter* PORTIA *and* LUCIUS.)

PORTIA.   I prithee,° boy, run to the Senate House.
     Stay not to answer me, but get thee gone.
     Why dost thou stay?
LUCIUS.   To know my errand, madam.
PORTIA.   I would have had thee there, and here again,   5
     Ere I can tell thee what thou shouldst do there.
     O Constancy, be strong upon my side!
     Set a huge mountain 'tween my heart and tongue!
     I have a man's mind, but a woman's might.
     How hard it is for women to keep counsel!   10
     Are thou here yet?
LUCIUS.   Madam, what should I do?
     Run to the Capitol, and nothing else?
     And so return to you, and nothing else?
PORTIA.   Yes, bring me word, boy, if thy lord look well,
     For he went sickly forth. And take good note   15
     What Caesar doth, what suitors press to him.
     Hark boy! What noise is that?
LUCIUS.   I hear none, madam.
PORTIA.   Prithee, listen well.
     I heard a bustling rumor° like a fray,°
     And the wind brings it from the Capitol.   20
LUCIUS.   Sooth, madam, I hear nothing.

(*Enter the* SOOTHSAYER.)

PORTIA.   Come hither, fellow. Which way has thou been?
SOOTHSAYER.   At mine own house, good lady.

1. prithee: pray thee; beg of you. **19. bustling rumor:** confused noise. **fray:** battle.

PORTIA.   What is 't o'clock?

SOOTHSAYER.   About the ninth hour, lady.

PORTIA.   Is Caesar yet gone to the Capitol?   25

SOOTHSAYER.   Madam, not yet. I go to take my stand
   To see him pass on to the Capitol.

PORTIA.   Thou hast some suit to Caesar, hast thou not?

SOOTHSAYER.   That I have, lady. If it will please Caesar
   To be so good to Caesar as to hear me,   30
   I shall beseech him to befriend himself.

PORTIA.   Why, know'st thou any harm's intended toward him?

SOOTHSAYER.   None that I know will be, much that I fear may
      chance.
   Good morrow to you. Here the street is narrow,
   The throng that follows Caesar at the heels,   35
   Of Senators, of praetors, common suitors,
   Will crowd a feeble man almost to death.
   I'll get me to a place more void,° and there
   Speak to great Caesar as he comes along.   (*Exit.*)

PORTIA.   I must go in. Aye me! How weak a thing   40
   The heart of woman is! O Brutus,
   The heavens speed thee in thine enterprise.
   Sure, the boy heard me. Brutus hath a suit
   That Caesar will not grant. Oh, I grow faint.
   Run Lucius, and commend me to my lord.   45
   Say I am merry. Come to me again,
   And bring me word what he doth say to thee.

                    (*Exeunt severally.**)

38. void: empty. * Exeunt severally: They leave by different exits.

Meaning and Method: Act II, Scenes 3 and 4

1. How does Artemidorus plan to warn Caesar? How does this addition
   to the plot help to increase tension and suspense?
2. If you were directing this scene, what parts of Portia's speech would
   you have her say half to herself? Which to the boy? Why is she so
   nervous that she forgets to give the boy a message? Do the Soothsayer's words add to her tension? Do they add to the tension of the
   audience?
3. What is the dramatic impact of having Portia standing side by side
   with the Soothsayer? (Consider each one's attitude toward Caesar and
   what each one knows or fears about the situation.)

Act III

SCENE 1. *Rome. Before the Capitol.*

(A *crowd of people; among them* ARTEMIDORUS *and the*
SOOTHSAYER. *Flourish. Enter* CAESAR, BRUTUS, CASSIUS, CASCA,
DECIUS, METELLUS, TREBONIUS, CINNA; ANTONY, LEPIDUS, POPI-
LIUS, PUBLIUS, *and others.*)

CAESAR. (*To the* SOOTHSAYER.)   The ides of March are come.
SOOTHSAYER. Aye, Caesar; but not gone.
ARTEMIDORUS. Hail, Caesar! Read this schedule.
DECIUS. Trebonius doth desire you to o'erread,
At your best leisure, this humble suit.   5
ARTEMIDORUS. O Caesar, read mine first; for mine's a suit
That touches Caesar nearer. Read it, great Caesar!
CAESAR. What touches us ourself shall be last served.
ARTEMIDORUS. Delay not, Caesar. Read it instantly!
CAESAR. What, is the fellow mad?
PUBLIUS.   Sirrah, give place.   10
CASSIUS. What, urge you your petitions in the street?
Come to the Capitol.

(CAESAR *goes up to the Senate House, the rest following.*)

POPILIUS. I wish your enterprise today may thrive.
CASSIUS. What enterprise, Popilius?
POPILIUS.   Fare you well.

(*Advances to* CAESAR.)

BRUTUS. What said Popilius Lena?   15
CASSIUS. He wished today our enterprise might thrive.
I fear our purpose is discovered.
BRUTUS. Look how he makes to Caesar. Mark him.
CASSIUS. Casca, be sudden, for we fear prevention.
Brutus, what shall be done? If this be known,   20
Cassius or Caesar never shall turn back,
For I will slay myself.
BRUTUS.   Cassius, be constant.
Popilius Lena speaks not of our purposes,
For, look, he smiles, and Caesar doth not change.

CASSIUS.   Trebonius knows his time; for look you, Brutus,   25
He draws Mark Antony out of the way.

(*Exeunt* ANTONY *and* TREBONIUS.)

DECIUS.   Where is Metellus Cimber? Let him go,
And presently prefer his suit to Caesar.
BRUTUS.   He is addressed. Press near and second him.
CINNA.   Casca, you are the first that rears your hand.   30
CAESAR.   Are we all ready? What is now amiss
That Caesar and his Senate must redress?
METELLUS.   Most high, most mighty, and most puissant°
Caesar,
Metellus Cimber throws before thy seat
A humble heart—(*Kneeling*)
CAESAR.   I must prevent thee, Cimber.   35
These couchings° and these lowly° courtesies
Might fire the blood of ordinary men,
And turn preordinance and first decree°
Into the law of children.° Be not fond,°
To think that Caesar bears such rebel blood   40
That will be thawed from the true quality
With that which melteth fools—I mean sweet words,
Low-crookèd curtsies, and base spaniel fawning.
Thy brother by decree is banished.
If thou dost bend and pray and fawn for him,   45
I spurn thee like a cur out of my way.
Know, Caesar doth not wrong; nor without cause
Will he be satisfied.
METELLUS.   Is there no voice more worthy than my own,
To sound more sweetly in great Caesar's ear   50
For the repealing° of my banished brother?
BRUTUS.   I kiss thy hand, but not in flattery, Caesar,
Desiring thee that Publius Cimber may
Have an immediate freedom of repeal.
CAESAR.   What, Brutus!

---

33. puissant (pyōō′ə·sənt): powerful; mighty. 36. couchings: low bowings. lowly:
humble. 38. preordinance . . . decree: traditional laws. 39. law of children:
laws which are changeable and whimsical, like the will of a child. fond: foolish.
51. repealing: recalling from exile.

CASSIUS.   Pardon, Caesar; Caesar, pardon.   55
   As low as thy foot doth Cassius fall,
   To beg enfranchisement° for Publius Cimber.
CAESAR.   I could be well moved, if I were as you.
   If I could pray to move, prayers would move me,
   But I am constant as the Northern Star,   60
   Of whose true-fixed and resting quality
   There is no fellow° in the firmament.
   The skies are painted with unnumbered sparks,
   They are all fire and every one doth shine;
   But there's but one in all doth hold his place.   65
   So in the world. 'Tis furnished well with men,
   And men are flesh and blood, and apprehensive,
   Yet in the number I do know but one
   That unassailable holds on his rank,
   Unshaked of motion. And that I am he,   70
   Let me a little show it, even in this;
   That I was constant Cimber should be banished,
   And constant do remain to keep him so.
CINNA.   O Caesar—
CAESAR.   Hence! Wilt thou lift up Olympus?°
DECIUS.   Great Caesar—
CAESAR.   Doth not Brutus bootless° kneel?   75
CASCA.   Speak, hands, for me!

   (CASCA *first, then the other conspirators and* MARCUS BRUTUS
   stab CAESAR.)

CAESAR.   *Et tu, Brute?°* Then fall, Caesar!   (*Dies.*)
CINNA.   Liberty! Freedom! Tyranny is dead!
   Run hence, proclaim, cry it about the streets!
CASSIUS.   Some to the common pulpits, and cry out,   80
   "Liberty, freedom, and enfranchisement!"
BRUTUS.   People and Senators, be not affrighted.
   Fly not, stand still. Ambition's debt is paid.
CASCA.   Go to the pulpit, Brutus.

57. **enfranchisement:** release. 62. **fellow:** equal. 74. **Olympus:** a mountain in Greece, the legendary home of the gods. 75. **bootless:** in vain. 77. *Et tu, Brute?*: *Latin,* "Even you, Brutus?"

DECIUS.   And Cassius too.

BRUTUS. Where's Publius?   85

CINNA. Here, quite confounded with this mutiny.

METELLUS. Stand fast together, lest some friend of Caesar's
   Should chance—

BRUTUS. Talk not of standing. Publius, good cheer
   There is no harm intended to your person,   90
   Nor to no Roman else. So tell them, Publius.

CASSIUS. And leave us, Publius, lest that the people,
   Rushing on us, should do your age some mischief.

BRUTUS. Do so, and let no man abide° this deed,
   But we the the doers.

(*Reenter* TREBONIUS.)

CASSIUS.   Where is Antony?   95

TREBONIUS. Fled to his house amazed.
   Men, wives, and children stare, cry out, and run
   As it were Doomsday.

BRUTUS.   Fates, we will know your pleasures.
   That we shall die, we know; 'tis but the time
   And drawing days out, that men stand upon.°   100

CASSIUS. Why, he that cuts off twenty years of life
   Cuts off so many years of fearing death.

BRUTUS. Grant that, and then is death a benefit,
   So are we Caesar's friends, that have abridged
   His time of fearing death. Stoop, Romans, stoop,   105
   And let us bathe our hands in Caesar's blood
   Up to the elbows, and besmear our swords.
   Then walk we forth, even to the market place,
   And, waving our red weapons o'er our heads,
   Let's all cry, "Peace, freedom, and liberty!"   110

CASSIUS. Stoop then, and wash. How many ages hence
   Shall this our lofty scene be acted over
   In states unborn and accents yet unknown!

BRUTUS. How many times shall Caesar bleed in sport,°
   That now on Pompey's basis° lies along°   115
   No worthier than the dust!

94. **abide:** pay the penalty for. 100. **stand upon:** worry about. 114. **in sport:** in drama (like this) viewed for entertainment. 115. **Pompey's basis:** the base of Pompey's statue. **along:** stretched out.

CASSIUS.   So oft as that shall be
  So often shall the knot of us be called
  The men that gave their country liberty.
DECIUS.   What, shall we forth?
CASSIUS.   Aye, every man away.
  Brutus shall lead, and we will grace his heels   120
  With the most boldest and best hearts of Rome.

(*Enter a* SERVANT.)

BRUTUS.   Soft! Who comes here? A friend of Antony's.
SERVANT.   Thus, Brutus, did my master bid me kneel;
  Thus did Mark Antony bid me fall down;
  And, being prostrate, thus he bade me say: 125
  Brutus is noble, wise, valiant, and honest;
  Caesar was mighty, bold, royal, and loving;
  Say I love Brutus, and I honor him;
  Say I feared Caesar, honored him, and loved him.
  If Brutus will vouchsafe that Antony   130
  May safely come to him and be resolved
  How Caesar hath deserved to lie in death,
  Mark Antony shall not love Caesar dead
  So well as Brutus living, but will follow
  The fortunes and affairs of noble Brutus   135
  Thorough° the hazards of this untrod state°
  With all true faith. So says my master Antony.
BRUTUS.   Thy master is a wise and valiant Roman—
  I never thought him worse.
  Tell him, so please him come unto this place,   140
  He shall be satisfied, and, by my honor,
  Depart untouched.
SERVANT.   I'll fetch him presently.   (*Exit.*)
BRUTUS.   I know that we shall have him well to friend.
CASSIUS.   I wish we may; but yet have I a mind
  That fears him much, and my misgivings still   145
  Falls shrewdly to the purpose.°

(*Reenter* ANTONY.)

BRUTUS.   But here comes Antony. Welcome, Mark Antony.

136. Thorough: through. **untrod state:** uncertain future. **146. Falls . . . purpose:** doubts the wisdom of what you are doing.

ANTONY.   O mighty Caesar; dost thou lie so low?
Are all they conquests, glories, triumphs, spoils,
Shrunk to this little measure? Fare thee well.   150
I know not, gentlemen, what you intend,
Who else must be let blood, who else is rank.°
If I myself, there is no hour so fit
As Caesar's death's hour, nor no instrument
Of half that worth as those your swords, made rich   155
With the most noble blood of all this world.
I do beseech ye, if you bear me hard,
Now, whilst your purpled hands do reek and smoke,
Fulfill your pleasure. Live a thousand years,
I shall not find myself so apt to die.   160
No place will please me so, no mean° of death,
As here by Caesar, and by you cut off,
The choice and master spirits of this age.
BRUTUS.   O Antony, beg not your death of us.
Though now we must appear bloody and cruel,   165
As by our hands and this our present act
You see we do. Yet see you but our hands
And this the bleeding business they have done.
Our hearts you see not. They are pitiful;
And pity to the general wrong of Rome—   170
As fire drives out fire, so pity pity—
Hath done this deed on Caesar. For your part,
To you, our swords have leaden° points, Mark Antony.
Our arms in strength of malice,° and our hearts
Of brothers' temper, do receive you in   175
With all kind love, good thoughts, and reverence.
CASSIUS.   Your voice shall be as strong as any man's
In the disposing of new dignities.°
BRUTUS.   Only be patient till we have appeased
The multitude, beside themselves with fear,   180
And then we will deliver you the cause
Why I, that did love Caesar when I struck him,
Have thus proceeded.
ANTONY.   I doubt not of your wisdom.
Let each man render me his bloody hand.

152. rank: in need of bleeding as a means of curing disease. 161. mean: means.
173. leaden: blunt. 174. in strength of malice: with the power to harm you.
178. disposing of new dignities: deciding who shall hold political office.

First, Marcus Brutus, will I shake with you.   185
Next, Caius Cassius, do I take your hand.
Now, Decius Brutus, yours; now yours, Metellus;
Yours, Cinna; and, my valiant Casca, yours;
Though last, not least in love, yours, good Trebonius.
Gentlemen all—alas, what shall I say?   190
My credit now stands on such slippery ground,
That one of two bad ways you must conceit° me,
Either a coward or a flatterer.
That I did love thee, Caesar, oh, 'tis true.
If then thy spirit look upon us now,   195
Shall it not grieve thee dearer than thy death
To see thy Antony making his peace,
Shaking the bloody fingers of thy foes,
Most noble! in the presence of thy corse?°
Had I as many eyes as thou hast wounds,   200
Weeping as fast as they stream forth thy blood,
It would become me better than to close
In terms of friendship with thine enemies.
Pardon me, Julius! Here wast thou bayed,° brave hart,°
Here didst thou fall, and here thy hunters stand,   205
Signed in thy spoil° and crimsoned in thy lethe.°
O world, thou wast the forest to this hart,
And this, indeed, O world, the heart of thee.
How like a deer strucken by many princes
Dost thou here lie!   210
CASSIUS. Mark Antony—
ANTONY.   Pardon me, Caius Cassius
The enemies of Caesar shall say this;
Then, in a friend, it is cold modesty.
CASSIUS. I blame you not for praising Caesar so;
But what compact mean you to have with us?   215
Will you be pricked in number° of our friends,
Or shall we on, and not depend on you?
ANTONY. Therefore I took your hands, but was indeed
Swayed from the point by looking down on Caesar.
Friends am I with you all and love you all,   220

---

192. conceit: imagine. 199. corse: corpse. 204. bayed: brought to bay; surrounded
by baying hunting dogs. hart: deer. 206. Signed in thy spoil: stained with your
slaughter. lethe: blood. 216. pricked in number: marked in the list; counted on.

Upon this hope, that you shall give me reasons
Why and wherein Caesar was dangerous.
BRUTUS.   Or else were this a savage spectacle.
Our reasons are so full of good regard
That were you, Antony, the son of Caesar,   225
You should be satisfied.
ANTONY.   That's all I seek;
And am moreover suitor that I may
Produce his body to the market place,
And in the pulpit, as becomes a friend,
Speak in the order of his funeral.   230
BRUTUS.   You shall, Mark Antony.
CASSIUS.   Brutus, a word with you.

(*Aside to* BRUTUS.)

You know not what you do. Do not consent
That Antony speak in his funeral.
Know you how much the people may be moved
By that which he will utter?
BRUTUS.   By your pardon.   235
I will myself into the pulpit first,
And show the reason of our Caesar's death.
What Antony shall speak, I will protest
He speaks by leave and by permission,
And that we are contented Caesar shall   240
Have all true rites and lawful ceremonies.
It shall advantage more than do us wrong.
CASSIUS.   I know not what may fall. I like it not.
BRUTUS.   Mark Antony, here, take you Caesar's body.
You shall not in your funeral speech blame us,   245
But speak all good you can devise of Caesar,
And say you do 't by our permission.
Else shall you not have any hand at all
About his funeral. And you shall speak
In the same pulpit whereto I am going—   250
After my speech is ended.
ANTONY.   Be it so
I do desire no more.
BRUTUS.   Prepare the body then, and follow us.

(*Exeunt all but* ANTONY.)

ANTONY. O, pardon me, thou bleeding piece of earth,
That I am meek and gentle with these butchers!   255
Thou art the ruins of the noblest man
That ever livèd in the tide of times.
Woe to the hand that shed this costly blood!
Over thy wounds now do I prophesy—
Which, like dumb mouths, do ope their ruby lips   260
To beg the voice and utterance of my tongue—
A curse shall light upon the limbs of men.
Domestic fury and fierce civil strife
Shall cumber° all the parts of Italy.
Blood and destruction shall be so in use,   265
And dreadful objects so familiar,
That mothers shall but smile when they behold
Their infants quartered with° the hands of war,
All pity choked with custom of fell deeds.°
And Caesar's spirit, ranging° for revenge,   270
With Ate° by his side come hot from hell,
Shall in these confines with a monarch's voice
Cry "Havoc,"° and let slip the dogs of war,
That this foul deed shall smell above the earth
With carrion men, groaning for burial.   275

(*Enter a* SERVANT.)

You serve Octavius Caesar,° do you not?
SERVANT. I do, Mark Antony.
ANTONY. Caesar did write for him to come to Rome.
SERVANT. He did receive his letters, and is coming;
And bid me say to you by word of mouth—   280

(*Seeing the body.*)

O Caesar!
ANTONY. Thy heart is big. Get thee apart and weep.
Passion, I see, is catching, for mine eyes,
Seeing those beads of sorrow stand in thine,
Began to water. Is thy master coming?   285

264. cumber: encumber; weigh down. **268. quartered with:** cut into pieces by.
269. All . . . deeds: Cruel (*fell*) deeds will become so common that people will
no longer feel pity. **270. ranging:** roaming; seeking. **271. Ate** (ā′tē): in Greek
mythology, the goddess of discord and revenge. **273. "Havoc":** To cry "Havoc"
is to give the signal for pillage and destruction. **276. Octavius Caesar:** grandson
of Caesar's sister Julia, who was adopted by Caesar as his heir. After 27 B.C., Octavius became Augustus Caesar, first emperor of Rome (27 B.C.–A.D. 14).

SERVANT.   He lies tonight within seven leagues of Rome.
ANTONY.   Post back with speed, and tell him what hath chanced.
　　Here is a mourning Rome, a dangerous Rome,
　　No Rome of safety for Octavius yet.
　　Hie hence, and tell him so. Yet, stay awhile.　　　　　　　290
　　Thou shalt not back till I have borne this corse
　　Into the market place. There shall I try,°
　　In my oration, how the people take
　　The cruel issue° of these bloody men;
　　According to the which, thou shalt discourse　　　　　　295
　　To young Octavious of the state of things.
　　Lend me your hand.

(*Exeunt with* CAESAR'S *body.*)

292. try: test; discover. 294. issue: deed; action.

Meaning and Method: Act III, Scene 1

1. From the historical accounts available to us it appears that Caesar never had a chance to read the actual letter of warning that he received, although he did have it with him up to the moment of his death. Shakespeare changes this, showing Caesar not only refusing to accept the letter, but irritated with the author of it. What reason does Caesar give for refusing to read it? In what way is Shakespeare's version more dramatic than the historical account?

2. Caesar appears as an "imperial" person, as a leader, in this scene. In what way are his behavior, his speech, and his attitude different in his public role from what they were when we saw him in private with his wife, Calpurnia? Is his character consistent or inconsistent?

3. Explain Caesar's last words "*Et tu, Brute? Then fall, Caesar!*"

4. Why does Mark Antony send a servant to Brutus and Cassius prior to appearing before them? How does he act toward Brutus and Cassius when he does meet them?

5. Why does Mark Antony not fear to reveal some of his feelings about Caesar before Brutus and Cassius? How are the feelings he reveals in his soliloquy (lines 254–75) different from those he has already publicly expressed? What does he prophesy? In what way are the events prophesied logical outcomes of the assassination of a revered leader? What similar events have occurred in recent history?

6. Brutus and Cassius constantly differ over tactics. What are the specific differences of opinion they have had about Mark Antony? Why does Cassius fear a funeral oration by Antony? Why does Brutus feel such a funeral speech can bring no harm?

SCENE 2.   *The Forum.*

(*Enter* BRUTUS *and* CASSIUS, *and a throng of* CITIZENS.)

CITIZENS.   We will be satisfied! Let us be satisfied!

BRUTUS.   Then follow me, and give me audience, friends.
Cassius, go you into the other street,
And part the numbers.
Those that will hear me speak, let 'em stay here;   5
Those that will follow Cassius, go with him;
And public reasons shall be rendered
Of Caesar's death.

FIRST CITIZEN.   I will hear Brutus speak.

SECOND CITIZEN.   I will hear Cassius, and compare their reasons,   10
When severally we hear them rendered.

(*Exit* CASSIUS, *with some of the* CITIZENS. BRUTUS *goes into the pulpit.*)

THIRD CITIZEN.   The noble Brutus is ascended. Silence!

BRUTUS.   Be patient till the last.
Romans, countrymen, and lovers! Hear me for my cause, and
be silent, that you may hear. Believe me for mine honor, and   15
have respect to mine honor, that you may believe. Censure°
me in your wisdom, and awake your senses, that you may
the better judge. If there be any in this assembly, any
dear friend of Caesar's, to him I say that Brutus' love to
Caesar was no less than his. If then that friend demand why   20
Brutus rose against Caesar, this is my answer: Not that I
loved Caesar less, but that I loved Rome more. Had you
rather Caesar were living, and die all slaves, than that Caesar
were dead, to live all freemen? As Caesar loved me, I weep
for him; as he was fortunate, I rejoice at it; as he was valiant,   25
I honor him; but, as he was ambitious, I slew him. There is
tears for his love; joy for his fortune; honor for his valor;
and death for his ambition. Who is here so base that would
be a bondman? If any, speak; for him have I offended. Who
is here so rude° that would not be a Roman? If any, speak;   30
for him have I offended. Who is here so vile that will not
love his country? If any, speak; for him have I offended.
I pause for a reply.

16. **Censure:** judge. 30. **rude:** barbarous; uncivilized.

ALL. None, Brutus, none!

BRUTUS. Then none have I offended. I have done no more to   35
Caesar than you shall do to Brutus. The question of his
death is enrolled° in the Capitol; his glory not extenuated,°
wherein he was worthy, nor his offenses enforced,° for
which he suffered death.

(*Enter* ANTONY *and others, with* CAESAR's *body.*)

Here comes his body, mourned by Mark Antony; who,   40
though he had no hand in his death, shall receive the
benefit of his dying, a place in the commonwealth—as which
of you shall not? With this I depart—that, as I slew my
best lover for the good of Rome, I have the same dagger for
myself when it shall please my country to need my death.   45

ALL. Live, Brutus! Live! Live!

FIRST CITIZEN. Bring him with triumph home unto his house!

SECOND CITIZEN. Give him a statue with his ancestors!

THIRD CITIZEN. Let him be Caesar!

FOURTH CITIZEN.   Caesar's better parts
Shall be crowned in Brutus!

FIRST CITIZEN.   We'll bring him to his house   50
With shouts and clamors!

BRUTUS.   My countrymen—

SECOND CITIZEN. Peace! Silence! Brutus speaks.

FIRST CITIZEN.   Peace, ho!

BRUTUS. Good countrymen. Let me depart alone,
And, for my sake, stay here with Antony.
Do grace to Caesar's corpse, and grace his speech   55
Tending to Caesar's glories, which Mark Antony,
By our permission, is allowed to make.
I do entreat you, not a man depart
Save I alone, till Antony have spoke.   (*Exit.*)

FIRST CITIZEN. Stay, ho, and let us hear Mark Antony!   60

THIRD CITIZEN. Let him go up into the public chair.
We'll hear him. Noble Antony, go up.

ANTONY. For Brutus' sake, I am beholding° to you.

(*Goes into the pulpit.*)

---

37. **enrolled:** preserved among the records. **extenuated:** belittled. **38. enforced:**
stressed. **63. beholding:** indebted; beholden.

FOURTH CITIZEN.   What does he say of Brutus?

THIRD CITIZEN.   He says, for Brutus' sake,
He finds himself beholding to us all.   65

FOURTH CITIZEN.   'Twere best he speak no harm of Brutus here!

FIRST CITIZEN.   This Caesar was a tyrant!

THIRD CITIZEN.   Nay, that's certain.
We are blest that Rome is rid of him.

SECOND CITIZEN.   Peace! Let us hear what Antony can say.

ANTONY.   You gentle Romans—

CITIZENS.   Peace, ho! Let us hear him.   70

ANTONY.   Friends, Romans, countrymen, lend me your ears.
I come to bury Caesar, not to praise him.
The evil that men do lives after them,
The good is oft interrèd with their bones.
So let it be with Caesar. The noble Brutus   75
Hath told you Caesar was ambitious.
If it were so, it was a grievous fault;
And grievously hath Caesar answered it.
Here, under leave of Brutus and the rest—
For Brutus is an honorable man;   80
So are they all, all honorable men—
Come I to speak in Caesar's funeral.
He was my friend, faithful and just to me.
But Brutus says he was ambitious;
And Brutus is an honorable man.   85
He hath brought many captives home to Rome,
Whose ransoms did the general coffers° fill.
Did this in Caesar seem ambitious?
When that the poor have cried, Caesar hath wept;
Ambition should be made of sterner stuff.   90
Yet Brutus says he was ambitious;
And Brutus is an honorable man.
You all did see that on the Lupercal
I thrice presented him a kingly crown,
Which he did thrice refuse. Was this ambition?   95
Yet Brutus says he was ambitious;
And, sure, he is an honorable man.
I speak not to disprove what Brutus spoke,
But here I am to speak what I do know.
You all did love him once, not without cause.   100

87. **general coffers:** public treasury.

What cause withholds you, then, to mourn for him?
O judgment, thou art fled to brutish beasts,
And men have lost their reason! Bear with me;
My heart is in the coffin there with Caesar,
And I must pause till it come back to me.   105

FIRST CITIZEN.   Methinks there is much reason in his sayings.
SECOND CITIZEN.   If thou consider rightly of the matter,
Caesar has had great wrong.
THIRD CITIZEN.   Has he, masters?
I fear there will a worse come in his place.
FOURTH CITIZEN.   Marked ye his words? He would not take   110
the crown,
Therefore 'tis certain he was not ambitious.
FIRST CITIZEN.   If it be found so, some will dear abide it!°
SECOND CITIZEN.   Poor soul! His eyes are red as fire with weeping.
THIRD CITIZEN.   There's not a nobler man in Rome than Antony.
FOURTH CITIZEN.   Now mark him, he begins again to speak.   115
ANTONY.   But yesterday the word of Caesar might
Have stood against the world. Now lies he there,
And none so poor to do him reverence.
O masters, if I were disposed to stir
Your hearts and minds to mutiny and rage,   120
I should do Brutus wrong, and Cassius wrong,
Who, you all know, are honorable men.
I will not do them wrong; I rather choose
To wrong the dead, to wrong myself and you,
Than I will wrong such honorable men.   125
But here's a parchment with the seal of Caesar—
I found it in his closet—'tis his will.
Let but the commons° hear this testament—
Which, pardon me, I do not mean to read—
And they would go and kiss dead Caesar's wounds   130
And dip their napkins° in his sacred blood,
Yea, beg a hair of him for memory,
And, dying, mention it within their wills,
Bequeathing it as a rich legacy
Unto their issue.°   135
FOURTH CITIZEN.   We'll hear the will! Read it, Mark Antony.

112. **dear abide it:** pay a severe penalty for it. 128. **commons:** common people.
131. **napkins:** handkerchiefs. 135. **issue:** descendants.

ALL.   The will! The will! We will hear Caesar's will!

ANTONY.   Have patience, gentle friends, I must not read it.
It is not meet you know how Caesar loved you.
You are not wood, you are not stones, but men;   140
And, being men, hearing the will of Caesar,
It will inflame you, it will make you mad.
'Tis good you know not that you are his heirs,
For, if you should, oh, what would come of it!

FOURTH CITIZEN.   Read the will! We'll hear it, Antony!   145
You shall read us the will! Caesar's will!

ANTONY.   Will you be patient? Will you stay awhile?
I have o'ershot myself to tell you of it.
I fear I wrong the honorable men
Whose daggers have stabbed Caesar. I do fear it.   150

FOURTH CITIZEN.   They were traitors! Honorable men!

ALL.   The will! The testament!

SECOND CITIZEN.   They were villains, murderers. The will! Read
the will!

ANTONY.   You will compel me, then, to read the will?
Then make a ring about the corpse of Caesar,   155
And let me show you him that made the will.
Shall I descend? And will you give me leave?

SEVERAL CITIZENS.   Come down.

SECOND CITIZEN.   Descend.

THIRD CITIZEN.   You shall have leave.   160

(ANTONY *comes down from the pulpit.*)

FOURTH CITIZEN.   A ring. Stand round.

FIRST CITIZEN.   Stand from the hearse, stand from the body.

SECOND CITIZEN.   Room for Antony, most noble Antony!

ANTONY.   Nay, press not so upon me. Stand far off.

SEVERAL CITIZENS.   Stand back! Room! Bear back!   165

ANTONY.   If you have tears, prepare to shed them now.
You all do know this mantle. I remember
The first time ever Caesar put it on.
'Twas on a summer's evening, in his tent,
That day he overcame the Nervii.°   170
Look, in this place ran Cassius' dagger through.
See what a rent the envious Casca made!
Through this the well-belovèd Brutus stabbed,

170. **Nervii:** a barbarian tribe conquered by Caesar during the Gallic Wars.

And as he plucked his cursèd steel away,
Mark how the blood of Caesar followed it,   175
As rushing out of doors, to be resolved
If Brutus so unkindly knocked, or no.
For Brutus, as you know, was Caesar's angel.
Judge, O you gods, how dearly Caesar loved him!
This was the most unkindest cut of all;   180
For when the noble Caesar saw him stab,
Ingratitude, more strong than traitors' arms,
Quite vanquished him. Then burst his mighty heart;
And, in his mantle muffling up his face,
Even at the base of Pompey's statuë,   185
Which all the while ran blood, great Caesar fell.
Oh, what a fall was there, my countrymen!
Then I, and you, and all of us fell down,
Whilst bloody treason flourished over us.
Oh, now you weep; and, I perceive, you feel   190
The dint° of pity. These are gracious drops.
Kind souls, what weep you when you but behold
Our Caesar's vesture° wounded? Look you here—
Here is himself, marred, as you see, with traitors.

FIRST CITIZEN.   Oh, piteous spectacle!   195

SECOND CITIZEN.   Oh, noble Caesar!

THIRD CITIZEN.   Oh woeful day!

FOURTH CITIZEN.   Oh traitors, villains!

FIRST CITIZEN.   Oh, most bloody sight!

SECOND CITIZEN.   We will be revenged!   200

ALL.   Revenge! About! Seek! Burn! Fire! Kill! Slay!
    Let not a traitor live!

ANTONY.   Stay, countrymen.

FIRST CITIZEN.   Peace there! Hear the noble Antony.

SECOND CITIZEN.   We'll hear him, we'll follow him, we'll die
    with him!

ANTONY.   Good friends, sweet friends, let me not stir you up.   205
To such a sudden flood of mutiny.
They that have done this deed are honorable.
What private griefs they have, alas, I know not,
That made them do it. They are wise and honorable,
And will, no doubt, with reasons answer you.   210

191. dint: blow; shock. 193. vesture: clothing.

I come not, friends, to steal away your hearts.
I am no orator, as Brutus is;
But, as you know me all, a plain blunt man
That love my friend; and that they know full well
That gave me public leave to speak of him.   215
For I have neither wit, nor words, nor worth,
Action, nor utterance, nor the power of speech,
To stir men's blood. I only speak· right on.
I tell you that which you yourselves do know;
Show you sweet Caesar's wounds—poor, poor, dumb   220
      mouths—
And bid them speak for me. But were I Brutus,
And Brutus Antony, there were an Antony
Would ruffle up your spirits and put a tongue
In every wound of Caesar that should move
The stones of Rome to rise and mutiny!   225

ALL. We'll mutiny!
FIRST CITIZEN. We'll burn the house of Brutus.
THIRD CITIZEN. Away, then! Come, seek the conspirators!
ANTONY. Yet hear me, countrymen. Yet hear me speak.
ALL. Peace, ho! Hear Antony. Most noble Antony!   230
ANTONY. Why, friends, you go to do you know not what.
      Wherein hath Caesar thus deserved your loves?
      Alas, you know not. I must tell you, then—
      You have forgot the will I told of.
ALL. Most true. The will! Let's stay and hear the will.   235
ANTONY. Here is the will, and under Caesar's seal.
      To every Roman citizen he gives,
      To every several° man, seventy-five drachmas.°
SECOND CITIZEN. Most noble Caesar! We'll revenge his death!
THIRD CITIZEN. Oh, royal Caesar!   240
ANTONY. Hear me with patience.
ALL. Peace, ho!
ANTONY. Moreover, he hath left you all his walks,
      His private arbors and new-planted orchards,
      On this side Tiber. He hath left them you,   245
      And to your heirs forever, common pleasures,
      To walk abroad, and recreate yourselves.
      Here was a Caesar! When comes such another?

238. several: individual. drachmas: silver coins.

FIRST CITIZEN.   Never, never! Come, away, away!
We'll burn his body in the holy place,   250
And with the brands fire the traitors' houses.
Take up the body.
SECOND CITIZEN.   Go fetch fire.
THIRD CITIZEN.   Pluck down benches.
FOURTH CITIZEN.   Pluck down forms,° windows, anything!   255

(*Exeunt* CITIZENS *with the body.*)

ANTONY.   Now let it work. Mischief, thou art afoot,   *accomplished*
Take thou what course thou wilt!   *his plan*

(*Enter a* SERVANT.)

                                                 How now, fellow!
SERVANT.   Sir, Octavius is already come to Rome.
ANTONY.   Where is he?
SERVANT.   He and Lepidus° are at Caesar's house.   260
ANTONY.   And thither will I straight to visit him.
He comes upon a wish. Fortune is merry,
And in this mood will give us anything.   *Success*
SERVANT.   I heard him say Brutus and Cassius
Are rid like madmen through the gates of Rome.   265
ANTONY.   Belike they had some notice of the people,
How I had moved them. Bring me to Octavius. (*Exeunt.*)

255. forms: benches. 260. Lepidus: one of Caesar's generals, who afterward became part of a three-man ruling body in Rome, along with Antony and Octavius.

Meaning and Method: Act III, Scene 2

1. Brutus insists that the choice for Romans was between freedom and
slavery. "Had you rather Caesar were living, and die all slaves, than
that Caesar were dead, to live all freemen?" Does Brutus offer any
facts to prove this really was the choice? *Was* Caesar ambitious? Why
does Brutus offer his life to the mob?
    During Brutus's speech a member of the crowd shouts "Let him be
Caesar!" What does he mean? What does this tell us about the ordinary Roman?
    Why is Brutus's oration written in prose while Mark Antony's is in
poetry? What qualities in Brutus allowed him to leave before Antony
gave his eulogy to Caesar?
2. When Mark Antony says "Now let it work. Mischief, thou art afoot, /
Take thou what course thou wilt!" we have good reason to suspect that

he has deliberately whipped up the mob to a pitch that will make his earlier prediction come true. How has he achieved his aim? Note the refrain of the words *ambition* and *honorable* throughout the speech. At what line, as you read, did you become aware that these words were being used ironically, that is, in a sense entirely opposite from their true meaning? At what point does Antony's voice break, almost in tears? Is he acting or is he really so broken up about Caesar's murder?

How does Antony get the mob to beg for the will? Why does he point to the bloody wounds after removing Caesar's mantle (lines 220–25)? Does Antony offer any facts to disprove Brutus's claim that Caesar was ambitious? Is the Fourth Citizen's response (line 110) a correct estimate of Caesar's ambition? Why does Antony claim to be "no orator . . . a plain blunt man" (lines 212–13)?

SCENE 3.   *A street in Rome.*

(*Enter* CINNA, *the poet.*)

CINNA.   I dreamed tonight that I did feast with Caesar,
   And things unluckily charge my fantasy.°
   I have no will to wander forth of doors,
   Yet something else leads me forth.

(*Enter* CITIZENS.)

FIRST CITIZEN.   What is your name?   5
SECOND CITIZEN.   Whither are you going?
THIRD CITIZEN.   Where do you dwell?
FOURTH CITIZEN.   Are you a married man, or a bachelor?
SECOND CITIZEN.   Answer every man directly.
FIRST CITIZEN.   Aye, and briefly.   10
FOURTH CITIZEN.   Aye, and wisely.
THIRD CITIZEN.   Aye, and truly, you were best.
CINNA.   What is my name? Whither am I going? Where do I
   dwell? Am I a married man or a bachelor? Then, to
   answer every man, directly and briefly, wisely and truly,   15
   wisely I say I am a bachelor.
SECOND CITIZEN.   That's as much as to say they are fools that
      marry.
   You'll bear me a bang° for that, I fear. Proceed directly.

2. things . . . fantasy: My imagination is burdened with thoughts of bad luck.
18. You'll . . . bang: You'll be struck.

CINNA. Directly, I am going to Caesar's funeral.

FIRST CITIZEN.   As a friend or an enemy?   20

CINNA. As a friend.

SECOND CITIZEN.   That matter is answered directly.

FOURTH CITIZEN.   For your dwelling—briefly.

CINNA. Briefly, I dwell by the Capitol.

THIRD CITIZEN.   Your name sir, truly.   25

CINNA. Truly, my name is Cinna.

FIRST CITIZEN.   Tear him to pieces! He's a conspirator.

CINNA. I am Cinna the poet, I am Cinna the poet!

FOURTH CITIZEN.   Tear him for his bad verses, tear him for his
     bad verses!   30

CINNA. I am not Cinna the conspirator!

FOURTH CITIZEN.   It is no matter, his name's Cinna! Pluck but
     his name out of his heart, and turn him going.

THIRD CITIZEN.   Tear him, tear him! Come, brands. Ho, fire-
     brands—to Brutus', to Cassius'! Burn all. Some to Decius'   35
     house and some to Casca's; some to Ligarius'. Away, go!

                                             (*Exeunt.*)

Meaning and Method: Act III, Scene 3

In this brief scene Shakespeare has used four actors to stand for a
mob and one actor to represent all its victims. What is the technique?
Does it work? If the playwright had used one actor to tell another that
mobs were killing innocent men, would the scene have been more exciting and convincing or less? Why?

Act IV

SCENE 1. *A house in Rome.*

(ANTONY, OCTAVIUS, *and* LEPIDUS, *seated at a table.*) *Power*

ANTONY. These many, then, shall die; their names are pricked.° *Crazy*
OCTAVIUS. Your brother too must die. Consent you, Lepidus?
LEPIDUS. I do consent—
OCTAVIUS.   Prick him down, Antony.
LEPIDUS. Upon condition Publius shall not live,
  Who is your sister's son, Mark Antony.   5
ANTONY. He shall not live. Look, with a spot I damn him.
  But, Lepidus, go you to Caesar's house.
  Fetch the will hither, and we shall determine   *Cheat the*
  How to cut off some charge in legacies.°   *people's money*
LEPIDUS. What, shall I find you here?   *from Caesar* 10
OCTAVIUS. Or here or at the Capitol.

(*Exit* LEPIDUS.)

ANTONY. This is a slight unmeritable man,
  Meet to be sent on errands. Is it fit,
  The threefold world divided, he should stand
  One of the three to share it?
OCTAVIUS.   So you thought him;   15
  And took his voice who should be pricked to die
  In our black sentence and proscription.
ANTONY. Octavius, I have seen more days than you;
  And though we lay these honors on this man
  To ease ourselves of divers slanderous loads,   20
  He shall but bear them as the ass bears gold,
  To groan and sweat under the business,
  Either led or driven, as we point the way.
  And having brought our treasure where we will,
  Then take we down his load, and turn him off,   25
  Like to the empty ass, to shake his ears,
  And graze in commons.°

1. **pricked:** written on a list of proscription (a list of condemned persons).
9. **How . . . legacies:** how to avoid paying off some of the legacies left by Caesar. 27. **graze in commons:** graze in community (*common*) fields.

OCTAVIUS.   You may do your will
     But he's a tried and valiant soldier.
ANTONY.   So is my horse, Octavius, and for that
     I do appoint him store of provender.°   30
     It is a creature that I teach to fight,
     To wind,° to stop, to run directly on,
     His corporal motion° governed by my spirit.
     And, in some taste,° is Lepidus but so.
     He must be taught, and trained, and bid go forth;   35
     A barren-spirited fellow; one that feeds
     On abjects,° orts,° and imitations,
     Which, out of use and staled by other men,
     Begin his fashion.° Do not talk of him,
     But as a property. And now, Octavius,   40
     Listen great things—Brutus and Cassius
     Are levying powers.° We must straight make head.°
     Therefore let our alliance be combined,
     Our best friends made, our means stretched,
     And let us presently go sit in council   45
     How covert° matters may be best disclosed,
     And open perils surest answered.
OCTAVIUS.   Let us do so; for we are at the stake,
     And bayed about with many enemies;
     And some that smile have in their hearts, I fear,   50
     Millions of mischiefs.   (*Exeunt.*)

30. I . . . provender: I provide fodder for him. 32. wind: turn. 33. corporal
motion: bodily action. 34. some taste: certain ways. 37. abjects: worthless things.
orts: scraps of food. 39. Begin his fashion: which he begins to use when they have
ceased to be fashionable with other men. 42. levying powers: raising armies.
make head: gather forces. 46. covert: secret.

Meaning and Method: Act IV, Scene 1

1. What kind of man is Lepidus? Does he seem to have a mind of his
   own? What does Mark Antony think of him? Why does Antony allow
   his nephew's name to be included on a list of those to be killed?
   What does this tell us about Mark Antony?
2. Characterize Octavius. Is he a match for Antony? What is his attitude
   toward Lepidus?

SCENE 2. *Camp near Sardis.* Before* BRUTUS's *tent.*

(Drum. Enter BRUTUS, LUCILIUS, LUCIUS, *and* SOLDIERS;
TITINIUS *and* PINDARUS *meet them.*)

BRUTUS. Stand, ho!
LUCILIUS. Give the word, ho, and stand!
BRUTUS. What now, Lucilius! Is Cassius near?
LUCILIUS. He is at hand, and Pindarus is come
  To do you salutation from his master.   5
BRUTUS. He greets me well. Your master, Pindarus,
  In his own change, or by ill officers,°
  Hath given me some worthy cause to wish
  Things done undone. But if he be at hand,
  I shall be satisfied.
PINDARUS.   I do not doubt   10
  But that my noble master will appear
  Such as he is, full of regard and honor.°
BRUTUS. He is not doubted. A word, Lucilius,
  How he received you. Let me be resolved.
LUCILIUS. With courtesy and with respect enough,   15
  But not with such familiar instances,
  Nor with such free and friendly conference,
  As he hath used of old.
BRUTUS.   Thou hast described
  A hot friend cooling. Ever note, Lucilius,
  When love begins to sicken and decay,   20
  It useth an enforcèd ceremony.°
  There are no tricks in plain and simple faith.
  But hollow men, like horses hot at hand,°
  Make gallant show and promise of their mettle;
  But when they should endure the bloody spur,   25
  They fall their crests,° and like deceitful jades,°
  Sink in the trial. Comes his army on?

(handwritten note: forced politeness)

---

* **Sardis:** capital city of Lydia, an ancient country in western Asia Minor. Brutus and Cassius fled to the East and returned to Greece to meet the army of Antony and Octavius. **7. In . . . officers:** because he has changed his nature or because of the deeds of unworthy subordinates. **12. full . . . honor:** worthy of respect. **21. enforcèd ceremony:** forced politeness. **23. hot at hand:** eager for the race. **26. fall . . . crests:** become crestfallen, spiritless. **jades:** poor-spirited nags.

LUCILIUS.   They mean this night in Sardis to be quartered.
The greater part, the horse in general,°
Are come with Cassius.

(*Low march within.*)

BRUTUS.   Hark! He is arrived.   30
March gently on to meet him.

(*Enter* CASSIUS *and his powers.*)

CASSIUS.   Stand, ho!
BRUTUS.   Stand, ho! Speak the word along.
FIRST SOLDIER.   Stand!
SECOND SOLDIER.   Stand!   35
THIRD SOLDIER.   Stand!
CASSIUS.   Most noble brother, you have done me wrong.
BRUTUS.   Judge me, you gods! Wrong I mine enemies?
And if not so, how should I wrong a brother?
CASSIUS.   Brutus, this sober form° of yours hides wrongs;   40
And when you do them—
BRUTUS.   Cassius, be content;   *Don't*
Speak your grief softly. I do know you well.   *make*
Before the eyes of both our armies here,   *a*
Which should perceive nothing but love from us,   *scene*
Let us not wrangle. Bid them move away;   45
Then in my tent, Cassius, enlarge your griefs,
And I will give you audience.
CASSIUS.   Pindarus,
Bid our commanders lead their charges off
A little from this ground.
BRUTUS.   Lucilius, do you the like, and let no man   50
Come to our tent till we have done our conference.
Let Lucius and Titinius guard our door.   (*Exeunt.*)

29. horse in general: all the cavalry. **40. sober form:** grave, dignified appearance.

SCENE 3.   BRUTUS's *tent.*

(*Enter* BRUTUS *and* CASSIUS.)

CASSIUS.   That you have wronged me doth appear in this:
   You have condemned and noted° Lucius Pella
   For taking bribes here of the Sardians;
   Wherein my letters, praying on his side
   Because I knew the man, were slighted off.   5
BRUTUS.   You wronged yourself to write in such a case.
CASSIUS.   In such a time as this it is not meet
   That every nice° offense should bear his comment.°
BRUTUS.   Let me tell you, Cassius, you yourself
   Are much condemned to have an itching palm,°   10
   To sell and mart your offices for gold
   To underservers.
CASSIUS.   I an itching palm!
   You know that you are Brutus that speaks this,
   Or, by the gods, this speech were else your last!
BRUTUS.   The name of Cassius honors this corruption,   15
   And chastisement doth therefore hide his head.°
CASSIUS.   Chastisement!
BRUTUS.   Remember March, the ides of March remember.
   Did not great Julius bleed for justice's sake?
   What villain touched his body, that did stab,   20
   And not for justice? What, shall one of us,
   That struck the foremost man of all this world
   But for supporting robbers, shall we now
   Contaminate our fingers with base bribes?
   And sell the mighty space of our large honors   25
   For so much trash as may be graspèd thus?
   I had rather be a dog, and bay the moon,
   Than such a Roman.
CASSIUS.   Brutus, bait not me!°
   I'll not endure it. You forget yourself,

2. noted: censured. 8. nice: petty. bear his comment: be carefully noted. 10. itching palm: an eager hand for taking bribes. 15–16. name . . . head: Since Cassius is so great a man, his corruption is not punished. 28. bait not me: Do not growl at me as though I were a bear. In the sport of bearbaiting, popular in Shakespeare's London, vicious dogs were released into a pit that contained an equally fierce bear tied to a stake. The animals often fought to the death.

To hedge me in.° I am a soldier, I,   30
Older in practice, abler than yourself
To make conditions.°

BRUTUS.   Go to. You are not, Cassius.

CASSIUS.   I am.

BRUTUS.   I say you are not.

CASSIUS.   Urge me no more, I shall forget myself.   35
Have mind upon your health! Tempt me no further.

BRUTUS.   Away, slight man!

CASSIUS.   Is 't possible?

BRUTUS.   Hear me, for I will speak.
Must I give way and room to your rash choler?°
Shall I be frighted when a madman stares?   40

CASSIUS.   O ye gods, ye gods! Must I endure all this?

BRUTUS.   All this! Aye, more. Fret till your proud heart break.
Go show your slaves how choleric you are,
And make your bondmen tremble. Must I budge?
Must I observe you? Must I stand and crouch   45
Under your testy humor? By the gods,
You shall digest the venom of your spleen,°
Though it do split you! For, from this day forth,
I'll use you for my mirth, yea, for my laughter,
When you are waspish.

CASSIUS.   Is it come to this?   50

BRUTUS.   You say you are a better soldier:
Let it appear so; make your vaunting true,
And it shall please me well. For mine own part,
I shall be glad to learn of noble men.

CASSIUS.   You wrong me every way; you wrong me, Brutus.   55
I said, an elder soldier, not a better.
Did I say better?

BRUTUS.   If you did, I care not.

CASSIUS.   When Caesar lived, he durst not thus have moved me.

BRUTUS.   Peace, peace! You durst not so have tempted him.

CASSIUS.   I durst not!   60

BRUTUS.   No.

CASSIUS.   What! Durst not tempt him!

BRUTUS.   For your life you durst not.

---

30. hedge me in: control me. **32. conditions:** decisions or rules. **39. choler:** anger;
wrath. **47. spleen:** rage; temper.

CASSIUS.   Do not presume too much upon my love.
  I may do that I shall be sorry for.
BRUTUS.   You have done that you should be sorry for.   65
  There is no terror, Cassius, in your threats,
  For I am armed so strong in honesty
  That they pass by me as the idle wind,
  Which I respect not. I did send to you
  For certain sums of gold, which you denied me.   70
  For I can raise no money by vile means.
  By heaven, I had rather coin my heart,
  And drop my blood for drachmas, than to wring
  From the hard hands of peasants their vile trash
  By any indirection.° I did send   75
  To you for gold to pay my legions,
  Which you denied me. Was that done like Cassius?
  Should I have answered Caius Cassius so?
  When Marcus Brutus grows so covetous,
  To lock such rascal counters° from his friends,   80
  Be ready, gods, with all your thunderbolts;
  Dash him to pieces!
CASSIUS.   I denied you not.
BRUTUS.   You did.
CASSIUS.   I did not. He was but a fool that brought
  My answer back. Brutus hath rived my heart.   85
  A friend should bear his friend's infirmities,
  But Brutus makes mine greater than they are.
BRUTUS.   I do not, till you practice them on me.
CASSIUS.   You love me not.
BRUTUS.   I do not like your faults.
CASSIUS.   A friendly eye could never see such faults.   90
BRUTUS.   A flatterer's would not, though they do appear
  As huge as high Olympus.
CASSIUS.   Come, Antony, and young Octavius, come!
  Revenge yourselves alone on Cassius,
  For Cassius is aweary of the world;   95
  Hated by one he loves; braved° by his brother;
  Checked like a bondman; all his faults observed,
  Set in a notebook, learned, and conned by rote,°

75. **indirection:** crooked means. 80. **rascal counters:** wretched coins. 96. **braved:** taunted. 98. **conned by rote:** learned by heart.

To cast into my teeth. Oh, I could weep
My spirit from mine eyes! There is my dagger,   100
And here my naked breast; within, a heart
Dearer than Plutus' mine,° richer than gold.
If that thou be'st a Roman, take it forth;
I, that denied thee gold, will give my heart.
Strike, as thou didst at Caesar; for, I know,   105
When thou didst hate him worst, thou lovedst him better
Than ever thou lovedst Cassius!

BRUTUS.   Sheathe your dagger.
Be angry when you will, it shall have scope,°
Do what you will, dishonor shall be humor.°
O Cassius, you are yokèd with a lamb   110
That carries anger as the flint bears fire,
Who, much enforcèd, shows a hasty spark,
And straight is cold again.

CASSIUS.   Hath Cassius lived
To be but mirth and laughter to his Brutus,
When grief and blood ill-tempered vexeth him?   115

BRUTUS. When I spoke that, I was ill-tempered too.

CASSIUS. Do you confess so much? Give me your hand.

BRUTUS. And my heart too.

CASSIUS.   O Brutus!

BRUTUS.   What's the matter?

CASSIUS. Have not you love enough to bear with me
When that rash humor which my mother gave me   120
Makes me forgetful?

BRUTUS. Yes, Cassius, and from henceforth,
When you are overearnest with your Brutus,
He'll think your mother chides, and leave you so.

POET. (*Within.*) Let me go in to see the generals.   125
There is some grudge between 'em, 'tis not meet
They be alone.

LUCILIUS. (*Within.*) You shall not come to them.

POET. (*Within.*) Nothing but death shall stay me.

(*Enter* POET, *followed by* LUCILIUS, TITINIUS, *and*
LUCIUS.)

102. **Plutus's mine:** all the riches of Plutus, god of wealth. 108. **scope:** free play.
109. **dishonor . . . humor:** Any insults you present will be regarded merely as
one of your fits of temper.

CASSIUS.   How now! What's the matter?

POET.   For shame, you generals! What do you mean?   130
    Love and be friends, as two such men should be,
    For I have seen more years, I'm sure, than ye.

CASSIUS.   Ha, ha! How vilely doth this cynic° rhyme!

BRUTUS.   Get you hence, sirrah. Saucy fellow, hence!

CASSIUS.   Bear with him, Brutus. 'Tis his fashion.   135

BRUTUS.   I'll know his humor when he knows his time.
    What should the wars do with these jigging fools?
    Companion,° hence!

CASSIUS.   Away, away, be gone!

(Exit POET.*)*

BRUTUS.   Lucilius and Titinius, bid the commanders
    Prepare to lodge their companies tonight.   140

CASSIUS.   And come yourselves, and bring Messala with you
    Immediately to us.

(Exeunt LUCILIUS *and* TITINIUS.*)*

BRUTUS.   Lucius, a bowl of wine!   *(Exit* LUCIUS.*)*

CASSIUS.   I did not think you could have been so angry.

BRUTUS.   O Cassius, I am sick of many griefs.

CASSIUS.   Of your philosophy you make no use   145
    If you give place to accidental evils.

BRUTUS.   No man bears sorrow better. Portia is dead.

CASSIUS.   Ha! Portia!

BRUTUS.   She is dead.

CASSIUS.   How 'scaped I killing when I crossed you so?   150
    Oh, insupportable and touching loss!
    Upon what sickness?

BRUTUS.   Impatient of my absence,
    And grief that young Octavius with Mark Antony
    Have made themselves so strong—for with her death
    That tidings came—with this she fell distract,   155
    And, her attendants absent, swallowed fire.

CASSIUS.   And died so?

BRUTUS.   Even so.

CASSIUS.   O ye immortal gods!

133. **cynic:** rude fellow. 138. **Companion:** fellow; used here as a word showing contempt.

(*Reenter* LUCIUS *with wine and taper.*)

BRUTUS.   Speak no more of her. Give me a bowl of wine.
In this I bury all unkindness, Cassius. (*Drinks.*)
CASSIUS.   My heart is thirsty for that noble pledge.   160
Fill, Lucius, till the wine o'erswell the cup.
I cannot drink too much of Brutus' love.   (*Drinks.*)
BRUTUS.   Come in, Titinius!

(*Exit* LUCIUS. *Enter* TITINIUS, *with* MESSALA.)

                          Welcome, good Messala.
Now sit we close about this taper here,
And call in question our necessities.   165
CASSIUS.   Portia, art thou gone?
BRUTUS.   No more, I pray you.
Messala, I have here receivèd letters
That young Octavius and Mark Antony
Come down upon us with a mighty power,
Bending their expedition toward Philippi.°   170
MESSALA.   Myself have letters of the selfsame tenor.
BRUTUS.   With what addition?
MESSALA.   That by proscription and bills of outlawry
Octavius, Antony, and Lepidus
Have put to death an hundred Senators.   175
BRUTUS.   Therein our letters do not well agree.
Mine speak of seventy Senators that died
By their proscriptions, Cicero being one.
CASSIUS.   Cicero one!
MESSALA.   Cicero is dead,
And by that order of proscription.   180
Had you your letters from your wife, my lord?
BRUTUS.   No, Messala.
MESSALA.   Nor nothing in your letters writ of her?
BRUTUS.   Nothing, Messala.
MESSALA.   That, methinks, is strange.
BRUTUS.   Why ask you? Hear you aught of her in yours?   185
MESSALA.   No, my lord.
BRUTUS.   Now, as you are a Roman, tell me true.

170. **Philippi:** a city in Macedonia (northern Greece).

MESSALA.   Then like a Roman bear the truth I tell—
    For certain she is dead, and by strange manner.
BRUTUS.   Why, farewell, Portia. We must die, Messala.   190
    With meditating that she must die once
    I have the patience to endure it now.
MESSALA.   Even so great men great losses should endure.
CASSIUS.   I have as much of this in art° as you,
    But yet my nature° could not bear it so.   195
BRUTUS.   Well, to our work alive. What do you think
    Of marching to Philippi presently?
CASSIUS.   I do not think it good.
BRUTUS.   Your reason?
CASSIUS.   This it is:
    'Tis better that the enemy seek us.
    So shall he waste his means, weary his soldiers,   200
    Doing himself offense, whilst we, lying still,
    Are full of rest, defense, and nimbleness.
BRUTUS.   Good reasons must, of force, give place to better,
    The people 'twixt Philippi and this ground
    Do stand but in a forced affection;   205
    For they have grudged us contribution.
    The enemy, marching along by them,
    By them shall make a fuller number up,
    Come on refreshed, new-added, and encouraged.
    From which advantage shall we cut him off,   210
    If at Philippi we do face him there,
    These people at our back.
CASSIUS.   Hear me, good brother—
BRUTUS.   Under your pardon. You must note beside,
    That we have tried the utmost of our friends,
    Our legions are brimful, our cause is ripe.   215
    The enemy increaseth every day;
    We, at the height, are ready to decline.
    There is a tide in the affairs of men,
    Which, taken at the flood, leads on to fortune;
    Omitted, all the voyage of their life   220
    Is bound in shallows and in miseries.

194. art: theory or belief acquired by study. **195. nature:** In contrast to *art, nature* is the personality and abilities one is born with.

On such a full sea are we now afloat,
And we must take the current when it serves,
Or lose our ventures.

CASSIUS.   Then with your will, go on.
We'll along ourselves, and meet them at Philippi.   225

BRUTUS.   The deep of night is crept upon our talk,
And nature must obey necessity,
Which we will niggard° with a little rest.
There is no more to say?

CASSIUS.   No more. Good night.
Early tomorrow will we rise and hence.   230

BRUTUS.   Lucius!

(*Enter* LUCIUS.)

My gown.

(*Exit* LUCIUS.)

                    Farewell, good Messala.
Good night, Titinius. Noble, noble Cassius,
Good night, and good repose.

CASSIUS.   O my dear brother!
This was an ill beginning of the night.
Never come such division 'tween our souls!   235
Let it not, Brutus.

BRUTUS.   Everything is well.

CASSIUS.   Good night, my lord.

BRUTUS.   Good night, good brother.

TITINIUS *and* MESSALA.   Good night, Lord Brutus.

BRUTUS.   Farewell, everyone.

(*Exeunt all but* BRUTUS. *Reenter* LUCIUS, *with the gown.*)

Give me the gown. Where is thy instrument?°

LUCIUS.   Here in the tent.

BRUTUS.   What, thou speak'st drowsily?   240
Poor knave, I blame thee not; thou art o'erwatched.°
Call Claudius and some other of my men.
I'll have them sleep on cushions in my tent.

LUCIUS.   Varro and Claudius!

228. niggard: satisfy stingily. **239. instrument:** lute. **241. o'erwatched:** weary from staying alert and watching for such a long time.

(*Enter* VARRO *and* CLAUDIUS.)

VARRO.   Calls my lord?   245

BRUTUS.   I pray you, sirs, lie in my tent and sleep.
It may be I shall raise you by and by
On business to my brother Cassius.

VARRO.   So please you, we will stand and watch your pleasure.

BRUTUS.   I will not have it so. Lie down, good sirs.   250
It may be I shall otherwise bethink me.
Look, Lucius, here's the book I sought for so;
I put it in the pocket of my gown.

(VARRO *and* CLAUDIUS *lie down.*)

LUCIUS.   I was sure your lordship did not give it me.

BRUTUS.   Bear with me, good boy, I am much forgetful.   255
Canst thou hold up thy heavy eyes awhile,
And touch thy instrument a strain or two?

LUCIUS.   Aye, my lord, an 't please you.

BRUTUS.   It does, my boy.
I trouble thee too much, but thou art willing.

LUCIUS.   It is my duty, sir.   260

BRUTUS.   I should not urge thy duty past thy might;
I know young bloods look for a time of rest.

LUCIUS.   I have slept, my lord, already.

BRUTUS.   It was well done; and thou shalt sleep again:
I will not hold thee long. If I do live,   265
I will be good to thee.

(*Music, and a song.*)

This is a sleepy tune. O murderous° slumber,
Lay'st thou thy leaden mace° upon my boy,
That plays the music? Gentle knave, good night.
I will not do thee so much wrong to wake thee.   270
If thou dost nod, thou break'st thy instrument;
I'll take it from thee. And, good boy, good night.
Let me see, let me see, is not the leaf turned down
Where I left reading? Here it is, I think.   (*Sits down.*)

---

267. murderous: because it deprives men of alertness. **268. mace:** the club or
staff with which an English law officer touched a person he was about to arrest.

(Enter the Ghost of CAESAR.)

How ill this taper burns! Ha! Who comes here?   275
I think it is the weakness of mine eyes
That shapes this monstrous apparition.
It comes upon me. Art thou anything?
Art thou some god, some angel, or some devil,
That makest my blood cold, and my hair to stare?°   280
Speak to me what thou art.
GHOST.   Thy evil spirit, Brutus.
BRUTUS.   Why comest thou?
GHOST.   To tell thee thou shalt see me at Philippi.
BRUTUS.   Well, then I shall see thee again?
GHOST.   Aye, at Philippi.   285
BRUTUS.   Why, I will see thee at Philippi, then.

(Exit Ghost.)

Now I have taken heart, thou vanishest.
Ill spirit, I would hold more talk with thee.
Boy, Lucius! Varro! Claudius! Sirs, awake!
Claudius!   290
LUCIUS.   The strings, my lord, are false.
BRUTUS.   He thinks he is still at his instrument.
    Lucius, awake!
LUCIUS.   My lord?
BRUTUS.   Didst thou dream, Lucius, that thou so criedst out?   295
LUCIUS.   My lord, I do not know that I did cry.
BRUTUS.   Yes, that thou didst. Didst thou see anything?
LUCIUS.   Nothing, my lord.
BRUTUS.   Sleep again, Lucius. Sirrah Claudius!

(To VARRO.)

Fellow thou, awake!   300
VARRO.   My lord?
CLAUDIUS.   My lord?
BRUTUS.   Why did you so cry out, sirs, in your sleep?
VARRO *and* CLAUDIUS.   Did we, my lord?
BRUTUS.   Aye. Saw you anything?
VARRO.   No, my lord, I saw nothing.

280. stare: stand on end.

CLAUDIUS.   Nor I, my lord.   305
BRUTUS. Go and commend me to my brother Cassius.
    Bid him set on his powers betimes before,°
    And we will follow.
VARRO *and* CLAUDIUS.   It shall be done, my lord.   (*Exeunt.*)

307. set . . . before: leave with his armies ahead of ours in good time.

Meaning and Method: Act IV, Scenes 2 and 3

1. Brutus and Cassius withdraw to Brutus's tent (probably the inner stage) to argue out of sight and ear of their staffs. Brutus accuses Cassius of having an "itchy palm," of accepting bribes. Does Cassius deny this accusation? What is ironic about Brutus's asking Cassius to send him money because he himself "can raise no money by vile means"?

2. It can be argued that Brutus proved himself a poor politician when he did not want Mark Antony killed along with Caesar, when he allowed Mark Antony to deliver a funeral eulogy, and when he left Mark Antony alone during that oration. In all these matters Brutus acted against Cassius' advice.

    In what way does he show himself a poor politician again in this scene? Why does Cassius yield so often to Brutus? Which one seems to reason philosophically? which practically?

3. What is meant by Brutus's lines 218–24, beginning, "There is a tide in the affairs of men"?

4. How did Portia die? Why did she kill herself? Why would Brutus feel guilt as well as grief at her death?

5. How does the scene with Lucius contrast with the angry scene between Brutus and Cassius? What characteristics of Brutus are revealed here? What characteristics are revealed by Brutus's reaction to the ghost?

Act V

SCENE 1. *The plains of Philippi.*

(*Enter* OCTAVIUS, ANTONY, *and* SOLDIERS.)

OCTAVIUS. Now, Antony, our hopes are answerèd.
    You said the enemy would not come down,
    But keep the hills and upper regions.
    It proves not so; their battles° are at hand;
    They mean to warn us at Philippi here,   5
    Answering before we do demand of them.
ANTONY. Tut, I am in their bosoms,° and I know
    Wherefore they do it. They could be content
    To visit other places, and come down
    With fearful bravery, thinking by this face   10
    To fasten in our thoughts that they have courage.
    But 'tis not so.

(*Enter a* MESSENGER.)

MESSENGER.   Prepare you generals.
    The enemy comes on in gallant show.
    Their bloody sign of battle° is hung out,
    And something to be done immediately.   15
ANTONY. Octavius, lead your battle softly on,
    Upon the left hand of the even field.
OCTAVIUS. Upon the right hand I. Keep thou the left.
ANTONY. Why do you cross me in this exigent?°
OCTAVIUS. I do not cross you; but I will do so.   20

(*March. Drum. Enter* BRUTUS, CASSIUS, *and* SOLDIERS;
    LUCILIUS, TITINIUS, MESSALA, *and others.*)

BRUTUS. They stand, and would have parley.
CASSIUS. Stand fast, Titinius. We must out and talk.
OCTAVIUS. Mark Antony, shall we give sign of battle?
ANTONY. No, Caesar, we will answer on their charge.
    Make forth; the generals would have some words.   25

---

4. battles: formations. **7. I am in their bosoms:** I know the secrets of their hearts. **14. bloody sign of battle:** red flag of defiance. **19. exigent:** critical moment; exigency.

OCTAVIUS.   Stir not until the signal.

BRUTUS.   Words before blows. Is it so, countrymen?

OCTAVIUS.   Not that we love words better, as you do.

BRUTUS.   Good words are better than bad strokes, Octavius.

ANTONY.   In your bad strokes, Brutus, you give good words. 30
    Witness the hole you made in Caesar's heart,
    Crying, "Long live! Hail, Caesar!"

CASSIUS.   Antony,
    The posture° of your blows are yet unknown;
    But for your words, they rob the Hybla° bees,
    And leave them honeyless.

ANTONY.   Not stingless too. 35

BRUTUS.   Oh, yes, and soundless too.
    For you have stol'n their buzzing, Antony,
    And very wisely threat before you sting.

ANTONY.   Villains, you did not so when your vile daggers
    Hacked one another in the sides of Caesar. 40
    You showed your teeth like apes, and fawned like hounds,
    And bowed like bondmen, kissing Caesar's feet,
    Whilst damnèd Casca, like a cur, behind
    Struck Caesar on the neck. O you flatterers!

CASSIUS.   Flatterers! Now, Brutus, thank yourself. 45
    This tongue had not offended so today
    If Cassius might have ruled.

OCTAVIUS.   Come, come, the cause. If arguing make us sweat,
    The proof of it will turn to redder drops.
    Look,
    I draw a sword against conspirators. 50
    When think you that the sword goes up° again?
    Never, till Caesar's three and thirty wounds
    Be well avenged, or till another Caesar
    Have added slaughter to the sword of traitors. 55

BRUTUS.   Caesar, thou canst not die by traitors' hands,
    Unless thou bring'st them with thee.

OCTAVIUS.   So I hope.
    I was not born to die on Brutus' sword.

BRUTUS.   Oh, if thou wert the noblest of thy strain,
    Young man, thou couldst not die more honorable. 60

---

33. posture: quality. **34. Hybla:** a mountain in Sicily famous for the honey produced there. **52. goes up:** returns to the scabbard.

CASSIUS.   A peevish schoolboy, worthless of such honor,
Joined with a masker and a reveler!°
ANTONY.   Old Cassius still!
OCTAVIUS.   Come Antony; away!
Defiance, traitors, hurl we in your teeth.
If you dare fight today, come to the field;   65
If not, when you have stomachs.

(*Exeunt* OCTAVIUS, ANTONY, *and* SOLDIERS.)

CASSIUS.   Why, now, blow wind, swell billow, and swim bark.°
The storm is up, and all is on the hazard.
BRUTUS.   Ho, Lucilius! Hark, a word with you.
LUCILIUS. (*Standing forth.*)   My lord?   70

(BRUTUS *and* LUCILIUS *converse apart.*)

CASSIUS.   Messala!
MESSALA (*Standing forth.*)   What says my general?
CASSIUS.   Messala,
This is my birthday, as this very day
Was Cassius born. Give me thy hand, Messala.   75
Be thou my witness that, against my will,
As Pompey was, am I compelled to set
Upon one battle all our liberties.
You know that I held Epicurus strong,°
And his opinion. Now I change my mind,   80
And partly credit things that do presage.°
Coming from Sardis, on our former ensign
Two mighty eagles fell, and there they perched,
Gorging and feeding from our soldiers' hands,
Who to Philippi here consorted us.   85
This morning are they fled away and gone.
And in their steads do ravens, crows, and kites
Fly o'er our heads and downward look on us,
As we were sickly prey. Their shadows seem

62. **masker . . . reveler:** one who spends his time in masquerades and night life.
67. **bark:** ship. 79. **held Epicurus strong:** was a firm believer in Epicurus. Epicurus (342?–270? B.C.), a Greek philosopher, taught, among other things, that
the gods (if they existed) were not interested in man; man, therefore, should not
waste his time believing in superstitions and omens. 81. **presage:** foretell the
future.

A canopy most fatal, under which   90
Our army lies, ready to give up the ghost.
MESSALA.   Believe not so.
CASSIUS.   I but believe it partly,
For I am fresh of spirit and resolved
To meet all perils very constantly.
BRUTUS.   Even so, Lucilius.
CASSIUS.   Now, most noble Brutus,   95
The gods today stand friendly, that we may,
Lovers in peace, lead on our days to age!
But since the affairs of men rest still incertain,
Let's reason with the worst that may befall.
If we do lose this battle, then is this   100
The very last time we shall speak together.
What are you then determinèd to do?
BRUTUS.   Even by the rule of that philosophy
By which I did blame Cato for the death
Which he did give himself°—I know not how,   105
But I do find it cowardly and vile,
For fear of what might fall, so to prevent
The time of life°—arming myself with patience
To stay° the providence of some high powers
That govern us below.
CASSIUS.   Then, if we lose this battle,   110
You are contented to be led in triumph
Through the streets of Rome?
BRUTUS.   No, Cassius, no. Think not, thou noble Roman,
That ever Brutus will go bound to Rome.
He bears too great a mind. But this same day   115
Must end that work the ides of March begun;
And whether we shall meet again I know not.
Therefore our everlasting farewell take.
Forever, and forever, farewell, Cassius!
If we do meet again, why, we shall smile;   120
If not, why then this parting was well made.
CASSIUS.   Forever, and forever, farewell, Brutus!

104–05. death . . . himself: suicide. **107–08. so . . . life:** by preventing life from ending naturally. **109. stay:** await.

If we do meet again, we'll smile indeed;
If not, 'tis true this parting was well made.

BRUTUS.   Why, then, lead on. Oh, that a man might know   125
The end of this day's business ere it come!
But it sufficeth that the day will end,
And then the end is known. Come, ho! Away! (*Exeunt.*)

Meaning and Method: Act V, Scene 1

1. What is the attitude of Cassius toward the coming battle at Philippi? In what way has he partially changed his basic attitude toward life?
   What is Brutus's attitude toward the battle to come? Why does he change his opinion about suicide?
2. What do lines 19–20 suggest about the relationship between Antony and Octavius?
3. Once again (lines 74–91) omens are used as foreshadowing. How do these lines indicate a change in Cassius's thinking regarding omens? How do they compare with his lines 142–43 of Act I, Scene 2, "The fault, dear Brutus, is not in our stars, / But in ourselves, that we are underlings"?
4. Why does Cassius remind Brutus (lines 45–47) of their earlier disagreement regarding the fate of Antony?
5. The purpose of the battle at Philippi is to avenge the murder of Caesar. Were Antony and Octavius justified in seeking revenge? Is revenge ever justified when it involves further killing? What evidence is there in the play of Shakespeare's attitude toward revenge?

SCENE 2.   *The field of battle.*

(*Alarum. Enter* BRUTUS *and* MESSALA.)

BRUTUS.   Ride, ride, Messala, ride and give these bills°
Unto the legions on the other side.

(*Loud alarum.*)

Let them set on at once, for I perceive
But cold demeanor° in Octavius' wing,
And sudden push gives them the overthrow.
Ride, ride, Messala. Let them all come down.   (*Exeunt.*)   5

1. **bills:** messages. 4. **cold demeanor:** lack of spirit.

SCENE 3.   *Another part of the field.*

(*Alarums. Enter* CASSIUS *and* TITINIUS.)

CASSIUS.   Oh, look, Titinius, look, the villains fly!
Myself have to mine own turned enemy.°
This ensign° here of mine was turning back.
I slew the coward, and did take it from him.
TITINIUS.   O Cassius, Brutus gave the word too early,   5
Who, having some advantage on Octavius,
Took it too eagerly. His soldiers fell to spoil,
Whilst we by Antony are all enclosed.

(*Enter* PINDARUS.)

PINDARUS.   Fly further off, my lord, fly further off!
Mark Antony is in your tents, my lord.   10
Fly, therefore, noble Cassius, fly far off!
CASSIUS.   The hill is far enough. Look, look, Titinius;
Are those my tents where I perceive the fire?
TITINIUS.   They are, my lord.
CASSIUS.   Titinius, if thou lovest me,
Mount thou my horse, and hide thy spurs in him   15
Till he have brought thee up to yonder troops,
And here again, that I may rest assured
Whether yond troops are friend or enemy.
TITINIUS.   I will be here again, even with a thought.   (*Exit.*)
CASSIUS.   Go, Pindarus, get higher on that hill;   20
My sight was ever thick.° Regard Titinius,
And tell me what thou notest about the field.

(PINDARUS *ascends the hill.*)

This day I breathèd first. Time is come round,
And where I did begin, there shall I end;
My life is run his compass. Sirrah, what news?   25
PINDARUS. (*Above.*)   O my lord!
CASSIUS.   What news?
PINDARUS. (*Above.*)   Titinius is enclosèd round about
With horsemen, that make to him on the spur!

2. **Myself . . . enemy:** I am now an enemy to my own men because they are
running away. 3. **ensign:** used both for the company's colors and the officer who
carried them. 21. **thick:** short. Cassius is nearsighted.

Yet he spurs on! Now they are almost on him!   30
Now, Titinius! Now some light.° Oh, he lights too.
He's ta'en! (*Shout.*) And, hark! They shout for joy.
CASSIUS.   Come down; behold no more.
Oh, coward that I am, to live so long
To see my best friend ta'en before my face!   35

(PINDARUS *descends.*)

Come hither, sirrah.
In Parthia did I take thee prisoner,
And then I swore thee, saving of thy life,
That whatsoever I did bid thee do,
Thou shouldst attempt it. Come now, keep thine oath.   40
Now be a free man, and with this good sword,
That ran through Caesar's bowels, search this bosom.
Stand not to answer. Here, take thou the hilts;
And, when my face is covered, as 'tis now,
Guide thou the sword.

(PINDARUS *stabs him.*)

             Caesar, thou art revenged   45
Even with the sword that killed thee. (*Dies.*)
PINDARUS.   So, I am free; yet would not so have been,
Durst I have done my will. O Cassius!
Far from this country Pindarus shall run,
Where never Roman shall take note of him.   (*Exit.*)   50

(*Reenter* TITINIUS *with* MESSALA.)

MESSALA.   It is but change,° Titinius; for Octavius
Is overthrown by noble Brutus' power,
As Cassius' legions are by Antony.
TITINIUS.   These tidings will well comfort Cassius.
MESSALA.   Where did you leave him?
TITINIUS.   All disconsolate,   55
With Pindarus, his bondman, on this hill.
MESSALA.   Is not that he that lies upon the ground?
TITINIUS.   He lies not like the living. Oh, my heart!
MESSALA.   Is not that he?
TITINIUS.   No, this was he, Messala,

31. **light**: descend; alight. 51. **change**: exchange; *that is*, the battle is a stalemate.

But Cassius is no more. O setting sun,   60
As in thy red rays thou dost sink to night,
So in his red blood Cassius' day is set;
The sun of Rome is set! Our day is gone;
Clouds, dews, and dangers come. Our deeds are done!
Mistrust of my success hath done this deed.   65
MESSALA.   Mistrust of good success hath done this deed.
O hateful error, melancholy's child,
Why dost thou show to the apt thoughts of men
The things that are not? O error, soon conceived,
Thou never comest unto a happy birth,   70
But kill'st the mother that engendered thee!
TITINIUS.   What, Pindarus! Where art thou, Pindarus?
MESSALA.   Seek him, Titinius, whilst I go meet
The noble Brutus, thrusting this report
Into his ears; I may say, thrusting it,   75
For piercing steel and darts envenomèd
Shall be as welcome to the ears of Brutus
As tidings of this sight.
TITINIUS.   Hie you, Messala,
And I will seek for Pindarus the while.

(Exit MESSALA.*)*

Why didst thou send me forth, brave Cassius?   80
Did I not meet thy friends? And did not they
Put on my brows this wreath of victory,
And bid me give it thee? Didst thou not hear their shouts?
Alas, thou hast misconstrued everything!
But, hold thee, take this garland on thy brow.   85
Thy Brutus bid me give it thee, and I
Will do his bidding. Brutus, come apace,
And see how I regard Caius Cassius.
By your leave, gods,—this is a Roman's part.
Come, Cassius' sword, and find Titinius' heart.   90

(Kills himself.)

(Alarum. Reenter MESSALA *with* BRUTUS, *young* CATO,
and others.)

BRUTUS.   Where, where, Messala, doth his body lie?
MESSALA.   Lo, yonder, and Titinius mourning it.

BRUTUS.   Titinius' face is upward.

CATO.   He is slain.

BRUTUS.   O Julius Caesar, thou art mighty yet!
Thy spirit walks abroad, and turns our swords   95
In our own proper° entrails.

everyone dies because of Caesar

(*Low alarums.*)

CATO.   Brave Titinius!
Look whether he have not crowned dead Cassius!

BRUTUS.   Are yet two Romans living such as these?
The last of all the Romans, fare thee well!
It is impossible that ever Rome   100
Should breed thy fellow. Friends, I owe more tears
To this dead man than you shall see me pay.
I shall find time, Cassius, I shall find time.
Come, therefore, and to Thasos send his body:
His funerals shall not be in our camp,   105
Lest it discomfort us. Lucilius, come;
And come, young Cato. Let us to the field.
Labeo and Flavius, set our battles on.
'Tis three o'clock; and, Romans, yet ere night
We shall try fortune in a second fight.   (*Exeunt.*) 110

mourning Cassius

96. **proper:** individual.

Meaning and Method: Act V, Scenes 2 and 3

1. Why does Brutus bid Messala to ride to Cassius and tell him to attack?
   How does Scene 2 increase the pace of the action and also add to the
   suspense?
2. Pindarus, Cassius' servant, tells Cassius what he sees on the distant
   hill because Cassius is nearsighted. How does Pindarus misinterpret
   the result of Brutus's attack? Has Cassius' dream affected his ability
   to evaluate what he is told by Pindarus? Cassius has had frequent differences as to tactics with Brutus. Is this fact related to his interpretation of the battle scene?
3. What do lines 94--96 mean? How do they remind us of Brutus's
   thoughts on suicide?
4. In what way are Cassius' behavior and the manner of his death a
   reflection on his character? How does Titinius's suicide also reflect on
   Cassius' character? Why is Pindarus now free?

5. After Cassius' suicide, Titinius says of him that "The sun of Rome is set" (line 63) and Brutus calls him "The last of all the Romans" (line 99). Why do they praise Cassius so highly? Is their praise justified?

SCENE 4.   *Another part of the field.*

(Alarum. Enter, fighting, SOLDIERS of both armies; then BRUTUS, young CATO, LUCILIUS, and others.)

BRUTUS.   Yet, countrymen, oh, yet hold up your heads!
CATO.   What bastard doth not? Who will go with me?
    I will proclaim my name about the field.
    I am the son of Marcus Cato, ho!
    A foe to tyrants, and my country's friend.   5
    I am the son of Marcus Cato, ho!
BRUTUS.   And I am Brutus, Marcus Brutus, I—
    Brutus, my country's friend. Know me for Brutus. *(Exit.)*
LUCILIUS.   O young and noble Cato, art thou down?
    Why, now thou diest as bravely as Titinius,   10
    And mayst be honored, being Cato's son.
FIRST SOLDIER.   Yield, or thou diest.
LUCILIUS.   Only I yield to die.

(Offering money.)

    There is so much that thou wilt kill me straight.
    Kill Brutus, and be honored in his death.
FIRST SOLDIER.   We must not. A noble prisoner!   15
SECOND SOLDIER.   Room, ho! Tell Antony, Brutus is ta'en.
FIRST SOLDIER.   I'll tell the news. Here comes the general.

(Enter ANTONY.)

    Brutus is ta'en, Brutus is ta'en, my lord.
ANTONY.   Where is he?
LUCILIUS.   Safe, Antony, Brutus is safe enough.   20
    I dare assure thee that no enemy
    Shall ever take alive the noble Brutus.
    The gods defend him from so great a shame!
    When you do find him, or alive or dead,
    He will be found like Brutus, like himself.   25

ANTONY.   This is not Brutus, friend, but, I assure you,
A prize no less in worth. Keep this man safe,
Give him all kindness. I had rather have
Such men my friends than enemies. Go on,
And see whether Brutus be alive or dead,   30
And bring us word unto Octavius' tent
How everything is chanced.   (*Exeunt.*)

SCENE 5.   *Another part of the field.*

   (*Enter* BRUTUS, DARDANIUS, CLITUS, STRATO, *and* VOLUMNIUS.)

BRUTUS.   Come, poor remains of friends, rest on this rock.
CLITUS.   Statilius showed the torchlight, but my lord,
   He came not back. He is or ta'en or slain.
BRUTUS.   Sit thee down, Clitus. Slaying is the word;
   It is a deed in fashion. Hark thee, Clitus.   (*Whispers.*)   5
CLITUS.   What, I, my lord? No, not for all the world.
BRUTUS.   Peace then! No words.
CLITUS.   I'll rather kill myself.
BRUTUS.   Hark thee, Dardanius.   (*Whispers.*)
DARDANIUS.   Shall I do such a deed?
CLITUS.   O Dardanius!
DARDANIUS.   O Clitus!   10
CLITUS.   What ill request did Brutus make to thee?
DARDANIUS.   To kill him, Clitus. Look, he meditates.
CLITUS.   Now is that noble vessel full of grief,
   That it runs over even at his eyes.
BRUTUS.   Come hither, good Volumnius; list a word.   15
VOLUMNIUS.   What says my lord?
BRUTUS.   Why, this, Volumnius:
   The ghost of Caesar hath appeared to me
   Two several times by night; at Sardis once,
   And, this last night, here in Philippi fields.
   I know my hour is come.
VOLUMNIUS.   Not so, my lord.   20
BRUTUS.   Nay, I am sure it is, Volumnius.
   Thou seest the world, Volumnius, how it goes;
   Our enemies have beat us to the pit.

(*Low alarums.*)

It is more worthy to leap in ourselves,
Than to tarry till they push us. Good Volumnius,   25
Thou know'st that we two went to school together.
Even for that our love of old, I prithee
Hold thou my sword hilts whilst I run on it.
VOLUMNIUS.   That's not an office for a friend, my lord.

(*Alarum still.*)

CLITUS.   Fly, fly, my lord; there is no tarrying here.   30
BRUTUS.   Farewell to you, and you, and you. Volumnius.
Strato, thou hast been all this while asleep;
Farewell to thee too, Strato. Countrymen,
My heart doth joy that yet in all my life   *This needed*
I found no man but he was true to me.   *people*   35
I shall have glory by this losing day   *for once*
More than Octavius and Mark Antony
By this vile conquest shall attain unto.
So fare you well at once; for Brutus' tongue
Hath almost ended his life's history.   40
Night hangs upon mine eyes; my bones would rest,
That have but labored to attain this hour.

(*Alarum. Cry within,* "Fly, fly, fly!")

CLITUS.   Fly, my lord, fly.
BRUTUS.   Hence! I will follow.

(*Exeunt* CLITUS, DARDANIUS, *and* VOLUMNIUS.)

I prithee, Strato, stay thou by thy lord.
Thou art a fellow of a good respect;   45
Thy life hath had some smatch° of honor in it.
Hold then my sword, and turn away thy face,
While I do run upon it. Wilt thou, Strato?
STRATO.   Give me your hand first. Fare you well, my lord.
BRUTUS.   Farewell, good Strato. (*Runs on his sword.*)   50
Caesar, now be still.   *Is happy*
I killed not thee with half so good a will. (*Dies.*)   *of dieing*

46. smatch: taste.

(*Alarum. Retreat. Enter* OCTAVIUS, ANTONY, MESSALA, LUCILIUS, *and the* ARMY.)

OCTAVIUS.   What man is that?

MESSALA.   My master's man. Strato, where is thy master?

STRATO.   Free from the bondage you are in, Messala.   55
The conquerors can but make a fire of him,
For Brutus only overcame himself,
And no man else hath honor by his death.

LUCILIUS.   So Brutus should be found. I thank thee, Brutus,
That thou hast proved Lucilius' saying true.   60

OCTAVIUS.   All that served Brutus, I will entertain° them.
Fellow, wilt thou bestow thy time with me?

STRATO.   Aye, if Messala will prefer° me to you.

OCTAVIUS.   Do so, good Messala.

MESSALA.   How died my master, Strato?   65

STRATO.   I held the sword and he did run on it.

MESSALA.   Octavius, then take him to follow thee
That did the latest service to my master.

ANTONY.   This was the noblest Roman of them all.
All the conspirators, save only he,   70
Did that they did in envy of great Caesar.
He only, in a general honest thought
And common good to all, made one of them.
His life was gentle,° and the elements
So mixed in him that Nature might stand up   75
And say to all the world "This was a man."

OCTAVIUS.   According to his virtue let us use him,
With all respect, and rites of burial.
Within my tent his bones tonight shall lie,
Most like a soldier, ordered honorably.   80
So call the field to rest, and let's away,
To part° the glories of this happy day.   (*Exeunt.*)

61. entertain: take into service. **63. prefer**: recommend. **74. gentle**: noble. **82. part**: share.

Meaning and Method: Act V, Scenes 4 and 5

1. Why does Lucilius pretend to be Brutus and offer money to the soldiers to kill him?
2. Why is Antony's decision not to kill Lucilius evidence of his practical

and clever nature? What character trait does he have that Brutus seemed to lack?

3. How does Brutus die? What are his emotions at the time of his death? How does his method of dying differ from Cassius'? Why did Brutus feel that he knew that "my hour is come"?

4. Reread lines 69–76. What are Antony's reasons for saying of Brutus: "This was the noblest Roman of them all"? How does he feel toward the other conspirators? What do Antony's remarks about Brutus and and the remarks by Strato and Lucilius have in common? Do you agree with their evaluation?

5. Why does Shakespeare give Octavius the final words of the play?

Meaning and Method: On the Play as a Whole

1. Is Brutus the hero or the villain of the play? Why? Consider his character, his motives in entering into the conspiracy, and the opinions and actions of his friends and servants.

2. How does Brutus's idealism lead to his misunderstanding, misjudging, or underestimating Cassius and Mark Antony?

3. Why is the war being fought? Are Octavius, Antony, and Lepidus fighting only to avenge the death of Caesar? Or are they also fighting because as the representatives of the new Roman government they have their own political interests to consider? Is there any evidence in the play to support either or both reasons?

4. Explain the following: Both Cassius and Brutus adopt drastically changed viewpoints when their philosophical views are challenged by immediate and threatening realities.

5. In the Elizabethan theater in which Shakespeare worked, little scenery was used. He therefore could not depend on setting to establish time, place, and mood. Instead, he had to let the audience know the setting through lines in the play.

   What lines in Act II, Scene 1, make the audience conscious that time is passing? Why is this awareness important?

   Where are the time and the place revealed in the opening lines of Act III, Scene 1? Why is the time important to the reaction of the audience?

6. In Act I, Scene 2, lines 53–80, there is an extended metaphor. What is it, and with what words has it been continued or expanded? What relation does the metaphor have to the characters and the play as a whole?

7. In Act IV, Scene 1, lines 18–27, there is an extended simile. What is it, and with what words has it been continued or expanded?

8. Tragedy, when applied to drama, is sometimes defined as the story of

a basically good and noble individual—usually a king or a man of great stature—who, through some fault in his character, brings about his own ruin and death. How does this definition apply to the character of Caesar? Could it apply equally well to Brutus? Why or why not? In what way were both of these men victims of the conspiracy?

Composition and Discussion

1. Write a character sketch in which you compare and contrast any two of the following: Caesar, Antony, Brutus, and Cassius.

2. What do you think is the main theme of *Julius Caesar*? Is it that well-meaning men can sometimes lead a country to disaster? Is it that power corrupts and leads to dictatorship? Is it that political murder may be justified? that oratory and propaganda may sway the masses? that the means justifies the end?

Using *Julius Caesar* as the basis for your arguments, be prepared to take part in a panel discussion offering what you think is the theme. You may use examples from history and literature to support your point of view.

3. Write an essay describing a political or historical event in which an individual has been caught in a conflict of loyalties, as Brutus was in *Julius Caesar*. Keeping these parallels in mind, show how history does or does not repeat itself.

4. Who exerts more influence throughout the play—Julius Caesar or Marcus Brutus? Would *The Tragedy of Marcus Brutus* be a better title? Why or why not?

5. In a few paragraphs discuss the role of prophecy in foreshadowing the action of the play and the role of fate in determining the lives of Caesar and Brutus. Consider the following:

(a) strange disturbances in nature
(b) sleeplessness
(c) the ghost of Caesar
(d) darkness
(e) healthiness and infirmities

6. The following are some expressions from *Julius Caesar* that have passed into our everyday language:

(a) an itching palm
(b) a dish fit for the gods
(c) a lean and hungry look
(d) masters of their fate
(e) the dogs of war

Select one of these and write what you think it means. Give details and particulars, and examples, real or imaginary, to support your explanation.

7. Do research for an oral report on some famous "soothsayers." Among these might be Nostradamus, Cassandra, and Jeane Dixon and her power of prophecy. Be ready to explain to the class the identity of each of these people, and what he or she predicted that actually came to pass.

8. Is political assassination ever justified? What was behind the assassinations of Abraham Lincoln, John F. Kennedy, Martin Luther King, Jr., Malcolm X, Robert Kennedy?

Write a composition expressing your views about one or more of these murders.

9. In a composition of several paragraphs, compare and contrast the character of Brutus with that of Dr. Stockmann in *An Enemy of the People*, specifically in relation to their roles as purported enemies of the people and as idealists seeking to help the people. Consider the success or failure of each, and the role played by political innocence in the career of each.

AS YOU LIKE IT

William Shakespeare

[1564–1616]

As You Like It is a lighthearted comedy that Shakespeare created by dramatizing a popular tale called Rosalynde, first published in 1590. Its author, Thomas Lodge, was probably inspired by the Italian pastoral plays of the sixteenth century in which members of the royal court are pictured as escaping from the formalities of court life to a charming countryside in which no one works—an idyllic setting populated by shepherds whose unreal days are devoted to love and the composing and singing of songs. Shakespeare retained most of Lodge's plot, changing the names of some characters and adding one or two others. He also retained the pastoral setting.

Shakespeare wrote his play in 1599, nine years after Lodge's book appeared. Possibly because of the popularity of satire in the decade between the writing of Lodge's and Shakespeare's works, Shakespeare's attitude toward his material was very different from that of Lodge. In As You Like It, he gently satirized romantic illusions and the pastoral tradition itself.

(For Shakespeare's life and works, see pages 176–82.)

CHARACTERS

Duke,
living in banishment

Frederick,
his brother, and usurper of
his dominions

Amiens | lords attending the
Jaques | banished Duke

Le Beau,
a courtier attending
Frederick

Charles,
wrestler for Frederick

Oliver | sons of Sir
Jaques | Rowland
Orlando | de Boys

Adam | servants
Dennis | to Oliver

Touchstone,
a clown

Sir Oliver Martext,
a vicar

Corin | shepherds
Silvius |

William,
a country fellow, in love
with Audrey

Hymen,
god of marriage

Rosalind,
daughter of the banished
Duke

Celia,
daughter of Frederick

Phebe,
a shepherdess

Audrey,
a country wench

Lords, Pages, and **Attendants**

Place.   Oliver's house; Duke Frederick's court; and the Forest
of Arden.

273

Act I

SCENE 1. *Orchard of* OLIVER'S *house.*

(*Enter* ORLANDO *and* ADAM.)

ORLANDO. As I remember it, Adam, it was upon this fashion:
Bequeathed me by will but poor a thousand crowns,° and,
as thou sayest, charged my brother, on his blessing,° to
breed° me well—and there begins my sadness. My brother
Jaques° he keeps at school, and report speaks goldenly   5
of his profit; for my part, he keeps me rustically° at
home, or, to speak more properly, stays me here at home
unkept. For call you that keeping for a gentleman of
my birth that differs not from the stalling of an ox?
His horses are bred better, for besides that they are   10
fair with their feeding, they are taught their manage,°
and to that end riders dearly° hired. But I, his brother,
gain nothing under him but growth, for the which his
animals on his dunghills are as much bound to him as I.°
Besides this nothing that he so plentifully gives me,   15
the something that nature gave me his countenance seems
to take from me.° He lets me feed with his hinds,° bars
me the place of a brother, and, as much as in him lies,
mines my gentility with my education.° This is it, Adam,
that grieves me, and the spirit of my father, which I   20
think is within me, begins to mutiny against this servi-
tude. I will no longer endure it, though yet I know no
wise remedy how to avoid it.

ADAM. Yonder comes my master, your brother.

ORLANDO. Go apart, Adam, and thou shalt hear how he will   25
shake me up.

---

2. Bequeathed . . . crowns: *that is,* my father left me in his will only a thousand crowns. **3. on his blessing:** if he wanted to receive his blessing. **4. breed:**
educate. **5. Jaques** (jă′kwēz). **6. rustically:** *that is,* simple and uneducated like a
rustic or country person. **11. manage:** training. **12. dearly:** expensively. **14. animals
. . . I:** his animals owe him as much as I do—nothing—for being allowed to
grow. **16–17. something . . . me:** *that is,* even the natural claims I have of him
as my brother he denies by his unfriendly treatment. **17. hinds:** laborers; hired
hands. **19. mines . . . education:** undermines my gentle birth by not giving me
an education.

(*Enter* OLIVER.)

OLIVER.   Now, sir! What make you here?

ORLANDO.   Nothing. I am not taught to make anything.

OLIVER.   What mar you then, sir?

ORLANDO.   Marry,° sir, I am helping you to mar that which   30
God made, a poor unworthy brother of yours, with idleness.

OLIVER.   Marry, sir, be better employed, and be naught° awhile.

ORLANDO.   Shall I keep your hogs and eat husks with them?
What prodigal portion° have I spent that I should come to
such penury?°   35

OLIVER.   Know you where you are, sir?

ORLANDO.   Oh, sir, very well, here in your orchard.

OLIVER.   Know you before whom, sir?

ORLANDO.   Aye, better than him I am before knows me. I know
you are my eldest brother, and, in the gentle condition   40
of blood, you should so know me.° The courtesy of
nations° allows you my better, in that you are the firstborn.
But the same tradition takes not away my blood, were
there twenty brothers betwixt us. I have as much of my
father in me as you, albeit° I confess your coming before   45
me is nearer to his reverence.°

OLIVER.   What, boy!°

ORLANDO.   Come, come, elder brother, you are too young in this.

OLIVER.   Wilt thou lay hands on me, villain?

ORLANDO.   I am no villain. I am the youngest son of Sir   50
Rowland de Boys; he was my father, and he is thrice
a villain that says such a father begot villains. Wert
thou not my brother, I would not take this hand from
thy throat till this other had pulled out thy tongue for
saying so. Thou hast railed on° thyself.   55

ADAM.   Sweet masters, be patient. For your father's remem-
brance, be at accord.

OLIVER.   Let me go, I say.

---

30. Marry: a mild oath meaning "by the Virgin Mary." **32. be naught:** be nothing; make yourself scarce. **34. prodigal portion:** part of my father's wealth; a
biblical allusion to the story of the Prodigal Son (*see* Luke 15:11–32). **35. penury:** extreme poverty. **40–41. gentle . . . me:** If you were a true gentleman,
you would treat me as one. **41–42. courtesy of nations:** customs of civilized society. **45. albeit:** although. **46. is . . . reverence:** gives you a greater claim to
be as highly regarded as he was. **47. What, boy:** *here,* Oliver strikes Orlando.
55. railed on: insulted.

ORLANDO. I will not, till I please. You shall hear me.
My father charged you in his will to give me good 60
education. You have trained me like a peasant, obscuring
and hiding from me all gentlemanlike qualities. The
spirit of my father grows strong in me, and I will
no longer endure it. Therefore allow me such exercises°
as may become a gentleman, or give me the poor allottery° 65
my father left me by testament. With that I will go buy
my fortunes.

OLIVER. And what wilt thou do? Beg, when that is spent?
Well,. sir, get you in. I will not long be troubled with
you, you shall have some part of your will. I pray you 70
leave me.

ORLANDO. I will no further offend you than becomes me for
my good.

OLIVER. Get you with him, you old dog.

ADAM. Is "old dog" my reward? Most true, I have lost my 75
teeth in your service. God be with my old master! He
would not have spoke such a word.

(*Exeunt* ORLANDO *and* ADAM.)

OLIVER. Is it even so? Begin you to grow upon° me? I will
physic your rankness,° and yet give no thousand crowns
neither. Holla, Dennis! 80

(*Enter* DENNIS.)

DENNIS. Calls your Worship?

OLIVER. Was not Charles, the Duke's wrestler, here to speak
with me?

DENNIS. So please you, he is here at the door and importunes
access to you. 85

OLIVER. Call him in. (*Exit* DENNIS.) 'Twill be a good way,
and tomorrow the wrestling is.

(*Enter* CHARLES.)

CHARLES. Good morrow to your Worship.

---

64. exercises: training. **65. allottery:** portion. **78. grow upon:** become troublesome to. **79. physic your rankness:** cure your foulness. In this case, rankness is a
medical term for a disorder requiring the bleeding of the patient.

OLIVER.   Good Monsieur Charles, what's the new news at the
new Court?   90

CHARLES.   There's no news at the Court, sir, but the old news;
that is, the old Duke is banished by his younger brother
the new Duke, and three or four loving lords have put
themselves into voluntary exile with him, whose lands
and revenues enrich the new Duke; therefore he gives them   95
good leave to wander.

OLIVER.   Can you tell if Rosalind, the Duke's daughter, be
banished with her father?

CHARLES.   Oh no, for the Duke's daughter, her cousin, so loves
her, being ever from their cradles bred together, that   100
she would have followed her exile or have died to stay
behind her. She is at the Court and no less beloved of
her uncle than his own daughter, and never two ladies
loved as they do.

OLIVER.   Where will the old Duke live?   105

CHARLES.   They say he is already in the Forest of Arden, and
a many merry men with him, and there they live like the
old Robin Hood of England. They say many young gentlemen flock to him every day, and fleet° the time carelessly,
as they did in the golden world.°   110

OLIVER.   What, you wrestle tomorrow before the new Duke?

CHARLES.   Marry do I, sir, and I came to acquaint you with a
matter. I am given, sir, secretly to understand that your
younger brother, Orlando, hath a disposition to come in
disguised against me to try a fall.° Tomorrow, sir, I   115
wrestle for my credit,° and he that escapes me without some
broken limb shall acquit him well. Your brother is but
young and tender, and, for your love, I would be loath to
foil° him, as I must for my own honor if he come in. Therefore, out of my love to you, I came hither to acquaint   120
you withal, that either you might stay him from his
intendment or brook° such disgrace well as he shall run
into, in that it is a thing of his own search, and altogether
against my will.

109. **fleet:** spend. 110. **golden world:** mythical golden age, before men learned to
be evil. 115. **try a fall:** attempt to throw me. 116. **credit:** reputation; good name.
119. **foil:** overthrow. 122. **brook:** endure.

OLIVER. Charles, I thank thee for thy love to me, which thou   125
shalt find I will most kindly requite. I had myself
notice of my brother's purpose herein, and have by under-
hand means labored to dissuade him from it, but he is
resolute. I'll tell thee, Charles—it is the stubbornest
young fellow of France, full of ambition, an envious   130
emulator° of every man's good parts, a secret and villainous
contriver against me his natural brother. Therefore use
thy discretion. I had as lief thou didst° break his neck
as his finger. And thou wert best look to 't, for if
thou dost him any slight disgrace, or if he do not   135
mightily grace himself on thee,° he will practice against
thee by poison, entrap thee by some treacherous device,
and never leave thee till he hath ta'en thy life by some
indirect means or other. For I assure thee, and almost
with tears I speak it, there is not one so young and so   140
villainous this day living. I speak but brotherly of him, but
should I anatomize° him to thee as he is, I must blush
and weep, and thou must look pale and wonder.

CHARLES. I am heartily glad I came hither to you. If he come
tomorrow, I'll give him his payment. If ever he go alone°   145
again, I'll never wrestle for prize more. And so, God keep
your Worship!

OLIVER. Farewell, good Charles. (*Exit* CHARLES.) Now will
I stir this gamester.° I hope I shall see an end of him, for
my soul, yet I know not why, hates nothing more than he.   150
Yet he's gentle,° never schooled, and yet learned, full of
noble device,° of all sorts enchantingly beloved, and indeed so much in the heart of the world, and especially of
my own people, who best know him, that I am altogether
misprized.° But it shall not be so long, this wrestler shall   155
clear all. Nothing remains but that I kindle° the boy thither,
which now I'll go about.   (*Exit.*)

130–31. **envious emulator:** jealous hater. 133. **had . . . didst:** would willingly
have you. 136. **grace . . . thee:** distinguish himself at your expense. 142. **anato-
mize:** dissect; analyze. 145. **go alone:** *that is,* walk without assistance and
support. 149. **stir . . . gamester:** incite this athlete (Orlando). 151. **gentle:** a
natural gentleman. 152. **noble device:** noble thoughts. 155. **misprized:** considered
worthless; despised. 156. **kindle:** incite. Oliver wishes to trick Orlando into challenging the wrestler.

Meaning and Method: Act I, Scene 1

1. How does the playwright make Orlando a sympathetic character and Oliver a villain in this scene? How does Oliver's treatment of Adam mark him as a cruel man?

2. A *soliloquy*—an extended speech in which a character alone on stage expresses his inner thoughts—is the means by which a playwright can give the audience needed background information. What does Oliver's soliloquy tell us about his feelings toward Orlando? What contradictions are there between what he says in the soliloquy and what he has just been saying to Charles? What do these contradictions indicate about Oliver's character?

SCENE 2.   *Lawn before the* DUKE's *palace.*

(*Enter* ROSALIND *and* CELIA.)

CELIA.   I pray thee, Rosalind, sweet my coz,° be merry.

ROSALIND.   Dear Celia, I show more mirth than I am mistress of, and would you yet I were merrier? Unless you could teach me to forget a banished father, you must not learn me how to remember any extraordinary pleasure.   5

CELIA.   Herein I see thou lovest me not with the full weight that I love thee. If my uncle, thy banished father, had banished thy uncle, the Duke my father, so thou hadst been still with me I could have taught my love to take thy father for mine. So wouldst thou if the truth of thy love   10
to me were so righteously tempered° as mine is to thee.

ROSALIND.   Well, I will forget the condition of my estate,° to rejoice in yours.

CELIA.   You know my father hath no child but I, nor none is like to have. And truly, when he dies, thou shalt be his   15
heir, for what he hath taken away from thy father perforce,° I will render thee again in affection. By mine honor, I will, and when I break that oath, let me turn monster. Therefore, my sweet Rose, my dear Rose, be merry.   20

ROSALIND.   From henceforth I will, Coz, and devise sports.°
Let me see, what think you of falling in love?

1. **coz:** cousin; in Shakespeare's day, any near relation. 11. **tempered:** proportioned; adjusted. 12. **estate:** situation; fortune. 16–17. **perforce:** by force. 21. **sports:** amusements.

CELIA. Marry, I prithee do, to make sport withal. But love
no man in good earnest, nor no further in sport neither
than with safety of a pure blush thou mayst in honor come   25
off again.

ROSALIND. What shall be our sport, then?

CELIA. Let us sit and mock the good housewife Fortune from
her wheel,° that her gifts may henceforth be bestowed
equally.   30

ROSALIND. I would we could do so, for her benefits are mightily
misplaced, and the bountiful blind woman doth most mistake in her gifts to women.

CELIA. 'Tis true, for those that she makes fair she scarce
makes honest, and those that she makes honest she makes   35
very ill-favoredly.

ROSALIND. Nay, now thou goest from Fortune's office to Nature's. Fortune reigns in gifts of the world, not in the lineaments of Nature.°

(*Enter* TOUCHSTONE.)

CELIA. No? When Nature hath made a fair creature, may she   40
not by Fortune fall into the fire? Though Nature hath given
us wit to flout at Fortune, hath not Fortune sent in this
fool to cut off the argument?

ROSALIND. Indeed, there is Fortune too hard for Nature, when
Fortune makes Nature's natural° the cutter-off of Nature's   45
wit.

CELIA. Peradventure° this is not Fortune's work neither, but
Nature's, who perceiveth our natural wits too dull to
reason of such goddesses, and hath sent this natural for
our whetstone;° for always the dullness of the fool is   50
the whetstone of the wits. How now, wit! Whither wander
you?

TOUCHSTONE. Mistress, you must come away to your father.

CELIA. Were you made the messenger?

28–29. Fortune . . . wheel: Chance or luck was personified in Roman mythology as the goddess *Fortuna*, a blind woman spinning men's fortunes on a
spinning wheel, creating and destroying as she pleased. Elizabethans attributed
many events to Fortune's wheel, as we do to luck. 38–39. lineaments . . . Nature: features, characteristics created by Nature. 45. natural: fool; one who is by
nature an idiot. 47. Peradventure: perhaps. 50. whetstone: sharpening stone for
a blade.

TOUCHSTONE.   No, by mine honor, but I was bid to come for   55
you.

ROSALIND.   Where learned you that oath, fool?

TOUCHSTONE.   Of a certain knight that swore by his honor they
were good pancakes, and swore by his honor the mustard
was naught.° Now I'll stand to it the pancakes were naught   60
and the mustard was good, and yet was not the knight
forsworn.°

CELIA.   How prove you that, in the great heap of your knowledge?

ROSALIND.   Aye, marry, now unmuzzle your wisdom.   65

TOUCHSTONE.   Stand you both forth now. Stroke your chins, and
swear by your beards that I am a knave.

CELIA.   By our beards, if we had them, thou art.

TOUCHSTONE.   By my knavery, if I had it, then I were. But if
you swear by that that is not, you are not forsworn. No   70
more was this knight swearing by his honor, for he never
had any, or if he had, he had sworn it away before ever
he saw those pancakes or that mustard.

CELIA.   Prithee who is 't that thou meanest?

TOUCHSTONE.   One that old Frederick, your father, loves.   75

CELIA.   My father's love is enough to honor him. Enough!
Speak no more of him, you'll be whipped for taxation° one
of these days.

TOUCHSTONE.   The more pity that fools may not speak wisely
what wise men do foolishly.   80

CELIA.   By my troth, thou sayest true, for since the little wit
that fools have was silenced, the little foolery that wise
men have makes a great show. Here comes Monsieur Le
Beau.

ROSALIND.   With his mouth full of news.   85

CELIA.   Which he will put on us, as pigeons feed their young.

ROSALIND.   Then shall we be news-crammed.

CELIA.   All the better. We shall be the more marketable.
(*Enter* LE BEAU.) *Bon jour*, Monsieur Le Beau. What's
the news?   90

LE BEAU.   Fair Princess, you have lost much good sport.

---

60. naught: *here*, bad. **62. forsworn:** shown to be a liar. **77. taxation:** *here*,
slander.

CELIA.   Sport! Of what color?°

LE BEAU.   What color, madam! How shall I answer you?

ROSALIND.   As wit and fortune will.

TOUCHSTONE.   Or as the Destinies decree.   95

CELIA.   Well said. That was laid on with a trowel.°

TOUCHSTONE.   Nay, if I keep not my rank—

ROSALIND.   Thou losest thy old smell.°

LE BEAU.   You amaze me, ladies, I would have told you of good
    wrestling which you have lost the sight of.   100

ROSALIND.   Yet tell us the manner of the wrestling.

LE BEAU.   I will tell you the beginning, and if it please your
    ladyships, you may see the end; for the best is yet to do,
    and here where you are they are coming to perform it.

CELIA.   Well, the beginning, that is dead and buried.   105

LE BEAU.   There comes an old man and his three sons—

CELIA.   I could match this beginning with an old tale.

LE BEAU.   Three proper° young men, of excellent growth and
    presence.°

ROSALIND.   With bills° on their necks, "Be it known unto all   110
    men by these presents."°

LE BEAU.   The eldest of the three wrestled with Charles, the
    Duke's wrestler, which Charles in a moment threw him, and
    broke three of his ribs, that there is little hope of life in
    him. So he served the second, and so the third. Yonder   115
    they lie, the poor old man, their father, making such pitiful
    dole over them that all the beholders take his part with
    weeping.

ROSALIND.   Alas!

TOUCHSTONE.   But what is the sport, monsieur, that the ladies   120
    have lost?

LE BEAU.   Why, this that I speak of.

TOUCHSTONE.   Thus men may grow wiser every day. It is the
    first time that ever I heard breaking of ribs was sport for
    ladies.   125

---

92. Sport . . . color: Celia pretends that Le Beau had said *spot*. In Shakespeare's
time, the two words were pronounced alike. **96. That . . . trowel:** *that is*, as a
bricklayer slaps down the mortar. **97–98. rank . . . smell:** a pun on two meanings
of *rank*, as a "position" and as "foul-smelling." **108. proper:** handsome. **109.
presence:** appearance. **110. bills:** advertisements. **110–111. "Be . . . presents":**
Rosalind makes a farfetched pun, a reference to the formula at the beginning of
many legal documents: "Know all men by these presents."

CELIA.   Or I, I promise thee.

ROSALIND.   But is there any else longs to see this broken music
in his sides? Is there yet another dotes upon rib-breaking?
Shall we see this wrestling, Cousin?

LE BEAU.   You must if you stay here, for here is the place   130
appointed for the wrestling, and they are ready to perform
it.

CELIA.   Yonder, sure, they are coming. Let us now stay and
see it.

(*Flourish of trumpets. Enter* DUKE FREDERICK, LORDS,
ORLANDO, CHARLES, *and* ATTENDANTS.)

DUKE FREDERICK.   Come on. Since the youth will not be en-   135
treated, his own peril° on his forwardness.

ROSALIND.   Is yonder the man?

LE BEAU.   Even he, madam.

CELIA.   Alas, he is too young! Yet he looks successfully.

DUKE FREDERICK.   How now, Daughter and Cousin! Are you   140
crept hither to see the wrestling?

ROSALIND.   Aye, my liege, so please you give us leave.

DUKE FREDERICK.   You will take little delight in it, I can tell
you, there is such odds in° the man. In pity of the challenger's youth I would fain° dissuade him, but he will not   145
be entreated. Speak to him, ladies, see if you can move
him.

CELIA.   Call him hither, good Monsieur Le Beau.

DUKE FREDERICK.   Do so. I'll not be by.

LE BEAU.   Monsieur the challenger, the Princess calls for you.   150

ORLANDO.   I attend them with all respect and duty.

ROSALIND.   Young man, have you challenged Charles the
wrestler?

ORLANDO.   No, fair Princess, he is the general challenger. I
come but in, as others do, to try with him the strength of   155
my youth.

CELIA.   Young gentleman, your spirits are too bold for your
years. You have seen cruel proof of this man's strength.
If you saw yourself with your eyes, or knew yourself with
your judgment, the fear of your adventure would counsel   160
you to a more equal enterprise. We pray you, for your

136. his . . . peril: He does it at his own risk. 144. in: against. 145. fain: gladly.

own sake, to embrace your own safety and give over this attempt.

ROSALIND.   Do, young sir, your reputation shall not therefore be misprized. We will make it our suit to the Duke that   165 the wrestling might not go forward.

ORLANDO.   I beseech you punish me not with your hard thoughts, wherein I confess me much guilty, to deny so fair and excellent ladies anything. But let your fair eyes and gentle wishes go with me to my trial. Wherein if I be   170 foiled, there is but one shamed that was never gracious; if killed, but one dead that is willing to be so. I shall do my friends no wrong, for I have none to lament me; the world no injury, for in it I have nothing. Only in the world I fill up a place which may be better supplied when I have   175 made it empty.

ROSALIND.   The little strength that I have, I would it were with you.

CELIA.   And mine, to eke out° hers.

ROSALIND.   Fare you well. Pray Heaven I be deceived in you!   180

CELIA.   Your heart's desires be with you!

CHARLES.   Come, where is this young gallant that is so desirous to lie with his mother earth?

ORLANDO.   Ready, sir, but his will hath in it a more modest working.°   185

DUKE FREDERICK.   You shall try but one fall.

CHARLES.   No, I warrant your Grace, you shall not entreat him to a second, that have so mightily persuaded him from a first.

ORLANDO.   You mean to mock me after, you should not have   190 mocked me before. But come your ways.

ROSALIND.   Now Hercules be thy speed,° young man!

CELIA.   I would I were invisible, to catch the strong fellow by the leg.   (*They wrestle.*)

ROSALIND.   Oh, excellent young man!   195

CELIA.   If I had a thunderbolt in mine eye, I can tell who should down.

179. **eke out:** support, supplement or increase. **184–85. more . . . working:** I do not intend to do anything so improper. **192. speed:** aid.

(*Shout.* CHARLES *is thrown.*)

DUKE FREDERICK.   No more, no more.

ORLANDO.   Yes, I beseech your Grace. I am not yet well
breathed.°   200

DUKE FREDERICK.   How dost thou, Charles?

LE BEAU.   He cannot speak, my lord.

DUKE FREDERICK.   Bear him away. What is thy name, young
man?

ORLANDO.   Orlando, my liege, the youngest son of Sir Rowland
de Boys.   205

DUKE FREDERICK.   I would thou hadst been son to some man else.
The world esteemed thy father honorable,
But I did find him still mine enemy.
Thou shouldst have better pleased me with this deed
Hadst thou descended from another house.   210
But fare thee well, thou art a gallant youth.
I would thou hadst told me of another father.

(*Exeunt* DUKE FREDERICK, TRAIN, *and* LE BEAU.)

CELIA.   Were I my father, Coz, would I do this?

ORLANDO.   I am more proud to be Sir Rowland's son,
His youngest son, and would not change that calling   215
To be adopted heir to Frederick.

ROSALIND.   My father loved Sir Rowland as his soul,
And all the world was of my father's mind
Had I before known this young man his son,
I should have given him tears unto° entreaties   220
Ere he should thus have ventured.

CELIA.   Gentle Cousin,
Let us go thank him and encourage him.
My father's rough and envious disposition
Sticks me at heart.° Sir, you have well deserved.
If you do keep your promises in love   225
But justly, as you have exceeded all promise,
Your mistress shall be happy.

---

200. breathed: exercised, breathing hard, out of breath from the exercise. **220.
unto:** added to. **224. Sticks me at heart:** pierces me to the heart.

ROSALIND.   Gentleman,

(*Giving him a chain from her neck.*)

Wear this for me, one out of suits° with Fortune,
That could° give more but that her hand lacks means.
Shall we go, Coz?   230
CELIA.   Aye. Fare you well, fair gentleman.
ORLANDO.   Can I not say I thank you? My better parts
Are all thrown down,° and that which here stands up
Is but a quintain,° a mere lifeless block.
ROSALIND.   He calls us back. My pride fell with my fortunes,   235
I'll ask him what he would. Did you call, sir?
Sir, you have wrestled well and overthrown
More than your enemies.
CELIA.   Will you go, Coz?
ROSALIND.   Have with you. Fare you well.

(*Exeunt* ROSALIND *and* CELIA.)

ORLANDO.   What passion hangs these weights upon my tongue?   240
I cannot speak to her, yet she urged conference.
O poor Orlando, thou art overthrown!
Or Charles or something weaker masters thee.

(*Reenter* LE BEAU.)

LE BEAU.   Good sir, I do in friendship counsel you
To leave this place. Albeit you have deserved   245
High commendation, true applause, and love,
Yet such is now the Duke's condition
That he misconstrues all that you have done.
The Duke is humorous.° What he is, indeed,
More suits you to conceive° than I to speak of.   250
ORLANDO.   I thank you, sir. And pray you tell me this:
Which of the two was daughter of the Duke
That here was at the wrestling?
LE BEAU.   Neither his daughter, if we judge by manners;
But yet indeed the lesser° is his daughter.   255

228. out of suits: not in the service of; not favored by. 229. could: would if she
could. 232–33. My better . . . down: I am behaving as if I had no manners.
234. quintain: block shaped like a man, used for jousting practice. 249. humorous:
here, moody; touchy. 250. conceive: imagine. 255. lesser: smaller.

The other is daughter to the banished Duke,
And here detained by her usurping uncle,
To keep his daughter company, whose loves
Are dearer than the natural bond of sisters.
But I can tell you that of late this Duke   260
Hath ta'en displeasure 'gainst his gentle niece,
Grounded upon no other argument
But that the people praise her for her virtues
And pity her for her good father's sake.
And, on my life, his malice 'gainst the lady   265
Will suddenly break forth. Sir, fare you well.
Hereafter, in a better world than this,
I shall desire more love and knowledge of you.
ORLANDO.   I rest much bounden to you. Fare you well.

(*Exit* LE BEAU.)

Thus must I from the smoke into the smother,°   270
From tyrant Duke unto a tyrant brother.
But heavenly Rosalind!   (*Exit.*)

270. smoke . . . smother: a saying, similar to "out of the frying pan into the fire."

Meaning and Method: Act I, Scene 2

1. In what way is the friendship between Rosalind and Celia unusual? Are there any fairy-tale qualities in their situation and relationship?
2. A touchstone is a criterion or standard by which the qualities of something are tested. A "fool" was a professional entertainer. In naming his character Touchstone, Shakespeare may have been pointing out that Touchstone is there to provide the standard by which the folly of the others may be measured.
   With this in mind, paraphrase and explain Touchstone's comment (lines 79–80), "The more the pity that fools may not speak wisely what wise men do foolishly."
3. What characters or situations in Scene 2 seem to be parallel with characters and situations in Scene 1?
4. How do Rosalind and Celia meet Orlando? How did Scene 1 prepare us for this meeting? How does Orlando affect the girls? How do we know that he and Rosalind are falling in love?
5. Why does Le Beau advise Orlando to leave quickly?

SCENE 3. *A room in the palace.*

(*Enter* CELIA *and* ROSALIND.)

CELIA.   Why, Cousin! Why, Rosalind! Cupid have mercy! Not
a word?

ROSALIND.   Not one to throw at a dog.

CELIA.   No, thy words are too precious to be cast away upon
curs, throw some of them at me. Come, lame me with rea-   5
sons.°

ROSALIND.   Then there were two cousins laid up, when the one
should be lamed with reasons and the other mad without
any.

CELIA.   But is all this for your father?   10

ROSALIND.   No, some of it is for my child's father. Oh, how full
of briers is this working-day world!

CELIA.   They are but burrs, Cousin, thrown upon thee in holiday foolery. If we walk not in the trodden paths, our very
petticoats will catch them.   15

ROSALIND.   I could shake them off my coat. These burrs are
in my heart.

CELIA.   Hem them away.°

ROSALIND.   I would try if I could cry hem and have him.

CELIA.   Come, come, wrestle with thy affections.   20

ROSALIND.   Oh, they take the part of a better wrestler than
myself!

CELIA.   Oh, a good wish upon you! You will try in time, in
despite of a fall. But, turning these jests out of service,
let us talk in good earnest. Is it possible, on such a sudden,   25
you should fall into so strong a liking with old Sir Rowland's
youngest son?

ROSALIND.   The Duke my father loved his father dearly.

CELIA.   Doth it therefore ensue that you should love his son
dearly? By this kind of chase, I should hate him, for my   30
father hated his father dearly, yet I hate not Orlando.

ROSALIND.   No, faith, hate him not, for my sake.

CELIA.   Why should I not? Doth he not deserve well?

5–6. **lame me with reasons:** make me lame by throwing arguments at me. 18.
Hem them away: Cough them up.

ROSALIND.   Let me love him for that, and do you love him
   because I do. Look, here comes the Duke.   35
CELIA.   With his eyes full of anger.

   (*Enter* DUKE FREDERICK, *with* LORDS.)

DUKE FREDERICK.   Mistress, dispatch you with your safest haste°
   And get you from our Court.
ROSALIND.   Me, Uncle?
DUKE FREDERICK.   You, Cousin.
   Within these ten days if that thou be'st found
   So near our public Court as twenty miles,   40
   Thou diest for it.
ROSALIND.   I do beseech your Grace,
   Let me the knowledge of my fault bear with me.
   If with myself I hold intelligence,°
   Or have acquaintance with mine own desires,
   If that I do not dream, or be not frantic°—   45
   As I do trust I am not—then, dear Uncle,
   Never so much as in a thought unborn
   Did I offend your Highness.
DUKE FREDERICK.   Thus do all traitors.
   If their purgation° did consist in words,
   They are as innocent as grace itself.   50
   Let it suffice thee that I trust thee not.
ROSALIND.   Yet your mistrust cannot make me a traitor.
   Tell me whereon the likelihood depends.
DUKE FREDERICK.   Thou art thy father's daughter, there's
         enough.
ROSALIND.   So was I when your Highness took his dukedom,   55
   So was I when your Highness banished him.
   Treason is not inherited, my lord,
   Or if we did derive it from our friends,
   What's that to me? My father was no traitor.
   Then, good my liege, mistake me not so much   60
   To think my poverty is treacherous.
CELIA.   Dear sovereign, hear me speak.
DUKE FREDERICK.   Aye, Celia, we stayed her for your sake,

---

37. **safest haste:** the quicker you go, the safer for you. 43. **If . . . intelligence:**
if I understood my own thoughts. 45. **frantic:** mad. 49. **purgation:** cleaning away
of sins or faults.

Else had she with her father ranged along.°
CELIA.   I did not then entreat to have her stay,   65
It was your pleasure and your own remorse.
I was too young that time to value her,
But now I know her. If she be a traitor,
Why so am I. We still have slept together,
Rose at an instant, learned, played, eat together,   70
And wheresoe'er we went, like Juno's swans,°
Still we went coupled and inseparable.
DUKE FREDERICK.   She is too subtle for thee, and her smooth-
        ness,
Her very silence and her patience,
Speak to the people, and they pity her.   75
Thou art a fool. She robs thee of thy name,
And thou wilt show more bright and seem more virtuous
When she is gone. Then open not thy lips.
Firm and irrevocable is my doom
Which I have passed upon her, she is banished.   80
CELIA.   Pronounce that sentence then on me, my liege.
I cannot live out of her company.
DUKE FREDERICK.   You are a fool. You, Niece, provide yourself.
If you outstay the time, upon mine honor,
And in the greatness of my word, you die.   85

(*Exeunt* DUKE FREDERICK *and* LORDS.)

CELIA.   O my poor Rosalind, whither wilt thou go?
Wilt thou change fathers? I will give thee mine.
I charge thee, be not thou more grieved than I am.
ROSALIND.   I have more cause.
CELIA.   Thou hast not, Cousin.
Prithee, be cheerful. Know'st thou not the Duke   90
Hath banished me, his daughter?
ROSALIND.   That he hath not.
CELIA.   No, hath not? Rosalind lacks then the love
Which teacheth thee that thou and I am one.
Shall we be sundered? Shall we part, sweet girl?
No. Let my father seek another heir.   95
Therefore devise with me how we may fly,
Whither to go and what to bear with us.

64. **ranged along**: wandered in his company. 71. **Juno's swans**: It was actually the
goddess Venus who possessed a chariot drawn by swans.

And do not seek to take your change upon you,°
To bear your griefs yourself and leave me out;
For, by this Heaven, now at our sorrows pale,   100
Say what thou canst, I'll go along with thee
ROSALIND.   Why, whither shall we go?
CELIA.   To seek my uncle in the forest of Arden.
ROSALIND.   Alas, what danger will it be to us,
Maids as we are, to travel forth so far!   105
Beauty provoketh thieves sooner than gold.
CELIA.   I'll put myself in poor and mean attire
And with a kind of umber° smirch my face.
The like do you. So shall we pass along
And never stir assailants.
ROSALIND.   Were it not better,   110
Because that I am more than common tall,
That I did suit me° all points like a man?
A gallant curtal ax upon my thigh,
A boar spear in my hand, and—in my heart
Lie there what hidden woman's fear there will—   115
We'll have a swashing and a martial° outside,
As many other mannish cowards have
That do outface° it with their semblances.
CELIA.   What shall I call thee when thou art a man?
ROSALIND.   I'll have no worse a name than Jove's own page,   120
And therefore look you call me Ganymede.
But what will you be called?
CELIA.   Something that hath a reference to my state,
No longer Celia, but Aliena.
ROSALIND.   But, Cousin, what if we assayed° to steal   125
The clownish fool out of your father's Court?
Would he not be a comfort to our travel?
CELIA.   He'll go along o'er the wide world with me,
Leave me alone to woo him. Let's away
And get our jewels and our wealth together,   130
Devise the fittest time and safest way
To hide us from pursuit that will be made
After my flight. Now go we in content
To liberty and not to banishment.   (*Exeunt.*)

98. **take your change upon you:** bear your changed fortunes by yourself. **108. umber:** brown earth-coloring. **112. suit me:** dress myself. **116. martial:** soldierlike. **118. outface:** hide. **125. assayed:** attempted.

Meaning and Method: Act I, Scene 3

1. Why was Rosalind banished? How does the Duke feel this banishment will benefit his daughter, Celia?
2. Why does Celia decide to go along with Rosalind? What is the purpose of their disguise? Why do they want Touchstone to accompany them?
3. How does the Duke's reactions to Rosalind indicate his insecurity?
4. What other kinds of tales have you read or heard in which a character is banished from a kingdom by a wicked man? How does this affect your attitude toward the play?

Act II

SCENE 1. *The Forest of Arden.*

(*Enter* DUKE SENIOR, AMIENS, *and two or three* LORDS, *like foresters.*)

DUKE SENIOR. Now, my comates and brothers in exile,
Hath not old custom° made this life more sweet
Than that of painted° pomp? Are not these woods
More free from peril than the envious Court?
Here feel we but the penalty of Adam,°   5
The seasons' difference, as the icy fang
And churlish chiding of the winter's wind,
Which, when it bites and blows upon my body,
Even till I shrink with cold, I smile and say
"This is no flattery. These are councilors   10
That feelingly° persuade me what I am."
Sweet are the uses° of adversity,
Which, like the toad, ugly and venomous,
Wears yet a precious jewel in his head.°
And this our life exempt from public haunt°   15
Finds tongues in trees, books in the running brooks,
Sermons in stones, and good in everything.°
I would not change it.
AMIENS.   Happy is your Grace,
That can translate the stubbornness of fortune
Into so quiet and so sweet a style.   20
DUKE SENIOR. Come, shall we go and kill us venison?
And yet it irks me the poor dappled fools,
Being native burghers° of this desert° city,
Should in their own confines° with forkèd heads°
Have their round haunches gored.

2. **old custom:** long experience. 3. **painted:** artificial. 5. **penalty of Adam:** Once Adam lost Paradise, he had to endure pain, such as that caused by the biting cold. 11. **feelingly:** through my feelings. 12. **uses:** advantages. 13–14. **toad . . . head:** This could refer to a common superstition, or to the jewel-like coloring and shape found on the head of some varieties of toads. 15. **exempt . . . haunt:** free from crowds. 16–17. **Finds . . . everything:** *that is,* there is a lesson to be learned everywhere in nature. 23. **burghers:** citizens. **desert:** deserted. 24. **confines:** territories. **forkèd heads:** arrows.

FIRST LORD.   Indeed, my lord,   25
   The melancholy Jaques grieves at that,
   And, in that kind, swears you do more usurp
   Than doth your brother that hath banished you.
   Today my Lord of Amiens and myself
   Did steal behind him as he lay along   30
   Under an oak whose antique root peeps out
   Upon the brook that brawls along this wood.
   To the which place a poor sequestered° stag,
   That from the hunter's aim had ta'en a hurt,
   Did come to languish, and indeed, my lord,   35
   The wretched animal heaved forth such groans
   That their discharge did stretch his leathern coat
   Almost to bursting, and the big round tears
   Coursed one another down his innocent nose
   In piteous chase. And thus the hairy fool,   40
   Much markèd of° the melancholy Jaques,
   Stood on the extremest verge of the swift brook,
   Augmenting it with tears.
DUKE SENIOR.   But what said Jaques?
   Did he not moralize° this spectacle?
FIRST LORD.   Oh yes, into a thousand similes.   45
   First, for his weeping into the needless stream,
   "Poor deer," quoth he, "thou makest a testament
   As worldlings do, giving thy sum of more°
   To that which had too much." Then, being there alone,
   Left and abandoned of his velvet friends,   50
   " 'Tis right," quoth he. "Thus misery doth part
   The flux° of company." Anon a careless herd,
   Full of the pasture, jumps along by him
   And never stays to greet him. "Aye," quoth Jaques
   "Sweep on, you fat and greasy citizens,   55
   'Tis just the fashion. Wherefore do you look
   Upon that poor and broken bankrupt there?"
   Thus most invectively° he pierceth through
   The body of the country, city, Court,

33. **sequestered:** separated from the others. 41. **markèd of:** noticed by. 44. **moralize:** make moral comments on. 48. **sum of more:** *that is,* adding your tears to the water. 52. **flux:** flow. 58. **invectively:** bitterly.

Yea, and of this our life, swearing that we   60
Are mere usurpers, tyrants, and what's worse,
To fright the animals and to kill them up
In their assigned and native dwelling-place.

DUKE SENIOR.   And did you leave him in this contemplation?

SECOND LORD.   We did, my lord, weeping and commenting   65
Upon the sobbing deer.

DUKE SENIOR.   Show me the place.
I love to cope° him in these sullen fits,
For then he's full of matter.°

FIRST LORD.   I'll bring you to him straight.   (*Exeunt.*)

67. cope: encounter. 68. matter: good sense.

Meaning and Method: Act II, Scene 1

1. The preference for living close to nature in the country rather than living in the city or at court is a characteristically "pastoral" one. Why does the banished Duke find his place of exile, the Forest of Arden, quite pleasant? How does he contrast it with life at court?
2. Jaques is described as "weeping and commenting / Upon the sobbing deer" (lines 65–66). What does this passage reveal to the audience about Jaques before he appears on stage? Would the effect be the same if, instead of hearing about the sentimental Jaques, we actually saw the scene with him and the deer? Why or why not?
3. Explain lines 12–14, the ones beginning with "Sweet are the uses of adversity." Do you agree or disagree with the thought expressed in them?

SCENE 2.   *A room in the palace.*

(*Enter* DUKE FREDERICK, *with* LORDS.)

DUKE FREDERICK.   Can it be possible that no man saw them?
It cannot be. Some villains of my Court
Are of consent and sufferance° in this.

FIRST LORD.   I cannot hear of any that did see her.
The ladies, her attendants of her chamber,   5
Saw her abed, and in the morning early
They found the bed untreasured of their mistress.

3. of consent and sufferance: accomplices, either by consent or by passively allowing the action.

SECOND LORD.   My lord, the roynish° clown at whom so oft
    Your Grace was wont to laugh is also missing.
    Hisperia, the Princess' gentlewoman,   10
    Confesses that she secretly o'erheard
    Your daughter and her cousin much commend
    The parts and graces of the wrestler
    That did but lately foil the sinewy Charles,
    And she believes, wherever they are gone,   15
    That youth is surely in their company.
DUKE FREDERICK.   Send to his brother, fetch that gallant hither.
    If he be absent, bring his brother to me.
    I'll make him find him. Do this suddenly,
    And let not search and inquisition° quail°   20
    To bring again these foolish runaways.   (*Exeunt.*)

8. **roynish:** scurvy; contemptible. 20. **inquisition:** inquiry. **quail:** falter; slacken.

SCENE 3.   *Before Oliver's house.*

(*Enter* ORLANDO *and* ADAM, *meeting.*)

ORLANDO.   Who's there?
ADAM.   What my young master? O my gentle master!
    O my sweet master! O you memory
    Of old Sir Rowland! Why, what make you here?
    Why are you virtuous? Why do people love you?   5
    And wherefore are you gentle, strong, and valiant?
    Why would you be so fond° to overcome
    The bonny prizer° of the humorous Duke?
    Your praise is come too swiftly home before you.
    Know you not, master, to some kind of men   10
    Their graces serve them but as enemies?
    No more do yours. Your virtues, gentle master,
    Are sanctified and holy traitors° to you.
    Oh, what a world is this when what is comely
    Envenoms° him that bears it!   15
ORLANDO.   Why, what's the matter?

7. **fond:** foolish. 8. **bonny prizer:** fine prize fighter. 13. **sanctified . . . traitors:** traitors who appear pious and holy. 15. **Envenoms:** poisons.

ADAM.   O unhappy youth!
    Come not within these doors, within this roof
    The enemy of all your graces lives.
    Your brother—no, no brother, yet the son—
    Yet not the son, I will not call him son   20
    Of him I was about to call his father—
    Hath heard your praises, and this night he means
    To burn the lodging where you use to lie
    And you within it. If he fail of that,
    He will have other means to cut you off.   25
    I overheard him and his practices.°
    This is no place, this house is but a butchery.
    Abhor it, fear it, do not enter it.
ORLANDO.   Why, whither, Adam, wouldst thou have me go?
ADAM.   No matter whither so you come not here.   30
ORLANDO.   What, wouldst thou have me go and beg my food?
    Or with a base and boisterous° sword enforce
    A thievish living on the common road?
    This I must do, or know not what to do
    Yet this I will not do, do how I can.   35
    I rather will subject me to the malice
    Of a diverted blood° and bloody brother.
ADAM.   But do not so. I have five hundred crowns,
    The thrifty hire° I saved under your father,
    Which I did store to be my foster nurse   40
    When service should in my old limbs lie lame,
    And unregarded age in corners thrown.
    Take that, and He that doth the ravens feed,
    Yea, providently caters for the sparrow,
    Be comfort to my age! Here is the gold,   45
    All this I give you. Let me be your servant.
    Though I look old, yet I am strong and lusty,°
    For in my youth I never did apply
    Hot and rebellious liquors in my blood,
    Nor did not with unbashful forehead° woo   50
    The means of° weakness and debility;

26. **practices:** plots. 32. **boisterous:** threatening. 37. **diverted blood:** one whose feelings have been turned from their natural course. 39. **thrifty hire:** saved-up pay. 47. **lusty:** vigorous. 50. **unbashful forehead:** vicious boldness. 51. **means of:** pleasures that bring.

Therefore my age is as a lusty winter,
Frosty, but kindly. Let me go with you,
I'll do the service of a younger man
In all your business and necessities.   55
ORLANDO. O good old man, how well in thee appears
The constant° service of the antique world,°
When service sweat for duty, not for meed!°
Thou art not for the fashion of these times,
Where none will sweat but for promotion,   60
And having that do choke their service up
Even with the having.° It is not so with thee.
But, poor old man, thou prunest a rotten tree
That cannot so much as a blossom yield
In lieu of all thy pains and husbandry.°   65
But come thy ways, we'll go along together,
And ere we have thy youthful wages spent
We'll light upon some settled low content.°
ADAM. Master, go on, and I will follow thee
To the last gasp, with truth and loyalty.   70
From seventeen years till now almost fourscore
Here livèd I, but now live here no more.
At seventeen years many their fortunes seek,
But at fourscore it is too late a week.°
Yet fortune cannot recompense me better   75
Than to die well and not my master's debtor.   (*Exeunt.*)

57. **constant:** faithful. **antique world:** "old days." 58. **meed:** reward. **61–62.
having . . . having:** and as soon as they have their reward, they cease to give
good service. 65. **husbandry:** economy. It may also refer to farming. 68. **settled
. . . content:** humble but contented way of living. 74. **too . . . week:** a week
too late, meaning "the time for such things has gone forever."

Meaning and Method: Act II, Scenes 2 and 3

1. How is tension developed in Scene 2? Why does Duke Frederick think
   Orlando is involved in Rosalind's and Celia's running away? How does
   the Duke propose to find the girls?
2. Why does Orlando leave his brother's house? Why does Adam go
   with him? In what way is this similar to the circumstances under
   which Celia accompanied Rosalind?
3. What social commentary does Orlando make on "old-time" and
   modern workers?

SCENE 4.   *The Forest of Arden.*

(*Enter* ROSALIND *disguised as* GANYMEDE, CELIA *disguised as* ALIENA, *and* TOUCHSTONE.)

ROSALIND.   Oh, Jupiter, how weary are my spirits!

TOUCHSTONE.   I care not for my spirits if my legs were not weary.

ROSALIND.   I could find in my heart to disgrace my man's apparel and to cry like a woman. But I must comfort the weaker   5
vessel, as doublet and hose° ought to show itself courageous to petticoat, therefore, courage, good Aliena.

CELIA.   I pray you bear with me, I cannot go no further.

TOUCHSTONE.   For my part, I had rather bear with you than bear you. Yet I should bear no cross° if I did bear you, for I think   10
you have no money in your purse.

ROSALIND.   Well, this is the forest of Arden.

TOUCHSTONE.   Aye, now am I in Arden, the more fool I. When I was at home, I was in a better place. But travelers must be content.   15

ROSALIND.   Aye, be so, good Touchstone.

(*Enter* CORIN *and* SILVIUS.)

Look you who comes here, a young man and an old in solemn talk.

CORIN.   That is the way to make her scorn you still.

SILVIUS.   Oh, Corin, that thou knew'st how I do love her!   20

CORIN.   I partly guess, for I have loved ere now.

SILVIUS.   No, Corin, being old, thou canst not guess,
Though in thy youth thou wast as true a lover
As ever sighed upon a midnight pillow.
But if thy love were ever like to mine—   25
As sure I think did never man love so—

---

6. **doublet and hose:** a man's attire. Rosalind is now dressed as Ganymede. *Doublet* means a short, close-fitting coat; *hose* refers not to stockings, as it does now, but to the breeches or trousers. 10. **bear . . . cross:** *literally,* endure no misfortune; but it also meant "have no money," as some Elizabethan coins had a cross on the reverse side.

How many actions most ridiculous
Hast thou been drawn to by thy fantasy?°
CORIN.   Into a thousand that I have forgotten.
SILVIUS.   Oh, thou didst then ne'er love so heartily!   30
If thou remember'st not the slightest folly
That ever love did make thee run into,
Thou hast not loved.
Or if thou hast not sat as I do now,
Wearing° thy hearer in° thy mistress' praise,   35
Thou hast not loved.
Or if thou hast not broke from company
Abruptly, as my passion now makes me,
Thou hast not loved.
Oh, Phebe, Phebe, Phebe!   (*Exit.*)   40
ROSALIND.   Alas, poor shepherd! Searching of thy wound,°
I have by hard adventure° found mine own.
TOUCHSTONE.   And I mine. I remember when I was in love I
broke my sword upon a stone and bid him take that for
coming a-night to Jane Smile. And I remember the kissing   45
of her batlet° and the cow's dugs that her pretty chopt°
hands had milked. And I remember the wooing of a
peascod° instead of her, from whom I took two cods° and,
giving her them again, said with weeping tears, "Wear these
for my sake." We that are true lovers run into strange   50
capers, but as all is mortal in nature, so is all nature in love
mortal in folly.°
ROSALIND.   Thou speakest wiser than thou art ware of.
TOUCHSTONE.   Nay, I shall ne'er be ware of mine own wit till I
break my shins against it.°   55
ROSALIND.   Jove, Jove! This shepherd's passion
Is much upon my fashion.°
TOUCHSTONE.   And mine, but it grows something stale with me.
CELIA.   I pray you, one of you question yon man
If he for gold will give us any food.   60
I faint almost to death.

---

28. fantasy: fancy; love. **35. Wearing:** wearing out. **in:** with. **41. Searching . . .
wound:** listening to you probing your wound. **42. hard adventure:** painful chance.
46. batlet: stick used for beating clothes during washing. **chopt:** chopped. **48.
peascod:** usually peapod, but here the whole plant. **cods:** pods. **52. mortal in
folly:** deadly in its foolishness. **54–55. Nay . . . it:** Note the pun in his lines.
57. upon my fashion: like my own.

TOUCHSTONE.   Holloa, you clown!°
ROSALIND.   Peace, fool. He's not thy kinsman.
CORIN.   Who calls?
TOUCHSTONE.   Your betters, sir.
CORIN.   Else are they very wretched.
ROSALIND.   Peace, I say. Good even to you, friend.
CORIN.   And to you, gentle sir, and to you all.   65
ROSALIND.   I prithee, shepherd, if that love or gold
    Can in this desert place buy entertainment,°
    Bring us where we may rest ourselves and feed.
    Here's a young maid with travel much oppressed
    And faints for succor.°
CORIN.   Fair sir, I pity her,   70
    And wish, for her sake more than for mine own,
    My fortunes were more able to relieve her.
    But I am shepherd to another man
    And do not shear the fleeces that I graze.°
    My master is of churlish° disposition   75
    And little recks° to find the way to Heaven
    By doing deeds of hospitality.
    Besides, his cote,° his flocks and bounds of feed,°
    Are now on sale, and at our sheepcote now,
    By reason of his absence, there is nothing   80
    That you will feed on. But what is, come see,
    And in my voice most welcome shall you be.
ROSALIND.   What is he that shall buy his flock and pasture?
CORIN.   That young swain° that you saw here but erewhile,
    That little cares for buying anything.   85
ROSALIND.   I pray thee, if it stand with honesty,
    Buy thou the cottage, pasture, and the flock,
    And thou shalt have° to pay for it of us.
CELIA.   And we will mend thy wages. I like this place
    And willingly could waste my time in it.   90
CORIN.   Assuredly the thing is to be sold.
    Go with me. If you like upon report

61. clown: rustic; country person; rube. **67. entertainment:** accommodation. **70. succor:** help to relieve her from distress. **74. do . . . graze:** do not sell the wool of the sheep I feed—because I am a hired shepherd and not the owner. **75. churlish:** miserly; stingy. **76. recks:** cares; reckons. **78. cote:** cottage. **bounds of feed:** pastures. **84. swain:** a poetic word, usually a term for a young man in love. **88. have:** have money.

The soil, the profit, and this kind of life,
I will your very faithful feeder be
And buy it with your gold right suddenly.   (*Exeunt.*)   95

Meaning and Method: Act II, Scene 4

1. What similarities and differences can you find between the real shepherds, Sylvius and Corin, and the make-believe shepherds, Ganymede and Aliena?
2. What are Sylvius' and Corin's attitudes toward love?

SCENE 5. *The forest.*

(*Enter* AMIENS, JAQUES, *and others.*)

AMIENS. (*Sings.*)
            Under the greenwood tree
            Who loves to lie with me,
            And turn° his merry note
            Unto the sweet bird's throat,
    Come hither, come hither, come hither.   5
            Here shall he see
            No enemy
    But winter and rough weather.
JAQUES. More, more, I prithee, more.
AMIENS. It will make you melancholy, Monsieur Jaques.   10
JAQUES. I thank it. More, I prithee, more. I can suck melancholy out of a song as a weasel sucks eggs. More, I prithee, more.
AMIENS. My voice is ragged. I know I cannot please you.
JAQUES. I do not desire you to please me, I do desire you to   15
    sing. Come, come, another stanzo.° Call you 'em stanzos?
AMIENS. What you will, Monsieur Jaques.
JAQUES. Nay, I care not for their names, they owe me nothing.° Will you sing?
AMIENS. More at your request than to please myself.   20

3. **turn:** harmonize. 16. **stanzo:** stanza. 18–19. **owe me nothing:** mean nothing to me.

JAQUES Well then, if ever I thank any man, I'll thank you. But
that they call compliment is like the encounter of two dog
apes,° and when a man thanks me heartily, methinks I have
given him a penny and he renders me the beggarly thanks.°
Come, sing, and you that will not, hold your tongues.   25

AMIENS. Well, I'll end the song. Sirs, cover the while.° The
Duke will drink under this tree. He hath been all this day
to look you.

JAQUES. And I have been all this day to avoid him. He is too
disputable for my company. I think of as many matters as   30
he, but I give Heaven thanks, and make no boast of them.
Come, warble, come.

SONG. (*All together here.*)

> Who doth ambition shun,
> And loves to live i' the sun,
> Seeking the food he eats,   35
> And pleased with what he gets,
> Come hither, come hither, come hither.
> Here shall he see
> No enemy
> But winter and rough weather.   40

JAQUES. I'll give you a verse to this note, that I made yesterday
in despite of my invention.°

AMIENS. And I'll sing it.

JAQUES. Thus it goes:

> If it do come to pass   45
> That any man turn ass,
> Leaving his wealth and ease
> A stubborn will to please,
> Ducdame,° ducdame, ducdame.
> Here shall he see   50
> Gross fools as he,
> And if he will come to me.

22–23. dog apes: male baboons. 24. beggarly thanks: excessive thanks, like those
of a beggar. 26. cover the while: set the table in the meantime. 42. in despite of
my invention: although I am no good at this sort of thing. 49. Ducdame: a three-
syllable word. Many commentators have tried to trace the origin of this word.
It is most probably one of the many meaningless syllables—like "hey nonny no"
—so often used to fill out the line of a song. Jaques' own explanation (*see* line 54)
is that it is a Greek invocation to call fools into a circle (that is, set them gossiping). It has greatly stimulated scholars to make learned guesses.

AMIENS. What's that "ducdame"?

JAQUES. 'Tis a Greek invocation to call fools into a circle. I'll
go sleep, if I can. If I cannot, I'll rail against all the firstborn   55
of Egypt.°

AMIENS. And I'll go seek the Duke. His banquet is prepared.
(*Exeunt severally.* *)

56. firstborn of Egypt: Jaques's meaning is not clear. Perhaps he means he will
scold or insult people of high position, such as the Duke. * *severally:* by different
doors.

Meaning and Method: Act II, Scene 5

1. Has Jaques turned out to have the characteristics the audience was led
to expect him to have? How does he regard the Duke?

2. Is the action of the play in any way advanced by this scene between
Jaques and Amiens? If it is not, what, then, is the purpose of the
scene?

3. Why has Amiens's song been called "lighthearted and cheerful"? Can
you set it to music or to a rhythmic reading?

SCENE 6. *The forest.*

(*Enter* ORLANDO *and* ADAM.)

ADAM. Dear master, I can go no further. Oh, I die for food.
Here lie I down, and measure out my grave. Farewell, kind
master.

ORLANDO. Why, how now, Adam! No greater heart in thee?
Live a little, comfort a little, cheer thyself a little. If this   5
uncouth forest yield anything savage, I will either be food
for it or bring it for food to thee. Thy conceit° is nearer
death than thy powers.° For my sake be comfortable,° hold
death awhile at the arm's end. I will here be with thee
presently, and if I bring thee not something to eat, I will   10
give thee leave to die. But if thou diest before I come, thou
art a mocker of my labor. Well said! Thou lookest cheerly,
and I'll be with thee quickly. Yet thou liest in the bleak air.
Come, I will bear thee to some shelter, and thou shalt not
die for lack of a dinner if there live anything in this desert.   15
Cheerly, good Adam!   (*Exeunt.*)

7. conceit: imagination. **8. powers:** strength. **comfortable:** comforted.

Meaning and Method: Act II, Scene 6

1. Why is the play broken up into so many brief scenes at this point? Discuss how they might have been staged for a performance at the Globe Theater.
2. What aspects of this scene are intended to remind the audience of an earlier scene in the same Act? What purpose might Shakespeare have had in introducing this parallelism?

SCENE 7. *The forest.*

(*A table set out. Enter* DUKE SENIOR, AMIENS, *and* LORDS *like outlaws.*)

DUKE SENIOR.   I think he be transformed into a beast,
    For I can nowhere find him like a man.
FIRST LORD.   My lord, he is but even now gone hence.
    Here was he merry, hearing of a song.
DUKE SENIOR.   If he, compact of jars,° grow musical,   5
    We shall have shortly discord in the spheres.°
    Go, seek him. Tell him I would speak with him.

(*Enter* JAQUES.)

FIRST LORD.   He saves my labor by his own approach.
DUKE SENIOR.   Why, how now, monsieur! What a life is this
    That your poor friends must woo your company?   10
    What, you look merrily!
JAQUES.   A fool, a fool! I met a fool i' the forest,
    A motley fool,° a miserable world!
    As I do live by food, I met a fool,
    Who laid him down and basked him in the sun,   15
    And railed on Lady Fortune in good terms,
    In good set terms,° and yet a motley fool.
    "Good morrow, fool," quoth I. "No, sir," quoth he.
    "Call me not fool till Heaven hath sent me fortune."
    And then he drew a dial° from his poke,°   20

5. **compact of jars:** made up of discordant sounds. 6. **discord . . . spheres:** In the old Ptolemaic theory of the universe, all planets were thought to revolve around the earth and to make music as they turned. If they were disturbed, the music would become discordant. 13. **motley fool:** *that is,* a professional fool. *Motley* was the many-colored costume worn by court jesters. 17. **good . . . terms:** carefully thought out and ordered words. 20. **dial:** watch. **poke:** pocket.

And looking on it with lackluster eye,
Says very wisely, "It is ten o'clock.
Thus we may see," quoth he, "how the world wags.°
'Tis but an hour ago since it was nine
And after one hour more 'twill be eleven,   25
And so, from hour to hour, we ripe and ripe,
And then, from hour to hour, we rot and rot,
And thereby hangs a tale." When I did hear
The motley fool thus moral on the time,
My lungs began to crow like chanticleer,°   30
That fools should be so deep-contemplative,°
And I did laugh sans° intermission
An hour by his dial. Oh, noble fool!
A worthy fool! Motley's the only wear.
DUKE SENIOR. What fool is this?   35
JAQUES. Oh, worthy fool! One that hath been a courtier,
And says if ladies be but young and fair,
They have the gift to know it. And in his brain,
Which is as dry as the remainder° biscuit
After a voyage, he hath strange places crammed   40
With observation, the which he vents°
In mangled forms.° Oh, that I were a fool!
I am ambitious for a motley coat.
DUKE SENIOR. Thou shalt have one.
JAQUES.   It is my only suit,°
Provided that you weed your better judgments   45
Of all opinion that grows rank° in them
That I am wise. I must have liberty
Withal, as large a charter° as the wind
To blow on° whom I please. For so fools have,
And they that are most gallèd° with my folly,   50
They most must laugh. And why, sir, must they so?
The "why" is plain as way to parish church.
He that a fool doth very wisely hit
Doth very foolishly, although he smart,

---

23. wags: moves along. 30. chanticleer: a rooster. 31. deep-contemplative: profoundly thoughtful. 32. sans: without. 39. remainder: leftover. 41. vents: utters. 42. mangled forms: quaint phrases. 44. suit: a pun on suit, meaning "petition" and "suit of clothes." 46. rank: abundantly, like weeds in a garden. 48. large a charter: as free a privilege. 49. blow on: censure. 50. gallèd: rubbed sore.

Not to seem senseless of the bob.° If not,   55
The wise man's folly is anatomized°
Even by the squandering° glances of the fool.
Invest° me in my motley, give me leave
To speak my mind, and I will through and through
Cleanse the foul body of the infected world,   60
If they will patiently receive my medicine.
DUKE SENIOR.   Fie on thee! I can tell what thou wouldst do.
JAQUES.   What, for a counter,° would I do but good?
DUKE SENIOR.   Most mischievous foul sin, in chiding sin.
For thou thyself hast been a libertine   65
As sensual as the brutish sting° itself,
And all the embossèd sores and headed evils
That thou with license of free foot hast caught
Wouldst thou disgorge into the general world.
JAQUES.   Why, who cries out in pride   70
That can therein tax any private party?°
Doth it not flow as hugely as the sea
Till that the weary very means do ebb?°
What woman in the city do I name
When that I say the city woman bears   75
The cost of princes on unworthy shoulders?
Who can come in and say that I mean her
When such a one as she such is her neighbor?
Or what is he of basest function°
That says his bravery is not on my cost,°   80
Thinking that I mean him, but therein suits°
His folly to the mettle° of my speech?
There then, how then? What then? Let me see wherein
My tongue hath wronged him. If it do him right,°
Then he hath wronged himself. If he be free,°   85

55. **Not . . . bob:** not to pretend that the taunt (*bob*) did not hurt him. **56. anatomized:** dissected. **57. squandering:** scattered. **58. Invest:** robe; dress. **63. counter:** valueless token. **66. brutish sting:** *that is,* lust. **70–71. who . . . party:** Who is attacking any particular person when he denounces pride? Satirists of the time, when rebuked for attacking individuals, usually replied that they were denouncing sin and not individual sinners. **72–73. Doth . . . ebb:** Does not pride flow in vast quantities until the source of pride (wealth) finally dries up? **79. basest function:** most degraded kind of employment. **80. bravery . . . cost:** his fine clothes have not cost me anything. **81. suits:** fits. **82. mettle:** material; *that is,* his protest shows that my words have fitted him. **84. If . . . right:** if my statements are correct. **85. free:** guiltless.

Why then my taxing like a wild goose flies,
Unclaimed of any man. But who comes here?

(Enter ORLANDO, *with his sword drawn.)*

ORLANDO.   Forbear, and eat no more.

JAQUES.   Why, I have eat none yet.

ORLANDO.   Nor shalt not, till necessity be served.

JAQUES.   Of what kind should this cock come of?   90

DUKE SENIOR.   Art thou thus boldened, man, by thy distress?
   Or else a rude despiser of good manners,
   That in civility° thou seem'st so empty?

ORLANDO.   You touched my vein at first.° The thorny point
   Of bare distress hath ta'en from me the show   95
   Of smooth civility. Yet am I inland-bred°
   And know some nurture.° But forbear, I say.
   He dies that touches any of this fruit
   Till I and my affairs are answered.

JAQUES.   An° you will not be answered with reason, I must die.   100

DUKE SENIOR.   What would you have? Your gentleness shall
         force
   More than your force move us to gentleness.

ORLANDO.   I almost die for food, and let me have it.

DUKE SENIOR.   Sit down and feed, and welcome to our table.

ORLANDO.   Speak you so gently? Pardon me, I pray you.   105
   I thought that all things had been savage here,
   And therefore put I on the countenance°
   Of stern commandment.° But whate'er you are
   That in this desert inaccessible,
   Under the shade of melancholy boughs,   110
   Lose and neglect the creeping hours of time,
   If ever you have looked on better days,
   If ever been where bells have knolled° to church,
   If ever sat at any good man's feast,
   If ever from your eyelids wiped a tear   115
   And know what 'tis to pity and be pitied,
   Let gentleness my strong enforcement be.
   In the which hope I blush, and hide my sword.

93. **civility**: courtesy. 94. **touched . . . first**: *that is*, your first guess is right. 96.
inland-bred: one who knows civilization. 97. **nurture**: good breeding. 100. **An**: if.
107. **countenance**: face; more generally, appearance. 108. **stern commandment**:
harsh, domineering behavior. 113. **knolled**: tolled.

DUKE SENIOR.   True is it that we have seen better day,
And have with holy bell been knolled to church,   120
And sat at good men's feasts, and wiped our eyes
Of drops that sacred pity hath engendered.
And therefore sit you down in gentleness
And take upon command what help we have
That to your wanting may be ministered.   125
ORLANDO.   Then but forbear your food a little while
Whiles, like a doe, I go to find my fawn
And give it food. There is an old poor man
Who after me hath many a weary step
Limped in pure love. Till he be first sufficed,   130
Oppressed with two weak evils, age and hunger,
I will not touch a bit.
DUKE SENIOR.   Go find him out,
And we will nothing waste till you return.
ORLANDO.   I thank ye, and be blest for your good comfort!
                                                (*Exit.*)
DUKE SENIOR.   Thou seest we are not all alone unhappy.   135
This wide and universal theater
Presents more woeful pageants than the scene
Wherein we play in.
JAQUES.   All the world's a stage,°
And all the men and women merely players.
They have their exits and their entrances,   140
And one man in his time plays many parts,
His acts being seven ages. At first the infant,
Mewling° and puking in the nurse's arms.
Then the whining schoolboy, with his satchel
And shining morning face, creeping like snail   145
Unwillingly to school. And then the lover,
Sighing like furnace, with a woeful ballad
Made to his mistress' eyebrow. Then a soldier,
Full of strange oaths and bearded like the pard,°
Jealous in honor,° sudden and quick in quarrel,   150
Seeking the bubble reputation°
Even in the cannon's mouth. And then the justice,

138. **All the world's a stage:** This was probably inspired by the motto of the new
Globe Theater—*Totus mundus agit histrionem* (The whole world plays the
actor). 143. **Mewling:** whimpering. 149. **pard:** leopard. 150. **Jealous in honor:**
sensitive about his honor. 151. **bubble reputation:** fame as quickly burst as a
bubble.

In fair round belly with good capon lined,
With eyes severe and beard of formal cut,
Full of wise saws° and modern instances,°   155
And so he plays his part. The sixth age shifts
Into the lean and slippered Pantaloon°
With spectacles on nose and pouch on side,
His youthful hose, well saved, a world too wide
For his shrunk shank, and his big manly voice,   160
Turning again toward childish treble, pipes
And whistles in his sound. Last scene of all,
That ends this strange eventful history,
In second childishness and mere oblivion,
Sans teeth, sans eyes, sans taste, sans everything.   165

(*Reenter* ORLANDO, *with* ADAM.)

DUKE SENIOR.   Welcome. Set down your venerable burden,
    And let him feed.
ORLANDO.   I thank you most for him.
ADAM.   So had you need.
    I scarce can speak to thank you for myself.
DUKE SENIOR.   Welcome. Fall to. I will not trouble you   170
    As yet, to question you about your fortunes.
    Give us some music, and, good Cousin, sing.
AMIENS. (*Sings.*)
        Blow, blow, thou winter wind.
        Thou art not so unkind
            As man's ingratitude.   175
        Thy tooth is not so keen,
        Because thou art not seen,
            Although thy breath be rude.
    Heigh-ho! Sing, heigh-ho! unto the green holly.
    Most friendship is feigning, most loving mere folly.   180
        Then, heigh-ho, the holly!
            This life is most jolly.

        Freeze, freeze, thou bitter sky,
        That dost not bite so nigh
            As benefits forgot   185

155. **saws:** sayings. **modern instances:** commonplace examples. 157. **Pantaloon:**
the foolish old man of Italian comedy.

        Though thou the waters warp,°
        Thy sting is not so sharp
           As friend remembered not.
    Heigh-ho! Sing, heigh-ho! unto the green holly.
    Most friendship is feigning, most loving mere folly.   190
        Then, heigh-ho, the holly!
           This life is most jolly.

DUKE SENIOR.   If that you were the good Sir Rowland's son,
    As you have whispered faithfully you were,
    And as mine eye doth his effigies° witness   195
    Most truly limned° and living in your face,
    Be truly welcome hither. I am the Duke
    That loved your father. The residue of your fortune,°
    Go to my cave and tell me. Good old man,
    Thou art right welcome, as thy master is.   200
    Support him by the arm. Give me your hand,
    And let me all your fortunes understand.   (*Exeunt.*)

186. **warp:** freeze. 195. **effigies:** images; likenesses. 196. **limned:** painted. 198.
residue of your fortune: rest of the story of your life.

Meaning and Method: Act II, Scene 7

1. What is the meaning of Jaques's wish to be a fool and his ambition "to wear a coat of motley"? Why does the Duke reprimand him for this ambition?

2. In Jaques's famous passage (lines 138–65), beginning "All the world's a stage . . ." how do each of the seven stages mentioned reflect his pessimistic and melancholy view of life? Did you notice that his dark view is sometimes lightened by touches of humor, as it is when he refers to "the . . . schoolboy . . . creeping like snail . . . to school"? Find other humorous touches. In what way are his words true? Untrue?

3. Notice that right at the end of Jaques's speech about the seven ages of man, Orlando and Adam enter. Do you think Shakespeare was deliberately undercutting the pessimistic sentiments just expressed? How do Orlando and Adam represent a more positive and joyful view of at least two of the stages of man?

4. Are Amiens's verses at the end of the scene in keeping with Jaques's melancholy outlook? Quote lines that prove your answer. Why is it fitting for this play to be interspersed with songs?

5. How is the fool's notion of time (lines 22–28) like and unlike that of Jaques's?

Act III

SCENE 1. *A room in the palace.*

(*Enter* DUKE FREDERICK, LORDS, *and* OLIVER.)

DUKE FREDERICK.   Not see him since? Sir, sir, that cannot be.
    But were I not the better part made mercy,
    I should not seek an absent argument
    Of my revenge, thou present.° But look to it.
    Find out thy brother, wheresoe'er he is.   5
    Seek him with candle, bring him dead or living
    Within this twelvemonth, or turn thou no more
    To seek a living in our territory.
    Thy lands and all things that thou dost call thine
    Worth seizure do we seize into our hands   10
    Till thou canst quit° thee by thy brother's mouth
    Of what we think against thee.
OLIVER.   Oh, that your Highness knew my heart in this!
    I never loved my brother in my life.
DUKE FREDERICK.   More villain thou. Well, push him out of   15
    doors,
    And let my officers of such a nature
    Make an extent upon° his house and lands.
    Do this expediently° and turn him going.

                                         (*Exeunt.*)

3–4. I . . . **present:** I should not look for your brother, but take vengeance
on you. 11. **quit:** acquit. 17. **Make . . . upon:** seize. 18. **expediently:** promptly.

Meaning and Method: Act III, Scene 1

1. What is Duke Frederick's threat if Oliver does not find Orlando within
a year?
2. How is this scene an example of irony of situation?

SCENE 2.   *The forest.*

(*Enter* ORLANDO, *with a paper.*)

ORLANDO. "Hang there, my verse, in witness of my love.
And thou, thrice-crownèd queen° of night, survey
With thy chaste eye, from the pale sphere° above,
Thy huntress' name that my full life doth sway.
O Rosalind! These trees shall be my books   5
And in their barks my thoughts I'll character,°
That every eye which in this forest looks
Shall see thy virtue witnessed everywhere.
Run, run, Orlando, carve on every tree
The fair, the chaste, and unexpressive° she."   (*Exit.*)   10

(*Enter* CORIN *and* TOUCHSTONE.)

CORIN. And how like you this shepherd's life, Master Touchstone?

TOUCHSTONE. Truly, shepherd, in respect of itself, it is a good
life; but in respect that it is a shepherd's life, it is naught.°
In respect that it is solitary, I like it very well; but in re-   15
spect that it is private,° it is a very vile life. Now, in respect it is in the fields, it pleaseth me well; but in respect
it is not in the Court, it is tedious. As it is a spare° life,
look you, it fits my humor well; but as there is no more
plenty in it, it goes much against my stomach. Hast any   20
philosophy in thee, shepherd?

CORIN. No more but that I know the more one sickens, the
worse at ease he is; and that he that wants money, means,
and content is without three good friends; that the property
of rain is to wet and fire to burn; that good pasture makes   25
fat sheep, and that a great cause of the night is lack of the
sun; that he that hath learned no wit by nature nor art°

2. **thrice-crownèd queen:** the goddess Diana was called so on earth; in heaven
she was Luna (the Moon); and in the underworld, or Hades, Persephone. Diana
was also the goddess of hunting and patroness of maidens; hence, the reference to
chaste in lines 3 and 10, and to *huntress* in line 4. **3. pale sphere:** the moon. **6.
character:** inscribe. **10. unexpressive:** inexpressible; beyond description. **13. naught:**
worthless. **16. private:** lonely; solitary. Touchstone, as a frequenter of the royal
court, prefers a public kind of life. **18. spare:** frugal. **27. nature . . . art:** In Elizabethan English, "nature" used in this way meant that which was born in man—
that is, natural ability; "art" was that which came with study and training—art
thus meant technical skill.

may complain of good breeding or comes of a very dull
kindred.

TOUCHSTONE.   Such a one is a natural° philosopher. Wast ever   30
in Court, shepherd?

CORIN.   No, truly.

TOUCHSTONE.   Then thou art damned.

CORIN.   Nay, I hope.

TOUCHSTONE.   Truly, thou art damned, like an ill-roasted egg all   35
on one side.

CORIN.   For not being at Court? Your reason.

TOUCHSTONE.   Why, if thou never wast at Court, thou never
sawest good manners. If thou never sawest good manners,°
then thy manners must be wicked, and wickedness is sin,   40
and sin is damnation. Thou art in a parlous° state, shepherd.

CORIN.   Not a whit, Touchstone. Those that are good manners
at the Court are as ridiculous in the country as the behavior
of the country is most mockable at the Court. You told me   45
you salute not at the Court, but you kiss your hands. That
courtesy would be uncleanly if courtiers were shepherds.

TOUCHSTONE.   Instance,° briefly, come, instance.

CORIN.   Why, we are still handling our ewes, and their fells,°
you know, are greasy.   50

TOUCHSTONE.   Why, do not your courtier's hands sweat? And is
not the grease of a mutton as wholesome as the sweat of a
man? Shallow, shallow. A better instance, I say, come.

CORIN.   Besides, our hands are hard.

TOUCHSTONE.   Your lips will feel them the sooner. Shallow   55
again. A more sounder instance, come.

CORIN.   And they are often tarred over with the surgery of our
sheep, and would you have us kiss tar? The courtier's hands
are perfumed with civet.°

TOUCHSTONE.   Most shallow man! Thou wormsmeat in respect   60
of a good piece of flesh indeed! Learn of the wise, and perpend.° Civet is of a baser birth than tar, the very uncleanly
flux of a cat. Mend the instance, shepherd.

---

30. natural: with a pun on "natural," meaning fool. **39. good manners:** with
double meaning—polite behavior and a moral life. **41. parlous:** perilous. **48.
Instance:** Give an example. **49. fells:** fleeces. **59. civet:** perfume obtained from
glandular secretions of the civet cat. **61–62. perpend:** consider.

CORIN.   You have too Courtly a wit for me. I'll rest.

TOUCHSTONE.   Wilt thou rest damned? God help thee, shallow   65
man! God make incision° in thee! Thou art raw.°

CORIN.   Sir, I am a true laborer. I earn that I eat, get that I
wear, owe no man hate, envy no man's happiness, glad of
other men's good, content with my harm,° and the greatest
of my pride is to see my ewes graze and my lambs suck.   70

TOUCHSTONE.   That is another simple sin in you, to bring the
ewes and the rams together and to offer to get your living
by the copulation of cattle; to be bawd° to a bellwether,°
and to betray a she-lamb of a twelvemonth to a crooked-
pated,° old, cuckoldy° ram, out of all reasonable match. If   75
thou beest not damned for this, the Devil himself will have
no shepherds. I cannot see else how thou shouldst 'scape.

CORIN.   Here comes young Master Ganymede, my new mistress' brother.

(*Enter* ROSALIND, *with a paper, reading.*)

ROSALIND.   (*Reads.*)   "From the east to western Ind,°   80
No jewel is like Rosalind.
Her worth, being mounted° on the wind,
Through all the world bears Rosalind.
All the pictures fairest lined°
Are but black to Rosalind.   85
Let no face be kept in mind
But the fair of Rosalind."

TOUCHSTONE.   I'll rhyme you so eight years together, dinners
and suppers and sleeping hours excepted. It is the right
butterwomen's rank to market.°   90

ROSALIND.   Out, fool!

TOUCHSTONE.   For a taste:
If a hart do lack a hind,°

---

66. **make incision:** cut to let blood—a common treatment for many complaints.
raw: inexperienced; unripe; green. 69. **content with my harm:** content to bear
my misfortunes. 73. **bawd:** go-between. **bellwether:** a wether, or ram, with a
bell about its neck that leads a flock of sheep. 74–75. **crooked-pated:** crooked-
headed. 75. **cuckoldy:** lecherous. 80. **Ind:** India. 82. **mounted:** blown about. 84.
lined: drawn. 89–90. **right . . . market:** Touchstone is comparing the pace of
Orlando's poem to the movement of old women going to market. 93. **hart, hind:**
male and female deer.

Let him seek out Rosalind.
If the cat will after kind,   95
So be sure will Rosalind.
Winter garments must be lined,
So must slender Rosalind.
They that reap must sheaf and bind,
Then to cart with Rosalind.   100
Sweetest nut hath sourest rind,
Such a nut is Rosalind.

This is the very false gallop° of verses. Why do you infect
yourself with them?

ROSALIND.   Peace, you dull fool! I found them on a tree.   105
TOUCHSTONE.   Truly, the tree yields bad fruit.
ROSALIND.   I'll graff° it with you, and then I shall graff it with a
medlar.° Then it will be the earliest fruit i' the country, for
you'll be rotten ere you be half ripe, and that's the right
virtue of the medlar.   110
TOUCHSTONE.   You have said, but whether wisely or no, let the
forest judge.

(*Enter* CELIA, *with a writing.*)

ROSALIND.   Peace! Here comes my sister, reading. Stand aside.
CELIA. (*Reads.*) "Why should this a desert be?
For it is unpeopled? No,   115
Tongues I'll hang on every tree,
That shall civil° sayings show;
Some, how brief the life of man
Runs his erring° pilgrimage,
That the stretching of a span°   120
Buckles in° his sum of age;
Some, of violated vows
'Twixt the souls of friend and friend.
But upon the fairest boughs,
Or at every sentence end,   125
Will I Rosalinda write,
Teaching all that read to know

---

103. gallop: *literally,* canter. The rolling motion of a canter is like the even stress
of Orlando's verses. **107. graff:** graft. **108. medlar:** (a) a pearlike fruit not eaten
until it is overripe; (b) a "meddler" in people's business. **117. civil:** civilized.
119. erring: wandering. **120. span:** the distance between the thumb and forefinger
of the stretched hand; about nine inches. **121. Buckles in:** encompasses.

The quintessence° of every sprite°
Heaven would in little° show.
Therefore heaven Nature charged   130
That one body should be filled
With all graces wide-enlarged.
Nature presently distilled
Helen's cheek, but not her heart,
Cleopatra's majesty,   135
Atalanta's better part,
Sad Lucretia's modesty.°
Thus Rosalind of many parts
By heavenly synod° was devised,
Of many faces, eyes, and hearts,   140
To have the touches dearest prized.
Heaven would that she these gifts should have,
And I to live and die her slave."

ROSALIND.   O most gentle pulpiter!° What tedious homily° of
love have you wearied your parishioners withal, and never   145
cried "Have patience, good people!"

CELIA.   How now! Back, friends! Shepherd, go off a little. Go
with him, sirrah.

TOUCHSTONE.   Come, shepherd, let us make an honorable retreat, though not with bag and baggage, yet with scrip° and   150
scrippage.°

(*Exeunt* CORIN *and* TOUCHSTONE.)

CELIA.   Didst thou hear these verses?

ROSALIND.   Oh, yes, I heard them all, and more too, for some
of them had in them more feet° than the verses would bear.

CELIA.   That's no matter. The feet might bear the verses.   155

ROSALIND.   Aye, but the feet were lame and could not bear

---

128. quintessence: the purest part. **sprite:** soul. **129. in little:** in miniature.
134–37. Helen's . . . modesty: Rosalind has the good qualities of four famous
women: Helen of Troy, in Greek mythology, the Queen of Sparta who betrayed
her husband; Cleopatra, Queen of Egypt at the time of Julius Caesar. She was a
queen most royal but unchaste; Atalanta, in Greek mythology, a swift runner who
was led aside by greed; and Lucretia (Lucrece), in Roman legend, a model wife
who, after being raped, killed herself. The legend is used by Shakespeare in his
poem "The Rape of Lucrece." **139. synod:** assembly. **144. pulpiter:** preacher.
homily: sermon. **150. scrip:** the shepherd's wallet. **151. scrippage:** a word invented by Touchstone to mean the contents of a wallet. He is also using it to
balance *baggage*. **154. feet:** A foot in poetry is a unit of metrical measurement.
Lines usually contain a regular number of feet.

themselves without the verse and therefore stood lamely in the verse.

CELIA. But didst thou hear without wondering how thy name should be hanged and carved upon these trees?   160

ROSALIND. I was seven of the nine days° out of the wonder before you came; for look here what I found on a palm tree. I was never so berhymed° since Pythagoras'° time, that I was an Irish rat, which I can hardly remember.

CELIA. Trow° you who hath done this?   165

ROSALIND. Is it a man?

CELIA. And a chain that you once wore about his neck. Change you color?

ROSALIND. I prithee—who?

CELIA. Oh Lord, Lord! It is a hard matter for friends to meet,   170 but mountains may be removed with earthquakes and so encounter.

ROSALIND. Nay, but who is it?

CELIA. Is it possible?

ROSALIND. Nay, I prithee now with most petitionary vehe-   175 mence,° tell me who it is.

CELIA. Oh, wonderful, wonderful, and most wonderful won- derful! And yet again wonderful, and after that, out of all hooping!°

ROSALIND. Good my complexion!° Dost thou think though I   180 am caparisoned° like a man, I have a doublet and hose in my disposition?° One inch of delay more is a South Sea of discovery.° I prithee tell me who is it quickly, and speak apace. I would thou couldst stammer, that thou mightst pour this concealed man out of thy mouth as wine comes   185 out of a narrow-mouthed bottle, either too much at once or none at all. I prithee take the cork out of thy mouth that I may drink thy tidings.

CELIA. So you may put a man in your belly.

161. seven . . . days: I have endured almost a nine-days wonder. 163. berhymed: rhymed to death. It was believed that in Ireland rats could be destroyed by incan- tations in rhyme. Pythagoras: an ancient Greek philosopher and mathematician, who taught the doctrine of the transmigration of souls; *that is*, that the human soul after death passed into the body of an animal. 165. Trow: know. 175–76. petitionary vehemence: pleading emphasis. 178–79. out . . . hooping: beyond any cry of wonder. 180. Good my complexion: Rosalind is trying not to blush. 181. caparisoned: *here*, dressed. 182. disposition: nature. 182–83. One . . . dis- covery: The slightest delay in telling me makes your story seem endless as the South Sea to a voyager.

ROSALIND. Is he of God's making? What manner of man? Is   190
his head worth a hat? Or his chin worth a beard?

CELIA. Nay, he hath but a little beard.

ROSALIND. Why, God will send more, if the man will be thank-
ful. Let me stay the growth of his beard if thou delay me
not the knowledge of his chin.°   195

CELIA. It is young Orlando, that tripped up the wrestler's heels
and your heart both in an instant.

ROSALIND. Nay, but the devil take mocking. Speak, sad brow°
and true maid.

CELIA. I' faith, Coz, 'tis he.   200

ROSALIND. Orlando?

CELIA. Orlando.

ROSALIND. Alas the day! What shall I do with my doublet and
hose? What did he when thou sawest him? What said he?
How looked he? Wherein went he? What makes he here?   205
Did he ask for me? Where remains he? How parted he with
thee? And when shalt thou see him again? Answer me in
one word.

CELIA. You must borrow me Gargantua's° mouth first. 'Tis a
word too great for any mouth of this age's size. To say aye   210
and no to these particulars is more than to answer in a
catechism.

ROSALIND. But doth he know that I am in this forest and in
man's apparel? Looks he as freshly as he did the day he
wrestled?   215

CELIA. It is as easy to count atomies° as to resolve the proposi-
tions of a lover,° but take a taste of my finding him, and
relish it with good observance. I found him under a tree,
like a dropped acorn.

ROSALIND. It may well be called Jove's° tree when it drops   220
forth such fruit.

CELIA. Give me audience, good madam.

ROSALIND. Proceed.

CELIA. There lay he, stretched along° like a wounded knight.

194–95. Let . . . chin: I can wait for his beard to grow, so long as you tell me
whose chin it is. **198. sad brow:** in sober earnest. **209. Gargantua's:** an allusion to
Rabelais's satirical tale of Gargantua, a peace-loving giant. François Rabelais
(1494?–1553?), was a French physician, satirist, and humorist. **216. atomies:**
specks of dust in a sunbeam. **216–17. resolve . . . lover:** solve a lover's problems.
220. Jove's: Jove is another name for Jupiter, supreme ruler of the Roman gods.
224. along: at full length.

ROSALIND.   Though it be pity to see such a sight, it well be-   225
comes the ground.

CELIA.   Cry "holloa"° to thy tongue, I prithee, it curvets° un-
seasonably. He was furnished like a hunter.

ROSALIND.   Oh, ominous! He comes to kill my heart.

CELIA.   I would sing my song without a burden.° Thou bringest   230
me out of tune.

ROSALIND.   Do you not know I am a woman? When I think,
I must speak. Sweet, say on.

CELIA.   You bring me out. Soft! Comes he not here?

(*Enter* ORLANDO *and* JAQUES.)

ROSALIND.   'Tis he. Slink by, and note him.   235

JAQUES.   I thank you for your company, but, good faith, I had
as lief have been myself alone.

ORLANDO.   And so had I, but yet, for fashion sake, I thank you
too for your society.

JAQUES.   God buy you.° Let's meet as little as we can.   240

ORLANDO.   I do desire we may be better strangers.

JAQUES.   I pray you mar no more trees with writing love songs
in their barks.

ORLANDO.   I pray you mar no more of my verses with reading
them ill-favoredly.°   245

JAQUES.   Rosalind is your love's name?

ORLANDO.   Yes, just.

JAQUES.   I do not like her name.

ORLANDO.   There was no thought of pleasing you when she was
christened.   250

JAQUES.   What stature is she of?

ORLANDO.   Just as high as my heart.

JAQUES.   You are full of pretty answers. Have you not been acquainted with goldsmiths' wives, and conned them out of
rings?°   255

ORLANDO.   Not so, but I answer you right painted cloth,° from
whence you have studied your questions.

227. holloa: hold up! whoa! curvets: prances. 230. burden: refrain. 240. God buy
you: God be with you. 245. ill-favoredly: with a pained expression. 254–55. out
. . . rings: Rings were often inscribed with little romantic sentences or mottoes.
Jaques hints that Orlando learned his poetry from memorizing (*conning*) these
trite little sayings. 256. painted cloth: This refers to a cheap substitute for fine
tapestries hung on walls. These coarse cloths were often decorated with proverbs
on good conduct.

JAQUES. You have a nimble wit. I think 'twas made of Atalanta's heels. Will you sit down with me? And we two will
rail against our mistress the world, and all our misery.   260

ORLANDO. I will chide no breather° in the world but myself,
against whom I know most faults.

JAQUES. The worst fault you have is to be in love.

ORLANDO. 'Tis a fault I will not change for your best virtue.
I am weary of you.   265

JAQUES. By my troth, I was seeking for a fool when I found
you.

ORLANDO. He is drowned in the brook. Look but in and you
shall see him.

JAQUES. There I shall see mine own figure.   270

ORLANDO. Which I take to be either a fool or a cipher.°

JAQUES. I'll tarry no longer with you. Farewell, good Signior
Love.

ORLANDO. I am glad of your departure. Adieu, good Monsieur
Melancholy.   275

(*Exit* JAQUES.)

ROSALIND. (*Aside to* CELIA.) I will speak to him like a saucy
lackey,° and under that habit play the knave with him. Do
you hear, forester?

ORLANDO. Very well. What would you?

ROSALIND. I pray you, what is 't o'clock?   280

ORLANDO. You should ask me what time o' day. There's no
clock in the forest.

ROSALIND. Then there is no truelover in the forest, else sighing
every minute and groaning every hour would detect the
lazy foot of Time as well as a clock.   285

ORLANDO. And why not the swift foot of Time? Had not that
been as proper?

ROSALIND. By no means, sir. Time travels in divers° paces with
divers persons. I'll tell you who Time ambles withal, who
Time trots withal, who Time gallops withal, and who he   290
stands still withal.

ORLANDO. I prithee who doth he trot withal?

ROSALIND. Marry, he trots hard with a young maid between the
contract° of her marriage and the day it is solemnized.

261. **breather:** living creature. 271. **cipher:** a nothing; an insignificant individual.
277. **lackey:** servant. 288. **divers:** different. 294. **contract:** formal betrothal.

If the interim be but a sennight,° Time's pace is so hard   295
that it seems the length of seven year.

ORLANDO.   Who ambles Time withal?

ROSALIND.   With a priest that lacks Latin and a rich man that
not the gout; for the one sleeps easily because he cannot
study, and the other lives merrily because he feels no pain,   300
the one lacking the burden of lean and wasteful learning,
the other knowing no burden of heavy tedious penury.
These Time ambles withal.

ORLANDO.   Who doth he gallop withal?

ROSALIND.   With a thief to the gallows, for though he go as   305
softly as foot can fall, he thinks himself too soon there.

ORLANDO.   Who stays it still withal?

ROSALIND.   With lawyers in the vacation, for they sleep between term and term and then they perceive not how Time
moves.   310

ORLANDO.   Where dwell you, pretty youth?

ROSALIND.   With this shepherdess, my sister. Here in the skirts°
of the forest, like fringe upon a petticoat.

ORLANDO.   Are you native of this place?

ROSALIND.   As the cony° that you see dwell where she is   315
kindled.°

ORLANDO.   Your accent is something finer than you could purchase in so removed a dwelling.

ROSALIND.   I have been told so of many. But indeed an old
religious° uncle of mine taught me to speak, who was in his   320
youth an inland man,° one that knew courtship too well,
for there he fell in love. I have heard him read many lec-
tures against it, and I thank God I am not a woman, to be
touched with so many giddy offenses as he hath generally
taxed their whole sex withal.   325

ORLANDO.   Can you remember any of the principal evils that he
laid to the charge of women?

ROSALIND.   There were none principal, they were all like one
another as halfpence are, every one fault seeming monstrous till his fellow fault came to match it.   330

ORLANDO.   I prithee recount some of them.

---

295. **sennight:** week. 312. **skirts:** outskirts. 315. **cony:** rabbit. 316. **kindled:**
brought forth. 320. **religious:** *that is,* hermitlike. 321. **inland man:** city dweller.

ROSALIND.   No, I will not cast away my physic but on those that
are sick. There is a man haunts the forest that abuses our
young plants with carving "Rosalind" on their barks, hangs
odes upon hawthorns and elegies on brambles—all, for-   335
sooth, deifying the name of Rosalind. If I could meet that
fancymonger,° I would give him some good counsel, for he
seems to have the quotidian° of love upon him.

ORLANDO.   I am he that is so love-shaked. I pray you tell me
your remedy.   340

ROSALIND.   There is none of my uncle's marks upon you. He
taught me how to know a man in love, in which cage of
rushes° I am sure you are not prisoner.

ORLANDO.   What were his marks?

ROSALIND.   A lean cheek, which you have not; a blue eye° and   345
sunken, which you have not; an unquestionable° spirit,
which you have not; a beard neglected, which you have
not—but I pardon you for that, for simply your having in
beard is a younger brother's revenue.° Then your hose
should be ungartered, your bonnet° unbanded, your sleeve   350
unbuttoned, your shoe untied, and everything about you
demonstrating a careless desolation. But you are no such
man, you are rather point-device° in your accouterments,°
as loving yourself than seeming the lover of any other.

ORLANDO.   Fair youth, I would I could make thee believe I love.   355

ROSALIND.   Me believe it! You may as soon make her that you
love believe it, which, I warrant, she is apter to do than to
confess she does. That is one of the points in the which
women still give the lie to their consciences. But, in good
sooth, are you he that hangs the verses on the trees wherein   360
Rosalind is so admired?

ORLANDO.   I swear to thee, youth, by the white hand of Rosalind, I am that he, that unfortunate he.

ROSALIND.   But are you so much in love as your rhymes speak?

ORLANDO.   Neither rhyme nor reason can express how much.   365

337. **fancymonger:** trader in love. 338. **quotidian:** fever that recurs daily. 342–43.
cage of rushes: cage of reed made for little birds. 345. **blue eye:** an eye with dark
rings underneath. Rosalind proceeds to poke fun at the standard picture of the
man in love as he was usually pictured by the Elizabethans. 346. **unquestionable:**
glum. 348–49. **having . . . revenue:** Your beard is a poor thing, like the income
of a younger brother. 350. **bonnet:** hat. 353. **point-device:** very neat. **accouterments:** equipment, trappings.

ROSALIND.   Love is merely a madness, and I tell you deserves
as well a dark house and a whip° as madmen do. And the
reason why they are not so punished and cured is that the
lunacy is so ordinary that the whippers are in love too. Yet
I profess curing it by counsel.   370

ORLANDO.   Did you ever cure any so?

ROSALIND.   Yes, one, and in this manner. He was to imagine me
his love, his mistress, and I set him every day to woo me.
At which time would I, being but a moonish° youth, grieve,
be effeminate, changeable, longing and liking, proud, fan-   375
tastical, apish, ° shallow, inconstant, full of tears, full of
smiles, for every passion something and for no passion truly
anything, as boys and women are for the most part cattle
of this color. Would now like him, now loathe him; then
entertain him, then forswear him; now weep for him, then   380
spit at him; that I drave my suitor from his mad humor°
of love to a living humor of madness, which was to for-
swear° the full stream of the world and to live in a nook
merely monastic.° And thus I cured him, and this way will
I take upon me to wash your liver° as clean as a sound   385
sheep's heart, that there shall not be one spot of love in 't.

ORLANDO..   I would not be cured, youth.

ROSALIND.   I would cure you if you would but call me Rosalind
and come every day to my cote and woo me.

ORLANDO.   Now, by the faith of my love, I will. Tell me where   390
it is.

ROSALIND.   Go with me to it and I'll show it you. And by the
way you shall tell me where in the forest you live. Will you
go?

ORLANDO.   With all my heart, good youth.   395

ROSALIND.   Nay, you must call me Rosalind. Come, Sister, will
you go?   (*Exeunt.*)

367. dark . . . whip: This was the common treatment given to lunatics. 374.
moonish: fickle; changeable as the moon. 376. apish: frivolous. 381. humor:
mood. 382–83. forswear: renounce with an oath. 384. merely monastic: as a
monk in a monastery. 385. liver: the seat of love in the human body, according to
ancient medical beliefs.

Meaning and Method: Act III, Scene 2

1. Shakespeare now offers a contrast to the sentiments about the pastoral
life expressed by the banished Duke in Act II, Scene 1, lines 1–18.

What faults does Touchstone find with country life? What values does Corin see in it? How do his arguments emphasize the earthy, unpoetical workaday aspects of the shepherd's life? How is their dialogue also a satirical comment on Court life?

2. A *parody* in literature aims to ridicule the attitude, style, or subject matter of one work by means of another. Compare the verses written by Orlando that Rosalind reads (lines 80–87) and Touchstone's parody of them (lines 93–102). What aspects of Orlando's verse is Touchstone ridiculing?

3. Read Orlando's verses to Rosalind beginning with "Why should this a desert be. . . ." (line 114). What praises of Rosalind does Orlando make? How would a twentieth-century girl react to such praises?

4. What is Jaques's reaction to Orlando's love for Rosalind? Why is this reaction consistent with Jaques's personality? Who seems to be the winner in this exchange of ideas and wit in lines 236–75?

5. Is Rosalind's decision not to remove her disguise in keeping with her character? Why or why not? She seems to find a mischievous joy in mocking the love-sick Orlando. Find some examples of her mirth and wit. In what way is the Elizabethan version of the "marks" of a youth in love (lines 345–52) different from those seen today?

6. How does this scene provide a glimpse of both sides of Rosalind's character: (a) the lovesick young woman, and (b) the witty, self-possessed young woman?

7. In this scene we meet an Orlando we have not known before— Orlando the lover—bemused, longing, enthralled, lovesick. If Orlando represents a kind of sentimental excess, how do the other incidents in the scene and the arguments of the other characters serve to evaluate this "romantic love"?

SCENE 3. *The forest.*

(*Enter* TOUCHSTONE *and* AUDREY; JAQUES *behind.*)

TOUCHSTONE.   Come apace,° good Audrey. I will fetch up your
goats, Audrey. And how, Audrey? Am I the man yet? Doth
my simple features content you?

AUDREY.   Your features! Lord warrant us! What features?

TOUCHSTONE.   I am here with thee and thy goats, as the most   5
capricious° poet, honest Ovid, was among the Goths.°

1. apace: quickly. 6. capricious: unpredictable; also a pun on *caper*, the Latin word for a goat, a selfish and hungry animal. Ovid . . . Goths: Ovid was banished from Rome for an intrigue with the daughter of the Emperor Augustus and forced to live with the *Getae* (Goths). This is the second pun on Goths and goats.

JAQUES. (*Aside*.)   Oh, knowledge ill-inhabited, worse than Jove in a thatched house!°

TOUCHSTONE.   When a man's verses cannot be understood, nor a man's good wit seconded° with the forward child under- 10 standing, it strikes a man more dead than a great reckoning in a little room.° Truly, I would the gods had made thee poetical.

AUDREY.   I do not know what "poetical" is. Is it honest in deed and word? Is it a true thing? 15

TOUCHSTONE.   No, truly, for the truest poetry is the most feign- ing,° and lovers are given to poetry, and what they swear in poetry may be said as lovers they do feign.

AUDREY.   Do you wish, then, that the gods had made me poetical? 20

TOUCHSTONE.   I do, truly, for thou swearest to me thou art honest.° Now if thou wert a poet, I might have some hope thou didst feign.

AUDREY.   Would you not have me honest?

TOUCHSTONE.   No, truly, unless thou wert hard-favored,° for 25 honesty coupled to beauty is to have honey a sauce to sugar.

JAQUES. (*Aside*.)   A material° fool!

AUDREY.   Well, I am not fair, and therefore I pray the gods make me honest. 30

TOUCHSTONE.   Truly, and to cast away honesty upon a foul° slut were to put good meat into an unclean dish.

AUDREY.   I am not a slut, though I thank the gods I am foul.

TOUCHSTONE.   Well, praised be the gods for thy foulness! Slut- ishness may come hereafter. But be it as it may be, I will 35 marry thee, and to that end I have been with Sir Oliver Martext,° the vicar of the next village, who hath promised to meet me in this place of the forest and to couple us.

JAQUES. (*Aside*.)   I would fain see this meeting.

AUDREY.   Well, the gods give us joy! 40

7–8. Jove . . . house: *that is*, a god living in a cottage. 10. seconded: supported. 11–12. great . . . room: *that is*, a huge bill for a private dinner party. 16–17. feigning: deceiving; creating a false appearance. 22. honest: chaste. 25. hard- favored: plain-faced; homely. 27. material: *here*, knowledgeable. 31. foul: ugly. 35–36. Sir Oliver Martext: a minister of the church was often a Bachelor of Arts, and so entitled *dominus*, which was translated as "sir." Oliver, however, seems to be only a local preacher who *mars texts* by his misinterpretations.

(*Enter* SIR OLIVER MARTEXT.)

TOUCHSTONE.   Sir Oliver Martext, you are well met. Will you
dispatch us here under this tree, or shall we go with you to
your chapel?

SIR OLIVER MARTEXT.   Is there none here to give the woman?

TOUCHSTONE.   I will not take her on gift of any man.   45

SIR OLIVER MARTEXT.   Truly, she must be given or the marriage
is not lawful.

JAQUES.   Proceed, proceed. I'll give her.

TOUCHSTONE.   Good even, good Master What-ye-call't. How do
you, sir? You are very well met. God 'ild° you for your last   50
company. I am very glad to see you. Even a toy° in hand
here, sir. Nay, pray be covered.°

JAQUES.   Will you be married, Motley?

TOUCHSTONE.   As the ox hath his bow,° sir, the horse his curb,°
and the falcon her bells,° so man hath his desires; and as   55
pigeons bill, so wedlock would be nibbling.°

JAQUES.   And will you, being a man of your breeding, be
married under a bush like a beggar? Get you to church,
and have a good priest that can tell you what marriage is.
This fellow will but join you together as they join wain-   60
scot;° then one of you will prove a shrunk panel, and like
green timber warp, warp.

TOUCHSTONE. (*Aside.*)   I am not in the mind, but I were better
to be married of him than of another. For he is not like
to marry me well, and not being well married, it will be a   65
good excuse for me hereafter to leave my wife.

JAQUES.   Go thou with me, and let me counsel thee.

TOUCHSTONE.   Come, sweet Audrey.
We must be married or we must live in bawdry.
Farewell, good Master Oliver: not—   70
            "O sweet Oliver,
            O brave Oliver,
            Leave me not behind thee—"
but—

---

50. **God 'ild:** God reward. **51. toy:** trifle. **52. be covered:** put on your hat. **54.
bow:** yoke; harness. **curb:** a chain or strap bracing the bit in a horse's mouth.
55. bells: small bells were tied to the trained falcon to help the trainer locate the
hawk when it landed. **56. nibbling:** *that is,* getting at a man. **60–61. wainscot:**
wooden paneling.

> "Wind° away,   75
>   Begone, I say,
>   I will not to wedding with thee."

(*Exeunt* JAQUES, TOUCHSTONE *and* AUDREY.)

SIR OLIVER MARTEXT.   'Tis no matter. Ne'er a fantastical knave
   of them all shall flout° me out of my calling.   (*Exit.*)

75. Wind: turn. **79. flout:** mock.

Meaning and Method: Act III, Scene 3

This scene, too, presents two people in "love." What seems to be
Touchstone's opinion of the value and permanence of love?

In what way does Shakespeare use Touchstone and Audrey to poke
fun at the love of Rosalind and Orlando? That is, what kind of love do
Touchstone and Audrey represent?

SCENE 4.   *The forest.*

(*Enter* ROSALIND *and* CELIA.)

ROSALIND.   Never talk to me, I will weep.

CELIA.   Do, I prithee, but yet have the grace to consider that
   tears do not become a man.

ROSALIND.   But have I not cause to weep?

CELIA.   As good cause as one would desire, therefore weep.   5

ROSALIND.   His very hair is of the dissembling° color.

CELIA.   Something browner than Judas's.° Marry, his kisses are
   Judas's own children.

ROSALIND.   I'faith, his hair is of a good color.

CELIA.   An excellent color. Your chestnut was ever the only   10
   color.

ROSALIND.   And his kissing is as full of sanctity as the touch
   of holy bread.

CELIA.   He hath bought a pair of cast° lips of Diana.° A nun of
   winter's sisterhood kisses not more religiously, the very   15
   ice of chastity is in them.

6. dissembling: deceptive; cheating. **7. Judas's:** Judas, the betrayer of Christ, was
portrayed with red hair in many paintings. **14. cast:** cast off. **Diana:** the Roman
goddess of chastity.

ROSALIND.   But why did he swear he would come this morning
and comes not?

CELIA.   Nay, certainly there is no truth in him.

ROSALIND.   Do you think so?   20

CELIA.   Yes, I think he is not a pickpurse nor a horse-stealer;
but for his verity in love, I do think him as concave as a
covered goblet° or a worm-eaten nut.

ROSALIND.   Not true in love?

CELIA.   Yes, when he is in, but I think he is not in.   25

ROSALIND.   You have heard him swear downright he was.

CELIA.   "Was" is not "is." Besides, the oath of a lover is no
stronger than the word of a tapster;° they are both the con-
firmer of false reckonings. He attends here in the forest
on the Duke your father.   30

ROSALIND.   I met the Duke yesterday and had much question
with him. He asked me of what parentage I was. I told him
of as good as he, so he laughed and let me go. But what
talk we of fathers when there is such a man as Orlando?

CELIA.   Oh, that's a brave man! He writes brave verses, speaks   35
brave words, swears brave oaths and breaks them bravely,
quite traverse,° athwart the heart of his lover—as a puisny°
tilter that spurs his horse but on one side breaks his staff
like a noble goose. But all's brave that youth mounts and
folly guides. Who comes here?   40

(*Enter* CORIN.)

CORIN.   Mistress and master; you have oft inquired
After the shepherd that complained of love
Who you saw sitting by me on the turf
Praising the proud disdainful shepherdess
That was his mistress.   45

CELIA.   Well, and what of him?

CORIN.   If you will see a pageant truly played
Between the pale complexion of true love
And the red glow of scorn and proud disdain,

22–23. **concave . . . goblet:** as hollow as a drinking cup with a cover. **28. tapster:**
the potboy in a tavern who brings the drinks. **37. traverse:** across. A tilter was
considered to be afraid if he directed his lance *athwart* (across) the body of his
opponent instead of giving a direct blow on his shield. **puisny:** inexperienced.

Go hence a little and I shall conduct you,   50
    If you will mark it.
ROSALIND.   Oh, come let us remove.
    The sight of lovers feedeth those in love.
    Bring us to this sight and you shall say
    I'll prove a busy actor in their play.   (*Exeunt.*)   55

Meaning and Method: Act III, Scene 4

1. How does Rosalind's plan for curing Orlando seem to be working out?
2. In line 31, Rosalind says, "I met the Duke yesterday." This is her
   long-banished father—and yet she speaks of this event as if it were
   an item in a local newspaper. Is this natural? realistic? Why did she
   not reveal who she was?

SCENE 5.   *Another part of the forest.*

(*Enter* SILVIUS *and* PHEBE.)

SILVIUS.   Sweet Phebe, do not scorn me, do not, Phebe.
    Say that you love me not, but say not so
    In bitterness. The common executioner,
    Whose heart the accustomed sight of death makes hard,
    Falls not the ax upon the humbled neck   5
    But first begs pardon. Will you sterner be
    Than he that dies and lives by bloody drops?

(*Enter* ROSALIND, CELIA, *and* CORIN, *behind.*)

PHEBE.   I would not be thy executioner.
    I fly thee, for I would not injure thee.
    Thou tell'st me there is murder in mine eye.   10
    'Tis pretty,° sure, and very probable,
    That eyes, that are the frail'st and softest things,
    Who shut their coward gates on atomies,
    Should be called tyrants, butchers, murderers!
    Now I do frown on thee with all my heart,   15
    And if mine eyes can wound, now let them kill thee.
    Now counterfeit° to swoon, why, now fall down.

11. pretty: a pretty notion. 17. counterfeit: pretend.

Or if thou canst not, oh, for shame, for shame,
Lie not, to say mine eyes are murderers!
Now show the wound mine eye hath made in thee.   20
Scratch thee but with a pin and there remains
Some scar of it. Lean but upon a rush,
The cicatrice° and capable impressure°
Thy palm some moment keeps. But now mine eyes,
Which I have darted at thee, hurt thee not,   25
Nor, I am sure, there is no force in eyes
That can do hurt.
SILVIUS.   O dear Phebe,
If ever—as that ever may be near—
You meet in some fresh cheek the power of fancy,°
Then shall you know the wounds invisible   30
That love's keen arrows make.
PHEBE.   But till that time
Come not thou near me. And when that time comes,
Afflict me with thy mocks, pity me not,
As till that time I shall not pity thee.
ROSALIND.   And why, I pray you? Who might be your mother   35
That you insult, exult, and all at once
Over the wretched? What though you have no beauty—
As, by my faith, I see no more in you
Than without candle may go dark to bed°—
Must you be therefore proud and pitiless?   40
Why, what means this? Why do you look on me?
I see no more in you than in the ordinary
Of nature's salework.° 'Od's my little life,°
I think she means to tangle my eyes too!
No, faith, proud mistress, hope not after it.   45
'Tis not your inky brows, your black silk hair,°
Your bugle° eyeballs, not your cheek of cream,
That can entame my spirits to your worship.
You foolish shepherd, wherefore do you follow her

23. cicatrice: scar. capable impressure: imprint retained. 29. fancy: love. 39. without . . . bed: *that is*, you're not so brilliant that you can go to bed by your own light. 43. salework: product of poor quality. 'Od's . . . life: a mild oath, "bless us." 46. black . . . hair: Black was not considered beautiful. 47. bugle: beady.

Like foggy south,° puffing with wind and rain?   50
You are a thousand times a properer° man
Than she a woman. 'Tis such fools as you
That makes the world full of ill-favored children.
'Tis not her glass,° but you, that flatters her,
And out of you she sees herself more proper   55
Than any of her lineaments° can show her.
But, mistress, know yourself. Down on your knees
And thank Heaven, fasting, for a good man's love.
For I must tell you friendly in your ear,
Sell when you can. You are not for all markets.   60
Cry the man mercy,° love him, take his offer.
Foul is most foul, being foul to be a scoffer.°
So take her to thee, shepherd. Fare you well.

PHEBE.   Sweet youth, I pray you, chide a year together.
I had rather hear you chide than this man woo.   65

ROSALIND.   He's fallen in love with your foulness and she'll
fall in love with my anger. If it be so, as fast as she
answers thee with frowning looks, I'll sauce her with bitter
words. Why look you so upon me?

PHEBE.   For no ill will I bear you.   70

ROSALIND.   I pray you do not fall in love with me,
For I am falser than vows made in wine.
Besides, I like you not. If you will know my house,
'Tis at the tuft of olives° here hard by.
Will you go, Sister? Shepherd, ply° her hard.   75
Come, Sister. Shepherdess, look on him better,
And be not proud. Though all the world could see,
None could be so abused in sight as he.
Come, to our flock.

(*Exeunt* ROSALIND, CELIA *and* CORIN.)

PHEBE.   Dead shepherd, now I find thy saw of might—
"Who ever loved that loved not at first sight?"°

50. **foggy south**: the south wind brought fogs and illness. 51. **properer**: more handsome. 54. **glass**: mirror. 56. **lineaments**: features. 61. **Cry the man mercy**: Ask his pardon. 62. **Foul . . . scoffer**: that is, you are ugly anyway, and uglier when you are disdainful. 74. **tuft of olives**: clump of olive trees. 75. **ply**: press. 80–81. **Dead . . . sight**: "Dead shepherd" is a reference to the poet and dramatist Christopher Marlowe, who was killed in a tavern brawl in 1593. "Who ever loved that loved not at first sight?" is a direct quotation from Marlowe's poem *Hero and Leander*, unfinished at the time of his death.

SILVIUS.   Sweet Phebe—
PHEBE.   Ha, what say'st thou, Silvius?
SILVIUS.   Sweet Phebe, pity me.
PHEBE.   Why, I am sorry for thee, gentle Silvius.
SILVIUS.   Wherever sorrow is, relief would be.   85
    If you do sorrow at my grief in love,
    By giving love your sorrow and my grief
    Were both extermined.
PHEBE.   Thou hast my love. Is not that neighborly?
SILVIUS.   I would have you.
PHEBE.   Why, that were covetousness.   90
    Silvius, the time was that I hated thee,
    And yet it is not that I bear thee love.
    But since that thou canst talk of love so well,
    Thy company, which erst° was irksome to me,
    I will endure, and I'll employ thee too.   95
    But do not look for further recompense
    Than thine own gladness that thou art employed.
SILVIUS.   So holy and so perfect is my love,
    And I in such a poverty of grace,°
    That I shall think it a most plenteous crop   100
    To glean the broken ears after the man
    That the main harvest reaps. Loose now and then
    A scattered smile, and that I'll live upon.
PHEBE.   Know'st thou the youth that spoke to me erewhile?°
SILVIUS.   Not very well, but I have met him oft,   105
    And he hath bought the cottage and the bounds
    That the old carlot° once was master of.
PHEBE.   Think not I love him, though I ask for him.
    'Tis but a peevish° boy, yet he talks well.
    But what care I for words? Yet words do well   110
    When he that speaks them pleases those that hear.
    It is a pretty youth—not very pretty—
    But, sure, he's proud, and yet his pride becomes him.
    He'll make a proper man. The best thing in him
    Is his complexion, and faster than his tongue   115
    Did make offense his eye did heal it up.
    He is not very tall, yet for his years he's tall.
    His leg is but soso, and yet 'tis well.

94. erst: formerly. **99. poverty of grace:** poor favor. **104. erewhile:** just now. **107. carlot:** carl; peasant. **109. peevish:** perverse; silly.

There was a pretty redness in his lip,
A little riper and more lusty red   120
Than that mixed in his cheek, 'twas just the difference
Betwixt the constant red and mingled damask.°
There be some women, Silvius, had they marked him
In parcels° as I did, would have gone near
To fall in love with him. But for my part,   125
I love him not nor hate him not, and yet
I have more cause to hate him than to love him.
For what had he to do to chide at me?
He said mine eyes were black and my hair black,
And, now I am remembered, scorned at me.   130
I marvel why I answered not again.
But that's all one, omittance is no quittance.°
I'll write to him a very taunting letter,
And thou shalt bear it. Wilt thou, Silvius?
SILVIUS.   Phebe, with all my heart.
PHEBE.   I'll write it straight,   135
The matter's in my head and in my heart.
I will be bitter with him and passing short.°
Go with me, Silvius.   (*Exeunt.*)

122. **mingled damask:** blended pink, the color of damask roses. 124. **parcels:** parts; each part separately. 132. **omittance is no quittance:** a legal proverb meaning that failure to collect a debt does not mean the debt has been forgotten. 137. **passing short:** exceedingly abrupt.

Meaning and Method: Act III, Scene 5

1. What manner of person is Phebe? How would you characterize her? Is she realistic? unrealistic? Why does she refuse Silvius and why does he nevertheless persist? What aspect of love does this scene present?
2. How does Rosalind (in her disguise as Ganymede) try to correct the situation? In what way does she complicate it?
3. In what respect is the "game" Rosalind is playing similar to that of Phebe's? In what way are Phebe and Orlando both "blind"?

Act IV

SCENE 1. *The forest.*

(*Enter* ROSALIND, CELIA, *and* JAQUES.)

JAQUES. I prithee, pretty youth, let me be better acquainted with thee.

ROSALIND. They say you are a melancholy fellow.

JAQUES. I am so, I do love it better than laughing.

ROSALIND. Those that are in extremity of either are abominable 5 fellows, and betray themselves to every modern censure° worse than drunkards.

JAQUES. Why, 'tis good to be sad and say nothing.

ROSALIND. Why, then 'tis good to be a post.

JAQUES. I have neither the scholar's melancholy, which is 10 emulation;° nor the musician's, which is fantastical; nor the courtier's, which is proud; nor the soldier's, which is ambitious; nor the lawyer's, which is politic;° nor the lady's, which is nice; nor the lover's, which is all of these. But it is a melancholy of mine own, compounded of many 15 simples,° extracted from many objects, and indeed the sundry° contemplation of my travels, in which my often rumination° wraps me in a most humorous° sadness.

ROSALIND. A traveler! By my faith, you have great reason to be sad. I fear you have sold your own lands to see other men's; 20 then to have seen much and to have nothing is to have rich eyes and poor hands.

JAQUES. Yes, I have gained my experience.

ROSALIND. And your experience makes you sad. I had rather have a fool to make me merry than experience to make me 25 sad—and to travel for it too!

(*Enter* ORLANDO.)

ORLANDO. Good day and happiness, dear Rosalind!

JAQUES. Nay, then, God buy you an you talk in blank verse.

(*Exit.*)

---

6. **modern censure:** trifling criticism. 11. **emulation:** jealous rivalry. 13. **politic:** crafty; sly. 16. **simples:** ingredients. 17. **sundry:** various. 18. **rumination:** meditation. **humorous:** moody.

ROSALIND.   Farewell, Monsieur Traveler. Look you lisp° and
wear strange suits. Disable° all the benefits of your own   30
country, be out of love with your nativity° and almost chide
God for making you that countenance° you are, or I will
scarce think you have swam in a gondola.° Why, how now,
Orlando! Where have you been all this while? You a lover!
An you serve me such another trick, never come in my   35
sight more.

ORLANDO.   My fair Rosalind, I come within an hour of my
promise.

ROSALIND.   Break an hour's promise in love! He that will divide
a minute into a thousand parts and break but a part of the   40
thousandth part of a minute in the affairs of love, it may be
said of him that Cupid hath clapped him o' the shoulder,°
but I'll warrant him heart-whole.

ORLANDO.   Pardon me, dear Rosalind.

ROSALIND.   Nay, an you be so tardy, come no more in my sight.   45
I had as lief be wooed of a snail.

ORLANDO.   Of a snail?

ROSALIND.   Aye, of a snail, for though he comes slowly, he carries
his house on his head—a better jointure,° I think, than you
make a woman. Besides, he brings his destiny with him.   50

ORLANDO.   What's that?

ROSALIND.   Why, horns, which such as you are fain to be
beholding to your wives for. But he comes armed in his
fortune and prevents the slander of his wife.

ORLANDO.   Virtue is no hornmaker, and my Rosalind is virtuous.   55

ROSALIND.   And I am your Rosalind.

CELIA.   It pleases him to call you so, but he hath a Rosalind of
a better leer° than you.

ROSALIND.   Come, woo me, woo me, for now I am in a holiday
humor and like enough to consent. What would you say to   60
me now an I were your very very Rosalind?

ORLANDO.   I would kiss before I spoke.

ROSALIND.   Nay, you were better speak first, and when you were

29. lisp: affect a foreign accent. 30. Disable: make slighting remarks about. 31.
nativity: place and moment of birth. 32. countenance: natural face. 33. swam
. . . gondola: that is, visited Venice, which was the goal of all travelers. 42.
clapped . . . shoulder: arrested him; made him prisoner. 49. jointure: money or
goods set aside for the wife if the husband dies. 58. leer: look.

graveled° for lack of matter, you might take occasion to kiss.
Very good orators, when they are out, they will spit, and
for lovers lacking—God warn° us!—matter, the cleanliest
shift° is to kiss.   65

ORLANDO. How if the kiss be denied?

ROSALIND. Then she puts you to entreaty and there begins new
matter.   70

ORLANDO. Who could be out, being before his beloved mistress?

ROSALIND. Marry, that should you if I were your mistress, or I
should think my honesty ranker° than my wit.

ORLANDO. What, of my suit?

ROSALIND. Not out of your apparel, and yet out of your suit.   75
Am not I your Rosalind?

ORLANDO. I take some joy to say you are, because I would be
talking of her.

ROSALIND. Well, in her person° I say I will not have you.

ORLANDO. Then in mine own person I die.   80

ROSALIND. No, faith, die by attorney.° The poor world is almost
six thousand years old, and in all this time there was not
any man died in his own person, videlicet,° in a love cause.
Troilus had his brains dashed out with a Grecian club, yet
he did what he could to die before, and he is one of the   85
patterns of love. Leander, he would have lived many a fair
year, though Hero had turned nun, if it had not been for a
hot midsummer night; for, good youth, he went but forth
to wash him in the Hellespont and being taken with the
cramp was drowned. And the foolish chroniclers of that age   90
found it was "Hero of Sestos."° But these are all lies. Men
have died from time to time and worms have eaten them,
but not for love.

ORLANDO. I would not have my right Rosalind of this mind, for
I protest her frown might kill me.   95

---

64. graveled: run aground. 66. warn: warrant. 66–67. cleanliest shift: the cleanest
way of getting around the difficulty. 73. ranker: fouler. 79. in her person: as her
representative. 81. by attorney: by proxy. 83. videlicit: namely. 84–91. Troilus
. . . Sestos: No one, says Rosalind, has really died for love, not even the great
lovers of legend, such as Troilus, the Trojan warrior who was madly in love with
Cressida, or Leander, the Greek youth who used to swim over the Hellespont to
visit Hero of Sestos and was finally drowned; historians in those days said that his
death was caused by Hero, but in truth, says Rosalind, it was a cramp.

ROSALIND. By this hand, it will not kill a fly. But come, now
I will be your Rosalind in a more coming-on° disposition,
and ask me what you will, I will grant it.

ORLANDO. Then love me, Rosalind.

ROSALIND. Yes, faith, will I, Fridays and Saturdays and all.   100

ORLANDO. And wilt thou have me?

ROSALIND. Aye, and twenty such.

ORLANDO. What sayest thou?

ROSALIND. Are you not good?

ORLANDO. I hope so.   105

ROSALIND. Why then, can one desire too much of a good
thing? Come, Sister, you shall be the priest and marry us.
Give me your hand, Orlando. What do you say, Sister?

ORLANDO. Pray thee, marry us.

CELIA. I cannot say the words.   110

ROSALIND. You must begin, "Will you, Orlando—"

CELIA. Go to. Will you, Orlando, have to wife this Rosalind?

ORLANDO. I will.

ROSALIND. Aye, but when?

ORLANDO. Why now, as fast as she can marry us.   115

ROSALIND. Then you must say, "I take thee, Rosalind, for wife."

ORLANDO. I take thee, Rosalind, for wife.

ROSALIND. I might ask you for your commission,° but I do take
thee, Orlando, for my husband. There's a girl goes before
the priest,° and certainly a woman's thought runs before   120
her actions.

ORLANDO. So do all thoughts, they are winged.

ROSALIND. Now tell me how long you would have her after you
have possessed her.

ORLANDO. Forever and a day.   125

ROSALIND. Say "a day," without the "ever." No, no, Orlando.
Men are April when they woo, December when they wed.
Maids are May when they are maids, but the sky changes
when they are wives. I will be more jealous of thee than a
Barbary cock pigeon over his hen, more clamorous than a   130
parrot against° rain, more newfangled° than an ape, more
giddy in my desires than a monkey. I will weep for nothing,

97. coming-on: encouraging. 118. commission: authority. 119–20. goes before the
priest: anticipates the priest's words. 131. against: in anticipation of. newfangled:
eager for novelties.

like Diana in the fountain,° and I will do that when you
are disposed to be merry. I will laugh like a hyen,° and that
when thou art inclined to sleep.   135

ORLANDO.   But will my Rosalind do so?

ROSALIND.   By my life, she will do as I do.

ORLANDO.   Oh, but she is wise.

ROSALIND.   Or else she could not have the wit to do this. The
wiser, the waywarder.° Make° the doors upon a woman's   140
wit and it will out at the casement.° Shut that and 'twill
out at the keyhole. Stop that, 'twill fly with the smoke out
at the chimney.

ORLANDO.   A man that had a wife with such a wit, he might say
"Wit, whither wilt?"°   145

ROSALIND.   Nay, you might keep that check° for it till you met
your wife's wit going to your neighbor's bed.

ORLANDO.   And what wit could wit have to excuse that?

ROSALIND.   Marry, to say she came to seek you there. You shall
never take her without her answer, unless you take her   150
without her tongue. Oh, that woman that cannot make her
fault her husband's occasion,° let her never nurse her child
herself, for she will breed it like a fool!

ORLANDO.   For these two hours, Rosalind, I will leave thee.

ROSALIND.   Alas, dear love, I cannot lack thee two hours!   155

ORLANDO.   I must attend the Duke at dinner. By two o'clock I
will be with thee again.

ROSALIND.   Aye, go your ways, go your ways, I knew what you
would prove. My friends told me as much, and I thought
no less. That flattering tongue of yours won me. 'Tis but 160
one cast away, and so come, death! Two o'clock is your
hour?

ORLANDO.   Aye, sweet Rosalind.

ROSALIND.   By my troth,° and in good earnest, and so God
mend me, and by all pretty oaths that are not dangerous,   165
if you break one jot of your promise or come one minute

---

133. **like Diana in the fountain:** like a fountain with the statue of Diana, always
weeping. 134. **hyen:** hyena. 139. **waywarder:** more frivolous. **Make:** shut. 141.
casement: window that opens on hinges. 145. **Wit, whither wilt:** "Wit (intelligence), where are you going?" This proverb was used to silence a person trying to
be overly clever. 146. **check:** rebuke. 151–52. **that . . . occasion:** that cannot
blame her husband as the cause of her own faults. 164. **troth:** true word.

behind your hour, I will think you the most pathetical
break-promise, and the most hollow lover, and the most
unworthy of her you call Rosalind, that may be chosen out
of the gross band of the unfaithful. Therefore beware my   170
censure and keep your promise.

ORLANDO.   With no less religion than if thou wert indeed my
Rosalind. So adieu.

ROSALIND.   Well, Time is the old justice that examines all such
offenders, and let Time try. Adieu.   175

(*Exit* ORLANDO.)

CELIA.   You have simply misused our sex in your love prate. We
must have your doublet and hose plucked over your head,
and show the world what the bird hath done to her own
nest.

ROSALIND.   O Coz, Coz, Coz, my pretty little coz, that thou   180
didst know how many fathom deep I am in love! But it
cannot be sounded. My affection hath an unknown bottom,
like the bay of Portugal.

CELIA.   Or rather, bottomless, that as fast as you pour affection
in, it runs out.   185

ROSALIND.   No, that same wicked bastard of Venus° that was
begot of thought, conceived of spleen, and born of madness,
that blind rascally boy that abuses everyone's eyes because
his own are out, let him be judge how deep I am in love.
I'll tell thee, Aliena, I cannot be out of the sight of Orlando.   190
I'll go find a shadow and sigh till he come.

CELIA.   And I'll sleep.   (*Exeunt.*)

186. bastard of Venus: Cupid.

Meaning and Method: Act IV, Scene 1

Rosalind continues to play her disguised role in her relation to Jaques
and to Orlando. What is her opinion of Jaques's melancholy spirit? By
teasing and abusing Orlando verbally, what does she learn about him?
Why does Celia criticize Rosalind for her words and actions?

SCENE 2.   *The forest.*

(*Enter* JAQUES, LORDS, *and* FORESTERS.)

JAQUES.   Which is he that killed the deer?

A LORD.   Sir, it was I.

JAQUES.   Let's present him to the Duke, like a Roman con-
queror, and it would do well to set the deer's horns upon
his head for a branch of victory. Have you no song, forester,   5
for this purpose?

FORESTER.   Yes, sir.

JAQUES.   Sing it. 'Tis no matter how it be in tune so it make
noise enough.

FORESTER.   (*Sings.*)

What shall he have that killed the deer?   10
His leather skin and horns to wear.
   Then sing him home.

(*The rest shall bear this burden.*)

Take thou no scorn to wear the horn,°
It was a crest ere thou wast born.
   Thy father's father wore it,   15
   And thy father bore it.
The horn, the horn, the lusty horn,
Is not a thing to laugh to scorn.   (*Exeunt.*)

13. horn: A man whose wife was unfaithful was traditionally ridiculed by the symbol of horns upon his head.

SCENE 3.   *The forest.*

(*Enter* ROSALIND *and* CELIA.)

ROSALIND.   How say you now? Is it not past two o'clock? And
here much° Orlando!

CELIA.   I warrant you with pure love and troubled brain he
hath ta'en his bow and arrows and is gone forth to sleep.
Look who comes here.   5

2. here much: a great deal of.

(*Enter* SILVIUS.)

SILVIUS.   My errand is to you, fair youth,
My gentle Phebe bid me give you this.
I know not the contents, but as I guess
By the stern brow and waspish° action
Which she did use as she was writing of it,   10
It bears an angry tenor.° Pardon me,
I am but as a guiltless messenger.
ROSALIND.   Patience herself would startle at this letter
And play the swaggerer—bear this, bear all.°
She says I am not fair, that I lack manners,   15
She calls me proud, and that she could not love me
Were man as rare as phoenix.° 'Od's my will!
Her love is not the hare that I do hunt.
Why writes she so to me? Well, shepherd, well,
This is a letter of your own device.   20
SILVIUS.   No, I protest I know not the contents.
Phebe did write it.
ROSALIND.   Come, come, you are a fool,
And turned into the extremity of love.
I saw her hand. She has a leathern° hand,
A freestone-colored° hand. I verily did think   25
That her old gloves were on, but 'twas her hands.
She has a huswife's hand, but that's no matter.
I say she never did invent this letter.
This is a man's invention and his hand.
SILVIUS.   Sure, it is hers.   30
ROSALIND.   Why, 'tis a boisterous° and a cruel style,
A style for challengers. Why, she defies me,
Like Turk to Christian. Women's gentle brain
Could not drop forth such giant-rude invention,
Such Ethiope° words, blacker in their effect°   35
Than in their countenance.° Will you hear the letter?

9. **waspish**: irritable. 11. **tenor**: intention. 14. **bear . . . all**: a person who could endure this would bear anything. 17. **phoenix**: a mythical bird. According to Egyptian mythology, only one such creature was alive at a time. Every five hundred years the phoenix built a nest of spices, which was set on fire by the rapid beating of the bird's huge wings. From the ashes of the phoenix consumed by fire a new phoenix was born. 24. **leathern**: tough-skinned. 25. **freestone-colored**: yellow-brown. 31. **boisterous**: violent. 35. **Ethiope**: *that is,* black. **effect**: intention. 36. **countenance**: appearance.

SILVIUS.   So please you, for I never heard it yet,
   Yet heard too much of Phebe's cruelty.
ROSALIND.   She Phebes me.° Mark how the tyrant writes.
   (*Reads.*) "Art thou god to shepherd turned   40
            That a maiden's heart hath burned?"
   Can a woman rail thus?
SILVIUS.   Call you this railing?
ROSALIND.   (*Reads.*)
            "Why, thy godhead laid apart,
               Warr'st thou with a woman's heart?"°   45
   Did you ever hear such railing?
            "Whiles the eye of man did woo me,
            That could do no vengeance to me."
   Meaning me a beast.
            "If the scorn of your bright eyne°   50
            Have power to raise such love in mine,
            Alack, in me what strange effect
            Would they work in mild aspéct!°
            Whiles you chid me, I did love,
            How then might your prayers move!   55
            He that brings this love to thee
            Little knows this love in me.
            And by him seal up thy mind,°
            Whether that thy youth and kind°
            Will the faithful offer take   60
            Of me and all that I can make,
            Or else by him my love deny,
            And then I'll study how to die."
SILVIUS.   Call you this chiding?
CELIA.   Alas, poor shepherd!   65
ROSALIND.   Do you pity him? No, he deserves no pity. Wilt
   thou love such a woman? What, to make thee an instrument and play false strains° upon thee! Not to be endured!
   Well, go your way to her, for I see love hath made thee a
   a tame snake, and say this to her: That if she loves me, I   70
   charge her to love thee. If she will not, I will never have her

---

39. She Phebes me: She scorns me. **44–45. Why . . . heart:** Why do you, a god
turned man, war with a woman's heart? **50. eyne:** eyes. **53. mild aspect:** gentle
looks. **58. seal up thy mind:** write your answer and send it by him. **59. kind:** nature. **68. strains:** melodies.

unless thou entreat for her. If you be a truelover, hence,
and not a word, for here comes more company.

(*Exit* SILVIUS.)

(*Enter* OLIVER.)

OLIVER.   Good morrow, fair ones. Pray you, if you know
    Where in the purlieus° of this forest stands   75
    A sheepcote fenced about with olive trees?
CELIA.   West of this place, down in the neighbor bottom.
    The rank° of osiers° by the murmuring stream
    Left on your right hand brings you to the place.
    But at this hour the house doth keep itself,   80
    There's none within.
OLIVER.   If that an eye may profit by a tongue,
    Then should I know you by description,
    Such garments and such years. "The boy is fair,
    Of female favor,° and bestows himself   85
    Like a ripe° sister, the woman low,
    And browner than her brother." Are not you
    The owner of the house I did inquire for?
CELIA.   It is no boast, being asked, to say we are.
OLIVER.   Orlando doth commend him to you both.   90
    And to that youth he calls his Rosalind
    He sends this bloody napkin. Are you he?
ROSALIND.   I am. What must we understand by this?
OLIVER.   Some of my shame, if you will know of me
    What man I am, and how, and why, and where   95
    This handkercher was stained.
CELIA.   I pray you tell it.
OLIVER.   When last the young Orlando parted from you
    He left a promise to return again
    Within an hour, and pacing through the forest,
    Chewing the food of sweet and bitter fancy,   100
    Lo, what befell! He threw his eye aside,
    And mark what object did present itself.
    Under an oak whose boughs were mossed with age
    And high top bald with dry antiquity,

75. **purlieus:** boundaries. 78. **rank:** row. **osiers:** willows. 85. **favor:** features. 86.
ripe: elder.

A wretched ragged man, o'ergrown with hair,   105
Lay sleeping on his back. About his neck
A green and gilded snake had wreathed itself,
Who with her head nimble in threats approached
The opening of his mouth. But suddenly,
Seeing Orlando, it unlinked itself   110
And with indented glides° did slip away
Into a bush, under which bush's shade
A lioness, with udders all drawn dry,°
Lay couching, head on ground, with catlike watch,
When that the sleeping man should stir. For 'tis   115
The royal disposition of that beast
To prey on nothing that doth seem as dead.
This seen, Orlando did approach the man
And found it was his brother, his elder brother.
CELIA.   Oh, I have heard him speak of that same brother, 120
    And he did render° him the most unnatural
    That lived amongst men.
OLIVER.   And well he might so do,
    For well I know he was unnatural.
ROSALIND.   But to Orlando. Did he leave him there,
    Food to the sucked and hungry lioness?   125
OLIVER.   Twice did he turn his back and purposed so.
    But kindness, nobler ever than revenge,
    And nature, stronger than his just occasion,°
    Made him give battle to the lioness,
    Who quickly fell before him. In which hurtling°   130
    From miserable slumber I awaked.
CELIA.   Are you his brother?
ROSALIND.   Was't you he rescued?
CELIA.   Was't you that did so oft contrive to kill him?
OLIVER.   'Twas I, but 'tis not I. I do not shame
    To tell you what I was, since my conversion   135
    So sweetly tastes, being the thing I am.
ROSALIND.   But—for the bloody napkin?
OLIVER.   By and by.
    When from the first to last betwixt us two

---

111. **indented glides**: wavy motion. 113. **udders . . . dry**: *that is,* hungry
and fierce. 121. **render**: describe. 128. **just occasion**: *that is,* his opportunity for
getting even with his wicked brother. 130. **hurtling**: noise of battle.

Tears our recountments° had most kindly bathed,
As how I came into that desert place,   140
In brief, he led me to the gentle Duke,
Who gave me fresh array and entertainment,°
Committing me unto my brother's love.
Who led me instantly unto his cave,
There stripped himself, and here upon his arm   145
The lioness had torn some flesh away,
Which all this while had bled, and now he fainted
And cried, in fainting, upon Rosalind.
Brief, I recovered him, bound up his wound,
And after some small space, being strong at heart,   150
He sent me hither, stranger as I am,
To tell this story, that you might excuse
His broken promise, and to give this napkin,
Dyed in his blood, unto the shepherd youth
That he in sport doth call his Rosalind.   155

(ROSALIND *swoons*.)

CELIA. Why, how now, Ganymede! Sweet Ganymede!

OLIVER. Many will swoon when they do look on blood.

CELIA. There is more in it. Cousin Ganymede!

OLIVER. Look he recovers.

ROSALIND. I would I were at home.

CELIA.   We'll lead you thither.   160
I pray you, will you take him by the arm?

OLIVER. Be of good cheer, youth. You a man! You lack a man's
heart.

ROSALIND. I do so, I confess it. Ah, sirrah, a body would think
this was well counterfeited!° I pray you tell your brother   165
how well I counterfeited. Heigh-ho!

OLIVER. This was not counterfeit. There is too great testimony
in your complexion that it was a passion of earnest.°

ROSALIND. Counterfeit, I assure you.

OLIVER. Well then, take a good heart and counterfeit to be a   170
man.

139. recountments: accounts of adventures. 142. entertainment: good treatment.
165. counterfeited: imitated; pretended. 168. passion of earnest: genuine emotion.

ROSALIND.   So I do. But, i' faith, I should have been a woman
   by right.

CELIA.   Come, you look paler and paler. Pray you draw home-
   ward. Good sir, go with us.   175

OLIVER.   That will I, for I must bear answer back how you
   excuse my brother, Rosalind.

ROSALIND.   I shall devise something. But I pray you commend
   my counterfeiting to him. Will you go?   (*Exeunt.*)

Meaning and Method: Act IV, Scene 3

1. Why does Rosalind deliberately misinterpret Phebe's letter?

2. In what way is Rosalind playing the same role here, in relation to
Sylvius, as we have seen her playing before in relation to Orlando?

3. What has befallen Orlando? What dramatic purpose is served by the
entrance of Oliver at this point? How does Rosalind betray her "femi-
ninity"?

4. Oliver's sudden conversion from the arch-villain of the piece to a
loving brother seems contrived and improbable. Some critics have
suggested that Shakespeare made Oliver's repentance so sudden because he was hurrying on toward the conclusion of the play. Might
there not be other explanations? Does Oliver's unlikely conversion
annoy you, or does it fit in with other improbable events that take
place in the Forest of Arden? In what way?

5. What new aspects of Orlando's character are revealed by Oliver's account of their adventure?

Act V

SCENE 1. *The forest.*

(*Enter* TOUCHSTONE *and* AUDREY.)

TOUCHSTONE.   We shall find a time, Audrey. Patience, gentle
   Audrey.

AUDREY.   Faith, the priest was good enough, for all the old
   gentleman's saying.

TOUCHSTONE.   A most wicked Sir Oliver, Audrey, a most vile   5
   Martext. But, Audrey, there is a youth here in the forest
   lays claim to you.

AUDREY.   Aye, I know who 'tis. He hath no interest in me in the
   world. Here comes the man you mean.

TOUCHSTONE.   It is meat and drink to me to see a clown. By my   10
   troth, we that have good wits have much to answer for—we
   shall be flouting,° we cannot hold.

(*Enter* WILLIAM.)

WILLIAM.   Good even, Audrey.

AUDREY.   God ye good even, William.

WILLIAM.   And good even to you, sir.   15

TOUCHSTONE.   Good even, gentle friend. Cover thy head, cover
   thy head, nay, prithee be covered.° How old are you, friend?

WILLIAM.   Five and twenty, sir.

TOUCHSTONE.   A ripe age. Is thy name William?

WILLIAM.   William, sir.   20

TOUCHSTONE.   A fair name. Wast born i' the forest here?

WILLIAM.   Aye, sir, I thank God.

TOUCHSTONE.   "Thank God," a good answer. Art rich?

WILLIAM.   Faith, sir, soso.

TOUCHSTONE.   "Soso" is good, very good, very excellent good.   25
   And yet it is not, it is but soso. Art thou wise?

WILLIAM.   Aye, sir, I have a pretty wit.

TOUCHSTONE.   Why, thou sayest well. I do now remember a
   saying, "The fool doth think he is wise, but the wise man
   knows himself to be a fool." The heathen philosopher,   30

12. **flouting:** jesting. 16–17. **cover . . . covered:** William is respectfully removing his cap.

when he had a desire to eat a grape, would open his lips
when he put it into his mouth, meaning thereby that
grapes were made to eat and lips to open. You do love this
maid?

WILLIAM.   I do, sir.   35

TOUCHSTONE.   Give me your hand. Art thou learned?

WILLIAM.   No, sir.

TOUCHSTONE.   Then learn this of me: To have is to have; for it
    is a figure in rhetoric that drink, being poured out of a
    cup into a glass, by filling the one doth empty the other,   40
    for all your writers do consent that *ipse*° is he. Now you
    are not *ipse*, for I am he.

WILLIAM.   Which he, sir?

TOUCHSTONE.   He, sir, that must marry this woman. Therefore,
    you clown, abandon—which is in the vulgar° leave,—the   45
    society—which in the boorish is company—of this female
    —which in the common is woman. Which together is,
    abandon the society of this female, or, clown, thou perishest;
    or, to thy better understanding, diest; or, to wit, I kill thee,
    make thee away, translate thy life into death, thy liberty   50
    into bondage. I will deal in poison with thee, or in bas-
    tinado,° or in steel, I will bandy with thee in faction,° I
    will o'errun thee with policy,° I will kill thee a hundred
    and fifty ways. Therefore tremble, and depart.

AUDREY.   Do, good William.   55

WILLIAM.   God rest you merry sir.   (*Exit.*)

(*Enter* CORIN.)

CORIN.   Our master and mistress seek you. Come, away, away!

TOUCHSTONE.   Trip,° Audrey! Trip, Audrey! I attend, I attend.
                                                        (*Exeunt.*)

41. *ipse*: *Latin*, he himself. 45. vulgar: common tongue. 51–52. bastinado: a
thrashing. 52. bandy . . . faction: strive with you by intrigue. 53. o'errun . . .
policy: overcome you by some crafty device. 58. Trip: walk quickly.

Meaning and Method: Act V, Scene 1

Does William seem particularly disappointed about losing Audrey?
Why is he a good victim for Touchstone's jests? Find examples of
Touchstone's humorous display of learning and logic.

SCENE 2.   *The forest.*

(*Enter* ORLANDO *and* OLIVER.)

ORLANDO.   Is 't possible that on so little acquaintance you should
like her? That but seeing you should love her? And, loving,
woo? And, wooing, she should grant? And will you persever
to enjoy her?

OLIVER.   Neither call the giddiness° of it in question, the pov-   5
erty of her, the small acquaintance, my sudden wooing,
nor her sudden consenting; but say with me, I love Aliena,
say with her that she loves me, consent with both that we
may enjoy each other. It shall be to your good, for my
father's house and all the revenue that was old Sir Row-   10
land's will I estate upon you, and here live and die a shepherd.

ORLANDO.   You have my consent. Let your wedding be tomorrow. Thither will I invite the Duke and all 's contented followers. Go you and prepare Aliena, for look you, here   15
comes my Rosalind.

(*Enter* ROSALIND.)

ROSALIND.   God save you, Brother.

OLIVER.   And you, fair Sister.   (*Exit.*)

ROSALIND.   O my dear Orlando, how it grieves me to see thee
wear thy heart in a scarf!   20

ORLANDO.   It is my arm.

ROSALIND.   I thought thy heart had been wounded with the
claws of a lion.

ORLANDO.   Wounded it is, but with the eyes of a lady.

ROSALIND.   Did your brother tell you how I counterfeited to   25
swoon when he showed me your handkercher?

ORLANDO.   Aye, and greater wonders than that.

ROSALIND.   Oh, I know where you are. Nay, 'tis true. There
was never anything so sudden but the fight of two rams,
and Caesar's thrasonical° brag of "I came, saw, and over-   30
came."° For your brother and my sister no sooner met but

5. giddiness: rashness. 30. thrasonical: boastful. 30–31. I . . . overcame: Julius
Caesar, after his victory over the King of Pontus, reported to the Senate in three
words: *Veni, vidi, vici.*

they looked, no sooner looked but they loved, no sooner
loved but they sighed, no sooner sighed but they asked one
another the reason, no sooner knew the reason but they
sought the remedy. And in these degrees have they made a   35
pair of stairs to marriage which they will climb incontinent,
or else be incontinent° before marriage. They are in the
very wrath° of love and they will together, clubs cannot
part them.°

ORLANDO.   They shall be married tomorrow, and I will bid the   40
Duke to the nuptial. But oh, how bitter a thing it is to
look into happiness through another man's eyes! By so
much the more shall I tomorrow be at the height of heart-
heaviness, by how much I shall think my brother happy in
having what he wishes for.   45

ROSALIND.   Why then, tomorrow I cannot serve your turn for
Rosalind?

ORLANDO.   I can live no longer by thinking.°

ROSALIND.   I will weary you then no longer with idle talking.
Know of me then, for now I speak to some purpose, that I   50
know you are a gentleman of good conceit.° I speak not
this that you should bear a good opinion of my knowledge,
insomuch I say I know you are. Neither do I labor for a
greater esteem than may in some little measure draw a
belief from you to do yourself good and not to grace me.   55
Believe then, if you please, that I can do strange things. I
have, since I was three year old, conversed with a magician
most profound in his art and yet not damnable.° If you do
love Rosalind so near the heart as your gesture cries it out,
when your brother marries Aliena, shall you marry her. I   60
know into what straits of fortune° she is driven, and it is
not impossible to me, if it appear not inconvenient to you,
to set her before your eyes tomorrow human as she is and
without any danger.

ORLANDO.   Speakest thou in sober meanings?   65

36–37. incontinent . . . incontinent: immediately . . . unrestrained. **38. wrath:**
passion. **38–39. clubs cannot part them:** When a brawl was started in London
streets, there was a cry of "clubs"; thereupon the apprentices in the shops seized
their clubs and swarmed out to separate the parties. **48. thinking:** *that is,* pretense. **51. conceit:** intelligence. **59. not damnable:** *that is,* his magic was not used
for wicked purposes. **61. straits of fortune:** difficult situations.

ROSALIND.   By my life, I do, which I tender° dearly, though I
say I am a magician. Therefore put you in your best array,
bid your friends, for if you will be married tomorrow, you
shall, and to Rosalind if you will.

(*Enter* SILVIUS *and* PHEBE.)

Look, here comes a lover of mine and a lover of hers.   70
PHEBE.   Youth, you have done me much ungentleness
To show the letter that I writ to you.
ROSALIND.   I care not if I have. It is my study°
To seem despiteful and ungentle to you.
You are there followed by a faithful shepherd.   75
Look upon him, love him, he worships you.
PHEBE.   Good shepherd, tell this youth what 'tis to love.
SILVIUS.   It is to be all made of sighs and tears,
And so am I for Phebe.
PHEBE.   And I for Ganymede.   80
ORLANDO.   And I for Rosalind.
ROSALIND.   And I for no woman.
SILVIUS.   It is to be all made of faith and service,
And so am I for Phebe.
PHEBE.   And I for Ganymede.   85
ORLANDO.   And I for Rosalind.
ROSALIND.   And I for no woman.
SILVIUS.   It is to be all made of fantasy,°
All made of passion, and all made of wishes,
All adoration, duty, and observance,°   90
All humbleness, all patience and impatience,
All purity, all trial, all observance,
And so am I for Phebe.
PHEBE.   And so am I for Ganymede.
ORLANDO.   And so am I for Rosalind.   95
ROSALIND.   And so am I for no woman.
PHEBE.   If this be so, why blame you me to love you?
SILVIUS.   If this be so, why blame you me to love you?
ORLANDO.   If this be so, why blame you me to love you?
ROSALIND.   Why do you speak too, "Why blame you me to   100
· love you?"

66. tender: regard. 73. study: deliberate purpose. 88. fantasy: imagination. 90.
observance: devotion.

ORLANDO.   To her that is not here, nor doth not hear.

ROSALIND.   Pray you, no more of this, 'tis like the howling of
Irish wolves against the moon. (*To* SILVIUS.) I will help
you if I can. (*To* PHEBE.) I would love you if I could. To-   105
morrow meet me all together. (*To* PHEBE.) I will marry
you if ever I marry woman, and I'll be married tomorrow.
(*To* ORLANDO.) I will satisfy you if ever I satisfied man,
and you shall be married tomorrow. (*To* SILVIUS.) I will
content you if what pleases you contents you, and you shall   110
be married tomorrow. (*To* ORLANDO.) As you love Rosalind,
meet. (*To* SILVIUS.) As you love Phebe, meet. And as I love
no woman, I'll meet. So, fare you well. I have left you
commands.

SILVIUS.   I'll not fail, if I live.   115

PHEBE.   Nor I.

ORLANDO.   Nor I.   (*Exeunt.*)

Meaning and Method: Act V, Scene 2

1. Now still another couple has fallen in love. What "kind" of love do
Celia and Oliver represent? Why is their love in keeping with the
spirit of the play? What effect does the love between Celia and
Oliver have on the relationship between Rosalind and Orlando?

2. How do Rosalind's remarks—"I am a magician" and "I have left you
commands"—emphasize her role or function in the play?

3. Rosalind's speech (lines 103–14) is really a series of riddles. How do
Orlando, Phebe, and Silvius interpret her words? What is the effect of
her words on a reader or an audience?

4. Do you agree or disagree with Silvius's description of love (*see* line 78
and lines 88–93)?

SCENE 3.   *The forest.*

(*Enter* TOUCHSTONE *and* AUDREY.)

TOUCHSTONE.   Tomorrow is the joyful day, Audrey, tomorrow
will we be married.

AUDREY.   I do desire it with all my heart, and I hope it is no
dishonest desire to desire to be a woman of the world. Here
come two of the banished Duke's pages.   5

(*Enter two* PAGES.)

FIRST PAGE.   Well met, honest gentleman.

TOUCHSTONE.   By my troth, well met. Come, sit, sit, and a song.

SECOND PAGE.   We are for you. Sit i' the middle.

FIRST PAGE.   Shall we clap into 't° roundly, without hawking°
or spitting or saying we are hoarse, which are the only   10
prologues° to a bad voice?

SECOND PAGE.   I' faith, i' faith, and both in a tune, like two
gypsies on a horse.

SONG

It was a lover and his lass,
    With a hey, and a ho, and a hey nonio,   15
That o'er the green cornfield did pass
    In the springtime, the only pretty ringtime,°
When birds do sing, hey ding a ding, ding.
Sweet lovers love the spring.

Between the acres of the rye,   20
    With a hey, and a ho, and a hey nonino,
These pretty country folks would lie,
    In the springtime, the only pretty ringtime,
When birds do sing, hey ding a ding, ding.
Sweet lovers love the spring.   25

This carol they began that hour,
    With a hey, and a ho, and a hey nonino,

---

9. clap into 't: get down to it. hawking: clearing the throat. 10–11. only pro-
logues: usual apologies. 17. ringtime: the time for wedding bells.

How that a life was but a flower
  In the springtime, the only pretty ringtime,
When birds do sing, hey ding a ding, ding.   30
Sweet lovers love the spring.

And therefore take the present time,
  With a hey, and a ho, and a hey nonino,
For love is crownèd with the prime°
  In the springtime, the only pretty ringtime,   35
When birds do sing, hey ding a ding, ding.
Sweet lovers love the spring.

TOUCHSTONE. Truly, young gentlemen, though there was no
  great matter in the ditty, yet the note° was very untunable.°
FIRST PAGE. You are deceived, sir. We kept time, we lost not   40
  our time.
TOUCHSTONE. By my troth, yes. I count it but time lost to hear
  such a foolish song. God buy you, and God mend your
  voices! Come, Audrey.   (*Exeunt.*)

34. **prime:** perfection. 39. **note:** tune. **untunable:** out of harmony.

Meaning and Method: Act V, Scene 3

What purpose is served by this scene?

SCENE 4. *The forest.*

(*Enter* DUKE SENIOR, AMIENS, JAQUES, ORLANDO, OLIVER,
and CELIA.)

DUKE SENIOR. Dost thou believe, Orlando, that the boy
  Can do all this that he hath promised?
ORLANDO. I sometimes do believe, and sometimes do not,
  As those that fear they hope and know they fear.

(*Enter* ROSALIND, SILVIUS, *and* PHEBE.)

ROSALIND. Patience once more, whiles our compact is urged.°   5

5. **compact is urged:** agreement is repeated.

You say if I bring in your Rosalind,
You will bestow her on Orlando here?
DUKE SENIOR.   That would I had I kingdoms to give with her.
ROSALIND.   And you say you will have her when I bring her?
ORLANDO.   That would I were I of all kingdoms king.   10
ROSALIND.   You say you'll marry me if I be willing?
PHEBE.   That will I, should I die the hour after.
ROSALIND.   But if you do refuse to marry me,
You'll give yourself to this most faithful shepherd?
PHEBE.   So is the bargain.   15
ROSALIND.   You say that you'll have Phebe if she will?
SILVIUS.   Though to have her and death were both one thing.
ROSALIND.   I have promised to make all this matter even.°
Keep you your word, O Duke, to give your daughter,
You yours, Orlando, to receive his daughter.   20
Keep your word, Phebe, that you'll marry me
Or else, refusing me, to wed this shepherd.
Keep your word, Silvius, that you'll marry her
If she refuse me. And from hence I go
To make these doubts all even.   25

(*Exeunt* ROSALIND *and* CELIA.)

DUKE SENIOR.   I do remember in this shepherd boy
Some lively touches of my daughter's favor.
ORLANDO.   My lord, the first time that I ever saw him
Methought he was a brother to your daughter.
But, my good lord, this boy is forest-born,   30
And hath been tutored in the rudiments
Of many desperate° studies by his uncle,
Whom he reports to be a great magician
Obscurèd° in the circle of this forest.

(*Enter* TOUCHSTONE *and* AUDREY.)

JAQUES.   There is, sure, another flood toward,° and these   35
couples are coming to the ark. Here comes a pair of very
strange beasts, which in all tongues are called fools.
TOUCHSTONE.   Salutation and greeting to you all!
JAQUES.   Good my lord, bid him welcome. This is the motley-

18. make . . . even: straighten out this matter. 32. desperate: dangerous. 34.
Obscurèd: living obscurely. 35. toward: about to occur.

minded gentleman that I have so often met in the forest.   40
He hath been a courtier, he swears.

TOUCHSTONE.   If any man doubt that, let him put me to my
purgation.° I have trod a measure.° I have flattered a lady.
I have been politic° with my friend, smooth with mine
enemy. I have undone three tailors.° I have had four   45
quarrels, and like to have fought one.

JAQUES.   And how was that ta'en up?

TOUCHSTONE.   Faith, we met, and found the quarrel was upon
the seventh cause.

JAQUES.   How seventh cause? Good my lord, like this fellow.   50

DUKE SENIOR.   I like him very well.

TOUCHSTONE.   God 'ild you, sir, I desire you of the like. I
press in here, sir, amongst the rest of the country
copulatives,° to swear and to forswear, according as
marriage binds and blood breaks. A poor virgin, sir, an ill-   55
favored thing, sir, but mine own. A poor humor of mine,
sir, to take that that no man else will. Rich honesty dwells
like a miser, sir, in a poor house, as your pearl in your foul
oyster.

DUKE SENIOR.   By my faith, he is very swift and sententious.°   60

TOUCHSTONE.   According to the fool's bolt,° sir, and such dulcet
diseases.°

JAQUES.   But for the seventh cause, how did you find the
quarrel on the seventh cause?

TOUCHSTONE.   Upon a lie seven times removed—Bear your body   65
more seeming, Audrey—as thus, sir. I did dislike the cut
of a certain courtier's beard. He sent me word if I said
his beard was not cut well, he was in the mind it was. This
is called the Retort Courteous. If I sent him word again "it
was not well cut," he would send me word he cut it to   70
please himself. This is called the Quip Modest. If again "it
was not well cut," he disabled my judgment.° This is called
the Reply Churlish. If again "it was not well cut," he

---

43. purgation: proving the truth of my claim. **trod a measure:** danced a formal
dance, a necessary accomplishment of a courtier. **44. politic:** crafty. **45. undone
three tailors:** *that is,* by not paying my debts to them. **54. copulatives:** people desirous of being mated. **60. sententious:** full of wise sayings. **61. According...
bolt:** ready to let fly at anything, following the proverb "A fool's bolt (arrow) is
soon shot." **61–62. dulcet diseases:** pleasant ailments; *that is,* the fool is enjoyable
entertainment. **72. disabled my judgment:** said my judgment was weak.

would answer I spake not true. This is called the Reproof
Valiant. If again "it was not well cut," he would say I lie. 75
This is called the Countercheck Quarrelsome. And so to
the Lie Circumstantial° and the Lie Direct.°

JAQUES.   And how oft did you say his beard was not well cut?

TOUCHSTONE.   I durst go no further than the Lie Circumstantial, nor he durst not give me the Lie Direct, and so we 80
measured swords and parted.

JAQUES.   Can you nominate in order now the degrees of the
lie?

TOUCHSTONE.   Oh, sir, we quarrel in print, by the book,° as you
have books for good manners. I will name you the degrees. 85
The first, the Retort Courteous; the second, the Quip
Modest; the third, the Reply Churlish; the fourth, the
Reproof Valiant; the fifth, the Countercheck Quarrelsome;
the sixth, the Lie with Circumstance; the seventh, the Lie
Direct. All these you may avoid but the Lie Direct, and you 90
may avoid that too, with an "If." I knew when seven
justices could not take up° a quarrel, but when the parties
were met themselves, one of them thought but of an "If,"
as "If you said so, then I said so," and they shook hands and
swore brothers. Your "If" is the only peacemaker, much 95
virtue in "If."

JAQUES.   Is not this a rare fellow, my lord? He's as good at
anything and yet a fool.

DUKE SENIOR.   He uses his folly like a stalking-horse,° and under
the presentation of that he shoots his wit. 100

(*Enter* HYMEN,* ROSALIND, *and* CELIA. *Still* † *music.*)

HYMEN.   Then is there mirth° in Heaven
When earthly things made even
    Atone° together.
Good Duke, receive thy daughter.
Hymen, from Heaven brought her, 105
    Yea, brought her hither,

---

77. **Circumstantial:** indirect. **Lie Direct:** *that is,* the direct accusation that the
speaker is a liar. 84. **quarrel . . . book:** Duelling manuals printed in Shakespeare's
time actually contained procedures just as fantastic as Touchstone's "seven causes."
92. **take up:** make up. 99. **stalking-horse:** *that is,* a decoy. * **Hymen:** god of marriage. † **Still:** soft. 101. **mirth:** joy. 103. **Atone:** unite.

That thou mightst join her hand with his
Whose heart within his bosom is.

ROSALIND. (*To* DUKE SENIOR.)   To you I give myself, for I am
yours. (*To* ORLANDO.) To you I give myself, for I am yours.   110

DUKE SENIOR.   If there be truth in sight, you are my daughter.

ORLANDO.   If there be truth in sight, you are my Rosalind.

PHEBE.   If sight and shape be true,
Why then, my love adieu!

ROSALIND.   I'll have no father, if you be not he.   115
I'll have no husband, if you be not he.
Nor ne'er wed woman, if you be not she.

HYMEN.   Peace, ho! I bar confusion.
'Tis I must make conclusion
Of these most strange events.   120
Here's eight that must take hands
To join in Hymen's bands
If truth holds true contents.°
You and you no cross shall part.
You and you are heart in heart.   125
You to his love must accord
Or have a woman to your lord.
You and you are sure together,
As the winter to foul weather.
Whiles a wedlock hymn we sing   130
Feed yourselves with questioning,
That reason° wonder may diminish,
How thus we met, and these things finish.

SONG

Wedding is great Juno's crown.
Oh, blessed bond of board and bed!   135
'Tis Hymen peoples every town.
High wedlock then be honorèd.
Honor, high honor and renown,
To Hymen, god of every town!

DUKE SENIOR.   O my dear niece, welcome thou art to me!   140
Even Daughter, welcome, in no less degree.

123. truth . . . contents: *that is,* if the truth is made up of all true things.
132. reason: explanation.

PHEBE.   I will not eat my word now thou art mine,
Thy faith my fancy to thee doth combine.

(*Enter* JAQUES DE BOYS.)

JAQUES DE BOYS.   Let me have audience for a word or two.
I am the second son of old Sir Rowland   145
That bring these tidings to this fair assembly.
Duke Frederick, hearing how that every day
Men of great worth resorted to this forest,
Addressed° a mighty power,° which were on foot,
In his own conduct,° purposely to take   150
His brother here and put him to the sword.
And to the skirts of this wild wood he came,
Where meeting with an old religious man,
After some question with him, was converted
Both from his enterprise and from the world,   155
His crown bequeathing to his banished brother,
And all their lands restored to them again
That were with him exiled. This to be true
I do engage° my life.
DUKE SENIOR.   Welcome, young man,
Thou offer'st fairly° to thy brothers' wedding.   160
To one his lands withheld, and to the other
A land itself at large, a potent dukedom.
First, in this forest let us do those ends
That here were well begun and well begot.
And after, every of this happy number   165
That have endured shrewd° days and nights with us
Shall share the good of our returnèd fortune
According to the measure of their states.
Meantime, forget this new-fallen dignity,
And fall into our rustic revelry.   170
Play, music! And you, brides and bridegrooms all,
With measure heaped in joy, to the measures° fall.
JAQUES.   Sir, by your patience. If I heard you rightly,
The Duke hath put on a religious life
And thrown into neglect the pompous Court?   175

---

149. **Addressed:** prepared. **power:** army. 150. **In his own conduct:** under his
own command. 159. **engage:** pledge. 160. **Thou offer'st fairly:** You made a good
present. 166. **shrewd:** bitter. 172. **measures:** dances.

JAQUES DE BOYS.   He hath.

JAQUES.   To him will I. Out of these convertites°
   There is much matter to be heard and learned.
   (*To* DUKE SENIOR.)   You to your former honor I bequeath,
   Your patience and your virtue well deserves it.   180
   (*To* ORLANDO.)   You to a love that your true faith doth
      merit.
   (*To* OLIVER.)   You to your land, and love, and great allies.
   (*To* SILVIUS.)   You to a long and well-deservèd bed.
   (*To* TOUCHSTONE.)   And you to wrangling, for thy loving
      voyage
   Is but for two months victualed.° So, to your pleasures.   185
   I am for other than for dancing measures.

DUKE SENIOR.   Stay, Jaques, stay.

JAQUES.   To see no pastime I. What you would have
   I'll stay to know at your abandoned cave.   (*Exit.*)

DUKE SENIOR.   Proceed, proceed. We will begin these rites,   190
   As we do trust they'll end, in true delights.   (*A dance.*)

177. convertites: converts to the religious life. 185. victualed: provisioned.

Epilogue

ROSALIND.   It is not the fashion to see the lady the epilogue,
   but it is no more unhandsome than to see the lord the
   prologue. If it be true that good wine needs no bush,° 'tis
   true that a good play needs no epilogue. Yet to good wine
   they do use good bushes, and good plays prove the better   5
   by the help of good epilogues. What a case am I in then,
   that am neither a good epilogue nor cannot insinuate° with
   you in the behalf of a good play! I am not furnished° like
   a beggar, therefore to beg will not become me. My way is
   to conjure° you, and I'll begin with the women. I charge   10
   you, O women, for the love you bear to men, to like as
   much of this play as please you. And I charge you, O men,
   for the love you bear to women—as I perceive by your

3. good . . . bush: good wine needs no advertisement—an old proverb arising from a custom practiced by shopkeepers in which a sign, identifying the
product being sold, was hung on the store front. The custom arose to assist shop-
pers who could not read. 7. insinuate: ingratiate myself. 8. furnished: dressed.
10. conjure: win you over by magic.

simpering none of you hates them—that between you and
the women the play may please. If I were a woman° I   15
would kiss as many of you as had beards that pleased me,
complexions that liked° me, and breaths that I defied not.
And I am sure as many as have good beards or good faces
or sweet breaths will, for my kind offer, when I make
curtsy bid me farewell.   20

(*Exeunt.*)

15. If . . . woman: Since there were no women actresses on the Elizabethan
stage, all female roles were played by young boys. 17. liked: pleased.

Meaning and Method: Act V, Scene 4 and Epilogue

1. What has happened to Duke Frederick, and how does this affect the
   other characters?
2. How does the entrance of Jaques de Boys serve as a means of ending
   the play? In what other way could the play have been ended?
3. The last act blends romance, burlesque (another word for parody), and
   satire. Find examples that prove this statement.
4. In what way are Rosalind's lines in the Epilogue in keeping with her
   character?

Meaning and Method: On the Play as a Whole

1. Is the main setting of the play—the Forest of Arden—a peaceful paradise only, or does it have elements of the real world in it? Discuss.
2. A romantic comedy is a play in which love is the predominant theme,
   evil has no real power to harm people, and highly improbable things
   happen as though they were quite natural. In what ways does this definition apply to *As You Like It*?
3. The plot of the play, and several of its characters, are very much like
   those of fairy tales. Can you think of any well-known fairy tales that
   also have meaning for the real world?
4. The play has much to say about three types of affection: the affection
   of master and servant, that between friends, and the affection between
   those who love one another. Which character or characters are involved with each type of affection, and what do their parts in the play
   have to say about affection?
5. Is Touchstone, as his name seems to imply, a measure against which
   the thoughts and actions of the other characters are to be tested? Or is
   he, as his costume of motley seems to suggest, a pure and simple fool?
   Discuss.

6. Would it be possible to present *As You Like It* on stage without the character of Jaques? Does he have some further value besides mere entertainment? Does he also satirize or ridicule, in a lighthearted way, some aspects of the real world? Is Jaques himself a type being satirized?

7. Shakespeare, when adapting Thomas Lodge's *Rosalynde* to the Elizabethan stage, created four new characters. What, if anything, do two of them—William and Audrey—add to the original story of romance in a forest paradise? Explain.

8. What bearing does the title of the play have on the life of Orlando when compared to that of Touchstone? On the happiness of the Duke when compared to the melancholy of Jaques? On the comments on country life made by Touchstone and by Corin? Did everything turn out as *you* would like it to?

Composition and Discussion

1. It is not necessary to write a serious drama to present serious ideas. Although a fine comedy entertains us, and permits an escape to the world of fantasy, it may still be capable of giving the audience insight into situations and people in the actual world.

Write a composition in which you explain and discuss one of the following ideas presented in *As You Like It*:

(a) "All the world's a stage,
      And all the men and women merely players."
      (Jaques to Duke Senior, II, 7, lines 138–39.)
      Agree or disagree: Apply to the world of today.

(b) "Love is merely a madness, and I tell you deserves as well a dark house and whip as madmen do."
      (Rosalind to Orlando, III, 2, lines 366–67.)
      Agree or disagree and give examples.

(c) "Those that are in extremity of either [melancholy or laughter] are abominable fellows, and betray themselves to every modern censure worse than drunkards."
      (Rosalind to Jaques, IV, 1, lines 5–7.)
      Explain. Why is the statement true or untrue?

(d) "The fool doth think he is wise, but the wise man knows himself to be a fool."
      (Touchstone to William, V, 1, lines 29–30.)
      Apply this statement to yourself or to a character in literature.

(e) "Sweet are the uses of adversity,"
      (Duke Senior to Amiens, II, 1, line 12.)
      Explain. Give examples to prove true or untrue.

2. To refer to Touchstone as a "wise man" might be quite reasonable, but is it fair to call Jaques a "fool"? (*See* Act II, Scene 7, lines 42–61.)

In spite of his faults, Jaques is one of the few characters who remains true to himself. While most of the other court refugees decide to return to civilization at the end of the play, Jaques firmly resolves to continue his melancholy existence in the company of the now solitary Duke Frederick. Jaques may be the most pessimistic and lonely inhabitant of the Forest of Arden, and the subject of most of the ridicule, but he is also the least changeable, the least foolish in love, and the least deceiving of the major characters in the play. Certainly, this makes him too admirable to play the part of a fool.

Be prepared to agree or disagree with this analysis. In an open-class discussion, give reasons for your answer. Discuss each of the points raised in the preceding paragraph.

   3. Write a paragraph on one of the following:
   (a) Rosalind, the "magician" in *As You Like It*
   (b) "Love at first sight" in *As You Like It*
   (c) The combination of foolishness and wisdom in the character of Rosalind
   (d) Shakespeare's use of the fool, as seen through Touchstone.

   4. Shakespeare often has his characters comment upon their surroundings so that the audience may be able to visualize a setting. The first scene in Act II serves to paint the Forest of Arden. Read the scene again, and then write a description of the Forest in your own words. You may be more detailed than Shakespeare, although you should keep the same feeling.

   5. Write a diary as though you were Rosalind or Celia from the day of your arrival in the Forest of Arden until your wedding day. You will, of course, use modern rather than Elizabethan English, but you will otherwise imagine yourself as living in the sixteenth century.

   6. Write an essay on the variations on the theme of love in *As You Like It*.

   7. Write a humorous essay on "The Seven Stages of Woman."

A Glossary
of Literary Terms

Act and Scene: An *act* is the major division of a play. From the time of the Elizabethans to the late nineteenth century, the English play was normally divided into five acts. Contemporary plays are usually divided into three acts.

   A *scene* is a subordinate unit of action within an act, and within each act there are often a number of scenes. The end of a scene is usually designated by the lowering of a curtain or by the entrance or exit of characters.

Allegory: a narrative in which the characters, the setting, and the action have a second meaning in addition to the story immediately apparent. An example of a straightforward allegorical drama is the English morality play, *Everyman*. Among the characters whom Everyman meets are Fellowship, Knowledge, and Good Deeds.

Alliteration: the recurrence of initial sounds (usually consonant sounds but sometimes vowel sounds) in successive or closely situated words in a line of poetry or prose.

Allusion: a reference to a presumably familiar person, place, or thing that usually has literary, historical, artistic, geographical, mythological, or scriptural significance.

Anachronism: from Greek *ana*, against, and *chronos*, time; an event that is "out of time." An anachronism refers to an event that did not take place—or could not have taken place—at the date indicated.

Antagonist: in drama or fiction, the character who opposes the protagonist, or chief character. *See* **Protagonist.**

Apostrophe: the direct address to a deceased or absent person as if he were present, or to an animal or thing, or an abstract idea or quality as if it could understand you.

Aside: in drama, lines spoken by an actor in an undertone to himself or aloud directly to the audience. It is a theatrical convention that an aside, which is heard by the audience, is assumed not to be heard by fellow actors on the stage.

Atmosphere and Setting: *Atmosphere* is the term used to describe the mental or emotional climate or mood of a literary work. *Setting* refers to the time and place in which the action of a story or play occurs. In drama, setting may also refer to the scenery—the physical set—on the stage.

Blank Verse: unrhymed poetry, in which each line usually has ten syllables. Five of the syllables are stressed—generally the second, fourth, sixth, eighth, and tenth syllables. For example, in Act I, Scene 2 of *Julius Caesar*, Caesar comments in blank verse on Cassius:

Yond CASSius HAS a LEAN and HUNgry LOOK.
He THINKS too MUCH, such MEN are DANgerOUS.

This arrangement of stressed and unstressed syllables in a ten-syllable line is called *iambic pentameter*.

Character and Characterization: A *character* is a fictional person created by an author. *Characterization* refers to the techniques an author uses to reveal the personality of the character he has created. In drama, the techniques of characterization include the following:
(a) the character's words, actions, and reactions to situations, events, and other people. This includes the comments the character makes to himself (*see* **Soliloquy**) and those made directly to the audience (*see* **Aside**).
(b) the character's physical appearance. This includes the physical appearance of the actor or actress selected to play the part, as well as the costume in which he or she is dressed.
(c) the comments and reactions of others to the character.
(d) the physical setting, which may reflect or emphasize the personality of the character.
The novelist or author of short stories may *tell* readers about a character, but with rare exceptions the playwright must *show*, not tell. However, characters can be described in the stage directions and in the preface, if there is one. *See* **Stage Directions**.

Chorus: in ancient Greek drama, a group of actors who comment upon and sometimes participate in the action of the play. In Elizabethan drama, the chorus (when used) is usually reduced to one actor, who presents an outline of the story and theme in a *prologue*.

Cliché: an expression that has been used so often that it has lost all freshness and originality. Some examples are *That's the way the cookie crumbles*, *It's a horse of a different color*, and *doing your own thing*. An author may deliberately use clichés as part of a character's speech to show the reader the way the character thinks and talks.

Climax and Anticlimax: The *climax* is that point at which the greatest intensity of interest, emotion, or suspense in drama or fiction occurs. The climax, often the most important event in the story, is usually very close to the turning point of the story or the final resolution. *Anticlimax* can be either dramatic or rhetorical. Dramatic anticlimax occurs in a narrative in which the "climax" is unexpected or is not a logical one, or in which its impact is far less than what the preceding action led the reader to expect. Rhetorical anticlimax is a ludicrous decrease in the importance or impressiveness of what is said.

Comedy: any literary work with a happy ending, but the word is most often applied to plays. Usually, the characters in a comedy are presented as general types rather than as realistic individuals. The characters and situations do not arouse deep emotional feelings in the audience, and the audience, in turn, does not experience a profound sense of identification. *See* **High Comedy** *and* **Low Comedy.**

Comic Relief: humor inserted into a play to break a serious mood.

Conflict: a struggle between two opposing forces or characters, either as man against man, man against society, man against nature, or man against himself. Concern with the outcome of the conflict is the basic element in suspense.

Connotation and Denotation: The *denotation* of a word is its literal or "dictionary" meaning as it is used in context. The *connotative* meanings include the associations one may have with the word.

Dénouement (dā·nōō·män′): the final unraveling or solution of the plot in drama or fiction. The dénouement usually follows the climax.

Dialogue: the lines spoken by the characters in a play or narrative.

Dynamic Character: one whose character changes in the course of the play or story. Its opposite is the *static character.*

Epilogue: a short section added to a completed play. It is usually spoken by one actor at the end of the play, and it may either comment upon the play, summarize it, bring the audience up to date, or ask for the indulgence of the critics and the applause of the audience.

Exposition: in drama, the part of the play in which the audience is given the background information it needs to know.

Fable: a short tale intended as moral instruction. Animals frequently serve as characters, as in Aesop's *Fables. See* **Parable.**

Falling Action: the action following the climax; sometimes called the *dénouement,* or the *resolution.*

Fantasy: in literature, any imagined story that creates a world of improbable events in unreal settings. In drama, the term *fantasy* does not refer to a major type of play—such as tragedy, comedy, or melodrama—but rather to any play set in a world of make-believe, whimsy, or imagination.

Farce: any play which evokes laughter by means of low comedy or ridiculous situations. Some plays that are not farces may have farcical scenes or farcical touches. *See also* **Low Comedy, Parody,** *and* **Satire.**

Figurative Language: language which makes use of *figures of speech*, word devices used to create fresher, more vivid, or more compact expression than ordinary, literal language would achieve.

Flashback: a scene inserted into a play, film, novel, or story showing events that happened at an earlier time.

Foil: a character, object, or scene that sets off another by contrast.

Foot: a unit used in measuring lines of poetry. Each foot usually contains at least one stressed syllable and one or two unstressed syllables (*see* **Meter**).

Foreshadowing: a technique whereby the author hints at events to come, the "shadow" of action that will be revealed later.

Hero and Heroine: the leading characters in a play; the protagonists.

High Comedy: humor based on intelligence and wit. High comedy is the term often applied to satiric comedy, in which the appeal is mainly intellectual. High comedy tends to be verbal rather than physical. *See* **Low Comedy.**

Humors: the four principal bodily fluids which, according to their proportions in the body, were believed to influence health and temperament. When all four humors were in balance, behavior was normal. When one fluid overbalanced another, the results were interpreted as follows:

Humors	Type of Personality If Humor Is in Excess	Characteristics
Blood	Sanguine	Kindly, joyful, amorous.
Phlegm	Phlegmatic	Unresponsive, cowardly, without intellectual liveliness.
Yellow Bile	Choleric	Easily angered, vengeful, stubborn, impatient.
Black Bile	Melancholic	Brooding, introspective, affected, sarcastic.

Hyperbole (hī·pûr′bə·lē): a deliberate overstatement, often for effect.

Imagery: a word picture, or image, used descriptively to represent things, actions, sensations, or ideas. Although most imagery is visual, it can also refer to the senses of hearing, touch, smell, and taste.

Irony: a figure of speech in which the implied meaning of a statement is the opposite of its literal or obvious meaning. Irony is usually the product of statement but may also arise from situations and events, or from the structure of a literary work.

Another type of irony, *irony of situation*, occurs when the outcome of a play or work of fiction is unexpected, or events turn out to be the opposite from what one had expected. For example, at the close of *Romeo and Juliet* the parents state that they will build a monument to commemorate their children's "true and faithful" love. This development is ironic since it was the parents' refusal to allow Romeo and Juliet to be in love while they were alive that resulted in their tragic death.

A third type of irony, sometimes called *dramatic irony*, occurs when a character on stage is kept ignorant of facts known to the audience, as Romeo is when he enters the tomb and believes Juliet to be dead. The lines, therefore, will have a double meaning—one for the characters that may be on stage, and another for the audience.

Legend: a story or tale, usually about a national, folk, or religious hero, that has been handed down, most often by word of mouth, from generation to generation. Legends are unauthenticated stories from earlier times that usually combine fact and fantasy. *See* **Myth.**

Low Comedy: humor based on slapstick and broad or off-color jokes. Most of the scenes between William and Phebe, the simple country people in *As You Like It*, are low comedy. Both high comedy and low comedy can appear in the same play, as they do in *As You Like It. See* **High Comedy.**

Malapropism: an unconscious error in speech or writing on the part of a character, but deliberate on the part of the author. Malapropisms result from substituting one word for another with a similar sound but entirely different meaning. An example of such an absurd misuse of words would be using the word *consolation* instead of *constellation* in the following sentence: "I enjoy visiting the planetarium and seeing the various *consolations*."

The term malapropism comes from Mrs. Malaprop, a character in Richard Sheridan's eighteenth-century comedy, *The Rivals*, who misuses words all the time.

Melodrama: a play in which extraordinary good is pitted against most terrible evil. Both hero and villain in melodrama will be types rather than fully developed characters, and good always triumphs despite tremendous odds. *See* **Stock Character.**

Metaphor: a figure of speech that compares one thing with another by speaking of the one as if it actually were the other. (Neither *like* nor *as* is used.)

Meter: an organized rhythmic pattern created by the repetition of the same foot, or group of stressed and unstressed syllables, throughout a poem.

Miracle Play: a medieval religious play which dramatized the lives of saints or stories from the Bible.

Monologue: an extended speech by one person on a stage. *See also* **Soliloquy.**

Mood: the prevailing feeling, atmosphere, or tone of a literary work.

Moral: the "teaching" or "lesson" in a work of literature. Sometimes this lesson is clearly stated, sometimes it is only hinted at, and at other times there is no lesson intended at all. *See* **Theme.**

Morality Play: a form of allegorical drama written in England in the fifteenth and sixteenth centuries. It was designed to present on stage different aspects of Christian morality. (*See* **Allegory.**)

Myth: usually a traditional story about the deeds of gods or heroes. Myths often attempt to explain natural phenomena, such as the origin of the sun.

Oxymoron: a figure of speech, consisting of two apparently contradictory terms, used to call attention to a truth contained within combined yet opposite terms. "Fiend angelical" is the oxymoron Juliet uses for Romeo, her lover, yet the murderer of one of her relatives.

Parable: a short tale making a moral or religious point. The New Testament parable of the Good Samaritan is a well-known example.

Parallelism: the use of identical or nearly identical grammatical constructions, sentence patterns, or paragraph structures within a passage or a work. Parallelism may also involve the repetition of character types or plot situations, usually for the purpose of emphasis or comparison and contrast.

Parody: a humorous imitation of the subject matter or style of an author. Parody may also apply to mimicry by one character of another.

Pastoral: pertaining to shepherds, country people, and the habits of rural life. In drama, a pastoral play is one which depicts a country setting somewhat artificially and idealistically.

Personification: a figure of speech in which human qualities are given to animals, abstract ideas, or inanimate objects. Sometimes characters in a play or story can be personifications of abstract qualities, as they are in the play *Everyman*, mentioned under **Allegory.**

Plot: the arranged pattern of related incidents and events in a literary work. Plot usually includes in its pattern the circumstances which begin the story, the complications leading to conflict, the rising action, the climax, and the final outcome or resolution.

A *subplot* is a second plot within a story, of lesser importance than the main plot. Plot and subplot are usually related to each other, and they are often united at some crucial point in the story.

Problem Play: a social drama, a play with a message, or a play dealing with serious political or religious problems.

Prologue: a brief opening section to a longer work. In many seventeenth- and eighteenth-century plays the prologue states the moral point or tells something about the theme or the plot.

Protagonist: the most important or leading character in a play or story.

Pun: a play on words involving the use of: (a) words with similar sounds but different meanings, as *odius* and *odorus*; (b) words with the same spelling but different meanings, as with the word *case* which may mean "a particular occurrence" or "a type of container"; (c) words with exactly the same sound but different meanings, as *son* and *sun*.

Realism: the attempt to present life as it actually is without distortion or idealization. Literary realism is generally opposed to the use of artificial language and to the presentation of noble heroes and heroines. It tries to give a picture that shows all of life's aspects—good and bad, beautiful and ugly.

Resolution: the events that follow the climax of a story or play. It is often used interchangeably with *falling action* and *dénouement*.

Rhyme: the repetition of similar or duplicate sounds in two or more words, especially at the end of lines of poetry. Shakespeare uses blank verse, which is unrhymed, for his plays, but he often uses a rhymed pair of lines—called a *couplet*—at the end of a scene or an act. The following lines appear at the end of Act I, Scene 2 of *Julius Caesar*:

> And after this let Caesar seat him *sure*,
> For we will shake him, or worse days *endure*.

Rhythm: in poetry, the recurrence or repetition of stressed and unstressed syllables in a regular pattern or manner. When rhythm in poetry is so strictly patterned that it can be measured in feet (*see* **Foot**), it is called meter (*see* **Meter**). Rhythm in prose is normally irregular and only approximate.

Rising Action: the events that lead up to the climax of a play or story. *See* **Climax and Anticlimax**.

Romanticism: a tendency or trend in literature, music, and art; romanticism pictures life in a picturesque, fanciful, exotic, emotional, or imaginative manner, and often reflects the writer's strong interest in nature and his love of the strange and supernatural.

Satire: the use of ridicule, sarcasm, wit, or irony in order to expose, set right, destroy, or laugh at a vice, human folly, or social evil. In drama, the satirical play is often comic, using farce and parody to give power to its ridicule. *See* **Farce** *and* **Parody.**

Scenario: a plot outline of a film or play. Usually a scenario includes the sequence of scenes and the characters in the play.

Sentiment and Sentimentality: *Sentiment* is honest emotion; *sentimentality* is excessive or artificial emotion, emotion unjustified by events.

Setting: *see* **Atmosphere and Setting.**

Simile: a figure of speech which makes a comparison betwen two unlike objects or qualities, usually by means of *like* or *as.*

Soliloquy: a monologue; an extended speech delivered by a character alone on stage in which he expresses his thoughts directly to the audience.

Stage Directions: the phrases, sentences, or paragraphs (*usually in italics and enclosed by parentheses*) which appear above, below, or adjacent to the dialogue of characters in a play.

Static Character: a character who does not change at all, or who remains almost entirely the same, throughout the course of a play or story.

Stock Character (Stereotype): a familiar, commonplace type of character. A stock character either possesses traits supposed to be characteristic of a particular class, or he reminds the reader of characters that he has often read about or seen on television.

Style: a writer's distinctive manner of expression; all those qualities and characteristics of language and ideas that distinguish one author's work and personality from another's.

Subplot: *see* **Plot.**

Symbol: something that stands for itself at a literal level, but which suggests something else—or several other things—at the same time. A symbol is frequently a concrete object or animal that represents a quality or an abstract idea. A light, for instance,, may symbolize knowledge and enlightenment.

Theme: the central idea of a literary work; the core of the discussion; the main point. In some works, especially novels and plays, the central theme may be accompanied by secondary themes.

Tone: the words and manner the author uses to communicate his attitude toward his subject, his audience, and even himself as a writer. Through the selection and arrangement of words, an author can achieve virtually the same effect as a speaker's tone of voice.

Tragedy: a play which presents painful situations, suffering, and death.

Tragic Flaw: the defect in the tragic hero which leads to his downfall.

Verse: language which is metrically composed; poetry. The term can be applied to a particular type of metrical structure, such as *blank verse,* or to a line of poetry, as in a *verse* from the Bible.

The Language Arts Program

The majority of language arts activities appear in the end-of-selection questions and assignments under the headings *Meaning, Method, Language,* and *Composition and Discussion.* Some language material, especially information about word origins, is covered in text footnotes.

General Skills

Characterization (inferring personality and/or attitudes of characters), 42, 43, 63, 84, 123, 172, 196, 202, 230, 238, 242, 255, 260, 264, 268, 269, 287, 298, 302, 311, 325, 328, 334, 349, 353; (recognizing techniques of characterization), 23, 123, 124, 146, 172, 196, 213–214, 218, 230, 255, 264, 279, 292, 295, 325, 340, 347

Characters (consistency in), 102, 173, 230, 325, 362; (motivations of), 23, 43, 63, 101, 102, 196, 230, 238, 239, 255, 265, 268, 269, 287, 292, 330, 334, 347; (naming), 43, 172, 287, 326, 362

Character sketch, 103, 175, 270

Comparing and/or contrasting characters, scenes, etc., 23, 83, 123, 145, 146, 172, 173, 174, 213, 218, 220, 230, 255, 260, 269, 287, 295, 298, 302, 305, 311, 324, 328, 334

Dictionary (using), 175

Evaluating critical opinions, 83, 173, 175, 347

Extending discussion beyond the immediate text, 101, 102, 103, 174, 230, 260, 292, 325, 363

Figurative language (interpreting), 196, 218, 238, 255, 269, 270, 295, 325, 353

Foreshadowing, 124, 196, 202, 270

Humor (recognizing humorous techniques), 123, 185, 186, 311, 325, 349

Models (guides for writing), 175–176, 270, 271, 364

Paragraph development (methods of), 175, 271, 364

Paraphrasing, 287

Plot (evaluating outcome of play), 102, 173, 362

Purpose (recognizing author's purpose), 83, 103, 174, 218, 269, 304, 305, 355

Reading aloud, 43

Repetition (dramatic effect of), 101, 239

Stage directions (importance of), 9, 123, 174

Stage productions, 43, 63, 174, 202, 220, 305

Titles (significance of), 103, 173, 270, 363

Literary Terms and Types

Anachronism, 186, 193fn.

Antagonist, 173

Atmosphere, 180

Backdrop, 178, 179

Climax, 63, 173

Comedy, 2–3, 83, 174, 272; (musical comedy), 175; (romantic comedy), 3, 173, 362
Conflict, 23, 43, 63, 102, 124, 146
Dénouement, 173
Description, 123, 146, 202, 353
Dialogue, 23, 42, 63, 123, 145, 146, 173, 180, 196, 202, 325
Drama (kinds of), 2–3
Elizabethan theaters, 178–180
Epilogue, 362
Exposition (background for a play), 23, 173, 185–186
Fairy tale, 287, 292, 362
Falling action, 173
Fantasy, 263
Figurative language, 14fn., 28fn., 46fn.
Foreshadowing, 124, 196, 202, 270
Hero and/or heroine, 103, 146, 173, 269
Humors, 210fn.
Irony, 103, 239, 255, 312
Metaphor, 43, 269
Motif, 174
Parody, 325, 362
Pastoral, 272, 295, 324
Personification, 280fn.
Plot, 146, 173, 174, 181, 185, 214, 220, 362
Point of view, 181
Problem play, 3, 5, 102
Props, 124, 173, 180
Protagonist, 103, 146, 173
Puns, 183fn., 186, 191fn., 282fn., 300fn., 306fn., 314fn., 325fn.
Realism, 124, 146, 173, 174
Repertory company, 180
Rising action, 173
Romanticism, 124, 146, 173, 174
Satire, 105, 123, 145, 146, 173, 174, 272, 325, 328, 362, 363
Sets, 180
Setting, 173, 269, 272, 362

Simile, 102, 269
Soliloquy, 196, 213, 230, 279
Stereotype, 175
Subplot, 146, 173
Suspense, 124, 146, 220, 264, 298
Symbolism, 43
Theme, 5, 103, 105, 174, 362
Tone, 146
Topic sentence, 175
Tragedy, 2–3, 270

Vocabulary Development

Adverbs, 123
Allusions, 20fn., 74fn., 81fn., 117fn., 131fn., 190fn., 191fn., 212fn., 223fn., 235fn., 245fn., 257fn., 258fn., 275fn., 310fn., 314fn., 318fn., 319fn., 325fn., 328fn., 333fn., 337fn., 342fn.
Mythology and folklore, 205fn., 229fn., 281fn., 313fn., 317fn., 319fn., 328fn., 337fn., 358fn.
Puns, 183fn., 186, 191fn., 282fn., 300fn., 306fn., 314fn., 325fn.
Word origins, 15fn., 77fn., 110fn., 113fn., 114fn., 117fn., 130fn., 133fn., 136fn., 137fn., 145fn., 163fn., 325fn.
Words from other languages, 56fn., 153fn., 223fn., 349fn.

Speaking and Listening

Panel discussion about man's responsibility to his family versus the need to act upon his convictions and beliefs, page 103
Discussing whether or not Arms and the Man is a "romantic comedy," 173
Discussing whether or not Shaw's characters in Arms and the Man are individuals or stereotyped instruments through which he gives his political, religious, and social beliefs, 175

Comparing and contrasting the characters of Brutus in *Julius Caesar*, and Dr. Stockmann in *An Enemy of the People*, following suggested guide, 271

Explaining one of several quotations from *As You Like It* and discussing the insights into situations and people that it gives the reader, 363

Explaining one of five quotations about people and/or ideas from *As You Like It*, 363

Essay on the variations on the theme of love in *As You Like It*, 364

Humorous essay on "The Seven Stages of Women," 364

Argumentation:

Using comparison and contrast to support your stand about the female characters in *Arms and the Man*, following suggested guide, page 175

Agreeing or disagreeing with topic sentence about the characters in *Arms and the Man*, and their unrealistic attitudes toward war, love, and social position, using examples from various sources to support your opinion, 175

Newspaper writing:

Two newspaper accounts (one biased, the other straightforward and objective) of the events that take place at a town meeting in *An Enemy of the People*, page 103

"Help Wanted" ad for school newspaper designed to attract actors and actresses for parts in *Arms and the Man*, following suggested guide, 175–176

Definition:

Defining and illustrating the various meanings of the term *idealism*, page 175

Applying the definition of *tragedy* to the lives of Caesar and Brutus, 270

Applying the definition of *romantic comedy* to *As You Like It*, 362

A
B
C
D
E
F
G
H
I
J